The Legacy of World War II
in European Arthouse Cinema

The Legacy of World War II in European Arthouse Cinema

Samm Deighan

McFarland & Company, Inc., Publishers
Jefferson, North Carolina

ISBN (print) 978-1-4766-8352-2
ISBN (ebook) 978-1-4766-4339-7

LIBRARY OF CONGRESS AND BRITISH LIBRARY
CATALOGUING DATA ARE AVAILABLE

Library of Congress Control Number 2021019251

© 2021 Samm Deighan. All rights reserved

No part of this book may be reproduced or transmitted in any form or by any means, electronic or mechanical, including photocopying or recording, or by any information storage and retrieval system, without permission in writing from the publisher.

Dirk Bogarde in the 1974 film *The Night Porter* (Lotar Film Productions)

Printed in the United States of America

*McFarland & Company, Inc., Publishers
Box 611, Jefferson, North Carolina 28640
www.mcfarlandpub.com*

For Ann and Richard

"In the morning light it was all as raw and frank as the voice of history which tells you not to fool yourself; this can happen in any city, to anyone, to you."—Christopher Isherwood, *Down There on a Visit* (1962)

Table of Contents

Acknowledgments — viii
Introduction: Memories That Scar — 1

1. Collaboration and Survival in Italian Neo-Realism — 5
2. Memory Beyond Consolation: French Cinema in the '50s — 24
3. Out of the Rubble: The Emergence of New German Cinema — 40
4. French Cinema in the '60s and the Myth of Resistance — 61
5. Postwar Perversion: Italian Cinema in the '70s — 76
6. The Punishment Begins: The Films of Rainer Werner Fassbinder — 95
7. Pasolini's *Salò* and Nazisploitation — 112
8. Innocent Children and Kafkaesque Doubles: Jewish Identity in French Cinema — 132
9. Apocalyptic Visions: The Holocaust on Screen in Poland — 153
10. The World Gone Mad: Czech and Slovak Cinema — 170
11. Ordinary Fascism World War II Films Behind the Iron Curtain — 188

Conclusion: The Trauma of Remembrance — 211
Chapter Notes — 213
Bibliography — 221
Index — 227

Acknowledgments

The genesis of this book was a graduate essay on Pier Paolo Pasolini written in 2010 at the University of Pennsylvania for Timothy Corrigan, a preeminent film historian whose work has focused on German Cinema. Over the years, I've never been able to stop thinking about Pasolini's *Salò* (1975) and the ways in which directors who survived the war depicted it in their films. This resulted in a sprawling series of essays and lectures on the subject of cinema and World War II, which this book has been developed from. Its real inspiration, however, comes from Christopher Gwin, my exacting high school German teacher who refused to let me drop his class, taught an unforgettable seminar on the Holocaust that changed the ways I think about violence and trauma, and organized a visit to Dachau during a class trip—all of which has had a lifelong impact on me.

There are a number of scholars and historians whose research made this book possible, including Saul Friendländer, Annette Insdorf, Antonin and Mira Liehm, Timothy Snyder, and many others cited in these pages who have done pioneering work exploring the effects of World War II and the Holocaust on contemporary culture. I also likely would not have written this book without a chance meeting with Marcel Ophuls, who came to the University of Pennsylvania for a lecture and (though he doubtlessly does not remember me) spoke so passionately and generously that I will always be grateful for the experience.

This book also would not have been written without the support of many of my colleagues: I have to thank Kat Ellinger and Mike White for their often daily support over the last few years and for the ongoing work we've done together on the Czech New Wave, which would also not have been possible without Second Run's kind and generous team of Mehelli Modi and Chris Barwick, who have hired us as a team to do commentaries on many of their vital Blu-ray releases of Czech and other Eastern European films. My chapters on Polish, Czechoslovakian, and Soviet cinema would not be the same without Jonathan Owen and Daniel Bird, the latter of whom would be a millionaire if he had a dollar for every one of my questions he answered. And for their generous support and encouragement over the last few years, I also need to thank Kier-la Janisse, Heather Drain, Alexandra Heller-Nicholas, Brandon Upson, Pete Tombs, Jared Auner, and Bret Wood—all of whom have either collaborated on projects with me, published my work, or hired me to do Blu-ray commentaries which enabled me to finish the book. Most of all, I need to thank Bill Ackerman, who read the first, messy chapters of this book five years ago, and who was the first person to tell me not only that I could write it, but that I should.

Introduction
Memories That Scar

It has been close to a century since World War II ended on September 2, 1945, yet the war has continued to be an incredibly popular subject for cinema—more so than the other wars to follow in the 20th century. There are perhaps two obvious reasons for this: first, the war affected the entire world, so there is no feasible way the subject could be exhausted; there are still many stories from different angles that have yet to be fully explored in either fictional or documentary films. Second, there is an obvious villain— Nazi Germany and their Axis allies—who have come to represent the ultimate symbol of human evil, a virus that spread through Europe and nearly destroyed the world. Historians like Saul Friedländer and Susan Sontag have described how Nazism, at least as it exists in the current cultural consciousness, has become mythologized, a mere symbol of the spectacle of evil.

And while there are certainly thousands of films about World War II and dozens of books about those films, there is a very specific focus to this book, and it is not intended to address or even mention every single film about the war. First, I'm only exploring films made in European countries that were occupied by Nazi Germany and their Axis allies. The major focus includes Germany, France, and Italy, as well as the Soviet Union and Eastern Bloc countries like Poland and Czechoslovakia. While Austria, Belgium, Denmark, Luxembourg, the Netherlands, Norway, and Greece were also subject to occupation during World War II, and countries like Finland were allied with Nazi Germany, I'm only including films countries that have enough titles under my specific purview to be examined as a group. The United Kingdom and its own occupied territories (like Iceland and the Faroe Islands) are not included, because they were actively at war with the Nazis but not occupied by them. Likewise, Sweden, Ireland, and Spain are not represented because of their neutral status—which means I have unfortunately had to exclude films like the Spanish masterpiece *Tras el cristal* (*In a Glass Cage*, 1986), one of the most harrowing horror films to explore the aftermath of Nazism.

Second, I'm particularly focusing on arthouse or "auteur" films with controversial or transgressive elements that present themes and viewpoints counter to mainstream World War II films. In general, arthouse films are not made for a mass market and instead serve to represent the artistic vision of a particular filmmaker and their group of collaborators. These films do not seek to entertain in a conventional way or to make a particular sized profit, as is the case with the mainstream cinema of markets like Hollywood. They are often experimental, challenging in content and form, and present radical interpretations of power, sex, politics, identity, and violence. The war is often presented in moral absolutes, with virtuous and heroic Allied forces on one side and the evil Axis powers on the other. But this book is primarily concerned with films that examine the reality that life during wartime exists in a moral grayscale, where compromise or collaboration are often necessary for the survival of an individual, a family unit, or an entire community.

While there are many, many mainstream World War II films, generally they seek not to tell genuine stories of war trauma, but to propagate myths. Steven Spielberg's *Schindler's List* (1993) is a classic example of this and Liel Liebovitz's scathing editorial on it sums up many of my own views. First, that *Schindler's List* and similar mainstream Holocaust films seek to dehumanize Nazis and make them into figures of superhuman evil, thus presenting the audience with a simple tale of black and white morality where it can be clearly understood who is good and who is evil. There is no moral complexity whatsoever. Second, the focus is rarely on Jewish characters, instead presenting them as token victims. As Liebovitz writes, "Schindler's Jews do not matter. They're abstractions, spiritual currency so that our 'hero' can pay his way toward salvation."[1] Stories like *Schindler's List* tend to beautify the Holocaust with a focus on survivors, obfuscating the sheer millions shot to death by killing squads, murdered in gas vans and later in gas chambers, and those who died of hunger, cold, and disease in concentration camps, ghettos, and on forced marches.

As Liebovitz writes, "Spielberg turned an infinitely complex reality into something even worse than kitsch: a spectacle."[2] Survivors like Elie Wiesel have argued that using the Holocaust as subject matter for cinema—for entertainment—is grossly offensive and that it can never present a remotely accurate picture of the reality. While it is not my place or within the scope of this book to say whether or not Holocaust and World War II films should exist or not, they do and in great numbers. This book does aim to explore films made by those who lived through the war—or in some cases, children of survivors born just as the war was ending—which present a more accurate representation of life in wartime and sink deep into the moral gray areas that often constitute survival. In that respect, I have chosen to loosely focus on films made between 1945 and 1985. This somewhat sweeping period does offer different interpretations of the war, but in most cases, it includes films made by directors who experienced the war firsthand.

The chapters move in a loosely chronological order, beginning in Chapter One with a discussion of Italian neo-realism in the '40s under directors like Roberto Rossellini, which set the stage for many of the arthouse depictions of World War II to follow. Chapter Two explores French cinema in the immediate postwar years through the '50s, namely the ways in which the Nazi occupation affected French culture and how directors like Alain Resnais and Jean Pierre Melville began to portray the war on screen. Chapter Three discusses the state of German cinema in 1945 and follows the rubble film in the late '40s through to the birth of New German Cinema in the '60s and the ways in which that movement challenged German memories of war and fascism. Chapter Four returns to French cinema in the '60s, particularly examining the way in which the myth of the French Resistance influenced national identity and how certain directors sought to overturn the image of rosy heroism. Chapter Five focuses on Italian cinema in the '70s and the ways in which arthouse directors began to experiment with cult movies tropes and erotica to present transgressive, somewhat gothic portraits of families in the grip of fascism. Chapter Six returns to Germany and explores the work of director Rainer Werner Fassbinder, the most prolific artist of his generation to make World

War II-themed films in Germany, particularly so many with a confrontational focus on power and violence.

Chapter Seven likewise focuses on Italian auteur Pier Paolo Pasolini and his 1975 film *Salò* and the ways in which it engages with World War II themed exploitation films that were becoming popular at the time. Chapter Eight looks at French cinema in the wake of Marcel Ophuls' 1969 documentary *The Sorrow and the Pity*, particularly in terms of how Jewish characters are explored in the films of the '70s and '80s. Chapters Nine, Ten, and Eleven all explore Soviet cinema, respectively focusing on Polish Holocaust films, Czechoslovakian films, and more broadly the few films made in the Soviet Union and Soviet satellite states that dared to push beyond the expected bounds of Soviet censorship. Where it is necessary, I discuss films from other countries, such as the United States, and mainstream films, particularly where they are used as a reference point.

To me, it seems like a particularly poignant time to explore these films. There are many unsettling political and historical parallels, such as the wave of right-wing politics and violence sweeping the world. But also the denial and repression of facts, science, and truth happening in various current governments, which were mainstays of fascist policy in the '30s. Many of the films explored in this book raise a series of questions that seem applicable to the current situation, but that are also perennial: What is power? How and why do we let it control us? How does fascism emerge in our societies? Why do so many choose to become collaborators or bystanders? What is violence? What is trauma? How does it change us? And can it be overcome?

In all of these retellings of the war, myth, legend, personal accounts, memory, fiction, fact, and truth overlap and make all of these narratives about so much more than just what happened during the war itself. In some cases, these films present newer, more honest interpretations of history as research is unearthed; they show that public opinion and national memory are similarly malleable, rarely fixed. Some of these films speak to the responsibility of bearing witness, while others raise questions of punishment and justice. Movies are not made by individuals and, historically speaking, nor are they viewed by individuals alone; cinema is largely a communal affair and all of the films in this book look at the way our stories are woven together and impact one another—for better or worse.

Many of the films featured here focus their narratives around the marginalized: women, Jews, and queer characters, those who are often cast on the sidelines in conventional war films. Their plots often deal with bodies, with unconventional depictions of sexuality, and with violence. The body itself becomes a way to understand wartime experience, to understand the horrors of genocide, to process trauma. The fundamentals of trauma theory tell us that memories must be recovered and the stories of these incidents must be told before we can process and move on from the horrors in our lives. In Chris Marker's experimental film *La Jetée* (1962), he notes: "Nothing sorts out memories from ordinary moments. Later on they do claim remembrance, when they show their scars." Marker, a member of the French Resistance and assistant on Resnais' seminal World War II documentary *Nuit et brouillard* (*Night and Fog*, 1956), makes the important point that perhaps what stands out so vividly in our memory are the things that wound and scar us.

In a larger sense connected to communal memory, the continued obsession with World War II is understandable. The history and the stories that live on represent the best and the worst of humanity, both unimaginable evil and incredible bravery. Throughout much of art and culture, the Holocaust is often used not just as the ultimate symbol of evil, but as a symbol of the worst trauma humanity has endured. While genocide has certainly been perpetrated before and after World War II, not on such an unimaginable scale. Many of the films in this book explore the effects of trauma and many offer the implication that this trauma can be endured or transcended. Whether that is a realistic assertion or a naive one, the defeat of the Nazis in 1945 has become an enduring message of hope in dark times that we too can endure—a message that continues to play out on screen.

1

Collaboration and Survival in Italian Neo-Realism

> "The cinema is the most powerful weapon."
> —Benito Mussolini, 1922

The European arthouse films discussed in this book offer a contrast to Hollywood productions from the postwar years, often in the sense that they offer up a more complicated view of life during wartime. In general, these films explore two themes: first, the conflation of fascism and sexual perversion, a leitmotif that extended from the 1940s through to the 1980s across a range of European countries; second, many of these films perhaps depressingly assert that surviving the war was often not a heroic act. Many of these films feature protagonists who are anything but heroic, including collaborators, opportunists, and morally ambivalent characters who can at best be described as self-serving. In order to understand the prevalence of World War II-themed films throughout Europe in the '70s and '80s, it's first necessary to discuss their origins in the Italian neorealist films of the '40s, where the themes of collaboration and sexual perversion first emerged in the work of director Roberto Rossellini.

Rossellini's renowned neorealist war trilogy—*Roma città aperta* (*Rome, Open City*, 1945), *Paisà* (*Paisan*, 1946), and *Germania anno zero* (*Germany Year Zero*, 1948)—provides the first major example of these themes within a newly liberated Europe. Drug addled prostitutes, morally compromised cabaret singers, fascist homosexuals, and pedophiles provide a stark contrast to Rossellini's heroic if sometimes demoralized Resistance fighters, grim soldiers, honest citizens, and hapless victims. The antagonistic character types presented in these three films—from collaborators and profiteers to Nazis—persisted throughout much of postwar European cinema.

Rossellini began shooting the first film in the trilogy, *Rome, Open City*, in the last months of World War II and his scripts for all three films focused on wartime devastation from Sicily to Berlin. Many of Rossellini's innovations resulted from the unavailability of conventional filmmaking means; the Italian film studios were shut down, so he had to make do with whatever funds, film equipment, props, sets, and actors were available, as all were scarce. As a result, these films have a stark, documentary feel that sharply contrasts the rosy, sentimental war films and propaganda pieces released by Hollywood in the '40s. It is no wonder they were considered revolutionary at the time. But in order to understand Rossellini's achievement, it is also necessary to understand the conditions under which he made *Rome, Open City*. Up until the bitter end of the war in 1945, Italy was a battle ground between Allied and Axis forces. The Allies had launched an invasion in January of 1943 and by July, Mussolini was arrested, and a new, provisional government was established under Marshal Pietro Badoglio. Between 1943 and 1944, the Allied armies struggled to push Nazi forces north out of Italy, a lengthy and brutal process. The U.S. Army didn't enter Rome until June of 1944, coinciding with the D-Day landing in France.

Like the majority of Italians, Rossellini was deeply affected by life during wartime and he had become a radically different filmmaker by 1945. Before the war and even during its early years, Rossellini could best be thought of as apolitical. Though he was never a card-carrying fascist, it was largely thanks to a friendly relationship with the Mussolini family and their professional support—particularly that of Benito's son Vittorio—that Rossellini was able to begin a career as a director. For example, his first film, *La nave bianca* (*The White Ship*, 1941), was funded by the Italian Navy, and his earliest work can be loosely described as war propaganda. His first three films are known as his "fascist trilogy," but this is more complicated than it seems, and it would not be accurate to draw a parallel between Rossellini's early films and, say, the Nazi propaganda created by Leni Riefenstahl.

While the emergence of neorealism is generally seen as a sharp break with Italian fascist cinema of the '30s, critics in more recent years have begun to reexamine this idea. Film historian Peter Bondanella writes,

> Italians were understandably anxious to forget the fascist years, which ended with the collapse of the regime and a bloody resistance struggle between 1943 and 1945 that assumed the proportions of a civil war before hostilities ended. Critics, film historians, politicians, and even veterans of the film industry who had learned their trades during the fascist period had every interest in emphasizing the originality and revolutionary quality of what succeeded the fascist cinema—Italian neorealism—and to denigrate everything that came before it.[1]

Like the National Socialists, cinema was of paramount importance to Mussolini's government. In the '30s, the fascists helped open a film school that still exists nearly a century later, while also launching Cinecittà, the most important studio system in Italian history. Film content was not as rigidly controlled as in Nazi Germany and the Italian fascist government took seriously cinema's ability to boost public morale and strengthen Italian cultural capital. While Goebbels claimed his Nazi cinema was modeled after Hollywood, the Italians sought this comparison more earnestly and produced relatively little propaganda in comparison to other totalitarian governments systems. Bondanella writes,

> Only rarely were commercial films expected to reflect the regime's ideology. Most Fascists were content to allow the film industry to provide mass public entertainment. Abundant evidence demonstrates that the fascist regime took a genuine interest in the health of the film industry and wanted it to flourish, without, however, insisting upon ideological purity in its products. In fact, the totalitarian regime's model was Hollywood, not the rigidly controlled popular culture of Soviet Russia or Nazi Germany.[2]

It would be fair to view this environment as a training ground for the neorealists, most of whom transitioned their careers from under the fascists to postwar life—in sharp contrast to many of the filmmakers working actively under Nazi rule, who were penalized or blacklisted after the war. Historians such as Bondanella have even argued that key characteristics of neorealism didn't emerge from thin air, but were first used by filmmakers working under the fascists. He writes, "The simple fact is that the use of nonprofessional actors, real locations, and documentary techniques was part of a growing trend toward film realism in the fascist cinema even before the advent of neorealism, and it is doubtless in this context that Rossellini learned of the effectiveness of such techniques."[3]

The first film in his neorealist trilogy, *Rome, Open City*, is the most conventional of the three and can be seen as an obvious transition point. While it is based on historical events and has a documentary-like quality to its cinematography, it is by far the most melodramatic and cinematically conventional film of the trilogy, though it does have a distinctly downbeat, defeatist tone—the universe of *Rome, Open City* is a place of senseless violence and betrayal. Film historians Carlo Celli and Marga Cottino-Jones write,

> "Open City" is a diplomatic term that refers to a city that in time of war has been declared by both sides to be free from all acts of military aggression. The title is an ironic testimony to the violence that marked the occupation period with a story of attempts of the Nazi occupation forces to capture CLN members carrying out guerrilla warfare. Nazi troops occupied Rome, and the Gestapo Headquarters in Via Tasso was full of prisoners being interrogated, tortured, and killed.[4]

The film was originally intended to be a documentary about Giuseppe Morosini, a Roman priest tortured and executed by the Gestapo for his involvement in the Resistance when he was just 24 years old. While a character based on Morosini, Don Pietro (Aldo Fabrizi), is one of the film's central protagonists, *Rome, Open City* ultimately follows several members of a Resistance group in Rome as they attempt to survive a Nazi purge. Dogged idealism gives way to tragedy and horror as beatings, torture, betrayal, suicide, and executions occur in quick succession. It is likely that Rossellini intended the audience of *Rome, Open City* to be able to recognize themselves within the film, particularly in the immediate months after the war ended; though Don Pietro is a dramatically heroic figure, the film presents many regular citizens caught up in the violent struggle of merely trying to survive in a war zone.

Unlike many later arthouse films, which often present more moral complexity, the film's characters are starkly divided into doomed heroes and nefarious villains. One of the most complex figures is Marina (Maria Michi), a singer in a cabaret—and implied prostitute—whose clientele is almost exclusively Nazis and fascists.[5] Marina ultimately betrays the Resistance group when her boyfriend, one of their number, callously breaks off his relationship with her and the Nazis woo Marina with a combination of drugs and expensive gifts. While this character type would become commonplace in later films, perhaps culminating in Bob Fosse's *Cabaret* (1972), Marina is an early if somewhat subdued example of one type of a collaborator: the morally compromised young woman who works in seedy cabarets and nightclubs and abandons both morals and politics in favor of physical comforts.

Marina admits that wealthy paramours pay for her clothing, furniture, and her apartment, while her job at the cabaret only supports her cigarette-smoking habit and keeps her outfitted in stockings; the latter were hard to find during the war years, as silk was expensive and fragile, while nylon was requisitioned for parachutes and other martial needs. Though she is not directly called a prostitute, it's clear that much of her income is derived from sexual relationships with men. She's also addicted to a sedative, which is given to her by Ingrid (Giovanna Galletti), a seductive German who has developed a very affectionate friendship—possibly sexual—with Marina. Ingrid works for the Nazi

Marina (Maria Michi) contemplates her beauty and its price (*Roma città aperta*, Excelsa Film, 1945).

commander Major Bergmann (Harry Feist) and the two conspire to lead Marina down a path of treachery.

Bergmann is likewise painted as a perverse, possibly homosexual character, with his debauchery a clear link to his immorality. Bondanella states, "Bergman's effeminate, homosexual mannerisms, along with equally exaggerated mannerisms of his female assistant, a lesbian named Ingrid, underline how closely audiences of Rossellini's time associated sexual deviancy with evil-doing in other areas of life."[6] The Gestapo stronghold—a site of interrogation, torture, and betrayal—is full of expensive liquor, crates of fine art, fur coats, historical treasures, and a gleaming piano. This connection drawn between opulence and immorality did not first emerge with Rossellini's film, but is something of a throwback to the Decadent literary and artistic movements popular from the fin-de-siècle through the early '20s. While Decadence is primarily associated with French and German writers, Italians like Gabriele D'Annunzio can also be considered part of this movement.

D'Annunzio's work often represents a link between decadence and moral evil. When discussing *Cabiria* (1914), a film partly written by D'Annunzio, Celli and Cottino-Jones note that his writing had

> an art nouveau or liberty emphasis on rarity, extravagance, luxury, and oriental motifs. It is an atmosphere that has often been equated with illicit sex, decadence, drugs, and illness, especially in authors such as Andre Huysmans, a source for D'Annunzio. The film's decor and plot exploited the transgressive elements implicit in such a setting and behavior, which was part of D'Annunzio's appeal and mirrored his lifestyle and reputation.[7]

In *Rome, Open City* there is a similar link drawn to the Nazi characters. Their decadence can be seen as a physical reflection of the film's black and white moral message, which sharply divides decadent fascists and their collaborators on one side and warm-hearted Christian and Marxist partisans living in abject poverty on the other.

The use of poverty as a fundamental characteristic of heroic characters can also be seen in other films from the period, such as Fritz Lang's *Cloak and Dagger* (1946). Though that film was made in Hollywood with an American star (Gary Cooper), the majority of the cast—including Austrian director Lang—was comprised of Central Europeans forced to flee their home countries to escape National Socialism. The film follows American intelligence agents on an espionage mission to rescue a nuclear scientist held by the Nazis. Notably, it includes a sequence through war-torn Italy, where it is suggested a beautiful young Resistance member (Lilli Palmer) is implied to have prostituted herself in order to survive. Essentially the opposite of Marina, she is a rare early example of a heroic variation on this character type.

The stark division between good and evil is a fundamental quality of these early neo-realist films, though it is far from unique to Italian cinema. Similar plots would occur in the immediate postwar films of countries like France and Germany, where many were desperate to distance themselves from fascist collaboration in any way possible. Bondanella writes,

> Immediately after the fall of the fascist state on 25 July 1943, there were a number of Italians who suddenly discovered themselves anti–Fascists, or at least hastened to avoid mention of their previously close ties to the regime and its leaders, whereas before that date they had been completely at home in the drawing rooms and salons of the regime's officials. Rossellini must certainly be numbered as one of these individuals, even though it is equally difficult to doubt the sincerity of his sudden "conversion" to making neorealist films in the immediate postwar period that are identified with an entirely different political ideology.[8]

This process of romanticizing the Resistance and painting its members as heroic was perhaps inevitable in both Italian and French cinema. However in the World War II-themed films of the '60s and '70s, many of the more transgressive filmmakers sought to overturn this mythologizing, Rossellini chief among them. In reality, Italian Resistance fighters, or partisans as they were more commonly known, were mostly soldiers. After a string of abysmal military failures from Italy's entrance into the war late in 1940 to the Allied invasion in 1943, soldiers from the virtually dissolved Italian Army fought back against the Nazis in the central and northern parts of Italy, often with the military weapons they had been issued and sometimes with the assistance of peasants.

Italy was in a state of civil war: occupied by Nazis in the north and Allied powers in the south, most anti-fascist groups refused to support or recognize the temporary Italian government under Badoglio until later in 1944. German forces regularly massacred partisans and citizens alike, and thousands more were deported to be used for forced labor. In addition to soldiers, partisans included police officers, escaped prisoners of war, refugees, and citizens fleeing from Italian cities. Towards the end of the war, partisan bands were often connected to political groups, such as the Communist Party, and fought against Nazis and Italian fascists as well. While these partisan armies were primarily rural, there were also smaller terrorist bands operating within cities. Celli and Cottino-Jones write, "The fact that some Italians had acted against Nazi/Fascism independently helped to create a political mythology that somewhat assuaged the feeling of collective responsibility after the war. The myth of the Resistance allowed Italians to attenuate the level of war guilt felt in Germany, for example."[9]

As would eventually be revealed about the French Resistance, the actual number of partisan fighters was a small portion of Italian citizens, with the conservative number believed to be around 200,000 people. Rossellini attempted to document some of these different types of partisans in his follow up to *Rome, Open City*. *Paisan* is a bleak portrait of this conflict that raged within Italy on many fronts for two years. Less melodramatic or sentimental than *Rome, Open City*, the film features a series of six vignettes about the Allied campaign north from Sicily and the gradual German retreat. The unifying theme is about the failure of communication during these months when Italians struggled to understand each other and struggled to interact with the various occupying forces.

With *Paisan*, Rossellini attempted to document the broader experience of Italians throughout the country during a time of war. The six stories feature widely different locations throughout Italy: Sicily, Naples, Rome, Florence, the Apennine Mountains, and the Po River Valley. It is worth noting that Italians from these separate regions generally saw themselves as being significantly different from one another. As a country, Italy was not unified until the 19th century and was thus a fairly new nation; citizens from different city states and rural regions often spoke widely different dialects and adhered to different cultural customs within their communities.

Unlike *Rome, Open City*, with its melodramatic trappings, *Paisan*, meaning "comrade" or "friend," is much closer to the documentary style associated with neorealism. Bondanella notes that it "remains much closer to the spirit of the newsreel documentary"[10] used so often during the war. Here, the focus has already begun to move away from *Rome, Open City*'s narrative structure of heroic Italian citizens versus decadent fascists. Unlike *Rome, Open City* or the final film in the trilogy, *Germany Year Zero*, sexual decadence is not a major theme of *Paisan*. The few depictions of sexuality within the film include an early scene where hiding German soldiers imply they are going to rape an Italian girl, while later, Maria Michi returns as a world weary prostitute who has a chance encounter with an American soldier (Gar Moore) she met and fell in love with months earlier. They are both so changed by their war experiences that neither recognizes the other, until the soldier tells her a story about the girl he is trying to find. Realizing it is her he's talking about, she sneaks off when he falls asleep but leaves him her home address, hoping they can begin a relationship. But he crumples up the note, believing it to be directions to a brothel.

The focus of *Paisan* is more generally on suffering—suffering not only from war itself, but felt in the postwar period thanks to poverty, loss, a broken government, political corruption, and attempts to recover in the aftermath of a devastating war. The bleak sense of defeat and futility introduced in *Rome, Open City* is even more pronounced in *Paisan*. Celli and Cottino-Jones argue that this exploration of human suffering and its causes is the real unifying characteristic of neorealist cinema. They write,

> More than any one stylistic element, there is a certain attitude that best describes neorealism, especially in film. That attitude includes a strong desire to uncover the truth about the widespread suffering in Italy, and to identify with the plight of the victims. Neorealism also criticizes the view of society as a mere collection of individuals who condone indifference to others' suffering.[11]

1. Collaboration and Survival in Italian Neo-Realism

If *Rome, Open City* follows the attempts of Italian citizens to survive the Nazi occupation and *Paisan* examines the devastating effects of two foreign armies clashing in Italy, *Germany Year Zero* is a harrowing portrait of survival in the immediate postwar years—Rossellini's masterpiece of suffering. While *Paisan* ends with the bombing of a city, this last film in Rossellini's war trilogy begins with the devastating aftermath. The bleak message of *Germany Year Zero* seems to be that just because fascist forces have been defeated and driven from Europe, the quality of life for everyday citizens has not really improved.

Germany Year Zero can be seen as something of a cross between Italian neorealism and German *Trümmerfilm* or rubble film, depressing dramas that depicted life in war-torn Europe among the crumbling, sepulchral ruins of German cities. Rossellini's dive into this subgenre follows the 12-year-old Edmund (Edmund Moeschke) as he struggles to help support his family. His father (Ernst Pittschau) was crippled in World War I, his older sister (Ingetraud Hinze) is nearly driven to prostitution to survive, and his older brother (Franz-Otto Krüger) refuses to register for work papers or food stamps because he fears he'll be arrested by Allied forces for his service as a German soldier. There's no work to be had, little food, and they're forced to share an apartment with another resentful family.

Alongside other children, Edmund steals food and is befriended by a former teacher, Herr Henning (Erich Gühne), an ardent Nazi and a pedophile. When Edmund approaches Henning for advice about how to help support his struggling family, Henning says, "The weak are destroyed so that the strong survive." He suggests that death would be the most honorable and beneficial outcome for Edmund's father. When Edmund's father laments that he doesn't have the courage to kill himself and states that his life is agony, Edmund poisons his tea, believing it to be an act of mercy.

The dejected Edmund (Edmund Moeschke) walks in the rubble of postwar Berlin (*Germania anno zero*, Tevere Film/SAFDI/Union Générale Cinématographique [UGC], 1948).

Germany Year Zero is distinct from the other two films in Rossellini's war trilogy because of its German setting and pervasive air of morbidity. *Rome, Open City* and *Paisan* both at least suggested a hopeful resolution, while the tone of *Germany Year Zero* is bitter and hopeless. The film opens with Edmund attempting to work as a gravedigger in a cemetery. When he is banished from that job for being too young and having no working papers, he passes a dead horse in the middle of the street being butchered for its meat. Occupying soldiers take a tourist photo in front of the spot where Hitler committed suicide and his body was burned. Edmund later plays one of Hitler's speeches on a portable record player in the ruins of the chancellery, because Henning is having him sell the record to soldiers looking for souvenirs.

This constant presence of death—emphasized by dialogue about failure, defeat, suffering, and suicide—is not only symbolic of wartime experience, but is also a reflection of Rossellini's personal grief. His son Romano died in 1946 of appendicitis and young Edmund Moeschke, whom Rossellini found at the circus, was cast because of his resemblance to Romano. All of the film's major actors, a cast of nonprofessionals, were found by Rossellini in Berlin and their starved, depressed faces are the perfect expression of *Germany Year Zero*'s themes, as are the bleak visions of a bombed out Berlin. In an article for *Cahiers du cinéma*, Rossellini writes,

> The city was deserted, the grey of the sky seemed to run in the streets and, from the height of a man, you could look out over all the roofs; in order to find the streets under the ruins, they had cleared away and piled up the debris; in the cracks of the asphalt, grass had started to grow. Silence reigned, and each noise, in counterpoint to it, underlined it even more; the bittersweet odour of rotting organic material constituted a solid wall through which one had to pass; you floated over Berlin.[12]

Edmund is ultimately consumed by this misery and commits suicide at the end of the film. Despite his best attempts, his life unravels: his father dies, he is rejected by the other homeless children, and Henning takes no responsibility for his influence on Edmund. Henning, who was once so enthusiastic about caressing Edmund, holding him on his lap, and sharing Nazi philosophy, slaps him in the face and calls him a monster when Edmund admits that he killed his father at Henning's suggestion. Teary eyed, Edmund wanders among the ruins and finds his way to the edge of an abandoned building destroyed by war. He sees his father's black coffin being carried down the street. His sister calls his name and he jumps to his death, his innocent body a harrowing symbol of mass trauma, guilt, and punishment.

These themes, particularly as they culminate in the film's shockingly downbeat ending, provide a stark contrast with American films made during this time. Many of the directors leaving the U.S. to shoot in war torn Europe were actually European émigrés. While their films do have some similarities to neorealism or the rubble film, there is a noticeable stamp of Hollywood propaganda to them. For example, Jacques Tourneur's *Berlin Express* (1948) is an early example of this trend. Essentially a postwar update of Hitchcock's *The Lady Vanishes* (1938), the film follows a group of people on a train searching for a missing peace activist. Though its location shots in Berlin and Frankfurt-am-Main evoke *Germany Year Zero*, the message of Tourneur's spy thriller is that the various citizens of the victorious Allied countries must work together to maintain peace and rebuild a new Europe together.

Other émigré directors from Germany and Austria working in Hollywood, like

Wilder, Fred Zinnemann, and Robert Siodmak—all of whom had previously teamed up for the influential, early German realist film about daily life in Weimar Germany, *Menschen am Sonntag* (*People on Sunday*, 1930), an important precursor to the neorealist films—produced films shot in Europe. Like Tourneur, they were stuck with the predictable Hollywood formula and messages of victory and optimism. Wilder's *A Foreign Affair* (1948) treads similar ground as *Berlin Express*. Even films determined to push the boundaries of acceptable Hollywood material, such as Fred Zinnemann's *The Search* (1948), remained staunchly in melodramatic territory. It follows concentration camp survivors and refugees trying to find loved ones and return home after the war. Though the film offers up some frank depictions of wartime atrocities, such as a harrowing sequence where children are terrified to climb into an ambulance because they still fear the Nazi gas vans—it ultimately has a Hollywood happy ending where good-hearted Americans help a young boy and his mother to reunite.

Even Hollywood produced documentaries like *The Death Mills* (1945), a short film that Wilder had a hand in creating, was required to soften or manipulate its subject matter. The film captured the horrors within the concentration camps but failed to mention that the victims of the Holocaust were overwhelmingly Jewish. Germans were allegedly required to watch this in order to receive their food ration cards at the close of the war.[13] However, Wilder was in Berlin for a more complex purpose than to direct films: he was also there to investigate the state of the German film industry and shape it to mimic the Hollywood model. Occupying Allied forces kept strict control over German media, allegedly in an effort to stamp out Nazi philosophies. In his book *Rubble Films*, Robert Shandley explains,

> All public utterances, whether mediated through the press, radio, literature, universities, theater, or music, were silenced. The Allies then began a thorough and deliberate process of filtering the voices that were allowed to speak.[14]

Cinema was particularly contentious, as the U.S. sought to create a mirror for Hollywood, while Soviet forces were more inclined to reintroduce authentic German voices.

The creation of the German rubble film,[15] thus came to echo the Hollywood films shot in Europe from this period. Both hinted at disturbing themes about the war, the Holocaust, and attempts of individuals to put their lives back together in the immediate postwar years, but on a largely superficial level. Unlike Rossellini's war trilogy, these films remained optimistic, and ultimately propagandistic, at heart. The rubble films exist in a sort of no man's land between the fall of the Reich in 1945 and the emergence of a stable, but divided Germany in the early '50s. Many of these transitional films are about the return of soldiers and refugees and play lip service to the traumas of World War II without fully addressing German responsibility. Shandley writes, "The rubble films were forced to seek out a language strong enough to confront recent German history while avoiding a confrontation with their German audience."[16]

Like the Germans, Italians were also slow to address these topics with any real depth—though Rossellini was not the only director making films about the war in the immediate years after it ended. Luchino Visconti helped direct a documentary about the partisan effort, *Giorni di gloria* (*Days of Glory*, 1945), primarily about the Ardeatine massacre, where Nazis killed more than 300 Italians in revenge for partisan violence. In Alessandro Blasetti's *Un giorno nella vita* (*A Day in the Life*, 1946) nuns and partisans put aside their differences to fight for the country. In Giuseppe di Santis' *Caccia tragica*

(*Tragic Hunt*, 1947), peasants and partisans alike are forced to turn to crime and violence in order to survive. Carlo Lizzani, who co-wrote the film, directed his own *Achtung! Banditi!* (*Attention! Bandits!*, 1951), about heroic resistance fighters on a mission to steal Nazi weapons. Francesco Maselli's *Gli sbandati* (*Abandoned*, 1955) focused on Resistance fighters.

Other directors, such as Alberto Lattuada, would experiment with darker neorealist films with the subgenre known as *neorealismo nero* or black neorealism, which borrowed from early film noir tropes. A key title is Aldo Vergano's *Il sole sorge ancora* (*Outcry*, 1946), which featured the involvement of real-life partisan fighters, including future director Gillo Pontecorvo. Even later films like *Estate violenta* (*Violent Summer*, 1959) and *Il federale* (*The Fascist*, 1961) feature protagonists who learn an important moral lesson as the narrative unfolds and realize the importance of rejecting fascism or throwing aside indifference to fight for Italy.

The above films are only a few examples, but in general these are more conventional in tone than Rossellini's trilogy, sticking to themes of Italian unity and heroic resistance. Put simply, neorealism came to mythologize the war and the Resistance itself. But by the late '50s and early '60s, some of the country's most prominent directors began to explore war themes with more depth. In her seminal book *Italian Film in the Light of Neorealism*, historian Millicent Marcus writes, "It took the Italian cinema twenty-five years to be able to look back at Fascism and war in a more complicated way."[17] In the '60s, established arthouse directors like Vittorio de Sica and Luchino Viscontiis began to focus on the war in their films—all building off the themes established by Rossellini in his neorealist trilogy.

Rossellini, however, was not interested in adhering to neorealist principles and continued to reinvent himself to the frustration of critics and audiences. His series of films with Ingrid Bergman largely abandoned war themes, with the exception of *Stromboli* (1950). Bergman stars as a Lithuanian refugee who frees herself from an internment camp by marrying an Italian (Mario Vitale), though she finds his home and community totally alien. Like *Germany Year Zero*, *Stromboli* explores the complicated notion that simply because war has ended, doesn't mean survival in its aftermath will be easy or that life will be enjoyable. Rossellini became increasingly focused on expressing human experience and suffering, with an emphasis on psychological realism and the experience of alienation in the postwar years. Bondanella argues,

> Italian neorealism had largely ignored psychological realism in an attempt to show how environment shaped character during the immediate postwar period, when unemployment and the reconstruction of Italy were the most important central facts of life.[18]

Rossellini sought to overturn this fixation and to look at the more complicated reality of the war. He came to focus on "the newly established protagonist of modernist cinema, the isolated and alienated individual."[19] With his 1959 film *General Della Rovere*, Rossellini effectively kicked off a trend of Italian arthouse films throughout the '60s that explored these more complex war themes. Bondanella writes,

> Rossellini moves the depiction of typical neorealist themes (the war, the Resistance) away from a strictly tragic tone to one that permits questioning and doubts about the nature of Italy's role in the war. Neorealist practice had transformed the Resistance into a myth; Rossellini allowed his audience to see the artifice concealed beneath the halos the saints of the Resistance wore.[20]

1. Collaboration and Survival in Italian Neo-Realism

The most important example of this is Rossellini's *Il generale della Rovere* (*General Della Rovere*, 1959), a departure from neorealist style but also a rare popular success for Rossellini. Fellow director Vittorio De Sica stars as Emanuele Bardone, a conman and opportunist exploiting his fellow citizens in Milan, particularly those suffering from various wartime tragedies. He is eventually arrested by the Gestapo and offered a deal from Colonel Müller (Hannes Messemer): he can face a military tribunal and execution, or he can agree to impersonate esteemed Italian Resistance fighter, General Della Rovere, who was accidentally killed by the Nazis. Bardone takes up this new persona and is installed in a local prison, where he is expected to infiltrate the Resistance network. But soon he finds that inhabiting Della Rovere's skin profoundly changes him.

Based on journalist Indro Montanelli's novel, itself inspired by a true story, *General Della Rovere* is in part so fascinating because it follows a character who is a liar and an actor by nature. Bardone begins the film masquerading as an invented character named Colonel Grimaldi, a dashing figure and World War I veteran who promises grief-stricken widows that he can get their arrested (and often secretly executed) husbands back… for a price. He primarily manipulates women—mothers and wives—and milks his two girlfriends for money to feed his gambling addiction. But for all his misdeeds, Bardone is a sympathetic, compelling figure who represents the often harrowing reality of survival in wartime.

By 1943, Italy was divided in two: the northern zone occupied by Nazis and the advancing Allied armies—mostly U.S. and British forces—in the South. After years under Mussolini, Italian citizens were unsure whether to trust the Axis or Allied forces and

Vittorio De Sica charms as a tragi-comic con artist who finds his identity while playing a role (*Il generale della Rovere*, Zebra Films/Société Nouvelle des Établissements Gaumont, 1959).

collaboration with the Nazis was widespread. Bardone can be seen to represent the vast gray area between citizens and soldiers, victims and perpetrators. *General Della Rovere* was one of the first Italian films that did not simply portray Nazis as villains, starkly contrasted with the Italian civilians as either victims or heroes. This bleak work is driven by an incredible performance from De Sica, who is transformed from a corrupt scoundrel to a hero of the Resistance, a man who becomes so caught up in the weighty presence of the General that he effectively becomes Della Rovere. He willingly dies in a firing squad without betraying any of the men who have come to admire him so much.

De Sica, who was a popular actor as well as a director, had often been typecast as a certain kind of charming comedic character. Bondanella argues that this is a type similar to Cary Grant's many roles where he "moves back and forth between a false persona he assumes in society (usually to romance a beautiful woman) and his authentic, more humble, and more likable personality."[21] Through De Sica's presence, Rossellini also introduces themes of irony, comedy, and even elements of the absurd into the war film, all themes that would more fully emerge in the '70s as younger directors similarly used them to explore World War II in more complicated ways.

Film historian Robert Gordon notes, "The late 1950s and early 1960s saw something of a step-change in attention to the Holocaust, in quantity and quality."[22] While Rossellini had essentially made his name with war-themed films in the '40s, his return to World War II material effectively opened the floodgates for other more controversial Italian films about the war. In Peter Burnett's book on the director, he explains that "one very significant aspect of the film is its return to the war and the Resistance, the scene of Rossellini's earlier victories. Strangely enough, it was one of the first Italian films to go back to that period, and in the wake of its financial success, a host of others quickly followed."[23] Examples in the immediate three years after the release of *General Della Rovere* include Gillo Pontecorvo's *Kapò* (1960), Rossellini's own *Era notte a Roma* (*Escape by Night*, 1960), Carlo Lizzani's *L'oro di Roma* (*The Gold of Rome*, 1961), and Liliana Cavani's documentary series *Storia del Terzo Reich* (*The History of the Third Reich*, 1961–1962).

In a parallel with Orson Welles' earlier film *The Stranger* (1946), also about a man who masquerades as someone else to survive during the war (Welles himself playing a Nazi hiding in New England), Rossellini apparently disliked *General Della Rovere* even though it was one of his only commercial successes. There is certainly something off-putting and unsettling at work in the film and its political message is perhaps deceptively conservative. Brunette describes *General Della Rovere* as "stylized," "artificial," and resisting "organic unity"[24] and notes how Rossellini quietly subverted the dramatic studio film producers were hoping for. In some ways, Rossellini seems to manipulate the tropes of neorealism and plays with the tension between what is real and unreal, factual and imagined. Brunette writes,

> There are also moments early in the film where presumably "real" people, that is, non-actors seemingly unaware of the camera's presence, are standing around watching wrecking crews knocking down actual bombed-out buildings, in a De Chirico–like reprise of the early scenes from *Germany Year Zero*. All of this contrasts continuously with the blatant unreality (because so tidy and *managed*) of the studio locations.[25]

This confusion between real and unreal, documentary and fiction, is even more pronounced within Bardone's character. The film's basic drama comes not from Bardone wanting to play a role—which he does in everyday life—but from the dissolution of his identity within the General, a cessation of role playing, which leads him directly to the firing squad. There is the implication that Bardone lacks a real identity and a genuine moral code. Can his talent for deception really be transformed into a heroic act? Philosopher Slavoj Žižek more literally describes what is so subversive about the unreality of Rossellini's film: "Is such a pathetic identification with the fake role the ultimate horizon of ethical experience? Can we imagine the inverse situation: the 'real' della Rovere is arrested, and the Resistance lets him know he has to dirty his image, to die as a miserable traitor, to do one last great service to the Resistance?"[26]

This illustrates an important transition from the early neorealist films to *General Della Rovere*, which is symptomatic of many of the films being addressed in this book: the movement away from a black and white morality, with good Allies on one side and evil fascists on the other, towards embracing a moral gray area that allowed for a more complex view of wartime life. The majority of these films present survival as a complicated endeavor which often required deception, seemingly immoral acts like theft, prostitution, or even murder, incredible sacrifices, and even the abandonment of one's own identity.

The next generation of Italian arthouse directors were undeniably influenced by *General Della Rovere*, particularly Bernardo Bertolucci and Pier Paolo Pasolini, whose work I will explore in later chapters, but most immediately Gillo Pontecorvo. The most obvious influence is in Rossellini's unconventional choice of a protagonist: a self-centered conman who ultimately turns anti-hero, rather than a brave hero of the Resistance who overcomes insurmountable odds to aid in Italy's defense. Released the year after *General Della Rovere*, Gillo Pontecorvo's *Kapò* (1960), an Italian-French co-production shot in Yugoslavia, mines similar territory. Edith (Susan Strasberg), a young Jewish girl, comes home from piano lessons to find the Jews of her town, including her parents, being forced into a truck for deportation. Though she has the opportunity to hide, she runs to her mother's side and the entire family is sent to a concentration camp (implied to be Auschwitz). At night, she wanders out of the children's section and an older prisoner, Sofia (Didi Perego), convinces her to take the identity of a non–Jewish woman named Nichole. This act saves her life, as the rest of her family is sent to the gas chamber.

But the grim situation of the camp begins to warp Edith, who is nearly driven mad by the brutal work detail, the cold, and the hunger. She betrays friends, steals food from other starving women, and, though she arrived at the camp as a virgin, she has sex with a German guard in exchange for food. After months at the camp, she becomes a favorite of the Germans and is made into a kapo, a lead prisoner in charge of the others who has more food, better clothing, and is allowed to avoid hard labor. But her comfortable life is interrupted by the arrival of Russian prisoners of war, particularly a soldier named Sascha (Laurent Terzieff), who reawakens memories of her old identity when she falls in love with him.

Director Gillo Pontecorvo was born into a wealthy Jewish family in Pisa. Like so many of his generation, World War II was the defining experience of his life. He relocated to Paris in the late '30s to escape anti-Semitism, but soon returned to Italy as a Communist partisan. In northern Italy, he became a Resistance leader for the final two years of the war. In general, his films are concerned with war, rebellion, and resistance and Pontecorvo remains best known for his later work, *La battaglia di Algeri* (*The Battle of Algiers*, 1966), about the war between France and Algeria in the '50s. However *Kapò* generated a

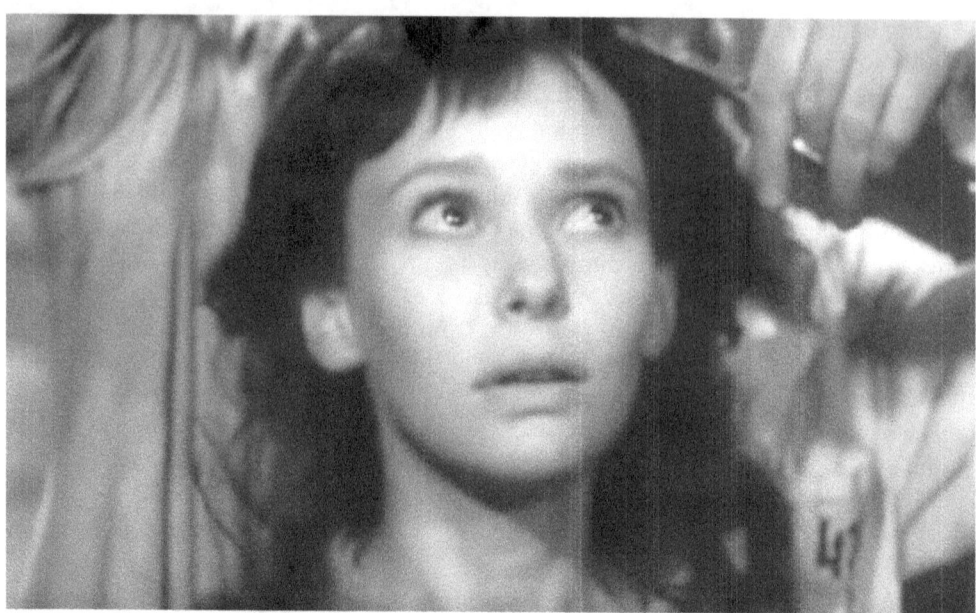

Edith (Susan Strasberg) has her hair shorn in *Kapò*, signifying the loss of her identity (*Kapò*, Cineriz/Vides Cinematografica/Zebra Films, 1960).

fair amount of controversy upon its release. Historian Mira Liehm's view of the film summarizes the common critical consensus of *Kapò*:

> The strength of all his fiction films lay in their documentaristic features rather than in the contrived narrative. In *Kapò*, his re-creation of the horrors of a concentration camp for women attains a high degree of authenticity, but he lapses into heavy-handed sentimentalism in his portrayal of a young Jewish prisoner who collaborates with the Germans.²⁷

His portrayal of concentration camp life offended many viewers and critics. French director and celebrated film critic Jacques Rivette called it "concentration camp pornography,"²⁸ referring particularly to a scene when a starving, despairing character played by Emmanuelle Riva throws herself on a barbed wire electric fence and commits suicide. In comparing this scene of *Kapò* with Alain Resnais's seminal Holocaust documentary *Nuit et brouillard* (*Night and Fog*, 1956), Jacques Lezra writes,

> The techniques of montage and the tracking shots in *Night and Fog*, in contrast to the tracking shot in *Kapò*, serve to refuse understanding. They refuse the temptation to travel into the other's place, to judge, as it were, from the position of the dead, to cross the electrified fence that separates the inside of the other's suffering from the journalistic or voyeuristic position the camera necessarily assumes outside the camp: they refuse, in brief, the temptation of reciprocity, the temptation of identification.²⁹

In this way, *Kapò* foreshadows two divergent types of Holocaust films that would emerge in the '70s and '80s: the violence and cruelty, shocking for its time, hints at more graphic, exploitative Holocaust-themed films of the '70s, like *Il portiere di notti* (*The Night Porter*, 1974). The sentimental elements, such as a robust musical score and the sudden, inexplicable romantic subplot, are evocative of the television series *Holocaust* (1978) and later mainstream films like *Schindler's List* (1993), meant to manipulate viewers' emotions while providing sanitized versions of history.

Perhaps *Kapò*'s most compelling element is its portrayal of Edith and her transformation from innocent schoolgirl to manipulative kapo. She remains the film's protagonist and, like Bardone of *General Della Rovere*, is strangely sympathetic despite her increasingly amoral behavior: she steals from a friend, encourages a woman to commit suicide, prostitutes herself, and uses her newfound power to exploit other prisoners. She abandons religion in favor of survival and doesn't reclaim her Jewish identity until her dying moments. Historian Annette Insdorf described this identity crisis as central to so many Holocaust-themed films from the period. She writes,

> When one was stripped of possessions, status, and external self-definition by Nazi brutality, the question of "who am I?" became problematic. And if one lost family or friends, the isolated self was all the more vulnerable to remorse, guilt, internalized aggression, and the assumption of other identities.[30]

Actress Susan Strasberg (daughter of famed acting coach Lee Strasberg) was likely cast as Edith because of the role that made her famous. In 1955, she was nominated for a Tony Award for her performance in *The Diary of Anne Frank* and she was also the first actress to appear in that role. Like Anne, Edith starts out as an innocent teenager. Pontecorvo seems to stress that it is the situation—life in a concentration camp—that is evil, not Edith herself.

In the following decade, this theme of false identity and even identity loss as a means of survival during wartime recurred throughout arthouse cinema, though more often than not these later films explored war survivors dealing with the repression of identity and memory years after the war. For example, the American film *The Pawnbroker* (1964), from director Sidney Lumet, follows a concentration camp survivor (Rod Steiger) who has relocated to Brooklyn and lives a life of agony and repressed memory in an urban ghetto. *The Pawnbroker* is one of the few American films from this period to examine identity, traumatic memory, and the Holocaust, themes that were just beginning to explode in European arthouse cinema in the wake of *General Della Rovere*.

Certainly in the early '60s, World War II and the Holocaust were suddenly popular themes in Italian cinema and expanded beyond the arthouse into a number of popular genres. For example, Luigi Comencini's *Commedia all'italiana* film *Tutti a casa* (*Everybody Go Home*, 1960), follows soldiers at an army base in northern Italy who abandon their posts and decide to flee home after the Wehrmacht take over the base. Carlo Lizzani's *Il gobbo* (*The Hunchback of Rome*, 1960) is a crime film in which a Resistance leader is unable to return to ordinary life after the war ends and becomes a gangster. *La lunga notte del '43* (*The Long Night of '43*, 1960) is a more conventional drama—despite its script from Pasolini—set in Ferrara during the very end of the war, when a married woman's affair with an army deserted is contrasted by a local fascist's attempts to consolidate power in a small town.

But after Rossellini and Pontecorvo, other directors began to gravitate towards these themes and more complex portrayals of wartime survivors, heroes, and villains. De Sica, a master of both comedy and melodrama, got his start with a series of romantic comedies in the '40s and went on to become a giant of neorealism with films like *Sciuscià* (*Shoeshine*, 1946), *Ladri di biciclette* (*Bicycle Thieves*, 1948), and *Umberto D.* (1952). Like Rossellini, he returned to the subject of World War II several times throughout his career and he often examined the themes of love, romance, and sexuality in a wartime context, often in collaboration with actress Sophia Loren. Beginning with *La ciociara* (*Two Women*, 1960), where a woman and her teenage daughter flee war-torn Rome, their war films together included *I sequestrati di Altona* (*The Condemned of Altona*, 1962), about a German family hiding a Nazi soldier, and *I girasoli* (*Sunflower*, 1970), where a woman searches for her missing soldier husband after the war.

Though *Two Women* is more of a conventional melodrama—and was extremely popular after its release, not only in Italy but also France and the United States—it explores a controversial theme: mass rape. Loren plays a widowed woman trying to care for her young daughter. They spend most of the war hiding out in the countryside for safety. After the Allied liberation of Rome, they resolve to head home, but are caught on the road by Moroccan soldiers—Allies—who gang rape both mother and daughter. This event is based on the *Marocchinate*, the mass rape and murder of thousands of women and girls in rural Italy following the Battle of Monte Cassino, which was perpetrated by Moroccan soldiers in the French Army. This was one of several films from the period to follow in the footsteps of Italian neorealism while addressing uncomfortable war themes, along with *L'oro di Roma* (*The Gold of Rome*, 1961) and *Le quattro giornate di Napoli* (*The Four Days of Naples*, 1962), about the bloody resistance against Nazi forces in Naples.

However, a key early example of more subversive filmmaking is De Sica's controversial *The Condemned of Altona* (1962), based on one of Jean Paul Sartre's final plays and his only fictional work to directly explore Nazism. This Italian-French coproduction concerns the Gerlach family, illustrious residents of Altona, a suburb of Hamburg. The family's patriarch (Fredric March) is dying of cancer, which brings an end to a 15-year deception: his son Franz (Maximilian Schell) is a Nazi war criminal who has been hidden by the family, hoping to spare him from prosecution. They have likewise kept him under the delusion that the war is still going on. But when Franz meets his brother's beautiful wife Johanna (Sophia Loren), their lives are forever changed.

Like *Two Women*, *The Condemned of Altona* came in the wake of films that followed *General Della Rovere*. But unlike films such as *The Four Days of Naples*, *The Condemned of Altona* is a more subversive examination of wartime themes. While exploring fascism as sexual perversion and issues of identity and memory, as many of the other films in this chapter, it also revolves around complex family dynamics and the strife between generations. These complicated family dynamics would come to dominate the World War II films to come like *The Four Horsemen of the Apocalypse* (1962), *Vaghe stelle dell'Orsa* (*Sandra*, 1965), *La caduta degli dei* (*The Damned*, 1969), and *Il giardino dei Finzi-Contini* (*The Garden of the Finzi-Continis*, 1970).

Millicent Marcus writes "for Italian Jews, Auschwitz was not the synecdoche, but the synonym for annihilation."[31] But the literal experience of Italians in the Holocaust was not addressed by the majority of these films, with the exception of *Kapò*, which are largely concerned with the symbolic weight of genocide and its aftermath. Many of these films focus far more on sexuality and the complicated relationships between men and women than they do about actual wartime events. The poet Ingeborg Bachmann declared that "fascism is the primary element in the relationship between a man and a woman,"[32] a statement that could be applied to many of these titles. In *The Condemned of Altona*, this is the overarching theme, which is explored in parallel to the family's complicated, histrionic dynamics.

Theater, both in terms of the Gerlach family drama but also in the literal sense, is an important element of De Sica's film. Annette Insdorf writes,

> Theater is both the source and narrative center of *The Condemned of Altona*. [The main characters] are agents of voice or exist primarily through their speech, in true theater style: Johanna is a stage actress, Werner is a trial lawyer, Leni reads aloud deceptive newspapers, Gerlach has cancer of the throat, and Franz's self-mystification ("One voice shall remain to cry no, not guilty," he screams) and subsequent disruption of the Brecht play are enacted through declamations.[33]

De Sica not only adapted Sartre's play, but used Bertolt Brecht's *Der aufhaltsame Aufstieg des Arturo Ui* (*The Resistible Rise of Arturo Ui*, 1941)—an anti-fascist play by way of *Richard III* that satirizes Hitler by portraying him as a Chicago gangster—as a play-within-a-play throughout the film.

One of the opening scenes finds Johanna in the middle of rehearsal for an unknown play set in 1938 and its climax—where Franz breaks out of the attic room he has been living in for 15 years and walks all the way to the theater—returns to the conclusion of *The Resistible Rise of Arturo Ui*. The kernel of Brecht's play was written in Denmark in 1934, when Brecht was already on the run from the Nazis, but not completed until 1941, when he was living in Finland and waiting for the visa that would soon take him to the U.S. It was not staged in Germany (or anywhere else) until 1958. Though it was intended for the American stage, it was turned down by U.S. producers while the country was still neutral in 1941.

The themes of Brecht and Sartre—*The Condemned of Altona* is a further exploration of his aphorism "man is condemned to be free"—overlap in the sense that both writers paralleled capitalist business enterprises with fascism. When Gerlach admits that he has only six months to live, he is placing both the boon and burden of the family business on his son Werner, who will not only inherit the company's billion dollars in assets, but also its history. Known for collaborating with the Nazis, the Gerlach estate went so far as to allow part of their extensive grounds to become a concentration camp where 30,000 Jews were murdered.

Though at first resistant, Werner discusses his surprising desire to take over the family business and change it for the better. He says to Johanna, "Every time I see a Mercedes Benz, I smell the stink of gas chambers." *The Condemned of Altona* rotates around this question of inheritance—financial, historical, and genetic—and its characters spout weighty sentiments like "History is sacred" (Franz) and "We are all raised as the children of criminals" (Gerlach). Johanna makes a heavy-handed Goethe reference—"Those that do not remember the past are condemned to repeat it"—and De Sica suggests that her lofty idealism and obsession with uncovering the truth will have fatal consequences. Like German director Rainer Werner Fassbinder would do a few years later, De Sica seeks to show that the world has conveniently forgotten the horrors of war and fascism and simply revealing the truth of its existence is not enough to destroy the dark impulses in the heart of humanity.

The sexual themes of *The Condemned of Altona* hint at perversion within the household. Early in Johanna and Franz's meetings, he assumes incorrectly that she is having an affair with his father. Instead, Johanna falls in love with her husband's mad brother, who she plans to run away with, while his sister Leni's actions are the most disturbing of all. She is unwholesomely obsessed with Franz and has been effectively keeping him prisoner by crafting and maintaining elaborate, post-apocalyptic fantasies. In Sartre's play, Franz must hide out because he was defending Leni from an attempted rape by an American soldier. Leni accidentally killed the man, hitting him with a bottle, but Franz

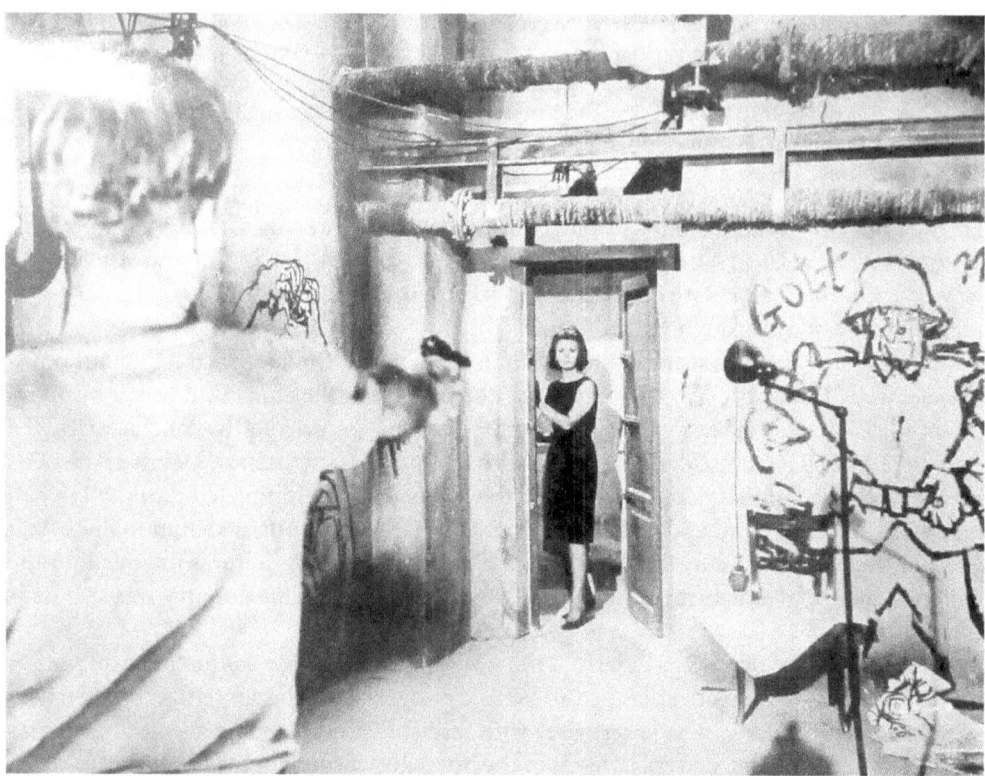

Johanna (Sofia Loren) confronts Franz (Maximilian Schell) in *The Condemned of Altona* (*I sequestrati di Altona*, Société Générale de Cinématographie (S.G.C.)/Titanus, 1962).

took responsibility. De Sica removed this plot element entirely and instead focuses on the complicated relationship between fiction, lies, fantasy, and truth woven by the respective members of the Gerlach family as representative of World War II Europe itself.

Another film from the same period that dealt with themes of sibling rivalry, troubled families, sexual perversion, and World War II was from another master of Italian neorealism, Luchino Visconti. Though born into a famed noble family in Milan, Visconti joined the Communist Party during the war and became a member of the Resistance. His partisan activities led to his arrest and imprisonment by the Nazis; he was due to be executed, but managed to escape just before Rome was liberated by the American Army. His film *Vaghe stelle dell'orsa…* (*Sandra*, 1965) follows a young woman, Sandra (Claudia Cardinale), who returns to her family estate in Volterra for a memorial ceremony dedicated to her late father, a scientist who died in Auschwitz. Her devoted American husband (Michael Craig) has no idea that the mansion is also home to a number of dark secrets. In a loose retelling of the myth of Orestes and Electra, Sandra believes that her mother (Marie Bell)—who is now mentally ill and requires constant care—teamed up with her stepfather (Renzo Ricci) to denounce her father as a Jew, an act that led directly to his death. The even darker secret is that Sandra and her estranged brother, the handsome Gianni (Jean Sorel), had an incestuous affair that they are in danger of renewing.

Though it has many parallels with *The Condemned of Altona*, Visconti's family melodrama is an elegantly layered construction that factors in references to World War II guilt, an unconventional love triangle, and a tragedy about the fading, yet corrupt splendor of

Italian aristocracy—which references from everything from pre–Roman Etruscan civilization with its dusty tombs and moldering urns to the glory of ancient Rome and the dazzle of Belle Epoque–era Europe. Sandra is almost literally unable to escape the ghosts of the past. The white dresses she wears mimic the sheet laid over her father's ceremonial bust, while the empty villa is as shadowy and menacing as a haunted house in a gothic horror film. The family has sunk into relative poverty and disgrace but attempts to maintain honor and keep up appearances. Curiously, it is only Sandra's American husband who looks towards the future and, tenderly, is able to overlook Sandra's past, providing she can abandon it herself.

Ultimately, though, war trauma is little more than subtext for the film. Marcus writes, "the Shoah becomes simply one more pretext for melodramatic plot developments."[34] In this way it has much in common with De Sica's later film *The Garden of the Finzi-Continis*, another bleak look at inheritances, corrupt aristocracy, and family breakdown during the war years. A wealthy Jewish family, the Finzi-Continis, ignore the looming fascist threat in late '30s Ferrara because they believe their aristocratic background and political connections will keep them safe. A subplot within the larger narrative follows a boy's (Lino Capolicchio) desperate love for the family's beautiful young daughter (Dominique Sanda). Marcus writes, "Within Giorgio's tale of unrequited love, unfolding against the background of the impending Holocaust, the garden represents a dangerous state of withdrawal, a space that, in psychoanalytic terms, suggests the operations of neurotic denial."[35]

Sandra and *The Garden of the Finzi-Continis* are indicative of the emerging struggle of World War II–themed films in the '60s and '70s: while some, such as *General Della Rovere*, grew out of neorealism and directly explored the aftermath of war itself, others used war trauma or its memory to explore more contemporary social issues such as sexuality and gender. While some directors married war themes to transgressive sexual content to flirt with taboos, others actually sought to explore issues of wartime guilt and responsibility in a more direct way. These concepts of inherited perversion and an inability to escape the past are common themes throughout these mildly perverse family melodramas of the early '60s but wouldn't reach their full potential until later in the decade with Visconti's *The Damned*, setting the stage for the perverse World War II arthouse fantasies of the '70s and '80s.

2

Memory Beyond Consolation

French Cinema in the '50s

"You think that people are all good or all bad. You think that good means light and bad means night? But where does night end and light begin? Where is the borderline? Do you even know which side you belong on?"—Henri Georges Clouzot's *Le corbeau* (1943)

As in Italy, French directors in the '40s had to contend with fascism—in the form of the Nazi occupation of France. While cinema was still censored by the Nazis, this was slightly more relaxed in occupied countries than it was in German-speaking territories the Nazis considered their homeland. In France, for example, films were not required to be as propaganda focused. But French filmmakers still had very few avenues to freely explore themes like subversion, resistance, or the horrors of life in wartime Europe; thus, there is no obvious French parallel to Italian neorealism. This required quite an about-face for French filmmakers: for example, the decade prior to occupation had been a golden age for French cinema. A precursor to neorealism, known as poetic realism, flooded screens with pessimistic dramas about the aftershock of World War I and the growing threat of fascism across Europe. Films like *Pépé le Moko* (1937), *Le grande illusion* (*The Grand Illusion*, 1937), *La règle du jeu* (*Rules of the Game*, 1939), and others prefigured the gloomy fatalism of both Italian neorealism and American film noir in the '40s. Lead characters were often downtrodden outcasts or frustrated criminals whose narratives end in bitterness, disillusionment, and death. These themes, unsurprisingly, were not allowed in French cinema after the German invasion.

The Nazis occupied France from June of 1940 to December of 1944. This can loosely be split into two periods: in the first, through November 1942, France was divided into the German occupied zone (*zone ocupée*) in the north, and the "free" zone (*zone libre*) in the south, which was ruled by the collaborationist Vichy government. This marked the expulsion of Jews, communists, and other political "undesirables" from the film industry. This persecution intensified at the end of 1942 in an incident in November of that year, when more than 10,000 Jews were rounded up, arrested, and sent to their deaths at Auschwitz. Known as Vel d'hiv, the French government denied involvement in this episode for decades, though many French citizens—including young students—were involved in the arrest and capture of their countrymen and expatriates.

Though cinema attendance was at an all-time high before the war, the studios were briefly shut down for the period of fighting and, as with Germany, Austria, Czechoslovakia, and many Eastern European countries, important artists fled Europe in the early years of the war. Reich Minister of Propaganda Joseph Goebbels decided that, for morale, the French studios would have to be reopened. The normal rules and censorship laws were put into effect and the Nazis began a French-German studio of their own, Continental-Films. Perhaps because of geographic and language barriers, French filmmakers were given more flexibility and occasionally managed to bend the strict rules that governed German cinema during the war years.

But by 1940, the state of French cinema was radically different than just a few years prior. Many important artists had fled, while some disappeared, were imprisoned in concentration camps, or settled into attempting to survive the occupation. Those that remained were forced to make films that focused on historic and fantastic subject matter, shying away from realism, overt depictions of the war, or narratives of occupied life. French movies primarily relied on escapism. As in Germany, film attendance soared despite the fact that most foreign language films were banned. The Nazis created a governing committee—the Comité d'Organisation des Industries du Cinéma (Organizational Committee for the Cinema Industry)—similar to the German Ministry of Culture. All professional cast and crew members were required to register, while Jews were excluded. The films themselves were not allowed to depict the Vichy government or Nazi occupiers, open rebellion toward or criticism of authority figures, or realist views of working class life. All films had to be approved by the C.O.I.C. and the German authority before they could be publicly screened.

To be a working member of the French cinema was difficult during this time. Those who left the country were scorned and declared cowards. French actors found it difficult to work in English-speaking territories and new audiences were often unwelcome and intolerant of their accents. When they returned to France, the reception was unfriendly and their careers were often damaged for years, sometimes permanently. The great star Jean Gabin, for instance, was hated for leaving France but found himself unpopular in America. He joined the Free French Navy, perhaps as an attempt to atone, but was not able to restore his professional reputation for another decade, despite the fact that he became a decorated soldier and re-entered Paris with the liberating army. Many of those who stayed home were accused of collaboration after the war, such as actors like Charles Boyer and Maurice Chevalier. Many in the industry were arrested, tried, and imprisoned.

However, some filmmakers were able to spread subtle messages of dissent through the use of fantasy, surrealism, and the supernatural: examples include Marcel Carné's *Les visiteurs du soir* (*The Devil's Envoys*, 1942), Guillaume Radot's *Le loup des Malveneur* (*The Wolf of the Malveneurs*, 1943), and Maurice Tourneur's *Le main du diable* (*Carnival of Sinners*, 1943). These films often took historical period settings and pitted their protagonists against devils and monsters. Many of these ultimately asserted that love and the inner life of the imagination were resistant to violence, control, and domination. Director and critic François Truffaut writes, "there was no place for subversion or protest in the films of this period [...] it is therefore understandable that cinema took refuge in historical films and films of fantasy and enchantment."[1]

There were some fantasy films too subversive to be made during this period; a few were banned during the screenwriting process, while the creators of others prudently waited until just after the war was over to realize their visions. As a result, the wave of fantasy films continued for some time after liberation through films like Carné's *Les enfants du paradis* (*The Children of Paradise*, 1945) and Jean Cocteau's *La belle et la bête* (*Beauty and the Beast*, 1946), which have come to be regarded as classics of French cinema. Unlikely teams formed and there was a lot of unexpected cinematic collaboration during the period. Wheeler Winston Dixon writes, "Adversity created an atmosphere—a hothouse, pressurized zone of creation—in which divergent artists gathered together to create works in defiance of a common enemy whose tyranny they were dedicated to abolish."[2]

Seemingly disparate artists like Cocteau and Robert Bresson teamed up for *Les Dames du Bois de Boulogne* (1945), a drama set during the occupation about a man (Paul Bernard) who is tricked by his scorned ex-lover (Maria Casarès) into marrying a prostitute (Élina Labourdette). Not overtly a film about resistance, its subtle themes are an example of how artists were forced to become creative during the period to get their message across. It is essentially a story about manipulation—at the hands of the scorned lover, Hélène—and the determination to love and to hope despite a seemingly bleak outcome. Dixon writes, "*Les Dames* is an attack on the 'caretakers' of the Vichy regime, who implicitly promised Parisians, and by extension all of France, that nothing would change under their rule, except perhaps the loss of a few personal liberties, and the disappearance of much of France's Jewish population."[3]

In general, directors were slow to turn to the subject of World War II in the immediate postwar years and the films that did followed the predictable formula of resistance and heroism also found in many of the popular Italian films in the '40s and '50s. Films like Henri Calef's *Jericho* (1946) glorified the Resistance, perhaps to an even more extreme degree than Italian films focusing on the same subject. For decades, French films criticizing the Resistance or even daring to show the complexity of survival in wartime were few and far between; this was a risky endeavor for directors because of the mythologizing that began to build up around the Resistance immediately as the war ended.

Rare early exceptions include Raymond Bernard's thriller *Un ami viendra ce soir* (*A Friend Will Come Tonight*, 1946) and René Clément's *La bataille du rail* (1946), both of which attempted to infuse war narratives with complexity. While both perpetuate the mythologizing of the Resistance, *A Friend Will Come Tonight*—which focuses on the inhabitants of a rural insane asylum working with the Resistance—at least approaches the topic of French anti-Semitism and France's role in the Holocaust, while also addressing the disorienting quality of life under occupation. This is likely because Bernard himself was Jewish and he had to hide out in rural France during the years of occupation, like so many other French Jews.

La bataille du rail follows the resistance efforts of rail workers who sabotaged German military trains. As with Italian neorealism, Clément's film included a cast made up of real-life rail workers and has certain documentary qualities. Clément actually got his start making documentary shorts, including one about trains, *Ceux de rail* (1942). *La bataille du rail* likewise resembles a documentary—an explanation for how train workers were able to sabotage the Nazis—and there is not much narrative structure to the film and little personal drama to speak of. Adrian Danks writes,

> In style and intent *La Bataille du rail* does have an equivalence with the contemporaneous works of Rossellini—*Open City* (1945) and *Paisa* (1946)—particularly in its patented combination of an intense immediacy and a somewhat distanced observation, the placing of characters within the detail of historical circumstances, and the reliance upon the close correspondences between the performers (often actual rail workers or Resistance fighters in Clément's film) and the roles that they play. Nevertheless, *La Bataille du rail*—despite an extremely visceral battle scene between Resistance rail workers and German troops on an armoured train—does not

attain the emotional intensity or the level of engagement attached to the character played by Anna Magnani in *Open City*, for instance.[4]

Regardless, it is another example of early postwar French cinema that aids in the myth that active, violent resistance was widespread among the French population.

An early exception to this trend is Henri-Georges Clouzot's *Manon* (1949), essentially a gloomy romantic melodrama that uses the war as a backdrop. Clouzot's film does explore themes of collaboration and the abandonment of morals in the face of survival—seemingly personal subject matter for the director. Clouzot was one of the few French directors to be persecuted both during and after the war and his case is a rather unusual one. His relationship with German cinema began in the early '30s: he spent the first decade of his professional life working as a screenwriter in Paris and then Berlin, where he oversaw the French versions of dual-language films. Fiona Watson writes,

> Clouzot began as a director of dubbing in Berlin at UFA's Neubabelsberg Studios between 1932 and 1938. He then became an assistant director, working for Litvak and Dupont, among others. He moved on to writing, (*Un Soir de rafle* [1931], *Le Duel* [1939], *Les Inconnus dans la maison* [1941]) and it was in Germany that he acquired a taste for the work of Fritz Lang, whose unflinching view of the sordid side of life can be detected throughout Clouzot's oeuvre.[5]

Clouzot had contracted tuberculosis early in life and suffered from poor health. His time in sanitariums also kept him from serving in the war and allowed him to read extensively, write scripts, and develop the grim impression of human nature that would heavily impact his work. He was allegedly fired from his position in Berlin due to his friendship with a number of Jewish producers. Despite this, he found work in Nazi-occupied France as a screenwriter and director for Continental-Films. One particular film he made for them, *Le corbeau* (*The Raven*, 1943), widely considered his masterpiece, promptly got him blacklisted from cinema by the Nazis, the Vichy government, the Catholic Church, and the French Resistance—a singular feat—due to its scathing subject matter.

In *The Raven*, a small village is plagued by an anonymous series of poison pen letters, which accuse a doctor (Pierre Fresnay) of adultery and of performing abortions. The letters soon spin out of control, revealing that everyone in town has at least one dark, dirty secret. The townsfolk are more than willing to inform on one another, and they become determined to find the guilty party—or at least a convenient scapegoat. A likely comment on life in Gestapo-infested Europe, *Le corbeau* is a film about blame, guilt, secrets, lies, and suspicion, apt subject matter during the occupation. It was rapidly banned by the conservative Vichy government due to its blatant anti–Nazi themes, though Clouzot claims that these were unintentional and that the film was written before the occupation even began.

Somewhat remarkably, it was also banned by the Resistance due to Clouzot's perceived collaboration with the Germans, and probably because the film blamed regular French citizens for their own submission and their willingness to cooperate. For this reason, it was also banned after the war and Clouzot was not permitted to direct another film until 1947. His sentence, which initially banned him from filmmaking for life, was overturned due to the support of Jean-Paul Sartre, Jean Cocteau, René Clair, and Marcel Carné, among other well-known artists and filmmakers.

One of Clouzot's finest works, *The Raven* captured the spirit of life in occupied France in a way that few films were able to at that time. An acerbic atmosphere of paranoia and misanthropy pervade the film. Though often compared to Hitchcock, Clouzot's films are darker and more nihilistic, lacking Hitchcock's generally lighthearted, conventional characters. This tone, so evident in *Le corbeau*, is subtly shared with other films made towards the end of the war. Due to this shared mood, Edward Baron Turk and other scholars have drawn a connection between the grim realist doldrums of *Le corbeau* and the fantasy works of the day, such as Carné's *Les visiteurs du soir*. Baron Turk writes,

> In its restraint, distance, and literary-pictorial inspiration, *Les visiteurs du soir* partakes of an emerging Occupation aesthetic which Evelyn Ehrlich felicitously names, "the cinema of isolation." [This includes] films set in purportedly realistic and contemporary contexts, such as Grémillion's *Lumière d'été* (1943), Bresson's *Les ange du péché* (1943), and Henri-Georges Clouzot's *Le corbeau* (1943).[6]

In general, these darker films were not as popular as the fantasy releases and many were banned or could not be screened until after liberation. Carné's *Les enfants du paradis* falls into this category, as does Robert Bresson's *Les dames du Bois de Boulogne* (1945). Additional films like Jacques Becker's *Goupi mains rouges* (*It Happened at the Inn*, 1943), Jean Grémillon's *Lumière d'été* (*Summer Light*, 1943), and *Le ciel est a vous* (*The Sky is Yours*, 1944), were scathing works of cold rage, meant to attack occupation life more openly and aggressively than the subtle, tragic works of fantasy they followed.

While equally bitter and scathing, Clouzot's *Manon* is a more melodramatic affair. This adaptation of Abbe Prevost's tragic novel, *Manon Lescaut* (1731), is updated to modern day; the film follows a member of the French Resistance, Robert (Michel Auclair),

Robert (Michel Auclair) tenderly buries Manon (Cecile Aubry) in the sand (*Manon*, Alcina, 1949).

who rescues the young prostitute Manon (Cecile Aubry) from angry villagers trying to execute her for alleged dalliances with German soldiers. Robert and Manon fall in love, but their relationship is doomed by his violent jealousy and her obsession with material gain. To avoid being arrested for murder, they stowaway on boat full of war refugees bound for Palestine. But what seems like a dream-like oasis is suddenly transformed into a wasteland of death and massacre when Robert, Manon, and the refugees are gunned down by desert bandits and left to rot in the sand.

It is perhaps an obvious comment on Clouzot's own experience during and after the war. Christopher Lloyd writes, "The subject of the film is the punishment and survival of former collaborators in post-war France (or elsewhere). There is little need to spell out the biographical parallels with Clouzot's own predicament."[7] *Manon* is yet another film—with many more to come later in the '60s and especially in the '70s—to suggest that dishonestly, manipulation, and amorality are the inevitable outcomes of an individual driven to survive at any cost. Truffaut wrote that *The Raven* "seemed to me to be a fairly accurate picture of what I had seen around me during the war and the post-war period—collaboration, denunciation, the black market, hustling."[8] This applies equally to the world of *Manon*, with its protagonists' descent into crime and violence. Robert and Manon are deeply flawed, often unlikable characters, but Clouzot suggests that they are not inherently evil, but merely products of a corrupt, violent world and they are beset by self-serving characters on all sides. Lloyd writes that with *Manon*, Clouzot is

> insisting more explicitly on the violence, immorality and rapacity of post-liberation France. […] Such deterministic fatalism, which conveniently acquits the protagonists of any real personal responsibility for immoral and criminal acts, doubtless struck a chord with contemporary audiences eager to forget or to excuse the humiliations and uneasy compromises brought by life under German occupation.[9]

Manon's visual world is steeped in postwar destruction, replete with bombed out cityscapes. The film takes a strange, dark turn into surrealist territory with its harrowing conclusion, which offers up a horrific fantasy about the fate of war refugees; they have survived years of life under the National Socialists and a grim journey over the sea only to perish in the desert in an act of seemingly random violence. This parallels the experience of real war survivors: not only Holocausts survivors, but soldiers returning home from the front, as well as regular French citizens displaced by the occupation. Lloyd writes,

> The return and reinsertion in French society of deportees and prisoners represented not only a psychological and social process of readjustment for the individuals concerned and their families, but also a significant political and logistical problem (demanding the creation of a ministry specifically dedicating to solving it), given the vast numbers involved. Apart from 700,000 conscripted civilians and 1.2 million soldiers returning from Germany and its satellite territories, several million people had been displaced within occupied France in the course of the war.[10]

The conclusion to *Manon* focuses directly on the refugee experience and takes a sharply tragic twist as many are unexpectedly killed, including Manon herself. Susan Hayward notes that some critics branded Clouzot as anti-Semitic because of this conclusion.[11] Around this time, he also directed the loosely similar short, "Retour de Jean," included in the anthology film *Retour à la vie* (*Return to Life*, 1949). In it, a concentration camp survivor (Clouzot regular Louis Jouvet) discovers a Nazi hiding out in a hotel and proceeds to torture the Nazi soldier to find out his motivations for such apparent evil. In the immediate postwar years, many branded as collaborators did all they could to distance themselves from apparent connections to fascism. In addition to the themes of *Manon*, Clouzot's conflation of victim and perpetrator in *Retour de Jean*—where the concentration camp survivor ultimately sees the war criminal as a human worthy of dignity—did nothing to endear him to his detractors.

A similarly complicated depiction of German soldiers can be found in Jean-Pierre Melville's *Le silence de la mer* (*The Silence of the Sea*, 1949). Born Jean-Pierre Grumbach, the Jewish Melville—who took the name of the American novelist as his *nom de guerre*—served in the French Army and was famously a fighter in the Resistance. Tim Palmer writes,

> As the Occupation began, he mingled there with both the Resistance and the underworld factions that exploited France's flourishing black market economy. Soon Melville became an active Resistance agent, involved to some degree with the underground networks *Combat* and *Libération*. After spending time in London, traveling via Gibraltar, Melville reentered the fray in Allied campaigns in North Africa and Italy before returning to Paris, a decorated veteran, in 1945, after his home country had been liberated.[12]

His experience in the war left an undoubtable stamp on his films, many of which are concerned with problems of masculinity and violence, and survival on the margins of society. Several, beginning with *Le silence de la mer*, are set during World War II, and perhaps due to his personal experiences, these films are fraught with complications and contradictions about the war itself. These are not the sort of black and white, morally polarized conventional war dramas popular at the time, but gritty and often nihilistic portraits of the struggle to survive. Notably, *Le silence de la mer* is adapted from a wildly popular novel of the same name written by the Resistance member "Vercors," an alias for Jean Bruller, which was published secretly in 1942. The novel, like Melville's film, portrays the German officer as a startlingly complex character, not the two-dimensional villain to be found in the majority of cinematic representations of Nazis. Melville fought long and hard for the rights to the novel—including agreeing to final approval of the complete film by Bruller and a panel of former Resistance fighters—resulting in a powerful debut.

The sense of moral ambiguity, so ubiquitous throughout Melville's films, is immediately felt in *Le silence de la mer*. A Frenchman (Jean-Marie Robain) and his young niece (Nicole Stéphane) are forced to share their home with a charming German officer (Howard Vernon), who has been assigned quarters with them. Determined to make friends, the idealistic officer speaks to them regularly in the evenings in increasingly thoughtful and sympathetic monologues, but in protest they maintain their silence and never respond. This relationship deeply impacts all three characters, particularly the German officer.

Though Melville is celebrated for his crime films, *Le silence de la mer* is more of a quiet melodrama, a genre he explored more often in his early years. Regardless, it is concerned with similar themes as his later crime films: loneliness, difficult relationships, communication problems, and alienation. Silence, which is such a major component of the film, allows the German officer to work out moral and philosophical issues concerning the war; in the beginning of the film, he believes it is a just goal that will ultimately benefit the greater good. But he comes to change his opinion and he volunteers himself for the Eastern Front, implying he has chosen certain death. The French characters, particularly the niece, have developed respect and maybe even affection for him, but they

Howard Vernon captivates as a handsome, erudite Nazi officer who is unusually presented as warm and wholly human (*La silence de la mer*, Melville Productions, 1949).

are incapable of expressing those feelings even when they become tragically aware they will never see him again. The overarching theme is that war, regardless of the victor, is a tragedy.

René Clément's *Jeux interdits* (*Forbidden Games*, 1952) is also worth mentioning, as it is another rare film from this period that looks at the subject of war not as the fight of good versus evil, but as a tragedy for all. During the Battle of France, a little girl's (Brigitte Fossey) family is killed, and she is taken in by a young boy (Georges Poujouly) and his parents. The two children process their war trauma by building their own pet cemetery, stealing crosses from a graveyard to mark the graves of pets and other local animals that have perished in the war. Though celebrated critically, the film was attacked in France for unfairly portraying the French people, particularly rural communities. It serves as an example of how filmmakers at this time were encouraged to portray French citizens as heroic and to mask the grim realities of war.

What is perhaps the single most important film from this period to challenge conventional depictions of World War II and shape the way war experience would be portrayed on screen was *Nuit et brouillard* (*Night and Fog*, 1955), Alain Resnais' documentary about the Holocaust and Nazi concentration camps. A central component of Holocaust narratives to emerge in the decades after the war—both cinematic or literary—is the issue of remembrance, of the sacred burden of bearing witness to unimaginable horror that the Nazis attempted to erase from history. For example, consider the story of Chełmno: in September of 1944, the Nazis scrambled to close the Chełmno extermination camp in occupied Poland. Known as Kulmhof to the Germans, it was used as an early killing center and is the first location where poison gas was used in mass killings during the Holocaust, with the total number of deaths believed to be between 150,000 and 180,000 people: primarily Jews from the Łódź Ghetto, but also from Hungary, Germany, and Austria, as well Polish-based Romani and Soviet prisoners of war. After a lengthy, indirect journey mostly by train, victims were locked in gas vans and suffocated to death, a slow method of killing compared to those used at camps like Auschwitz and Treblinka.

When this process was abandoned, the SS attempted to completely erase the existence of Chełmno, as they would later with the other death camps, in an operation known as Aktion 1005. The few remaining prisoners were murdered in vans—some 25,000 people—and a few surviving thousand were transported to Auschwitz-Birkenau. A manor house at the site and all operational buildings were leveled. All the bodies were exhumed by a group of about 80 Sonderkommando—Jewish prisoners used in grueling work details—and then burned in an open-air pit much like the kind later used during the closing of Auschwitz. Their bones were then crushed with mallets—later an industrial machine—and dumped in batches in the local river by night. Following this, most of the 80 Sonderkommando were executed. All documents relating to the camp were destroyed. Even the rubble from the buildings was removed and sent back to Germany, along with the gas vans.

All memory of Chełmno likely would have been lost if it were not for a handful of survivors. Three testified along with a gas van driver in the Adolf Eichmann trial in 1961 and later in the Chełmno trials of the late '60s, though it is believed that seven men survived in total. The most well-known of these, Simon Srebnik, was only fifteen-year-old at the time he miraculously survived his own execution; though he was shot in the head by the SS, he managed to recover.

Bearing witness, giving testimony, and sharing memories of previously unknown horrors became a staple of Holocaust discourse since the 1960s. With the advent of the Eichmann trial—when the Holocaust became an international news item for the first time since the war—there has been an onslaught of memoirs, documentaries, fictional novels, poetry collections, narrative films, and websites like the World Memory Project, as well as numerous physical memorials and museum like Yad Vashem in Israel and the United States Holocaust Memorial Museum in Washington, D.C. Many of these attempt the herculean task of documenting the memories of survivors and unraveling the relationship between memory, identity, trauma, and survival.

But in the immediate postwar years into the 1950s, this mass trauma was marked by a near impenetrable silence. Despite the Nuremberg trials of 1945 and 1946, most Holocaust perpetrators remained at large. Some went into hiding—most notoriously in South America—while others were simply reintegrated into society in Germany or other parts of Europe. Their crimes remain unpunished and, in most cases, unacknowledged examples of what philosopher Hannah Arendt would soon controversially describe as the banality of evil.

On the tenth anniversary of the liberation of the concentration camps, the first major documentary film about the Holocaust emerged. Resnais was commissioned to make a short film about the camps, which became *Night and Fog*. The film was inspired by a 1954 book published in France about eyewitness accounts of Jews being deported to concentration camps, as well as a historical exhibition on the subject from the same year. Resnais, who spent the war years studying acting, attending film school, and then briefly on the German front as a soldier, was reluctant to undertake the project because of his lack of first-hand experience. He wound up collaborating with novelist Jean Cayrol, a survivor of the notoriously brutal labor camp Mauthausen-Gusen.

Resnais' film cuts back and forth between black-and-white historical footage and his own color shots of the abandoned and overgrown camps of Auschwitz and Majdanek in occupied Poland, Struthof in occupied France, and Mauthausen in occupied Austria. Prolific French actor Michel Bouquet narrates, providing explanations of Nazi ideology, a brief history of the Third Reich's rise and fall, and a discussion of the kind of treatment concentration camp prisoners experienced: torture, medical experimentation, beatings, starvation, disease, forced prostitution, and death. There are graphic shots of emaciated bodies in piles, a room filled with women's hair (cut from victims), and shots of the process Nazis used to render soap from human fat. The film ends on an open-ended note, asking who was responsible for the atrocities and how they can be prevented in the future—perhaps an obvious allusion at the time to the French war in Algeria.

The title *Night and Fog* is a direct reference to the *Nacht und Nebel* decree made by Himmler in December of 1941. He ordered that any "foreign" persons within the Reich— which is to say anyone who was not a German national—found to be resisting should disappear without a trace into the night and fog. This meant that they should be unceremoniously executed and disposed of or arrested and transported quietly to a concentration camp where they were likely to be killed soon after arrival. The film's primary image of "night and fog" is an eerie shot of a transport train arriving at Auschwitz.

Though *Night and Fog* was threatened by both French censors and the German government, it was eventually shown at the Cannes Film Festival and in French theaters. Perhaps strangely, it was also protested by Israel for its generic message. Like other documentary films in the mid- to late '40s, the Jewish identity of the majority of the victims of the Holocaust was not directly addressed. While Truffaut called it the greatest film ever made—and it is a moving work of power and pathos—it is hardly a comprehensive portrait of Holocaust experience. Claude Lanzmann, director of the nine-hour Holocaust documentary *Shoah* (1985), summarized much of the criticism:

> It is a film about the living, about the survivors.... There are piles of bodies of those who died of typhus at Bergen-Belsen that, when the camps were opened, were filmed by the Allied news services, footage that appears in *Nuit et brouillard*, but there were no gas chambers in Bergen-Belsen, in Dachau, in Sachsenhausen or in Buchenwald. *Nuit et brouillard* is a beautiful, idealistic film about the deportations, the word "Jew" is mentioned only once during its long litany, and the tears it elicits are the sign of its formidable powers of consolation.[13]

It can certainly be read as a film that attempts to compare the events of the Holocaust with contemporary atrocities and thus focuses on survival against the odds and the promise of a hopeful future. Resnais himself said, "The constant idea was not to make a monument to the dead, turned to the past. If this existed, it could happen again; it exists now in another form."[14] And despite its limitations—it would of course be impossible to relate every Holocaust experience in one film—*Night and Fog* raises important issues that would surround the Holocaust in all forms of art, media, memorial, and study: the complementary issues of guilt and responsibility; the intertwining themes of memory, trauma recovery, bearing testimony, and preventing future horrors; and maintaining identity in the face of dehumanization and mass murder.

Perhaps the reason the film has not been eclipsed by more contemporary, popular

The close-up of a concentration camp uniform in *Night and Fog* is the closest Resnais comes to focusing on the Jewish victims of the Holocaust (*Nuit et brouillard*, Argos Films, 1956).

efforts like *Sophie's Choice* (1982), *Schindler's List* (1993), or *The Pianist* (2002) is that it presents these themes with unflinching simplicity and without overt sentimentality. Phillip Lopate writes, "The rap against most Holocaust films is that they exploit the audience's feelings of outrage and sorrow for commercial ends; and, by pretending to put us vicariously through such a staggeringly incomprehensible experience, they trivialize, reducing it to sentimental melodrama."[15]

Lopate also discusses that the film is better described as non-fiction or "anti-documentary" rather than strictly documentary, as it presents certain truths—and certainly emotional truths—without a barrage of facts, narration, or exposition. The film itself tells us that "words are insufficient" and that no picture or description exists that can truly relate this horror.

Resnais continued this theme with his follow up film, *Hiroshima mon amour* (*Hiroshima My Love*, 1959), about the nebulous relationship between a Japanese man and a French woman in the postwar years. Written by French novelist Marguerite Duras, the film was originally intended to be a follow up documentary about the bombing of Hiroshima which marked the end of World War II. Not wanting to directly repeat his efforts on *Night and Fog*, this French-Japanese co-production instead follows a loose narrative surrounding the nameless "She" (Emmanuelle Riva) and "He" (Eiji Okada), and their lengthy conversations about love, identity, memory, forgetfulness, loss, and the atomic bomb.

It is gradually revealed that while he survived the bombing—he was out of the country serving in the Japanese army at the time—she equates it with her own memories of suffering in wartime France. There, she loved a German soldier who was killed on the eve of their planned departure. In turn, she was imprisoned by villagers and had her head shaved, due to her alleged collaboration with the Nazis. She nearly went mad with grief. Years later, she travelled to Japan to act in a French film about the bombing of Hiroshima.

Their repetitive conversations present a simple argument. She tries to relate to the horror at Hiroshima, while he refutes this at every turn. He says, "You are not endowed with memory. You saw nothing in Hiroshima. Nothing." The film lies somewhere between an expressionistic documentary like *Night and Fog* and a traditional war-themed melodrama like *Casablanca*—the lovers actually meet at a café named after the 1942 film. Resnais and Duras brilliantly blend private and public, personal and universal tales of trauma and memory. This is essentially the story of one woman's devastating wartime experience as paralleled with collective trauma on a scale previously unknown to humankind. Insdorff writes that this is effective because "films that depict a character's memory of a horrific past—and that character's enslavement by it—can have more consistency and integrity than a movie that purports to show the past in an objective way."[16]

The couple's relationship is inextricably bound into Japan's postwar trauma. Just as millions have lost their lives—and names—in Hiroshima, Nagasaki, Auschwitz, Treblinka, and across countless battlefields around the world, the film's two protagonists remain nameless. She is an actress, preparing to re-tell, even to relive the story of Hiroshima, while he is an architect, working to build new structures and re-create lost buildings. Flashbacks of her head being shaved in France mirrors the images of hair lost during the atomic blast and afterwards as an effect of the radiation. There is the sense that her French body is the locus point for other bodies—particularly German and Japanese—and her need to confess, to hold on to and live in the past, is a universal need.

Women's bodies were often the site of guilt, vengeance, and retribution in the immediate days and months after the occupation ended in France. Peter Cowie states,

> After WWII, the French people turned on those who had collaborated with the occupying Nazis and the Vichy regime of Maréchal Pétain. Women who had slept with German officers were identified and if they weren't tried, they were publicly humiliated by having their hair shorn and then being forced to parade in that condition for many weeks or months thereafter.[17]

Cowie cites the harrowing experience tale of famed actress Arletty, star of *Les visiteurs du soir* and *Les Enfants du paradis*, among other films, who became a scapegoat for women who had affairs with German officers. James Lord explains,

> Arletty was too well known for the mere humiliation of having her head shaved, her naked skull tarred with a swastika and in this abject state paraded through the street to confront the jeers and spittle of the mob. Prison would be none too good for her, people said, looking forward to severe retribution for the moral treason of which they found her guilty.[18]

This type of public revenge was often undertaken by communities as a sort of mob justice. Cowie explains, "Resnais has pointed out with a certain irony that the people involved in shaving Riva's hair are not Resistance fighters, so much as shopkeeper types, as happened in the majority of cases."[19] This factual element of the woman's experience in *Hiroshima mon amour* fits in with some of the other documentary aspects Resnais included. She has an obsession with numbers and throughout their conversation repeats statistics: "200,000 dead. 80,000 wounded. In nine seconds." Resnais echoes this dialogue with shots of Hiroshima, including a museum dedicated to the atrocity, hospitals, the city's architecture, newspaper articles, photographs, and even a miniature model of the city. These totems of memory are beset with images of flesh: wounds, scars, radiation burns, and androgynous, shadowy scenes of the couple holding and caressing each other in the dark.

Part of what makes the film so unique is that their sexual and romantic relationship—which has no history of its own—is vividly impacted by the past. *Hiroshima mon amour* is celebrated as influential for its inventive uses of flashbacks and an ambiguous temporal structure that lapses between past and present at will. It is the first of many World War II-themed films to adopt this structure, which effectively delivers several poetic if tragic statements about the nature of identity and memory. Kent Jones writes that the film's tension lies in this relationship: "In fact, it's the anguish of past, present, and future: the need to understand exactly who and where we are in time, a need that goes perpetually unsatisfied."[20] Time in *Hiroshima mon amour* is elusive and frustrating. It reflects the circular nature of the two characters' identities, which are bound up with past trauma, present reality, and future potential, and the fundamental tension between the three.

Resnais also explores three key themes that would reappear almost obsessively in the World War II films released in the decades after it: the need to confess past guilt and traumatic experiences; the need to share memory; and the need to try to understand seemingly incomprehensible horrors. How, for instance, could one begin to comprehend the reality of events that were new to human history, such as the Holocaust—government sanctioned segregation, deportation, ghettos, concentration camps, and extermination

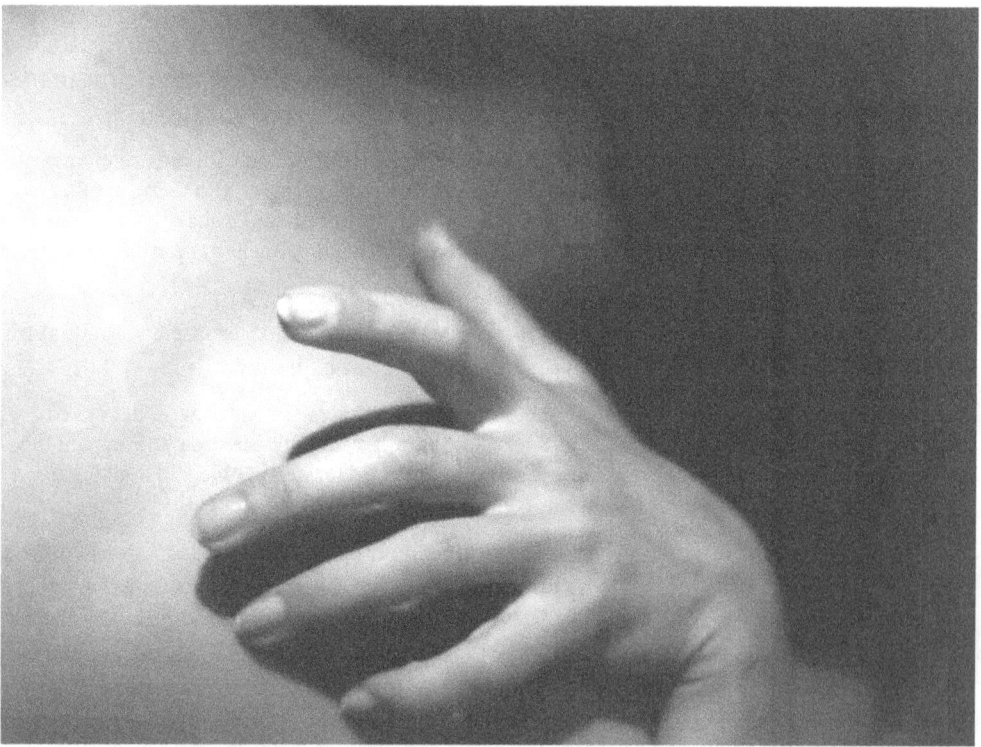

Hands on naked flesh is a common motif in *Hiroshima, mon amour* (Argos Films/Como Films/Daiei Studios/Pathé Entertainment, 1959).

done with factory-like efficiency—or the atomic blasts that killed hundreds of thousands and impacted Japanese life down to the very soil of the earth.

Yet, while the question of remembering and understanding events is vital, it is also agonizing. She calls it a "memory beyond consolation" and is horrified at the prospect of forgetting her German lover, but the memory of him includes the memory of the torture, shaming, and imprisonment that accompanied her love for him. This agonizing experience is a critical part of her identity, but also a moment of horror, an act that should be fixed in the memory so it can never recur. Within her story—and the film at large, as in *Night and Fog*—there is an unspoken warning that the past is perhaps destined to repeat itself. Kate Kennelly writes that

> A fundamental principle linking *Night and Fog* and *Hiroshima mon amour* is their conception of the traumatic past as an enduring reality that lurks in the present. [...] Resnais undertook what he called "formal experiments," which would unsettle the spectator through abrupt flashbacks, emotional estrangement, and self-reflexive commentaries on the inadequacy of the documentary in reconstructing these tragedies.[21]

Future films about the Holocaust and Nazi occupation would adapt some of his methods—both fictional and documentary—specifically to connect past traumas with present events. For example, Robert Bresson's *Un condamné à mort s'est échappé ou Le vent souffle où il veut* (*A Man Escaped or: The Wind Bloweth Where It Listeth*, 1956) is another important film from this period to included similarly abstract "formal experiments" and documentary-like elements. Based on the memoirs of Resistance member André Devigny, the film follows Fontaine (François Leterrier) as he is imprisoned by the Gestapo and attempts to escape in a lengthy and meticulous process. He figures out how to unlock his handcuffs, then later saws through the wooden panel on his doors so he can wander the prison freely at night, then fashions a rope.

A Man Escaped includes relatively few details specific to World War II: a shot in the opening credits informs us that the film is set at Montluc prison in Lyon, a military prison that was adapted for use by the Gestapo, who tortured and killed thousands there, including several massacres. Resistance fighters like Devigny were housed there, as well as leaders like Raymond Aubrac and Jean Moulin, and historian Marcus Bloch, among others. We learn that Fontaine is a member of the Resistance and the prison guards are unmistakably Germans. But the majority of the film—which has an otherworldly, spiritual quality, like much of Bresson's work—is focused on the painstaking minutiae of Fontaine's attempt to escape. Bresson himself explains,

> It was a very precise, technical story about the escape. I remember reading it, and I recall that it affected me the ways things of great beauty do. It was written in an extremely stark, precise, precise tone; even the construction of the narrative was beautiful. It had grandeur. At the same time, there was a coldness mixed with simplicity that made it seem like it was written from the heart, which is very rare. [...] I maintained a tone bordering on documentary, to preserve the sense of reality at all times.[22]

It is important to note that Bresson had also been imprisoned by the Germans; he was not in a Gestapo prison but had lived in a prisoner-of-war camp for about a year. Many of his films are concerned with the experience of imprisonment and attempted liberation. This tension between imprisonment and freedom takes on a spiritual focus, with the specific narrative or historical plot details hovering distantly in the background. Tony Pipolo describes the religious quality of his films. Some of these, such as *Les anges*

Montluc prison in *A Man Escaped*, a former Gestapo torture center where over 15,000 people were incarcerated and close to 1,000 were executed. *Un condamné à mort s'est échappé ou Le vent souffle où il veut*, SNE Gaumont/Nouvelles Éditions de Films (NEF), 1956).

du péché (*The Angels of Sin*, 1943) and *Journal d'un curé de campagne* (*Diary of a Country Priest*, 1951) are concerned with religious figures, such as priests and nuns. But Fontaine takes on a similar quality. Pipolo writes, "The protagonist of *A Man Escaped* is a soldier and a man of action, but, like his predecessors, he is also a spiritual force, inspiring hope in his fellow prisoners."[23] And in this sense, *A Man Escaped* takes on a far broader symbolic context that goes beyond World War II to the theme of society as a prison. The central conflict within the film is not really between French Resistance fighters and German soldiers; rather it is between an imprisoned man and the very walls of the prison itself.

Likewise, another controversial film from this time, *La traversée de Paris* (*The Trip Across Paris*, 1956) is not really about the conflict between good-hearted French citizens and the evil Nazis occupying their country. Director Claude Autant-Lara is more focused on exposing the bleak realities of life during occupation because of the fundamentally flawed nature of humanity in general. This darkly cynical comedy follows a down on his luck taxi-driver (Bourvil)—who has become a black-market delivery driver—and a cantankerous painter (Jean Gabin) who are attempting to deliver black market meat across the city of Paris despite the curfew and other occupation regulations. They get into a number of scrapes, thanks to the rude and impulsive behavior of the artist, who turns out to be world-famous and only interested in assisting with the black market schemes for his own amusement. His recklessness is particularly encouraged by the treatment he receives from the Germans, who exempt him automatically from any disciplinary actions.

The film treats collaboration as an everyday fact of life and the French citizens it depicts regard the black-market trade casually. Autant-Lara was no stranger to controversy throughout his career; his previous film *Le blé en herbe* (*The Game of Love*, 1954), about a relationship between a teenage boy and an older woman, resulted in death threats and went to court for obscenity in the U.S. Unlike the majority of World War II–themed films from the '50s and '60s, *The Trip Across Paris* is one that seemingly lacks any innocent victims—this is a Paris populated by war profiteers, Gestapo informants, and those who otherwise found a way to benefit from the occupation. Such bitter, honest portrayals of occupied life wouldn't really become commonplace on screen in France until the '70s.

3

Out of the Rubble

The Emergence of New German Cinema

"From one day to the next, the past was swept away, and it remained gone for the next twenty-five years."—Saul Friedländer, *Reflections of Nazism*

In comparison to Italian neorealism or the French cinema of the '50s, there was a relative dearth of similar films in immediate postwar Germany. It wasn't really until the genesis of New German Cinema in the late '60s that native filmmakers began to explore World War II and its troubled legacy within their own country. In terms of West Germany,[1] the reason for this lies in the foundation of a postwar national cinema, which was largely taken over by American occupiers. This was a reflection of the situation within the country as a whole. From Germany's surrender in May of 1945, it was divided into four zones occupied by the militaries of the Soviet Union in the east, the U.S. in the south, France in the southwest, and Britain in the northwest. The European boundaries redrawn by the Nazis—such as countries they had occupied or territories they claimed were actually part of Germany—were declared invalid. The pre–World War II map of Europe was also somewhat redrawn, particularly to the east, where a number of territories were claimed by the Soviets.

In the immediate years after the war, Allied forces attempted to punish war criminals in the ongoing Nuremberg trials, begin the complicated overall denazification process, and find a solution to the difficult problem of dealing with millions of refugees—both Germans prisoners of war outside the country attempting to return home and the various eight million refugees within Germany who had been held in concentration camps, still only a relatively small percentage compared to those who had died in death camps, of disease, starvation, or overwork in labor camps. There were also over 12 million Germans living in eastern territories who were expelled once these lands were taken over by Soviet forces. About half left the area and returned to Germany before the war ended, but many died during the final months of the war; the rest were either expelled and forced to return to Germany, though a few were naturalized.

Germany had become a nation where millions were taken from their homes and geographically dislocated, imprisoned, tortured, traumatized, and murdered—both those targeted by the Nazis, as well as the German soldiers and citizens subjected to the Soviets at the end of the war. The majority of the latter group settled in West Germany and many of them villainized the Soviet Union and demanded reparations. The takeover by Allied and Soviet forces complicated life in the immediate postwar years, no thanks to the influence of the French, who were determined to keep Germans from reforming their own governmental organizations. The country didn't really begin to stabilize until 1949, when they were allowed to form their own divided governments: the Federal Republic of Germany in West Germany, a parliamentary democracy, and the German Democratic Republic, a socialist republic overseen by the Soviets in the east.

Military disarmament, the question of reparations, and denazification were paramount in these years, but the process was complicated. While swastikas, Nazi flags, and other paraphernalia were banned, denazification was not such a simple process. Many former Nazis and members of the German military were reabsorbed into society without punishment, while reparations for victims of the Holocaust were only granted to an absurdly small percentage of actual survivors. The general attitude, particularly by the '50s, was the idea that regular Germans weren't guilty—but were victims of the war itself, regardless of whether they were Nazi Party members or not. Nazis came to be associated primarily with the SS and were viewed as a small, criminal, and sadistic percentage of actual German society. In other words, very few were held accountable and even the German military, the Wehrmacht, were glorified and painted as heroes.

Denazification of the film industry was essentially impossible, but in the years just after the war, the Americans at least insured Hollywood dominance over the market and a complete lack of independent voices within German cinema. Thomas Elsaesser writes,

> The famous "Zero Hour" for West German society and industry also seemed to apply to film-making, fostering illusions of autonomy and independence. At the same time, since parts of the old UFA organization survived both the nationalization of the central production unit at Neubabelsberg (which became the East German State company DEFA), and the Allied Forces' deconcentration measures, there was an ominous impression of the continuity with the infamous recent past of German cinema.[2]

West German cinema generally stuck to safe and inoffensive subject matter. For example, out of the Western countries, German cinema had a surprising lack of what could be described as genre movies in the postwar years—a distinct absence of horror, science fiction, and fantasy, with the exception of a handful of low budget horror films and the *krimi* subgenre of crime films based on the pulp mystery novels of British writer Edgar Wallace that took off in the '60s. Many notable horror film and thriller directors, such as Fritz Lang and Otto Preminger, had relocated to the United States in the years before the war and many of them chose to remain.

An exception to this was the *Trümmerfilm* or rubble film, loosely a West German equivalent to neorealism. So called because of their visual fixation on bombed-out Germany, these films were generally dramas that explored postwar life. Like a lot of French films that painted the country in a positive light, replete with heroic Resistance fighters, the rubble film served a similar function in West Germany. Erik Renstschler argues that, somewhat like film noir in the United States, the rubble film isn't specifically a genre, but rather a series of films made in a certain time and place, under specific conditions, with thematic and stylistic similarities. He writes,

> The rubble film is rather a series of feature films produced in Germany between 1946 and 1949 which confront postwar realities. Spanning a number of narrative formulas and employing a variety of styles, *Trümmerfilme* share a historical situation, a production context, and a political mission. With Germany's film industry out of commission, its studios demolished or seized, and many of its key figures compromised by their Nazi era activities, the first movies

after a year's hiatus (the so-called "Filmpause") bore the mark of material shortcoming and artistic uncertainty. [...] Rubble films took stock of a shattered nation and registered a state of physical and psychological ruin.[3]

Topically speaking, these films focused on a return to life after the end of the war: soldiers and refugees returning home; the difficulties of daily existence in the late '40s, and the confrontation of poverty, suffering, and loss; Germany's rather naive attempts to wipe its Nazi past clean and start with a blank slate; and issues of guilt, responsibility, and punishment. In these films, though the recent past and present are often bleak, there is the sense that the future will be bright. Nazism is rarely referred to and the war itself serves as the general antagonist. Like the majority of French films made during this period, in essence they attempt to rewrite history and instill a sense of national pride.

Rentschler writes, "The mission of the *Trümmerfilm* lay in clearing away the rubble, restoring human agency, and creating the conditions for a future community."[4] These films were not meant to offer an explanation for past horrors or even, in many cases, to admit their existence in literal terms. For contemporary viewers, there is a shocking lack of acknowledgment that the Holocaust even took place at all. Much like the French films of the period, the rubble films attempt to help forge a new national identity, one that relied heavily on optimism and which encouraged the German people to cooperate with their Allied occupiers. It is impossible to discuss these films without noting the obvious influence of Hollywood and there is certainly a touch of propaganda to these films.

Robert Shandley admits that the rubble films "played an important role in the formation of a collective attitude towards the past, one that shaped many public debates in Germany in the decades thereafter."[5] This determination to forget or ignore the past stayed with Germany in the following decades and would not be directly confronted in film until the New German Cinema of the '60s and '70s through directors like Rainer Werner Fassbinder and Volker Schlöndorff. Instead, the majority of the rubber films contain uplifting messages and happy endings. A primary example is *Die Mörder sind unter uns* (*Murderers Among Us*, 1946), where a military surgeon suffering from post-traumatic stress disorder joins forces with a concentration camp survivor to send a former Nazi to trial.

The survivor, an artist named Susanne (Hildegard Knef), attempts to return home but finds that a surgeon, Dr. Mertens (Ernst Wilhelm Borchert)—now a bitter alcoholic—has taken up residence there. Dr. Mertens allows Susanne to move back in and she in turn doesn't force him to leave. They develop an uneasy friendship, though Mertens struggles to work because he is incapacitated by his memories of war trauma. Susanne learns that his former superior officer (Arno Paulsen), is not only still alive, but has a thriving business where he turns old military helmets into pants and pans. He is ultimately revealed to be a war criminal; Dr. Mertens is only prevented from killing him in revenge by his love for Susanne, though his former superior is prosecuted as a war criminal.

Murderers Among Us was one of the first postwar German films; it was produced by DEFA (Deutsche Film-Aktiengesellschaft), which was the first film production company founded after the war. It would become the state studio of the German Democratic Republic, though that government would not officially form for another three years. Located in Berlin, this studio was founded under the Soviets, who believed that cinema would be a crucial way to educate and shape postwar Germany. But many of the messages

Refugees ride a train through the rubble on their way home in *Murderers Among Us* (*Die Mörder sind unter uns*, Deutsche Film [DEFA], 1946).

in *Murderers Among Us* were also pushed onto West Germany society, such as the theme that the past should be left behind and the only way to recover from war trauma is to let go of bad memories and move towards a hopeful future. There is the subtle suggestion, through the character of Susanne, that forgetfulness might just be the best medicine.

Rentschler argues that Susanne, the concentration camp survivor of *Murderers Among Us*, attempts to leave her past behind once she is able to return home and start with a clean slate.

> Released from a concentration camp, where she has spent the last three years of the war, she makes a beeline for her former residence, her make-up intact and her spirits undaunted. No sooner has she reoccupied her apartment than she goes to work clearing away the debris. For her the past is not an issue; she is willing and able to leave it behind.[6]

This way of thinking certainly ties into the belief—which would essentially become gospel under the Adenauer government of the '50s—that it was something that happened *to* Germany; not something perpetrated by the country and its citizens. Likewise, it is not up to traumatized citizens to punish war criminals, rather they should be turned in for state-sponsored justice.

Other rubble film examples include *In jenen Tagen* (*In Those Days*, 1947), about different accounts of resistance in Germany. Made by Helmut Käutner, who had several of his films banned by the Nazis and thus was seen as a figure of resistance in terms of early postwar German cinema, *In Those Days* helped create the template for rubble films that depicted ordinary Germans as fundamentally opposed to Nazis values even when they were forced to accept them as part of daily life. Many of the rubble films had their own political agendas; for example *Lang ist der Weg* (*Long Is the Road*, 1948), related the story of Polish Holocaust survivors and was the first of these films to directly refer to the Holocaust itself, rather than just portraying the war in more general terms. Made in partnership with the U.S. Army, the film was meant to raise sympathy for Jewish refugees who were hoping to emigrate to Palestine and who would ultimately found the new state of Israel. Like *Murderers Among Us*, its overall message is about the hopeful future to emerge after surviving such devastation.

Likewise, *Morituri* (1948)[7] followed a group of escaped concentration camp prisoners who are helped to freedom by a Polish doctor and then liberated by the Soviet army. *Morituri* was produced by Artur Brauner for his Central Cinema Company (CCC Films) and has some potentially biographical moments for the producer—it was certainly a deeply personal project. Brauner, a Polish Jew, survived the Holocaust by fleeing to the Soviet Union, though several of his family members were killed in the massacre at Babi Yar. He was determined to make a series of films about the war during this period, though *Morituri* remains the most well-known of these. However *Morituri* bombed at the box office and was even protested in Germany. Apparently, theater owners were afraid to show it, fearing violence from Nazi sympathizers.[8]

Brauner was forced to produce more commercial films to stay afloat, though was ultimately successful enough that CCC Films came to produce a wide range of German-language postwar favorites. He used the money to set up shop in a former Nazi factory where poison gas was made. Brauner said, "Out of the poison-gas factory I wanted to make a dream factory."[9] His long, fruitful career including producing works by Fritz Lang, Vittorio De Sica, Robert Siodmak, and Andrzej Wajda, among others, many of which were critically and financially successful films about the Holocaust, including more recent efforts like *The Last Train* (2006).

However, the German cinema of the '50s—produced during the so-called *Wirtschaftswunder* or economic miracle under Konrad Adenauer—typically avoided any controversial subject matter and audiences obviously preferred lighthearted escapism. The concept of *Vergangenheitsbewältigung*, literally overcoming or coming to terms with the past, was not a focus of German culture until the late '60s. Probably the most popular genre from the late '40s through the early '70s was the *Heimatfilm*, a series of sentimental domestic melodramas. Trafficking in moral absolutes and generally set in Germany's sweeping rural vistas, they reinforced the illusion of a simpler, purer time when life was about honor, family, and the importance of tradition. Rentschler writes,

> The *Trüummerfilm*'s panoramas of destruction with their spiritual void and material lack will yield to the *Heimatfilm*'s more soothing countryside panoramas. The features of the Adenauer era will take leave of the rubble film's *Albträume*[10] and embrace the *Alpenträume* of a *Schönes Deutschland*.[11] Bleak prospects of a world without shelter will give way to a vast abundance of homeland films in the 1950s with their intact communities, pastoral havens, and flourishing cottage industries. Enacting the structured opposition between the terms *Zusammenbruch* and *Neubau* (collapse and reconstruction), homeland films will function as celluloid *Neubauten*, temporary domiciles, mass-produced and quickly produced for displaced and disenfranchised masses.[12]

There are a few exceptions during this period, particularly from filmmakers who fled Nazism for Hollywood but were lured back, often by producers like Artur Brauner. A key exception is Peter Lorre's *Der Verlorene* (*The Lost One*, 1951), the actor's sole effort as writer and director. He also starred in this bleak film about the horrors of Nazism and war. Lorre, who effectively helped begin film noir in the U.S. with his appearance in films like *The Stranger on the Third Floor* (1940) and *The Maltese Falcon* (1941), also brought it to Europe when he returned there for a few years after the war. *The Lost One* is one of the few German films that could be considered film noir and it is a uniquely depressing entry with an overwhelming sense of defeat that culminates in the protagonist's suicide—certainly unusual subject matter for German cinema of the period.

Lorre plays Dr. Rothe, a physician hired to perform experiments for the Nazis. In a series of flashbacks, he relates how he discovered that his fiancée (Renate Mannhardt) was selling government secrets to the Allies. He murdered her and his Nazi associates helped him cover it up so that it looked like suicide by hanging, rather than murder by strangulation. He became increasingly paranoid thanks to overwork, depression, and the oppressive attentions of his landlady (Johanna Hofer), who is also his dead fiancée's mother. After committing a few other murders, Rothe goes into hiding under an assumed name after the war—until he runs into a former colleague and, out of exhaustion, ends his life by jumping in front of a train.

Though the film is obsessed with death, wartime destruction, and decay, Lorre doesn't overtly depict Nazism. There are plenty of veiled references to the war, such as air raid sirens, a refugee camp, medical experimentation, and bombings. The evils of Nazi bureaucracy are shown in the scene where Hösch (Karl John) and Winkler (Helmuth Rudolph)—respectively a fellow scientist and a Nazi leader—help Rothe cover up his fiancée's murder and joke about her alleged suicide.

Due to a variety of issues, including his health and financial troubles, Lorre's life was difficult during the making of the film and his bitterness is palpable. He was suffering from a morphine addiction and had spent time in a sanitarium where he received

Peter Lorre finds blood on his face in *The Lost One*, in a shot inspired by Fritz Lang's *M* (1931) (*Der Verlorene*, Arnold Pressburger Filmproduktion, 1951).

electroshock therapy. He temporarily fled a frustrating career in Hollywood and hoped to help revitalize the German film industry. But Lorre's experience of professional and personal misery in the postwar years was far from unique and these frustrations were shared to different degrees by exiles, Holocaust survivors, and the millions whose lives were forever changed by war. The theme of suicide, so prominent in *The Lost One*, was a fixture of German society during this period.

Historian Peter Gay explains that the wave of war-related suicides began around the same time the Nazis came into power and was particularly prominent among writers and artists. For example, many of the Expressionists playwrights and their work faded into obscurity because "many of them killed themselves during the Nazi period."[13] This subject was so prominent in German literature as to have its own subgenre. Gay writes,

> There was a whole genre of novels dealing with the suicides of young high school students—*Schülerselbstmordromane*—and its popularity reflected widespread interest in a grave phenomenon. In early 1929 Friedrich Torberg published a characteristic suicide novel, *Der Schüler Gerber*, and prefaced his story with the laconic comment that in a single week—January 27 to February 3, 1929—he had read in the newspapers of ten such suicides. And Ernst Toller, himself to die by his own hand in 1939, dedicated his autobiography to "the memory of my nephew Harry who, in 1928, at the age of eighteen, shot himself."[14]

Even many of those who survived the war remained obsessed by it and had difficulty forging new lives. French philosopher Albert Camus captured this sense of futility, absurdity, and despair in one of his major philosophical works, *Le Mythe de Sisyphe* (*The Myth of Sisyphus*, 1942). Written during the French occupation and Camus' time in the Resistance, this treatise concerns whether or not it is acceptable to commit suicide in the face of an absurd world. Writer Klaus Mann, son of novelist Thomas Mann, called for a mass suicide just years before his own. Mann, like many of his contemporaries, fled Germany for the U.S. and was a staunch anti–Nazi, showing up on their blacklist alongside several of his family members. He created an anti-fascist journal, *Decision*, and served in Italy with the U.S. Army, but was unable to reconcile the events of the war. Andrew Pulver writes, "As the cold war developed, however, he became increasingly depressed about the future. In 1949, in an essay entitled Europe's *Search for a New Credo*, he called for a 'movement of despair,' suggesting that a 'suicide wave' of intellectuals would shock the world out of its 'lethargy.'"[15]

While this idea may seem extreme, Mann was not the first to think of it. In 1936, film producer Stefan Lux shouted, "This is the final blow," and committed suicide in the League of Nations' assembly room in an attempt to rouse the world to the Nazi persecution of Jews. Lux's case—and hundreds more—are described in David Lester's book *Suicide and the Holocaust*. He lists numerous motivations: refugees for whom the journey of escape was impossible, émigrés who were not accepted by any new country, those who learned their loved ones were murdered, Resistance members attempting to escape capture and torture, acts of political resistance, and so on. A high number of these include Jewish suicides during Nazi occupation—he cites 500 in Austria in 1938 alone—as well as Jews attempting to escape deportation, such as 1,200 people in Łódź, Poland, then the location of the second largest ghetto in occupied Europe.

Germans also committed suicide, often in mass numbers at the end of the war. Soldiers killed themselves to evade capture and to escape prosecution. German citizens were convinced by their government—in perhaps the most outrageous example of government propaganda encouraging suicide—that the arriving Soviet army were barbarians who would rape (this turned out to be true), imprison, and torture them. Christian Goeschel describes how entire families and even small villages killed themselves, specifically between January and May of 1945. Hitler, who shot himself months later, said, "It's only a second. Then one is redeemed of everything and finds tranquility and eternal peace."[16]

The suicides continued after the war, due to survivor's guilt, post-traumatic stress disorder, and the years of displacement and poverty faced by many. Famous artists, writers, and intellectuals like Klaus Mann, Bruno Bettelheim, Tadeusz Borowski, Paul Celan, Primo Levi, and Jean Amery—who wrote *On Suicide: A Discourse on Voluntary Death* (1976) two years before killing himself—all brought about their own deaths throughout the ensuing years. Primo Levi's suicide, in particular, remains a well-tread subject due to the fact that it occurred late in life, when the writer was 67, and was the result of a fall which it has been speculated was an accident. Adam Kirsch writes that Levi's story is a familiar one:

> The long-delayed suicide of the Holocaust survivor is a story whose outlines we know too well. Jean Amery, who survived Gestapo torture and Auschwitz, took an overdose of sleeping pills in 1978; Paul Celan, who spent the war in a slave labor camp in Romania and saw his parents murdered, drowned himself in the Seine in 1970; Jerzy Kosiński, who survived in hiding during the Nazi occupation of Poland, asphyxiated himself in a bathtub in 1991. By jumping from a third-story landing, Levi seemed to be delivering the same message: he had borne the burden of an intolerable experience as long as he could, until his strength gave out and he had to let it drop.[17]

Some of these writers, such as Klaus Mann, present a semi-hopeful view of suicide as a returning to the past and an escape from the unbearable memory of trauma, which is also a theme in Lorre's *The Lost One*. Disturbingly, Lorre spends much of the film smiling defeatedly. He speaks of death constantly; his own, Germany's, and the deaths of the women around him. There is no way to return home, to the idealized past, before war and violence. In general, the other rubble films avoided this depressing theme, generally choosing to focus on the idea of building a hopeful future. A notable exception includes *Liebe 47* (*Love '47*, 1949), about a young couple who meet because they have both decided to kill themselves. They share their wartime experiences with each other and decide to live after all.

This is a similar theme in Rossellini's *Germany Year Zero*, which can be loosely considered a rubble film because of its shooting locations. Like *Germany Year Zero*, the landscape in Lorre's *The Lost One* is hellish and foreboding. The expressionist-influenced cinematography from Vaclav Vich transforms Hamburg into a skeletal, gray place on the brink of death. Lorre used a complex and somewhat confusing narrative structure that builds a sense of dread and paranoia through flashbacks and disturbed memories. Are the events unfolding on screen Rothe's paranoid fantasy or a violent reality? Either way, his plight is symbolic of the psychosis experienced during wartime. Like Lang's *M* (1931), which made Lorre a star, much of the film's plot is partially based on a real-life crime. Though it was influenced by Guy de Maupassant's story "Le Horla" (1887), *The Lost One* was also inspired by a news story about a Hamburg doctor who murdered his assistant and committed suicide.

A loosely similar example is director Robert Siodmak's *Nachts, wenn der Teufel kam*

(*The Devil Strikes at Night*, 1957), also inspired by a historical murderer. Siodmak was one of several directors lured back to Germany in the postwar years by producer Brauner. It took the Dresden-born director a few years after the end of the war, but he eventually returned to his home country to film *Die Ratten* (*The Rats*, 1955), about a starving woman who sells her child, and *The Devil Strikes at Night*. This thriller follows a serial killer operating in World War II Germany. Based on real-life alleged murderer Bruno Lüdke, Siodmak's film focused on government corruption, as an innocent man is initially blamed because Nazi authorities don't want to take responsibility for their inability to find the real killer. This is somewhat ironic, as Lüdke's guilt has been questioned in more recent years.

While *The Devil Strikes at Night* is a serial killer thriller, it has what is perhaps an obvious political subtext. Bernard Hemingway writes,

> *The Devil Strikes At Night* has been compared to Fritz Lang's *M* (1931), but this is only partly justified. Both films deal with a serial killer but whereas the killer and the fear he engenders amongst the ordinary citizenry is the centrepiece of Lang's film, Siodmak's killer is only a pretext for the director's main concern, which is a coming-to-terms with the Nazi era. The systemic murders carried out by the mentally deficient Lüdke (his only victim that we see is a slatternly waitress) are contrasted with the brutal logic of the genocidal Nazis.[18]

Like other rubble films, Siodmak does make an effort to give the film some realistic, documentary-like qualities. This is true not just in terms of the details of Lüdke's crimes, but in his attempts to capture life under the Gestapo. In this way it feels more like a historical drama than a straightforward thriller. Unlike Lang's *M*, it stops short of scathing social analysis and mimics the rubble films' depiction of Nazis as exaggerated caricatures, as a corrupt, sadistic minority controlling a country of otherwise innocent Germans forced to compromise for their own survival. In this sense, *The Devil Strikes at Night* is an example of a slightly later offshoot of the rubble film, which emphasizes the decadence of Nazism and made direct reference to the Holocaust. Other examples include *Des Teufels General* (*The Devil's General*, 1955), with Curd Jürgens starring as a proud Luftwaffe general critical of the Third Reich, who is caught between would-be liberators and Nazi extremists.

Aside from some of these exceptions, the unfortunate combination of bland mainstream films obviously influenced by Hollywood and the overall lack of a vibrant national cinema frustrated a group of young filmmakers and artists enough that they banded together and released a petition known as the Oberhausen Manifesto in 1962. This was the genesis of the group of directors whose loose movement ultimately came to be described as New German Cinema. Unified less by style or theme and more by time, place, and cinematic aims, it's difficult to discuss their films as a cohesive whole. Elsaesser explained,

> Four factors have shaped the New German Cinema: a system of public funding for feature film production; a legal framework for television co-production; an international reputation for four or five individual directors and, finally, the politicized and media-conscious student movement of the late 1960s and 1970s.[19]

Filmmakers like Alexander Kluge, Werner Herzog, Volker Schlöndorff, and Wim Wenders explored an arthouse sensibility somewhat similar to the French New Wave. Their films emphasized realism, were generally set in present day Germany, and often dealt with social and political issues faced by the country's citizens. Roughly beginning in 1966 with Alexander Kluge's *Abschied von gestern* (*Yesterday's Girl*), the early efforts of New German Cinema generally shied away from directly exploring World War II-themes, though there are a few notable exceptions. A particularly early turning point in this movement and its response to the atrocities of the past can be found in a short film made by Kluge and Peter Schamoni, *Brutalität in Stein* (*Brutality in Stone*, 1960). Their film was meant to be a deeply critical examination of the Nazi legacy by contrasting destroyed Nazi buildings and monuments. Rentschler writes,

> The Nazi garbage pile of history provides a testimony in stone: the heroic style, monumental appeal, and large scale of depleted and unfinished structures bear witness to misguided grand illusions. This short documentary recollects shards and reflections of a collective dream, juxtaposing the fragments of today with the immodest designs of Nazi city planners, refashioning historical debris into a deconstructed museum of memories. Kluge's rubble film is a parody of a Nazi *Kulturfilm*.[20]

This turning point in the '60s coincided with an important series of trials that brought the Holocaust sharply back into public attention. While some Nazi leaders were tried and executed in the Nuremberg trials immediately after the war, there were a series of secondary trials held later, throughout Germany, aimed at prosecuting war criminals who had so far evaded capture. This began with the notorious capture and arrest of Adolf Eichmann, one of the architects of the Holocaust, by Mossad, the Israeli intelligence service. He was effectively kidnapped in Argentina in 1960 and brought to Jerusalem for a trial that began in 1962. The widely publicized trial and recorded proceedings included testimonials from many Holocaust survivors, bringing to light for the first time some of the atrocities that occurred at the Nazi death camps.

While Eichmann was found guilty on several counts and executed by hanging, not all of the concentration camp trials held in Germany itself had similar outcomes and some of them seemed to be held merely to suggest that some official effort was being made. Overall, these trials were aimed at uncovering those responsible for Aktion Reinhardt, or Operation Reinhardt, the Nazi code name for the plan that orchestrated the Holocaust and established both death camps, concentration camps, and other forms of systematic murder. Separate trials were held throughout the '60s for the death camps: Auschwitz, Belzec, Sobibor, Treblinka, Chełmno, and Majdanek. While the trials resulted in new information about what actually occurred and brought much about the Holocaust to light, justice was not exactly served. Many of the SS officers on trial for war crimes at Chełmno were cleared, while others received piteously short sentences.

These trials, particularly the Auschwitz trials held in Frankfurt, brought to light a series of philosophical questions. Because of legal precedent, those SS officers and other soldiers who worked in the camps could only be charged with murder if they were found to have killed people while not following orders. Those who killed while following orders could only be charged as accomplices. This resulted in a hopelessly skewed series of trials where the prosecution was forced to operate under the supposition that within a totalitarian government—such as Nazi Germany—only those who made decisions and served as leaders could be held responsible. Those serving under them were only accomplices following orders. Thus, thousands of former Nazis, many of whom actively participated in the Holocaust, were reintegrated into German society and escaped facing any consequences.

The seeds sown with the rubble films—which suggested that Nazis were a small, aberrant fraction of German society—allowed the nation to distance itself from guilt and to avoid feeling responsible. Some of the early New German films confronted these issues of guilt and responsibility, such as Volker Schlöndorff's film *Der junge Törless* (*Young Törless*, 1966), which examines latent fascism in the interwar period. Based on an autobiographical novel by Robert Musil, the film follows the teenage Thomas Törless (Mathieu Carrière), who is newly enrolled in a military academy. He is befriended by two of the institution's crueler boys, Reiting (Fred Dietz) and Beineberg (Bernd Tischer). They have caught another boy named Basini (Marian Seidowsky) stealing and, in exchange for not turning him into the school's authorities, have made him their slave. In addition to humiliating and beating him, it is implied that sexual abuse also occurs. Törless is both fascinated and repulsed by their actions, leading him to an intense period of introspection that results in an emotional and soon physical withdrawal from school.

While *Young Törless* may feel like something of an outlier in early New German Cinema—for example, Schlöndorff is more stylistically conventional than some of his colleagues—his feature length debut helped set the stage for the years to come. Film historian Timothy Corrigan writes,

> Through the early 1960s, Schlöndorff had apprenticed in France (where he'd been educated as a teenager) with several of the major figures in the French New Wave, including Louis Malle, Alain Resnais, and Jean-Pierre Melville. This connection would be a crucial springboard for Schlöndorff's career, since it provided him with an early training in the stylistics and politics of an alternative cinema, while at the same time making him aware of his own country's lack of an active national cinema.[21]

It's particularly important to examine the film in the context of how it attempts to make sense of the past, one of the overarching themes of New German Cinema. Corrigan writes that *Young Törless* attempts to "investigate the terms of the present by uncovering the losses, repressions, and denials of the German past."[22] Certainly one horrific element

Törless (Mathieu Carrière) looks away from the vicious beating of a classmate in *Young Törless* (*Der junge Törless*, Franz Seitz Filmproduktion, Nouvelles Éditions de Films [NEF], 1966).

of the film is not that the boys' sadistic inclinations are present in the first place, but that these impulses are so commonplace and so willingly accepted. Basini, of course, is notably struggling with money and it is implied that he is from a slightly lower class background than boys like Reiting or Beineberg, in addition to having Jewish heritage.

Schlöndorff presents Törless's complicity as the true horror of the film. He knows Reiting and Beineberg are cruel and their actions are wrong, but he merely accepts events as they unfold and, instead of rebelling, is content to leave school and return to the isolated comforts of home in what Corrigan describes as "a frighteningly stoic withdrawal."[23] Once he has uncovered the extent of the boys' behavior towards Basini, Törless writes in his notebook, "I must be sick, insane. Why else would things that others find normal disgust me?" He comes to the conclusion that "perfectly normal people can do terrible things." *Young Törless* expresses a sentiment earlier described by one of Germany's greatest posts, Friedrich Hölderlin, in his novel *Hyperion* (1799):

> It is a hard saying, and yet I say it because it is the truth: I can conceive of no people more dismembered than the Germans. You see workmen, but no human beings, thinkers but no human beings, priests but no human beings, masters and servants, youths and staid people, but no human beings.[24]

This was followed by Hans Jürgen Pohland's *Katz und Maus* (*Cat and Mouse*, 1967), another tale of homoeroticism, sadism, and fascism in schoolboys. One of the most neglected films of early New German Cinema, it was also among the most scandalous. In 1966, a man named Pilenz (Wolfgang Neuss) returns to Danzig, his hometown, and wonders whatever happened to a former classmate, Joachim Mahlke (played by both Lars and Peter Brandt). Pilenz remembers that Mahlke was ostracized for his enormous Adam's apple, but found popularity through his diving skills. After stealing a medal from a soldier, he's expelled from school, but regains his honor by joining the war effort and becoming a soldier himself, until his disappearance.

Pohland, who generally served as a producer rather than a director, struggled to find someone to helm the film and was allegedly in talks with Polish director Andrzej Wajda before taking on the job himself. Based surprisingly faithfully on a 1961 novella by Günter Grass, the material was controversial from the start. Magdalena Saryusz-Wolska writes, "To some it was an iconoclastic work, pornographic even, that depicted German youth in a disgraceful way, while others read it with satisfaction as a critical and ironic text about recent German history."[25] In addition to the book's graphic depictions of masturbation and the theft and then desecration of a revered war medal, Pohland's choice of actors was both unconventional and ill-timed. Saryusz-Wolska writes,

> Pohland's casting decisions as well as the political situation in the German Federal Republic contributed to the film's failure. Joachim Mahlke was played by the sons of Willy Brandt, who at the time of shooting (the summer holidays of 1966) was still mayor of West Berlin. When the previews showed one scene of them masturbating before the camera—although nothing overly graphic was depicted—and another in which one of them places the Iron Cross in his underpants, scandal broke out.[26]

Brandt was also then leader of the Social Democratic Party and in 1969 would assume the role of Chancellor for the country.

The fraught sexual and political content essentially destroyed the film's reputation and instead of going on to develop a cult audience, as was the case with equally scandalous though later World War II–themed arthouse films, it has been more or less forgotten.

It is, however, important to note Pohland's use of time and memory within the film. Seemingly inspired by the French New Wave, the narrator, Pilenz, physically injects himself into his own memories even as he is relating them. Carrie Smith-Prei writes, "Like the original text, the film problematizes the nature of memory by positioning that the narrator, Pilenz, constructs himself just as he constructs the memories of his childhood in wartime Danzig."[27]

This idea of the unreliable narrator was an important component of earlier cinematic movements like film noir, but its use in *Cat and Mouse* speaks to a deeper issue within German culture, namely the inability to relate past traumas to present circumstances. Smith-Prei explains, "Pilenz's body resists the narrative at the same time that it creates it, carving out the imaginary space of memory for the plot to unfold while puncturing the social construction of masculinity towards which Mahlke strives."[28] *Cat and Mouse* and *Young Törless*, along with Werner Herzog's *Lebenszeichen* (*Signs of Life*, 1968) and Werner Schroeter's *Der Bomberpilot* (1970), are marked by depictions of sexualized bodies, rigid gender constructs, and a use of narration that not only suggests the contrast between past and present, but unites the two temporal spaces.

Signs of Life, Herzog's feature-length debut, concerns three German soldiers on leave recovering from minor war injuries in Nazi-occupied Greece. The young Stroszek (Peter Brogle) has married a Greek woman (Athina Zacharopoulou) and is living a life of leisure and relaxation while the war seems little more than a distant memory. But solitude, boredom, and purposelessness do not agree with Stroszek and one day he snaps, taking a munitions depot in an ancient fortress hostage to the dismay of the entire island, particularly German command, who are unsure how to resolve the situation quickly and quietly.

Like many of Herzog's later films, *Signs of Life* is about the maddening absurdity of modern life. While Herzog doesn't specifically make any observations about the struggles of wartime or life under occupation, he does depict a side of war and military life not often shown on screen—particularly in World War II films. Herzog portrays Stroszek's mental break and the ensuing violence as the poetic if somewhat inevitable outcome when a man is made to feel impotent and useless. While this certainly applies to inactive military duty, it is also more broadly about the repetitive quality of daily life. *Signs of Life* reflects the sense of impending violence that American novelist Carson McCullers also describes in her 1941 novella about perverse events at an army base, *Reflections in a Golden Eye*. In the opening paragraph, she asserts, "An army post in peacetime is a dull place. Things happen, but then they happen over and over again."[29]

In *Signs of Life*, the soldiers eat, drink, play cards, and repeat the same small talk until Stroszek suddenly has a mental breakdown. His violence—which could easily result in tragedy considering that he's armed, trained, and sitting on top of a fully stocked munitions depot—is ineffectual, yet somehow lyrical. He sets a chair on fire, shoots bullets aimlessly into the sky, and sets off rockets that harm no one and look more like a dazzling fireworks display than an act of war. His worst offense is that he kills a donkey.

These themes are taken even further in Werner Schroeter's experimental TV film *Der Bomberpilot* (*The Bomber Pilot*, 1970). The loose plot follows three women in a traveling cabaret troupe living and performing during the Third Reich. Their musical revue falls apart when one of the girls has a nervous breakdown and they struggle through a series of odd jobs and bouts with mental illness, until reuniting a few years later and deciding to travel to the United States for their great revival tour. All three actresses unusually grant their own names to their characters: Carla Egerer a.k.a. Carla Aulaulu, who worked regularly with Fassbinder at this time on films like *Götter des Pest* (*Gods of the Plague*, 1970), *Warum läuft Herr R. Amok?* (*Why Does Herr. R Run Amok?*, 1970), and *Pioniere in Ingolstadt* (*Pioneers in Ingolstadt*, 1971); Mascha Rabben of Fassbinder's *Welt am Draht* (*World on a Wire*, 1973); and Magdalena Montezuma, Schroeter's muse and collaborator until her death in 1984.

Fassbinder spoke regularly of Schroeter's profound influence, not just on himself but on New German Cinema as a whole. Schroeter was perhaps the most experimental of the country's filmmakers, as expressed in *Der Bomberpilot*, something contemporary viewers will likely be astonished was made for television. *Der Bomberpilot* is really the first true example of a cult film from New German Cinema and very little about it is conventional. There are numerous instances where Schroeter either breaks the fourth wall or defies normative conventions of filmmaking entirely, including frequent lapses into fantasy, song and dance numbers that seem intentionally bad, and on-going voice overs from a clearly unreliable narrator. There are plenty of satirical elements and, perhaps oddly, this seems like a bridge between Vera Chytilová's Czech film *Sedmikrásky* (*Daisies*, 1966) and the Nazisploitation films of the '70s with its poor editing and awkward dubbing, vibrant colors that enhance a sense of kitsch, and exaggerated performances.

Michelle Langford wrote, "Schroeter articulates history as a particularly subjective and fragmentary form of remembering."[30] While the girls idealize the war

Werner Schroeter reimagines the Third Reich as a failed camp spectacle with Carla Egerer, Mascha Rabben, and Magdalena Montezuma in *Der Bomberpilot* (Werner Schroeter Filmproduktion, 1970).

years—particularly Carla, who longs for the Viennese choir boys she seduced—all three are plagued with personal difficulties: mental collapse, suicide attempts, existential angst, trouble in love, and the crushing depression of daily life. A sense of postwar guilt and collective misery is reflected in the song and dance numbers that occur throughout the film. Schroeter would frequently use musical elements in his movies and even directed opera. Here he presents a blend of everything from Strauss—using a particularly scathing version of "Wiener Blut" with lyric references to blasé attitudes about remembering the past—to pop music like Elvis. However during the girls' performances, they seem to be drunk, drugged, or involved in some sort of slapstick routine. Langford writes, "Their movements are uncoordinated, awkward and a-rhythmic, the very antithesis of the highly ordered spectacle of the Nazi revues and revue films to which they allude. In doing so, they evoke a kind of 'false memory' of that period of history."[31]

Their haphazard saluting to the swastika flag that opens the film is, in itself, something of the ultimate "fuck you" to fascist culture and political rhetoric. Schroeter's blend of anarchism and pathos present in *Der Bomberpilot* has no equal in New German Cinema. According to Langford, the girls

> seem to mock the order and hierarchy of the Nazi revue by their lack of discipline, the vastly different shapes and sizes of the girls' bodies and their arrangement according to no apparent hierarchical order. Rather than alleviating chaos, they are its very embodiment. Through their bodies and their "faults of performance," Schroeter's girls situate themselves at the juncture of the fault lines between history and memory.[32]

Der Bomberpilot marks a turning point in New German Cinema, at least in terms of how the movement would begin to reflect on Germany's past and the legacy of fascism. The majority of directors working under this umbrella examined turmoil in contemporary Germany. But Elsaesser writes that by the mid- to late '70s, "political questions, social issues, current affairs and historical topics began to be treated in fiction films and documentaries in a manner unknown before in the Federal Republic."[33] New German Cinema's *enfant terrible*, Rainer Werner Fassbinder, whose work will be explored in a later chapter, was responsible for the bulk of this. There are, however, a handful of other West German productions from the late '70s and through the '80s worth discussing that also explore these themes.

Another experimental example from the period is *Hitler, ein Film aus Deutschland* (*Hitler: A Film from Germany*, 1977), Hans-Jürgen Syberberg's more than seven-hour opus co-produced by the BBC. A radical exercise in theatrical excess, it almost has more in common with opera than it does conventional cinema—Wagner is a constant, almost spectral presence and his tomb even appears several times—and this is a film that demands much of its viewers. It would be fair to describe it as a fully immersive experience, rather than merely a cinematic event, an endurance test the like of which can only really be compared to Claude Lanzmann's marathon Holocaust documentary *Shoah* within the context of war-themed films.

Syberberg wrote the film and also acts as narrator, though there is no conventional plot, rather a series of experimental vignettes that touch upon different topics in German history, mythology, and politics. The film is divided into four parts. The first, *Der Gral: Von der Weltesche bis zur Goethe-Eiche* (*The Grail: From the Cosmic Ash-Tree to the Goethe Oak*), explores the personality cult that surrounded Hitler. The second, *Ein deutscher Traum ... bis ans Ende der Welt* (*A German Dream.... Until the End of the*

World), examines Germanic mythology and culture, particularly the elements that fed into Nazi ideology. The third part, *Das Ende eines Wintermärchens und der Endsieg des Fortschritts* (*The End of a Winter's Tale and the Final Victory of Progress*) specifically discusses anti-Semitism and the Holocaust, while the final section, *Wir Kinder der Hölle erinnern uns an das Zeitalter des Grals* (*We Children of Hell Recall the Age of the Grail*), is mostly made up of extraneous, generally satirical material from the script being read aloud, often with the assistance of a Hitler puppet.

The film's most outspoken supporter, Susan Sontag, writes,

> The assumptions are familiar, crude, plausible. But they hardly prepare us for the scale and virtuosity with which he conjures up the ultimate subjects: hell, paradise lost, the apocalypse, the last days of mankind. Leavening romantic grandiosity with modernist ironies, Syberberg offers a spectacle about spectacle: evoking "the big show" called history in a variety of dramatic modes—fairy tale, circus, morality play, allegorical pageant, magic ceremony, philosophical dialogue, Totentanz—with an imaginary cast of tens of millions and, as protagonist, the Devil himself.[34]

It's difficult to provide a concise description of the film, due to its deeply experimental nature, but Syberberg uses a handful of common filmic devices and themes throughout. Like the British master of excess, Ken Russell, biography was a focus of much of Syberberg's career and here he uses Hitler as both a symbolic and a historical figure, sitting somewhere at the crossroads of fact, fiction, fantasy, myth, culture, and death cult, like a perverse reinterpretation of Walter Benjamin's musings on *Angelus Novus*. In *Theses on the Philosophy of History*, Benjamin writes of the angel:

> His face is turned toward the past. Where we perceive a chain of events, he sees one single catastrophe which keeps piling wreckage upon wreckage and hurls it in front of his feet. The angel would like to stay, awaken the dead, and make whole what has been smashed. But a storm is blowing in from Paradise; it has got caught in his wings with such violence that the angel can no longer close them. This storm irresistibly propels him into the future to which his back is turned, while the pile of debris before him grows skyward. This storm is what we call progress.[35]

Syberberg uses Hitler as the locus point for German history and national identity, which he seems to view as inherently evil. He blends together accounts of Hitler's daily rituals and the biographies of his closest companions and collaborators, alongside references to German cultural figures like Goethe, Wagner, Brecht, and Thomas Mann, in a sort of cultural exorcism. Sontag writes,

> Nazism is known by allusion, through fantasy, in quotation. Quotations are both literal, like an Auschwitz survivor's testimony, and, more commonly, fanciful cross references-as when the hysterical SS man recites the child murderer's plea from Lang's *M*; or Hitler, in a tirade of self-exculpation, rising in a cobwebby toga from the grave of Richard Wagner, quotes Shylock's "If you prick us, do we not bleed?"[36]

The theme of death, loss, mourning, and especially the expiation of guilt are predominant throughout. The concept of *Trauerarbeit*, meaning "grieving" or literally "grief work," was first explored in connection to genocide and German guilt by psychologists Alexander and Margarete Mitscherlich in a 1967 text. This is integral to Syberberg's themes and curiously predates the German public's gradual understanding of the subject.

This essentially came with the release of *Holocaust*, an American TV series that aired in Germany in 1979. Written and created by Gerald Green and directed by *Roots'* Marvin J. Chomsky, this four-part series related the fictional story of a bourgeois family of German Jews—a doctor (Fritz Weaver), his pianist wife (Rosemary Harris), and their adult children (including a daughter-in-law played by a young Meryl Streep)—most of whom are deported to Auschwitz after experiencing things like Nazi persecution, rape, violence, specific events like Kristallnacht, and some of the more notorious aspects of the Holocaust such as the Warsaw Ghetto, various concentration camps, and the gas chambers.

It is difficult not to fixate on the series' more lurid, sensational aspects. Controversy at the time related to whether it was appropriate to use the Holocaust as a source of popular entertainment, not even considering the number of inaccurate (or even blatantly incorrect) elements. Regardless, this was the first time that a vast number of not only American viewers, but also Europeans were exposed to personal stories relating to World War II, Nazi genocide, and the Holocaust. Annette Insdorf writes, "It is primarily through motion pictures that the mass audience knows—and will continue to learn—about the Nazi era and its victims."[37] *Holocaust*'s importance to mainstream German culture is not that it really resolved any issues about German history and the lingering effects of war trauma, but that it raised a series of complicated questions that haunted German history, culture, and contemporary society.

Some of these questions fortunately challenged the theories put forth by German academics of the day. Elsaesser writes,

> Jürgen Habermas detected in the writings of German academic historians, foremost among them Ernst Nolte and Andreas Hillgruber, an unacceptably revisionist project, desired to historicize the Nazi period in order to "normalize" it, by comparing the extermination of Jews, as Nolte seemed to do, to earlier genocides (the Boer war, the destruction of the Heroes, the Ottoman massacre of the Armenians, Stalin's Gulags) and later ones (Idi Amin's Uganda, the killing fields of Pol Pot). The most controversial revisionist argument, however, was Hillgruber who implicitly juxtaposed the victims of the concentration camps with the hundreds of thousands of women and children killed in the Allied bombing raids that resulted in the firestorms of Dresden and Hamburg, or the several million civilians who perished during the mass-expulsions from the Eastern provinces of the Reich after capitulation.[38]

The claims of the *Holocaust* TV series—and the arguments of historians such as Hillgruber—were addressed with renewed vigor by New German Cinema filmmakers like Schlöndorff. His controversial black-comedy-based Günter Grass novel of the same name, *Die Blechtrommel* (*The Tin Drum*, 1979), examines not only issues of anti–Semitism, but also anti–Polish sentiment thanks to its setting of Gdańsk, once known as Danzig to its extensive German population. Poland's main seaport, the city has a storied history that includes Prussian occupation, Polish rule, a period of independence, and it remains an ideal site to symbolize cultural tensions.

The film follows Oskar Matzerath (David Bennent, son of actor Heinz Bennent who also has a small but memorable role in *The Tin Drum*), a boy who decides, when he is three years old, that he is going to stop growing. Oskar's family life is complicated, as his mother (Angela Winkler) is involved with both her husband, the pro–Nazi Alfred (Mario Adorf), and her cousin, the pro–Polish Jan (Daniel Olbrychski), who Oskar believes is actually his father. Obsessed with his toy drum, Oskar discovers an unusual talent: he can make his voice shatter glass, which he does whenever anyone tries to take his drum away. Lost in a world of fantasy, Oskar exists alongside of, though not really in, the interwar world of Danzig, while the emerging Nazi party is overtaking the city.

Hugely successful, even winning a Palme d'Or and an Academy Award, *The Tin Drum* was nonetheless controversial for reasons similar to Hans Jürgen Pohland's earlier Grass adaptation, *Katz und Maus*: a child actor was depicted in scenes with sexual content. Bennent was just twelve years old at the time of filming but has several sex scenes throughout the second half of the film, as his character Oskar has become a teenager despite the fact that his physical appearance remains unchanged. The film was banned for child pornography allegations in various parts of North America, but the deeper controversy is related to Grass's source material and Schlöndorff's adaptation of it (which was approved by the author). In a sense, Schlöndorff's views on his home country seem to echo Fassbinder's feeling that Germany was inherently a place of racism, prejudice, and cruelty. In his diary, Schlöndorff declares, "Germany, to this day, is the poisoned heart of Europe."[39]

The film and its source material both belie a sense of bitter resentment about Germany itself. Erik Rentschler writes,

> The film's source had occasioned much controversy and scandal when it came out in 1959. Grass' book assailed the German past and scorned the German present with its solemn religiosity, prudish domesticity, and unrelenting conservatism. Contemporary critics denounced the work's lack of piety, its pornographic indulgence, and its utter disregard for established values and institutions. As an angry intervention and a virulent provocation, Grass' epic portrait stood out as the most prominent German novel of the postwar era.[40]

The Tin Drum is partly based on Grass's own life—he grew up in Gdańsk and served in the Wehrmacht as a young man; his early three novels are referred to as the Danzig trilogy, which includes *The Tin Drum* and *Cat and Mouse*. The novel also reflects Grass's desire to create German art completely opposed to Nazi propaganda and the values it represented. Grass discussed his motivation for writing *The Tin Drum* and the Danzig trilogy in general as an inevitable he act:

Volker Schlöndorff uses Nazi spectacle as a symbol of mass stupidity and evil in *The Tin Drum*.

I was twelve years old when the war started and seventeen years old when it was over. I am overloaded with this German past. In the fifties and the sixties, the Adenauer period, politicians didn't like to speak about the past, or if they did speak about it, they made it out to be a demonic period in our history when devils had betrayed the pitiful, helpless German people. They told bloody lies. It has been very important to tell the younger generation how it really happened, that it happened in daylight, and very slowly and methodically. One of the best things we have after forty years of the Federal Republic is that we can talk about the Nazi period. And postwar literature played an important part in bringing that about.[41]

Grass's novel and Schlöndorff's film both comment on German culture by also adapting one of the country's most popular literary forms, the *Bildungsroman*, essentially a coming of age novel with an educational component. Rentschler writes,

A twisted variation on the German *Bildungsroman*, Oskar's education between the fronts of German and Polish history becomes an exercise in alienation and deformation. The film imbues the boy's negativity with a subversive power; his acts of refusal both issue from and militate against the experience of history.[42]

In this way it connects back to Schlöndorff's *Young Törless*, quite a different, if equally subversive film about the experience of a schoolboy growing up in an inherently sadistic world.

Much of *The Tin Drum* is focused on family: Oskar's relationship with his mother and his familial background in general, for example, Schlöndorff relates the comic story of how his grandparents came to be together. The film is also concerned with his difficult passage between childhood and maturity—essentially a reinterpretation of themes found in *Heimatfilme*—and Schlöndorff was not the only director to explore this against the backdrop of World War II. Though dramatically different in both tone and style, Helma Sanders-Brahms' *Deutschland bleiche Mutter* (*Germany Pale Mother*, 1980) also focuses on the relationship between a protagonist and their parents.

Sanders-Brahms' film also has some parallels with Fassbinder's *Die Ehe der Maria Braun* (*The Marriage of Maria Braun*, 1978), in the sense that the central story is about a soldier and his bride who are separated by war and cannot sustain the initial passion of their romance. But it also has far more parallels with Andrzej Zuławski's *Trzecia czesc nocy* (*The Third Part of the Night*, 1971),[43] based on the director's father's experiences struggling to survive in war-torn Poland. Likewise, *Germany Pale Mother* is based on the life of Sanders-Brahms' mother; both films feature, albeit in a fictionalized form, the births of the directors. In this case, Hanne (Elisabeth Stepanek) explains how her parents, Lene (Eva Mattes) and Hans (Ernst Jacobi), met and fell in love just before the war. They were married, but Hans was shipped off to the Eastern front and Lene attempted to survive in wartime Germany with such obstacles as air raids, poverty, starvation, and childbirth. Though Lene and Hans reunite after the war, in the ruins of Berlin, their relationship falls apart and Lene remains, bereft and disfigured, to contemplate the wreckage of her life.

The film resulted in plenty of public and critical derision. Elsaesser writes,

Germany Pale Mother, her international success, was not only accused of riding the Nazi nostalgia wave, but, as the story of a mother-daughter relationship, cashing in on a fashionable subject. This instinct for the *Zeitgeist* on the part of a director who had by then styled herself as an *Autor* was not well received, and Sanders-Brahms became next to Syberg the least-loved film director in Germany.[44]

She certainly pulled influences from a number of diverse sources, including the feminist branch of New German Cinema, Brecht (the title is a reference to a poem he wrote the year he was forced to leave Germany, which is recited at the beginning of the film by his own daughter), Nazi propaganda, in particular newsreels and radio broadcasts, and even German art. This film is perhaps not sensational in the same way as the *Holocaust* miniseries, but it is a uniquely feminist spin on melodrama. *Germany Pale Mother* presents a polarized world where women are little more than victims, fighting tooth and nail for survival. Their bodies are the literal sites of history and politics. In some respects, *Germany Pale Mother* is an interesting counterpart to *The Tin Drum*—both films represent the utter failure of the domestic unit as the outcome of war. Existing in the often-discomfiting space between history and memory, elements of fairytale and magical realism intrude in a narrative that also includes rotting corpses, rape, anti-Semitic violence, depression, and suicide.

A similar cry of rage and bitterness can be found in one final film worth mentioning, which is loosely connected with the New German Cinema movement: Christoph Schlingensief's *100 Jahre Adolf Hitler: Die letzte Stunde im Führerbunker* (*100 Years of Adolf Hitler*, 1989). Influenced by everyone from Pasolini to Fassbinder, Schlingensief was younger and generally more experimental than the other New German Cinema directors (Schroeter and Syberberg notwithstanding), but this film presents a fascinating if grotesque conclusion to the trend of satirizing—or even exploiting—the darkest days of German history as a form of cinematic exorcism.

The film *100 Years of Adolf Hitler* has a satirical, even comedic tone, and is loosely evocative of Chaplin's *The Great Dictator* (1940), if that film had been fueled by Surrealism and a cocaine bender several weeks long. Claustrophobic and nightmarish, this is a far cry from the much later, lauded *Der Untergang* (*The Downfall*, 2004), a dramatic look at Hitler's last days in his Berlin bunker. The relatively plotless film follows the frenzied chaos that occurs over the period of a few days in Hitler's bunker just before Germany experienced defeat at the hands of the Allies. This is largely aided and abetted by the mental degradation of Hitler (Udo Kier) and the ensuing violent, often sexually explicit actions of his entourage, which includes Göring (Alfred Edel), Goebbels (Dietrich Kuhlbrodt)—and his abusive, incestuous behavior towards his wife (Margit Carstensen) and daughter (Marie-Lou Sellem)—Waffen SS General Hermann Fegelein (Volker Spengler), Martin Bormann (Andreas Kunze), and Eva Braun (Brigitte Kausch), among others.

In response to a retrospective of Schlingensief's career that came just after his untimely death from lung cancer in 2010, *Der Spiegel* describes the film as "a great massacre of references" and a "carnage of images."[45] Schlingensief is quoted as saying, "I carry fear inside of me," in reference to the horror of German history, and this was the first of a loose trilogy he called his "Germany Trilogy," which includes a film about the reunification of East and West Germany, *Das deutsche Kettensägen Massaker* (*The German Chainsaw Massacre*, 1990) and *Terror 2000: Intensivstation Deutschland* (*Terror 2000: Germany Out of Control*, 1994), about the days following reunification.

The perfect way to conclude a discussion of World War II–themed films in New German Cinema, *100 Years of Adolf Hitler* is intentionally a satire that recycles old themes—while also attempting to shock—with the end goal of expurgating Hitler's cultural currency. Udo Kier played Hitler several times throughout his career, though always with a comedic angle meant to mock one of the most hated figures of the 20th century rather than a serious attempt to confront history. Through a beloved cult actor like Kier,

Hitler is made safe, campy, comedic; as a symbolic figure, he is exhausted of all serious value and drained of historical weight. *Der Spiegel* explains, "This is the Schlingensief principle: images against images, thoughts against thoughts and Hitler against Hitler. In the end, the debris Schlingensief dredges up serves a thoroughly German purpose—self-purification."[46]

4

French Cinema in the '60s and the Myth of Resistance

"In France Resistance immediately entered the realm of legend."—André Bazin[1]

By the 1960s, France gradually returned to its status as a global power thanks to extensive physical and psychological rebuilding at the hands of President Charles de Gaulle and his Fifth Republic. In many ways, de Gaulle represents the relationship between postwar France and the myth of heroic resistance. De Gaulle was *the* national war hero: he commanded armies against the Nazis and later led the Free French government and the Resistance in exile from London. He returned to Paris as a liberating force and led the provisional government from 1944 to 1946. He rescued the country again in 1959, returning to politics after a lengthy break, to found the Fifth Republic amidst the ashes of the disastrous Fourth Republic. He served as president for the next decade, until he resigned in 1969, grappling with crises like the Algerian War and the Cold War. His policy of "national independence," in which he believed France should neither be dependent on nor subservient to any other nation was closely tied to his vision of nationalistic pride.

This vision fed directly into the narrative of a heroic France, whose citizens resisted Nazi occupation on a wide scale. Throughout the '60s, certain filmmakers—particularly those operating under the auspices of French arthouse cinema and the emerging French New Wave—sought to dispel some of these myths and shed light on the truth about collaboration in France. This coincided with the capture and arrest of Adolf Eichmann in 1960 and his subsequent trial in Israel in 1961, which made the Holocaust a subject of international focus. As I explained in the previous chapter, this very public trial brought the full horrors of the concentration camps into public consciousness for the first time. It is impossible to discuss the World War II-themed films of the '60s from any country without considering the impact of this monumental trial. It led to a series of concentration camp trials throughout the decade and many countries were forced to reckon with their own role in Nazi genocide and its legacy.

One of the first French directors to approach this subject was Jean-Pierre Melville. In an earlier chapter, I discussed Melville's *The Silence of the Sea*, the director's debut film, which established him as an independent voice within French cinema and set the stage for a theme that would recur throughout his work: World War II and its impact on ordinary French citizens. As I mentioned, Melville served in the French Army and was a member of the Resistance. But his films eschew the French tendency to portray the Resistance and French participation in the war overall in black and white terms. While somewhat glorifying resistance work, they betray a complexity that likely speaks to Melville's own harrowing experiences in the war. Notably, he would not marry his preferred genre, the crime thriller, to war themes until towards the end of his career with *L'armée des ombres* (*Army of Shadows*, 1969).

The Silence of the Sea is essentially a pensive melodrama about a Nazi officer who is stationed to live with a French father and daughter in their country home. Through the officer's attempts to make friendly conversation, the father and daughter develop a new understanding of him, themselves, and the war itself. Melville's second film about the war, the unusual *Léon Morin, prêtre* (*Léon Morin, Priest*, 1961), could perhaps best be described as a philosophical melodrama. Ginette Vincendeau argues that these three primary war films are not only about Melville's own experiences, but of the national response to the memories of war and the way that myth transformed over the decades. She writes that the importance of these three films is "not only a function of Melville's *private* experience, but of how they explore and rework the *public* 'myth' of the Resistance."[2] Vincendeau also argues that the films of the '60s, such as *Léon Morin, Priest*, had likely shifted gears in the way World War II was represented because of the political events of the '50s. She writes that "the rise of the European Community, the French defeat in Indo-China in 1954 and the beginning of the Algerian war shifted the figure of the enemy from the German to the colonial 'other.'"[3] *Léon Morin, Priest* certainly does not put Nazis front and center as its antagonists; rather, conflict is shown to be internal, within one French woman.

Léon Morin, Priest follows Barny (Emmanuelle Riva), a young French communist who has recently been widowed and is raising her daughter alone in the French Alps during the war. Though she claims to no longer be religious, she seeks confession with

Emmanuelle Riva brings the fiery, resistant Barny to life in *Léon Morin, Priest* (*Die Blechtrommel*, Franz Seitz Filmproduktion, 1979).

Father Morin (Jean-Paul Belmondo), a handsome young priest, initially as a way to mock or ridicule him. Barny constantly attempts to provoke him, arguing about religion and politics. But instead of getting angry or turning her away, Morin responds by challenging her in turn and, partly fueled by her attraction to him, brings her to question everything about her life. The two begin to meet regularly for these conversations and their relationship takes a complicated turn.

In typical Melville fashion, the relationship between Barny and Morin is far more complicated than just an illicit affair; though there is an obvious attraction between the two and Morin plays on Barny's sexual frustration, their relationship never proceeds that far though Barny eventually attempts to seduce Morin. A distance always remains between the two. On the surface, *Léon Morin, Priest* is a film about life during the occupation, when totalitarian forces controlled everything from sex and politics to identity itself. Ingeniously and somewhat transgressively, Morin uses sexual desire as a force for spiritual awakening. Though attraction and desire may seem at odds with a Catholic priest's usual means of imparting spiritual wisdom, Morin seems to recognize that desperate times may call for unconventional measures. Michael Sragow writes,

> Morin uses his charisma, his surly, forthright charm, and his delight in religious argument to revive the faith or at least the curiosity of Catholic women, even outright sinners. He acts with bracing economy when he does something as simple as tug a flirt's skirt down below her knee. The movie reaches its peak of sexual melodrama when he smashes a hatchet into a stump. It's both a startling expression of his masculine might and an absolute statement of his determination to be abstinent.[4]

In many ways, *Léon Morin, Priest* is about people—especially women, as the village is largely absent of men as they are away at war—who deny the effects of adversity on their lives. Barny claims that relocating to the small town in the Alps, initially occupied by Italian soldiers, is a refuge from Paris and the frontlines of the war, which feel so far removed from the mountains. But German soldiers replace the Italians and life in the town begins to change. Melville shows this process and the gradual, sometimes subtle ways in which political repression can impact emotions, desires, and spiritual beliefs. Barny was married to a Jewish man—thus her own daughter is half-Jewish—and other Jewish characters come to suffer throughout the film, such as Sabine (Nicole Mirel), an office manager.

Like all of Melville's war films, *Léon Morin, Priest* is based on an autobiographical text written by a member of the Resistance—in this case, Béatrix Beck's *Léon Morin, prêtre* (also known as *The Passionate Heart* in English), written in 1952. And like Melville's other World War II films, it focuses on moral ambiguity as a fundamental component of life during wartime. Gary Indiana writes in the film "moral clarity is elusive at best, and even the most righteous people are a mess of contradictions."[5] But it also avoids the more obvious trappings of World War II cinema; aside from some signifiers that are essentially relegated to the background, Melville is more interested in analyzing human nature. As he would express far more directly a few years after this with *Army of Shadows*, *Léon Morin, Priest* rejects the notion that people are either inherently good or bad, and rather their moral choices are a direct result of their environment.

Barny may be an outspoken communist who sets out to challenge conventional morality and traditional religion, and while she does argue against collaboration, she is not exactly a figure of resistance. The film's primary concern is not about who elected to join the Resistance and the only overt "resistance" actions concern the concealment of Judaism, such as Barny's baptism of her daughter and a Jewish scholar shaving off his traditional facial hair and taking a new name. Vincendeau notes that despite being Jewish himself, Melville

> significantly reduces the Jewish strand of the narrative. In the novel Barny hides a Jewish couple and their child; in the released film this remains as a baffling moment when she takes a little boy to the country on her bicycle. Nazi atrocities are equally off-screen, "deportations" left vague in relation to Jewishness. More strikingly, the German presence is unthreatening.[6]

In this way, *Léon Morin, Priest* is an example of the refusal in French cinema—but also throughout other European films from the '60s—to admit the fact that the victims of the Holocaust were overwhelmingly Jewish. Likewise, there is a certain reluctance to accept personal responsibility for Nazi atrocities in countries like France that collaborated with their occupiers. But *Léon Morin, Priest* is not a film about external action, rather it is concerned with contemplation, with the events and conversations that transforms an individual's psyche. Really, *Léon Morin, Priest* is about the power of desire, of longing, and its ability to transform a person or even a community—particularly when what we desire is unattainable, or worse, or revealed to be a disappointment.

Another important example is Jean Dewever's *Les honneurs de la guerre* (*The Honors of War*, 1960). Though it has a relatively straightforward plot and is perhaps not as philosophically complex as *Léon Morin, Priest*, it is a far cry from the standard depiction of the average Frenchman as a Resistance fighter. Its bold anti-war message was responsible for the film being censored and the government was outraged over its depiction of Resistance fighters, who are shown to be flawed survivors rather than heroic fighters. Essentially a tale of German soldiers versus French citizens, the film is set in 1944 after the town of Nanteuil has already been liberated and the German forces defeated. But German soldiers—many of them young, wounded, and hopeless—try to survive, assuming they will be arrested by the liberating Allied forces. Peace, however, is not destined to last. Tensions with the locals, including sniper attacks from the French, drive both groups inevitably back towards violence.

The Honors of Wars was particularly scathing about the French rewriting of history: some of the townsfolk who become snipers and shoot at the relatively defenseless German soldiers have suddenly adapted the determination to resist—but only when it's convenient and they are personally in little danger. Matters are made worse by a German commanding officer who arrives on the scene and goads his men to attack, even though it is clear they have already lost. The film's ultimate themes are the senselessness of war and the human tendency towards self-aggrandizement. Perhaps the most revolutionary element of *The Honors of War* is to show the Germans and French as being essentially the same; they just happen to speak two different languages. While the majority of mainstream films in the postwar years depicted the French as brave or at least well-intentioned and the Germans as evil sadists, Dewever—alongside a handful of other directors like Melville—sought to show that all people are fundamentally the same, equally capable of goodness or violence.

Films like *Fortunat* (1960) are more the norm. In this melodrama, Michèle Morgan stars as the wife of a Resistance leader who is being pursued by the Nazis. A rough, blue collar poacher (Bourvil) decides to help her and his life is transformed. This is essentially a class comedy with romantic undertones and a tragic finale, but the war is narratively used as a way to unite people from different backgrounds. It is also an example of a somewhat popular subgenre during the decade: Resistance-themed comedies that featured ordinary French citizens as heroes. Such comedies became increasingly popular throughout the decade, as evidenced by films like Jean-Paul Rappeneau's *La vie de château* (*A Matter of Resistance*, 1965), set just before D-Day. The iconic Catherine Deneuve stars as a bored housewife in a rural village whose husband (Philippe Noiret) tries to ignore the fact that war has erupted throughout the country. He also refuses to take his wife to Paris, where she fantasizes about living. A German officer (Carlos Thompson) and a French spy (Pierre Brasseur) have both fallen for her and try to seduce her away from her husband.

In a different way, *Un taxi pour Tobrouk* (*Taxi for Tobruk*, 1960) is also about people putting aside their differences to come together during war, though it is a more serious drama. French soldiers must transport a German officer (Hardy Krüger) across the desert, but are forced to band together. It shows war as being fundamentally absurd, particularly in the way it pits people against one another, and can be read more as commentary on the French-Algerian War—at the time, it was becoming increasingly popular to use World War II to criticize France's involvement with Algeria. Another popular example of this is Henry Verneuil's *Week-end à Zuydcoote* (*Weekend at Dunkirk*, 1964), a gritty war film that seems like another obvious commentary on the Algerian War. Though it stars French icon Jean-Paul Belmondo, the film presents a brutal look at the realities of war as a group of French soldiers must decide whether to flee Dunkirk for England or stay and fight the arriving Germans.

A film from the mid-'60s that does explore the Resistance in a more subversive way is Claude Chabrol's *La Ligne de démarcation* (*The Line of Demarcation*, 1966). Like Melville, Chabrol was a figure not quite of the French New Wave, but adjacent to it—though he had actually effectively kicked off the New Wave with *Le beau Serge* in 1958. Like Melville, Chabrol lived through the war, though he was a teenager during these years and as the son of an affluent bourgeois family he grew up in relative safety in the countryside, though allegedly both his parents were in the Resistance. An avid cinema fan since childhood, Chabrol worked as a film critic and in 20th Century–Fox's publicity office in Paris before moving on to a career as a director, bankrolled by his wife's wealthy family. It was he who helped New Wave directors like Godard, Rohmer, and Rivette secure jobs or funding for their early films. The most prolific of these young directors—Chabrol averaged one film per year for much of his lengthy career—he followed *Le beau Serge* with a number of well-regarded early films like *Les cousins* (*The Cousins*, 1959) in the late '50s and early '60s, which is loosely regarded as the first boom of his career.

But by the mid–60s, he had yet to establish himself as the master of grim crime films and seedy melodrama, which would come later in the '70s. This was a period when funding had largely dried up for many of the New Wave directors, but the ever-practical Chabrol offered himself up as a director-for-hire during this period. Several of his films from this time are forgotten spy spoofs and *The Line of Demarcation* essentially stands alone as his triumph of the mid-'60s. And yet in retrospect, a film about the Nazi occupation seems like an obvious way for Chabrol to explore many of the themes that would recur throughout his career: violence, betrayal, backstabbing, revenge, and guilt. James Monaco writes that unlike Hitchcock or Fritz Lang, to whom Chabrol is often compared, "everyone is always guilty in Chabrol's films."[7]

The Line of Demarcation is one of his least seen or discussed films. A relatively subdued film for Chabrol, it was one of the first French movies to openly declare that not every Frenchman was heroic during the occupation and many were content to serve as collaborators. Some were even double agents or greedily profited from the war. As with Melville, Chabrol based the film on a memoir, *Mémoires d'un agent secret de la France libre et La Ligne de démarcation* (*Memoirs of a Secret Agent of Free France and The Line of Demarcation*) by Gilbert Renault, a celebrated French agent, who published the book under his wartime code name, Colonel Rémy.

The film takes place in 1941 in Jura, a village divided in half by a river that marked the line of demarcation between France and the Nazi-occupied territory. Pierre (Maurice Ronet), an officer and aristocrat, is newly released from imprisonment by the Nazis and returns home to learn that his chateau has been transformed into headquarters for the area's German command and that his English wife, Mary (American actress and French New Wave star Jean Seberg), has secretly joined the Resistance. It is dangerous work. The local chapter is plagued by informants and traitors and Pierre is deeply ambivalent about his wife's involvement. But when she is arrested, Pierre begins to rethink his participation in the war and considers where his loyalties really lie.

Chabrol admitted that he took some liberties with Rémy's memoirs, which followed the expected moral absolutes. Michael Coates-Smith and Garry McGee note that "he duped the veteran on set, pretending to shoot a scene which he had decided to cut. This was one in which Rémy heavy-handedly contrasts the 'honorable Wehrmacht and the ruthless Gestapo.'"[8] Chabrol allegedly told each actor that his or her own character was the protagonist of the film and the resulting product feels unsentimental and curiously dispassionate, somewhat like Rossellini's earlier *Rome, Open City*. Coates-Smith and McGee write,

> The director often seems scrupulously detached from his narrative. Clearly he didn't take the film as solemnly as some would have wished, and while it honors the real courage of many of its characters [...] there is an occasional hint of tongue-in-cheek about the moral demarcation line we are being offered.[9]

The film follows a particular rhythm; for every scene featuring heroic resistance work, there is an example of cowardly, predatory behavior. One particularly chilling exchange follows a smuggler (Roger Dumas) who promises to help an entire Jewish family escape occupied territory. But he betrays them; he bleeds them dry financially and is indirectly responsible for their murder. Darragh O'Donoghue argues that Chabrol frequently used the "transfer of guilt" concept from Hitchcock, which he and Eric Rohmer discuss in their book on the British master of suspense. O'Donoghue explains that this "transfer of guilt"

> was the process whereby either the antisocial feelings or actions of the hero were transferred to a "villain" character who could be identified, punished and removed, thereby purging the hero, the narrative world and the moral economy of the film.[10]

It can be argued that the smuggler who callously sends a Jewish family to their deaths with the excuse that he was just trying to survive and trying to take care of his own family is a miasma that pollutes every character in the film, particularly those who remain complacent. This would be explored more fully in years to come through films like Louis Malle's *Lacombe Lucien* (1974) and Joseph Losey's *Mr. Klein* (1976), but Chabrol was the first to explicitly confront this idea of complacency as a moral evil in *The Line of Demarcation*'s story of contrasting couples—the officer and his wife in the Resistance and the treacherous doctor (Daniel Gélin) and his tragic wife (Stéphane Audran). At this period in the mid-'60s, Chabrol's portrayal of collaboration and opportunism as being widespread and commonplace was quite daring.

But in terms of the mechanics of filmmaking, *The Line of Demarcation* is remarkable in the way it shows a community as a living organism where each member is affected by the actions of another—and the ways in which personality responsibility and moral beliefs can transform the fate of an entire group. This is also a reflection of Chabrol's style of filmmaking; unlike many of the other so-called New Wave auteurs, he considered working with a team vital to his work and a loose family followed him throughout the many decades of his career, including cinematographer Jean Rabier, editor Jacques Gaillard, and composer Pierre Jansen, all of whom participated in *The Line of Demarcation*.

Chabrol is not typically seen as a political director, but throughout his career he often used crime and suspense plots to confront controversial social issues. *The Line of Demarcation* is certainly political in the way that it explores French complicity in Nazi crimes as well as the broader issues of how the French contributed to the Nazi occupation of their own country—he would return to this theme much later with films like *Une affaire de femme* (*Story of Women*, 1988), about a woman who becomes an abortionist and takes advantage of the occupation to lift herself out of poverty, and *L'Œil de Vichy* (*The Eye of Vichy*, 1993), an experimental documentary that explores Vichy-era propaganda. Chabrol said Vichy "was not a government. It began simply as stupidity, and became a horror. It led to all sorts of things—denunciations by Frenchmen against each other, against Communists, Jews. It was terrible."[11]

The Nazi occupation of France began in 1940, after the French forces were defeated, and resulted in the division of the country into two zones: *zone norde* (or the "north

The entire town is complicit in Chabrol's *The Line of Demarcation* (*La ligne de démarcation*, Les Productions Georges de Beauregard/Rome Paris Films/Société Nouvelle de Cinématographie [SNC], 1966).

zone") and *zone libre* (or the "free zone"), located in the southern part of the country. Paris, along with the north-western sections of the country, were ruled by German military forces and their French pawns. Vichy, a city in roughly south-central France, was designated the headquarters of the "free" part of the country, thus lending its name to the collaborationist government as a whole. Occupation included strict laws surrounding curfews, rationing of foods and good, harsh control of the press, raiding of cultural treasures, and the mistreatment of Jews, who were forced to wear yellow stars and barred from public, as well as from the workforce in many cases.

The primary focus of life during occupation was survival. While rebellions increasingly occurred and a formal Resistance was founded, there were also French citizens who attempted to manipulate the situation to their own advantage. While some took advantage of Germans, others exploited the many desperate Jews trying to hide or flee. Thousands of Jews were arrested and sent to Auschwitz and black markets thrived. While later narratives sought to present these years in black and white terms with the honorable, heroic French bravely resisting Nazi brutality, in reality it was a moral gray area—the type of environment repeatedly explored by Chabrol throughout his films. His focus was often on ordinary middle class life, where he sought to show that regular people were neither inherently good nor evil, but certainly capable of evil, violence, and exploitation and they could be inevitably pushed in this direction by certain situations. Jonathan Kirshner writes that his films

> share common thematic concerns, regarding jealousy, marital fidelity, interpersonal power dynamics, and shifting loyalties across triangular relationships. [...] Bourgeoisie rituals come under anthropological interrogation; domestic geography is surgically precise (dwellings, simple and palatial, are meticulously designed); and there is Chabrol's signature delight in lingering over meals, especially at crucial junctures. Almost invariably, there is murder, always, there is guilt, the weight of which is shared by more than one character.[12]

This idea of communal guilt and responsibility as a theme for World War II films was relatively new at that time, but more and more directors began to explore these narratives as the decade went on, particularly into the '70s. Films like Alexandre Astruc's *La longue marche* (1966) or Costa-Gavras' *Un homme de trop* (*Shock Troops*, 1967), both about desperate Resistance fighters, began to introduce more of a moral gray scale to the proceedings. More typical were productions like René Clément's huge budget historical epic *Paris brûle-t-il* (*Is Paris Burning?*, 1966), about the liberation of the city by Allied forces, which was packed with international stars, or comedies like French-UK coproduction *La grande vadrouille* (1966).

But while some of the country sought to glorify and celebrate the 20th anniversary of the Nazi defeat, other members of French society—students, workers, and those affiliated with the political left—became increasingly dissatisfied with the old guard, symbolized by de Gaulle himself. Many of the New Wave directors actively participated in the protests and riots that shut down Paris in 1968 and led to widespread change in France—and around the world, as many other countries were plagued with similar issues. The films made during this period and into the early '70s began to build on the themes of *The Line of Demarcation* and sought to overturn the myth of widespread heroic resistance in France.

One particularly violent example is Alain Robbe-Grillet's *L'homme qui ment* (*The Man Who Lies*, 1968), certainly one of the more unusual war-themed films from the period. It can loosely be connected to a series of films from the '60s and '70s that use World War II narratives to raise deeper philosophical questions about the nature of truth, memory, identity, and trauma. American examples include films like *The Pawnbroker* (1964), where a Holocaust survivor has relocated to New York and is tormented by his memories of Nazi terror, which are aggravated by urban violence. But *The Man Who Lies* is not this sort of straightforward, mostly linear narrative, rather it borrows from surreal and absurdist traditions and is difficult to categorize.

This French-Italian-Czechoslovak production follows a man (Jean-Louis Trintignant) who arrives at a small village. He claims to be Boris Varessa, best friend of a local Resistance hero, Jean Robin, who was executed during the war. Boris uses this alleged friendship to ingratiate himself into the lives of the women in Robin's family home. He seduces the widow, sister, and maid in turn, telling each a different story about his relationship to Robin and his role in the war.

Robbe-Grillet developed a reputation for elusive, challenging material thanks to: his prominence as a writer in the *nouveau roman* movement, which attempted to challenge conventional fiction; his script for Alain Resnais' enigmatic masterpiece *L'année dernière à Marienbad* (*Last Year at Marienbad*, 1961); and his own films as a director which include *Trans-Europ-Express* (1966) and *L'Eden et après* (*Eden and After*, 1970). His work often questions the nature of truth, identity, and desire. *The Man Who Lies* is concerned with the way narrative shapes identity and how this parallels history.

False stories and invented narratives were a reality of survival in World War II. Jews of all ages adopted or were given new names, as Jewish men and women were legally forced by the Nazis to add "Israel" or "Sarah" to their respective first names. Partisans and resistance members assumed code names and adopted new identities, while after the war many surviving Nazis fled to different towns, cities, or countries under fake names. Narratives about personal identity also changed tone and shape with the outcome of the war. For example, a year after *The Man Who Lies* was released, French director Marcel Ophuls released *Le Chagrin et la pitié* (*The Sorrow and the Pity*, 1969). This documentary about widespread French collaboration with the Nazis—which Ophuls established was the rule, not the exception—came after decades of much of French society bragging about their active roles in the Resistance.

Boris is the living expression of this phenomenon. At the start of the film, he's shot to death by soldiers, but awakens the next day and takes the name Boris Varessa from a tombstone he passes. Like an actor trying out different roles, he tells each person he meets different stories about himself; sometimes the details change subtly, while other times the stories are dramatically different. Occasionally he's a hero of the Resistance and Jean Robin's best friend, other times he *is* Jean Robin, while others still he's a traitor responsible for Robin's death.

Visually, the film is fixated on the concepts of memory and identity. Portraits, drawings, old photographs, and mirrors crowd Robin's family castle, which is itself the signifier of a pre-war era. These various images are used to complicate events, a visual reflection of the ever-changing narratives and histories presented by Boris. T. Jefferson Kline writes that Boris "compulsively reinvents his stories, leading his listeners ever further from any possibility of coherence. Robbe-Grillet's liar doesn't necessarily lie; he simply builds and rebuilds his reality in obsessively repeated and inverted versions of himself."[13]

These alternate realities and factual inconsistencies are not merely verbal and Robbe-Grillet's camera is plagued with visual discrepancies. Toby McKibbin writes,

One of Alain Robbe-Grillet's recurring tropes appears in *The Man Who Lies* via execution as sex game with Sylvie Bréal (*L'homme qui ment*, Como Films/Compagnie Cinématographique de France/Lux Film, 1968).

In *The Man Who Lies*, the voiceover informs us that the central character is entering an empty bar, yet the camera shows us that the bar is full. Are we to assume that the lie takes place in the audio or in the visual, or are we to accept that since they contradict each other we can trust neither sound nor image?[14]

The film's numerous contradictions and inconsistencies can be found throughout Robbe-Grillet's films and novels and are a key characteristic of his work. His interest is often in presenting varying interpretations of a particular event or character, while attempting to remain morally unbiased. He refuses to lead the reader or viewer in a certain direction, as is the case with most film and literature, where we are expected to side with a particular protagonist or viewpoint. Arguably, this could connect to Robbe-Grillet's own experience growing up with parents who were essentially Nazi sympathizers. In an interview with *The Paris Review*, Robbe-Grillet himself discussed the fact that his parents were "Germanophile" during the war. He said, "Well, they *were* Germanophile—so what? I don't hide it. I don't try to justify or condemn it—I tell the story. And this had never been done before."[15] Robbe-Grillet was referring to his fictionalized autobiography, *Le miroir qui revient* (*Ghosts in the Mirror*, 1984), but he could have just as easily been discussing his films. He explains,

> All these characters, whether real or imagined, make up the content of my imaginary world. It doesn't matter which has been born of experience and which belongs to the imagination. I would be sad if I had to differentiate—I don't live like that.[16]

Despite his unconventional way of portraying identity, character, and narrative, this doesn't distract from the historical fact that many people during the war years knew—or were themselves—a Boris Varessa, an individual who was at once doomed victim, selfish manipulator, bystander, and perpetrator. Along with directors like Melville, Ophuls, and others, Robbe-Grillet highlights the fact that black and white thinking, where one person is clearly a hero or a villain, simply does not reflect the truth of wartime experience for the majority of people.

According to an interview included in the recent British Film Institute home video release of *The Man Who Lies*, which made the film available to audiences for the first time in decades, Robbe-Grillet admits that he took some of his inspiration from real events. He was invited to film in Slovakia and heard of a nearby castle where a woman waited for her brother, a Resistance member who disappeared during the war. Robbe-Grillet also acknowledges that he took inspiration from Franz Kafka's *Das Schloß* (*The Castle*, 1926), a surreal tale of nightmarish bureaucracy that Kafka died before completing. A nameless narrator, known only as K., is accidentally summoned to a forbidding castle, the site of authority over a small village. Because he does not know the complex bureaucratic system—which the locals view as perfect and incorruptible—he begins to discover and thus unintentionally reveal its flaws.

When referring to *The Castle* and its influence, Robbe-Grillet quoted Descartes: "If I dream of something with enough power, when I wake up I don't know whether it was a dream or reality."[17] This nightmare state present in Kafka's *The Castle* is a critical foundation for *The Man Who Lies*, and would come to be a profound influence on other Holocaust films through the '70s, and '80s, such as the East German film *Jakob, der Lügner* (*Jakob the Liar*, 1975), the American film *The Man in the Glass Booth* (1975), and Joseph Losey's French production *Mr. Klein* (1976).[18] Many World War II-themed films in the '60s, '70s, and '80s began to explore the relationship between truth and memory, and particularly between the myth of heroism and the reality of survival.

Another important film to explore these themes—and one of the most classic World War II films made in France—is Melville's *Army of Shadows*, released the following year in 1969. Though it lacks the surreal or absurdist qualities of *The Man Who Lies* and embraces a sense of stark realism, *Army of Shadows* is a far darker film and has gradually come to be seen as one of the great masterpieces of Melville's career. This loosely biographical effort was based on a 1943 book by Joseph Kessel, an Argentinian-born writer who lived the majority of his life in France and had served in the French military in both world wars. Kessel participated in the Resistance and used some of his own experience for the novel, as well as stories related to him by other Resistance fighters. *Army of Shadows* also touches on Melville's own experiences in the Resistance. In an interview Melville said, "In this film, for the first time, I show things that I have seen, that I have experienced."[19]

The film follows Philippe Gerbier (Melville regular Lino Ventura), a Resistance leader in Marseille. Gerbier's various grim adventures include his arrest at the hands of the Gestapo and a stint in a prisoner of war camp, even though no evidence against him could be found. He works diligently on a plan to escape the camp, but is unexpectedly sent to Paris for further questioning, which allows him to finally stage an escape. Back in Marseille, Gerbier must arrange for the execution of a young informant (Alain Libolt) who betrayed him, which is carried out by Gerbier himself and three other Resistance members.

A charismatic pilot (Jean-Pierre Cassel) is brought into the fold and meets other

Melville as a suspected Resistance member in a trailer for *Army of Shadows* that questions "Who are they?" (*L'armée des ombres*, Les Films Corona/Fono Roma, 1969).

vital Resistance members, such as Mathilde (Simone Signoret), central to the network even though she appears to just be a housewife. Gerbier travels to headquarters in London and meets a philosopher (Paul Meurisse) who is revealed to be the secret leader of the Resistance. But Gerbier is forced to cut his trip short to rescue a Resistance member who has been arrested and is being tortured in a Gestapo prison. In the attempt, Gerbier himself is arrested and is only able to escape execution because of a brilliant plan of Mathilde's. Unfortunately when Mathilde herself is arrested, it seems the entire network will unravel.

Harrowing as it is, many of the scenes in the film were taken from or at least inspired by real life. For example, Robert O. Paxton explains that the opening at the internment camp

> is based on the experiences of Jean Pierre-Bloch, a colleague of Melville's in Free France. Pierre-Bloch (he was born Jean-Pierre Bloch but later changed the hyphenation) was a socialist journalist and politician who escaped from a prisoner of war camp in 1940 and organized early parachute drops in the Dordogne region. In 1942, he reached London, where de Gaulle put him in charge of civilian intelligence operations in the Central Office of Information and Action. In 1943, he became minister of the interior in the provisional government set up by de Gaulle in Algiers, and he played a major role in establishing this government in France upon the liberation.[20]

Likewise, the sequence where Gerbier escapes from Gestapo headquarters in Paris was filmed at the Hôtel Majestic, the actual hotel used as the historical headquarters. The escape itself was based on a story told to Melville by Paul Rivière. Rivière was a leader of the Resistance and was in charge of the Rhône-Alpes region, where it was his task to organize the transport of important personnel from France to London and, critically, he took charge of covert plane landings and the airdrop of supplies. These are merely two examples out of dozens, but illustrate how *Army of Shadows* serves as more than just a fictional representation of what life in the Resistance might have been like—as is the case with many films that take it as their focus.

This unrelentingly bleak film—shot in muted gray, black, and blue tones by cinematographers Pierre Lhomme and Walter Wottitz—is marked by its sense of bitterness and moral ambiguity. While most World War II films present combat as fundamentally heroic, here violence is seen as an inevitable if reprehensible means to an end. It's a film about the realities of survival in wartime and one that, above all, depicts the French Resistance in its formative months. Though Melville was open about his own involvement in the Resistance, he reportedly never boasted of his exploits and worked to overturn the widespread practice—popular for several decades after the war—of claiming involvement with the Resistance. Coincidentally, Melville's film was released the same year as Marcel Ophüls's scathing documentary, *The Sorrow and the Pity*,[21] which exposed the level of complicity and collaboration among the French during the Nazi occupation.

Army of Shadows had a somewhat complicated reception, however. The tide had begun to turn in the early '60s, in terms of the public opinion towards glorifying the Resistance and painting its members as widespread throughout France or as gallant heroes. Growing public criticism of the war with Algeria began to shift focus away from sympathizing with the French military; de Gaulle himself ended the war in 1962 when he was pressured to grant Algeria independence. *Army of Shadows* certainly does not glorify resistance work as being easy or even effective, but it was criticized for praising de Gaulle himself. He is depicted in the film as a side character, but by the late '60s he had fallen out of favor with the French public, particularly its youth, leading to his resignation in 1969. As Melville served under de Gaulle, his loyalty to him is perhaps understandable.

In de Gaulle's famous speech marking the liberation of Paris in 1944, he described the country's capital as, "Outraged Paris! Broken Paris! Martyred Paris, but liberated Paris!" This conflicting sense of broken yet liberated bodies ties into the mythic reimagining of the Resistance itself, a vision that both Ophüls and Melville sought to destroy. Particularly in Melville's film, there is no united French brotherhood of resistors, no courage, no bravery, no glory, only inevitable failure: collaboration, betrayal, loss, psychological torment, physical torture, death. Even if he occasionally depicts ordinary French citizens as being sympathetic to or quietly aiding the Resistance, Melville portrays resistance as merely an act of treading water—attempting to survive in the face of insurmountable odds and almost certain death. Like many of the best World War II-themed films to come after it, particularly from the '70s, *Army of Shadows* blurs the lines between victim and perpetrator, between resistance fighter, collaborator, and everyday citizen, making it clear that in this fatal battle for survival, there are no clear cut lines between right and wrong.

As discussed in an earlier chapter, Melville was born Jean-Pierre Grumbach and took on his *nomme de guerre* to avoid attracting attention to his Jewish background and it was a name he used in the Resistance. His experiences have not been fully documented and unlike other notable war personalities, such as de Gaulle who actually retired from politics (however temporarily) in the late '40s to write his war memoirs, Melville only went into detail occasionally during interviews. It's known that he served in the 71st artillery regiment when he was just in his early 20s. Anthony Lane reports that:

He was conscripted into the Army in October, 1937, and was still there at the start of the war. In 1940, he was evacuated to England from Dunkirk; returning to France, he joined the Resistance in the South. Details remain hazy, but we know that he served with the Free French forces, first in North Africa and later in the campaigns to liberate Italy and France.[22]

He first offered his services to the Free French apparently months earlier, when he was still in Marseille, where he distributed pamphlets for the Resistance; an underground press was one of their many initiatives during the war. But his journey from the Army to the Resistance was not quite so simple. Adam Schatz writes that he arrived in Barcelona, waiting to be transported to Gibraltar before making his way to London. But the ship failed to start.

> The boat was seized by a Spanish patrol. Grumbach was detained for more than a month on suspicion of being a spy or a commando, then transferred to a naval prison, where he remained until late May, when he was cleared after an investigation. A month later he boarded a ship to London with a group of eighty other French citizens. "The volunteer Grumbach produced a very good impression," his interrogator in London wrote, and issued him a Number One visa. To the left of the photograph on his FFC visa, Grumbach wrote: "I wish to serve under the name of Melville, Jean-Pierre."[23]

Melville's own experiences in the military and specifically in the Resistance undoubtedly inspired his depiction of men suspicious and untrusting to the point of paranoia. The death of a young, suspected traitor, which comes early in the film, is sickening. Later, the execution of the film's only main female character (Simone Signoret) is inevitable, yet tragic; it is obvious she has agreed to talk to the Gestapo to prevent the torture and death of her teenage daughter, but the Resistance members cannot allow her life to be spared. Their rules are sacrosanct. Real-life Resistance member and philosopher Albert Camus writes in *Lettres à un ami allemand* (literally "Letters to a German Friend" but known as *Resistance, Rebellion, and Death* in English, 1960), "The seas, rains, necessity, desire, the struggle against death—these are things that unite us all. We resemble one another in what we see together, in what we suffer together."[24] The characters of *L'armée des ombres* are largely united by this sense of suffering.

Generally speaking, Melville's films are defined by operatic if unsentimental violence, rituals of masculinity, and the operations of underground societies. In this way, *Army of Shadows* bears much in common with Melville's crime films and can be seen as an existential thriller, much like Joseph Losey's later, *Mr. Klein* (1976), which shares its themes of sacrifice and martyrdom. *Army of Shadows* also evokes the earlier resistance thrillers Fritz Lang made during his exile in England and America during the war: *Man Hunt* (1941), about a British aristocrat who "hunts" Hitler for sport and is in turn pursued by the Gestapo; *Ministry of Fear* (1944), about a man released from a mental institution who accidentally comes into the possession of microfilm the Nazis want; and *Hangmen Also Die!* (1943), inspired by the assassination of Nazi leader Reinhard Heydrich by the Czech Resistance. Like *Army of Shadows*, *Hangmen Also Die* is unsentimental and often grim in its portrayals of justice and retribution.

Originally known as "437" or "Never Surrender" (the title of a moving poem written within the film), *Hangmen Also Die* portrays not only Nazis as villains; mobs of citizens and opportunistic capitalists are equally suspect. A particularly nihilistic scene eventually cut from the end of the film apparently involved the execution of hostages (as revenge for Heydrich's assassination) above a mass grave, an event with historical basis.

Recent history, it seemed, was too much for Hollywood. Melville also seems to have been influenced by Lang's *Cloak and Dagger* (1946). Generally considered one of Lang's minor efforts, its portrayal of violence has a chillingly inevitable quality. One scene of the film was lifted almost directly for Hitchcock's Cold War thriller *Torn Curtain* (1966), where a member of the Resistance engages in a silent fight to the death with a Gestapo agent that is bloodless but no less shocking—a sequence also evoked in *Army of Shadows* for the murder of a young Nazi guard.

Like Lang's war-themed thrillers, *Army of Shadows* is so effective because it unexpectedly follows the pattern established by Melville's crime films. For a war film, it is deeply cynical and utterly lacks any sentimentalism about violence—key qualities of Melville's crime thrillers. The harsh, overwhelmingly masculine world of crime, violence, and revenge that began with *Le doulos* (1962)—the first of several of Melville's crime films where any notion of black and white morality is quickly abolished—and continued in films like *Le deuxième souffle* (1966), *Le samouraï* (1967), *Le cercle rouge* (1970), and *Un flic* (1972). While many of these are fatalistic in nature—for example, most of his films end with the deaths of all major characters—none are quite as bleak and unforgiving as *Army of Shadows*. It asserts that resistance against a totalitarian regime almost always means torture and death for those involved—something later echoed by Ophüls in his 1988 war documentary, *Hôtel Terminus*, where numerous women give testimony about their treatment at the hands of the Gestapo. Melville and Ophüls assert that resistance is not about the survival of an individual, but the survival of a society, the preservation of a very way of life, one that necessarily entails unimaginable sacrifice. As Camus writes, "Men like you and me who in the morning patted children on the head would a few hours later become meticulous executioners."[25]

5

Postwar Perversion
Italian Cinema in the '70s

"Personal morals are dead. We are an elite society where everything is permissible."—Luchino Visconti's *The Damned* (1969)

World War II-themed films were increasingly popular in 1970s Italy, with many of the period's major arthouse directors exploring the subject. Many of these films mark an evolution from the neorealism of the '40s and '50s, in the sense that they continue to explore themes of decadence and sexual perversion particularly as they are conflated with fascism, however on a much larger, often more baroque scale than the earlier films. This leitmotif extended from Italian neorealism in the 1940s to German cinema of the 1980s. As discussed in my earlier chapter on Italian neorealism, the concept of inherited perversion and an inability to escape the past was a common theme throughout the mildly perverse family melodramas of the early '60s, but wouldn't reach its erotic, exploitation-fueled climax until the release of Luchino Visconti's *La caduta degli dei* (*Götterdämmerung*, 1969), better known to English speaking audiences as *The Damned*.

Here Visconti continued to develop themes introduced in *Sandra*. *The Damned* returns to corrupt industrialists and perverse sons, again loosely inspired by myth—this time from Germanic folklore by way of Wagner—but reimagined as a much larger, less intimate production. *The Damned* is set during the Nazi rise to power in the early '30s and is far more than just a sweeping family melodrama. Baron Joachim Von Essenbecks (Albrecht Schoenhals) is the head of a steel dynasty but struggles to bring his company into the rapidly changing world and his squabbling heirs don't make things any easier. His self-indulgent daughter-in-law Sophie (Ingrid Thulin) allows her son Martin (Helmut Berger), the company's heir, to explore his passions unchecked—which include transvestitism and pedophilia—while her fiancé Friedrich (Dirk Bogarde) is a factory manager angling for more power. A manipulative SS officer, Aschenbach (Helmut Griem), convinces Friedrich to murder the Baron and frame the company's liberal vice president, Herbert (Umberto Orsini), who is forced to go into hiding while his wife and children are sent to Dachau.

Sophie, meanwhile, hopes to get the upper hand on Aschenbach by fingering her own brother, Konstantin (Rene Kolldehoff), a homosexual SA officer who is subsequently murdered on the Night of the Long Knives. The sudden imbalance of family power allows Martin to become truly monstrous: he rapes his prepubescent cousin, as well as a young Jewish girl who lives in his apartment complex, and eventually attacks his own mother.

He forces Sophie and Friedrich to marry and then kill themselves, so that Martin is left as the primary heir to the family fortune along with his cousin Günther (Renaud Verley). The two are united in thoughts of power and violence, and become little more than puppets of the SS.

The Damned was a truly transformative moment in World War II-themed cinema. Subject matter found routinely throughout the arthouse films of the '70s was effectively introduced here by Visconti: everything from *Cabaret* (1972), Liliana Cavani's *Il portiere di notti* (*The Night Porter*, 1974), Lina Wertmüller's *Pasqualino Settebellezze* (*Seven Beauties*, 1975), and Pasolini's *Salò* (1975), among other films, either borrow from it or build on its themes. These include the baroque sense of style, perverse sexual elements, factual historical details, Shakespearean tragedy, and epic melodrama. This lengthy work—with a running time of more than 150 minutes—parallels an increasingly bloody family drama with historical moments of violent triumph in the early years of National Socialism. The Reichstag fire in February of 1933 and the Night of the Long Knives in June of 1934 elegantly bookend the von Essenbach squabbles for power.

Visconti said, "what has always interested me is the analysis of a sick society"[1] and he certainly had no shortage of real-life examples to inspire him. The von Essenbachs were loosely based on the Krupp family, a steel and ammunition dynasty from Essen whose patriarch, Gustav, and heir, Alfried, were initially skeptical of Hitler but became avowed, almost obsessive Nazis. When Alfried took charge in 1941, the company became Germany's primary arms supplier and began taking control of similar corporations in occupied territory. Alfried consolidated family power, ousting any rivals and fellow heirs, and began to use slave labor from concentration camps for his business. Despite being found guilty of war crimes, the company survived and Alfried managed to hold on to most of his assets after the war.

The von Essenbachs are an obvious mirror for the Krupp family, but Visconti uses them as a cross-section of the kind of German society that flourished under Nazi rule: upper class opportunists (Sophie), well-positioned perverts (Martin and Konstantin), angry young men in need of direction (Günther), and ambitious mid-level managers (Friedrich). As a result, one of Visconti's pet themes—the fall of the aristocracy—is brilliantly melded with the Nazi's rise to power, nationalistic fervor, and reactionary fascism. Herbert, the company vice president and politically liberal fall guy, says Nazism is a monster of their own creation, born in their factories and flourishing with their money. Visconti proves that it is also spread by men like Friedrich, who serves as a Macbeth-like figure driven to monstrous acts by his ambition, but who remains one of the few characters capable of self-reflection and moral insight.

All this is orchestrated by Helmut Griem's Aschenbach, representative of the ultimate cinematic Nazi. He's a charming, sociopathic, blond Satan who carefully manipulates individual family members to his own ends, turning them against each other until only Martin and Günther remain. And perhaps curiously, it is Helmut Berger's fastidious yet devious Martin who serves as the film's unforgettable protagonist. A figure of debauched beauty and nearly unchecked perversion, Martin acts as a transformative, corrupting agent throughout the film.

He turns the Baron's high class birthday dinner into a cabaret drag show, where he dresses as Marlene Dietrich and sings "Kinder, heut' abend, da such' ich mir was aus" (known in English as "A Man, Just a Regular Man") from *Der blaue Engel* (*The Blue Angel*, 1930). The plotting and misdeeds of the other characters are contrasted by his

In *The Damned*, Martin (Helmut Berger) entertains and terrorizes his family with a drag performance during a celebratory banquet (*La caduta degli dei [Götterdämmerung]*, Italnoleggio Cinematografico/Praesidens/Pegaso Cinematografica, 1969).

multiple acts of pedophilia—his own uncle blackmails him over this—and his *coup de grace* includes incest. He finally overthrows his controlling mother, the Lady Macbeth-like Sophie, and rapes her in an act that seems at least partially consensual. She is reduced to a near-comatose state after this and Martin forces her to go through with a wedding to Friedrich. Their nuptials are consummated with an act of double suicide, leaving a coiffed Martin in a freshly pressed SS uniform to his fate as head of the family.

While Martin's acts nearly landed the film with an X-rating, his scenes are far from the only moments of perversion. Visconti devotes a lengthy, extended sequence to a recreation of the Night of the Long Knives, when the SS purged the ranks of the *Sturmabteilung* or SA, murdering and arresting most of their number, including their leader and one of Hitler's closest associates, Ernst Röhm. Over a thousand people were arrested and though the final death total is unknown, it is believed to be in the hundreds. The SA were known for their fearsome street violence and rowdiness, as well as for their alleged homosexuality. While Röhm and a few of the SA leaders were more or less openly gay, this fact was manipulated by Hitler and the SS for purely political reasons; they wanted the German public to believe they were taking steps to destroy the corrupt, unruly branch of the Nazi party. Visconti also played up this aspect of the SA's reputation and presents them as rabble rousers who carouse in an idyllic lake setting—the spa town of Bad Wiessee where the purge actually occurred—with the night increasingly descending into drunkenness and a mass orgy before the morning's operatic bloodshed.

While *The Damned* was building on themes introduced in the '40s by Rossellini and Italian neorealism, in many ways it changed the landscape in terms of depictions of World War II on screen in the '70s. It serves as a marked contrast to some of the more restrained war dramas of the time. While directors like Pasolini had begun to present the war in more symbolic terms in his segment of the anthology film *Amore e rabbia* (*Love and Anger*, 1969), war-themes were generally relegated to conventional moralistic tales like De Sica's *I girasoli* (*Sunflower*, 1970), which features Marcello Mastroianni and Sophia Loren as a couple torn apart by war. But younger directors began to follow Visconti's lead, particularly in terms of combining World War II narratives with extravagant sex and violence.

A key early example that followed closely on the heels of *The Damned* was *Il conformista* (*The Conformist*, 1970), an early masterpiece from up-and-coming director and Pasolini protégé Bernardo Bertolucci, who explored the subjects of homosexuality and fascism from a new angle. Based on a novel by Italian journalist Alberto Moravia, *The Conformist* jumps forwards and backwards in time as it follows the murky career of Marcello Clerici (Jean-Louis Trintignant), an employee of the Fascist secret police in Italy, who is set with the task of assassinating his former professor, Luca Quadri (Enzo Tarascio), in Paris.

Though the film is narratively disjointed, it eventually becomes clear that Marcello took a position with the government and married his wife Giulia (Stefania Sandrelli) in order to fit in, to conform. Millicent Marcus writes, "Marcello seeks to obliterate his sense of deviancy by conforming to the social mores and political ideology of 1930s Italy."[2] Everything in his private life seems in disarray. As a boy, he was teased at school and molested by a chauffeur (European cult treasure Pierre Clémenti), who he believes he murdered after the assault. He resents his family's wealth and privilege, though his father (Giuseppe Addobbati) is confined to an insane asylum after years working as a torturer for the previous government. His mother (Italian singer Milly, sister of Totò) is in a morphine-soaked prison of her own making at an isolated estate and spends her few waking hours in sexual bliss with her Japanese chauffeur. Marcello's only friend is the blind Italo (José Quaglio), whom he violently betrays.

Seemingly nothing is sacred to Marcello and he repeatedly sacrifices even his own sexual desires. He uses his honeymoon with Giulia as a convenient ruse to travel to Paris to murder the professor. And though he seems to fall in love with his ideological opposite—Anna (Dominique Sanda), the professor's young wife—he passively observes her murder. Anna is the film's most complex character and is the key to its revolving door of mutable identity and fluid reality. Dominique Sanda actually appears in the film three times: not only as Anna, but as a secretary in an Italian fascist office and as a prostitute in a French brothel, seemingly haunting Marcello throughout the film's various settings.

At first, she appears to reciprocate Marcello's affections, but is possibly just playing an elaborate game with him. She allows him to see her partially naked and flirts with him, but aggressively bites his lip when he kisses her and sets out to seduce his wife. This culminates in the film's most erotic scene—a slow tango between Anna and Giulia—which is also its most claustrophobic moment. Anna leads a room full of drunken revelers to dance inexorably towards Marcello in an undulating, oppressive spiral that traps him at the center of the room. Through the film, but particularly in this scene, it becomes clear that Marcello does not actually seek to fit in, but merely wants to maintain the appearance of doing so. Being part of the crowd fills him with a quiet terror.

The film's sexual politics make much of this ambiguity—whether or not Anna and Marcello are homosexual, bisexual, or merely opportunists—and Marcello himself seems uncertain. Despite being an avowed atheist, he submits to Giulia's demands that he confess his sins to a Catholic priest before marriage, boasting of acts that include homosexuality, murder, and premarital heterosexual intercourse. Marcus explains, "Marcello is

Anna (Dominique Sanda) leads Giulia (Stefania Sandrelli) in an erotic tango (*Il conformista*, Mars Film/Marianne Productions/Maran Film, 1970),

marked from the outset by a love of violence and by a feminine sultriness which leads him to be seduced and to react with homicidal vengeance time and time again."[3]

He admits that he has chosen Giulia because she is mundane and boring, but she is hardly less damaged than Marcello himself. In a parallel with his own childhood sexual abuse at the hands of the chauffeur, Giulia admits that she began a sexual relationship with her 60-year-old uncle when she was only a teenager—the very man to give her away at their wedding. But Bertolucci makes it clear that Marcello's most perverse act is not his nebulous sexuality or even the murders he has committed, but his desire to conform above all else. He is neurotic, self-loathing, and admits that what he wants most is to appear normal. He says what he wants is "the impression of normalcy. Stability, security. In the morning when I'm dressing in the mirror I see myself. And compared to everyone else, I feel I'm different."

Marcello is a strange amalgamation of repulsion and attraction. He is never completely presented as a victim, but as a sort of cowardly predator, waiting for opportune moments to reveal his true nature: one devoid of personality, scruples, or even real desire. The film's tragedy, which culminates in Anna's death, is at once muted and enhanced by Marcello's skewed understanding of identity and reality. In the middle of a French forest, she escapes the car where her husband is being murdered and perhaps could have fled to safety with Marcello—who is located in the rear car—but when she sees his face, she begins to scream uncontrollably until the other fascist agents gun her down. This is the film's only truly emotional sequence, brutal in its intensity, and it serves as a sort of ultimate climax that counters the repeated acts of denial throughout.

It is tempting to view *The Conformist* as a film about the evils of sexual repression, but this interpretation is too simple. Marcus writes, "Far from insisting that underneath every Fascist lurks a repressed homosexual, Bertolucci presents Marcello's idiosyncratic sexuality as one example of the general need to deny personal differences, which would lead an insecure, threatened individual to identify with an all-powerful state."[4] Both political and sexual, *The Conformist* is a deeply psychological reading of fascism that makes a number of important parallels to the contemporary understanding of fascism as a death cult. Marcello's attempts to conform can be understood through Freud's writings on the death drive. In *On Metapsychology*, he writes, "the hypothesis of a death instinct, the task of which is to lead organic life back into the inanimate state."[5] Marcello's actions—to join the secret police as a potential, if failed assassin—are not the attempts of a man to embrace "normal" middle class life, but the complete erasure of self.

Conversely, in Claude Lanzmann's memoirs, *The Patagonian Hare: A Memoir* (2013), he writes of the pre-war attempts of Jews to disappear into mainstream German society as a similar impulse: "Assimilation is another form of annihilation, a triumph of forgetting."[6] This impulse to erase one's identity and culture is akin to a form of self-death. Marcello attempts to shed the upper middle-class excess symbolized by his parents, but what he views as "normal" it is easy to see as violent, destructive, sadistic, and perverse, hinting at the true core of his identity.

His level of detachment seems almost existentialist in nature and it is easy to draw parallels to Dostoyevsky's Raskolnikov from *Crime and Punishment* and Camus' Meursault of *The Stranger*. But unlike these other fictional murderers, Marcello is symbolically impotent, unable to commit real acts of murder on his own. One of Bertolucci's biggest changes from Moravia's novel is that he moves Marcello to the scene of the crime. In the book, other agents carry out the professor's murder while Marcello is safely miles away. Bertolucci places him in the car behind the assassination, calmly witnessing the deaths of the professor and his wife. This theme of the car or the vehicle is a powerful one throughout the film and there is almost constantly the sense that Marcello is being passively driven through the events of his life, beginning with the chauffeur who brings about his initiation into sex, violence, and trauma.

Moravia said that Marcello "was a pitiable character—pitiable because a victim of circumstance, led astray by the times, a *traviato*."[7] *Traviatio*, meaning "corrupted," takes on a further layer in the film, as Bertolucci makes Marcello into a wholly unreliable narrator. Where the novel moves from Marcello's childhood trauma linearly through the anti-fascist uprising at the end of the war, Bertolucci's moves backwards and forwards in time at will, making multiple viewings almost a guaranteed prerequisite to comprehending the narrative as a whole.

Bertolucci subverts conventional reality at every turn—not just with the film's dizzying sense of time, but with its overwhelming visual style and inventive cinematography. While upper-class decadence also fuels other war-themed films from the period, *The Conformist* attempts to capture the surreal or hallucinatory qualities of life in a fascist regime. This Italian-French-West German affair was shot by the great cinematographer Vittorio Storraro and, perhaps unlike similar efforts from the decade, makes brilliant use of the fascist stylistic palette. In particular, Bertolucci and Storrarro focus on the art deco favored in the '30s, wide open spaces—such as Roman ruins that double as an outdoor asylum—cluttered sitting rooms, and starkly white design and architecture.

This is undoubtedly one of Bertolucci's finest achievements, though it was not his first attempt to explore the relationship between war trauma, inheritance, identity, sexuality, and truth. *Strategia del ragno* (*The Spider's Stratagem*, 1970), made the same year as *The Conformist*, is sort of a curious successor to Visconti's *Sandra* and was released just before *The Conformist*. Written by Bertolucci and based on Argentinian writer Jorge Luis

Borges' story "Theme of the Traitor and the Hero," *The Spider's Stratagem* follows a young man's return to his home village, Tara, years after his father's wartime murder.

Athos Magnani, Jr. (Giulio Brogi portrays both father and son) has been summoned home by Draifa (Alida Valli), his father's mistress. Haunted by her lover's memory, Draifa is determined that Athos should discover who killed his father. But Athos uncovers a series of contradictory clues and misleading witnesses, such as that a fortune teller foresaw his father's death and that he received a strange letter of warning. His father was an avowed anti-fascist and has since become a local hero with streets named after him and monuments to his bravery peppering the city. General consensus is that he was murdered by a fascist—during a performance of Giuseppe Verdi's opera *Rigoletto*—but Athos soon uncovers contradictory evidence that he may have been killed by anti-fascists working with the local police.

Ultimately these clues don't lead anywhere and Athos Jr., is sucked further into Tara's strange web. And though the film is set up as a mystery—not unlike *Sandra*, where a famous hero's child attempts to solve his murder—that's not the really sole purpose of the film. *The Spider's Stratagem* functions as more of a series of dreamlike vignettes rather than a fully formed, linear narrative. As with *The Conformist*, Bertolucci uses sudden flashbacks, disorienting camera angles, and closely follows the dissolution of the protagonist's identity. Athos loses himself not only in the quest to find his father's murderer, but in his father's memory itself. Through the parallel stories of father and son, Bertolucci charts the overlap between political, historical, and psychological, focusing

The eerie town of Tara in *The Spider's Stratagem* appears to be frozen in time, aging but never advancing beyond the war (*Strategia del ragno*, RAI Radiotelevisione Italian/Red Film, 1970).

as much on communal trauma as individual. And though the film has little sexual perversion to speak of, there is the subtle suggestion of incest. It is Draifa, Athos's mistress, who brings his son to the town. She presses him to solve his father's murder, but also proceeds to seduce him and seems to confuse the identities of father and son as the film progresses.

There are numerous surreal elements, which make this feel more like a Fellini film than *The Conformist* and looks ahead somewhat to Fellini's *Amarcord* (1973). In that film, a boy who grows up in a closed off Italian village in the '30s populated with absurd characters who all refuse to take any moral responsibility for the growing wave of fascism. In both *The Spider's Stratagem* and *Amarcord*, these provincial towns seem to exist in a frozen state, unable to advance with the rest of the world. In *The Spider's Stratagem*, Athos has stepped into a place that has not advanced in any way since the end of the war. The town's citizens are all older and it seemingly lacks a younger generation. While Athos has to deal with occasional abuse from them, he also has surreal encounters such as a sequence where visiting circus performers try to capture an escaped lion. Art, too, plays an obviously important role in the film. In addition to a dance sequence and his father's death taking place at the opera, Bertolucci contrasts Athos with Magritte's painting "La reproduction interdite," where a man is looking into a mirror but it only reflects the back of his head. Athos also constantly compares the crime of his father's murder to various scenes in Shakespeare, namely *Julius Caesar* and *Macbeth*.

All in all, *The Spider's Stratagem* is remarkably similar to *Sandra* and acts as something of a test run for many of the themes more fully developed in *The Conformist*. Films like *The Damned*, *The Conformist*, and *The Spider's Stratagem* serve as important departures from the other war-themed films of the period, particularly in the sense that they are critical of the Italian people—of anyone driven to collaborate with fascist terror or even ignorant or lazy enough to ignore the horrors being perpetrated. While some mainstream efforts touched on these subjects, such as George Pan Cosmatos's *Rappresaglia* (*Massacre in Rome*, 1973), with Richard Burton as Gestapo chief who orchestrates the massacre of hundreds of Italians in retribution for a partisan attack; or Carlo Lizzani's *Mussolini: Ultimo atto* (*Last Days of Mussolini*, 1974).

Though it is not an Italian film, it is also necessary to briefly discuss Bob Fosse's American musical *Cabaret* (1972) and its source material, which had an undeniable influence on films from the period that combined decadence and fascism. *Cabaret* is based on Christopher Isherwood's *Goodbye to Berlin* (1939), a short autobiographical novel about the writer's time in pre-war Germany. Though he expatriated to New York in the '40s, Isherwood and his lifelong friend, the poet Wystan Auden, had travelled extensively in Europe during the '30s and it is these adventures that informed Isherwood's early novels. The characters in his fiction, particularly Sally Bowles, were hugely influential to pop-culture depictions of World War II and the understanding of life in '30s Germany.

Auden and Isherwood both wrote passionately against fascism in the early years of their careers and experienced much of it firsthand. In 1936, they travelled to China to write *Journey to a War*, one of the first English-language books on the Sino-Japanese War that bled into World War II. This experience was likely the inspiration for Auden's thoughts on the subject:

> War is bombing an already disused arsenal, missing it, and killing a few old women. War is a handful of lost and terrified men in the mountains, shooting at something moving in the

undergrowth. War is waiting for days with nothing to do; shouting down a dead telephone; going without sleep, or sex, or a wash. War is untidy, inefficient, obscure, and largely a matter of chance.[8]

Before this experience in China, Auden served as an ambulance driver in the Spanish Civil War and witnessed more than his share of death and violence. Most importantly, the two writers also directly experienced the rise of Nazism first hand thanks to their years in Berlin in the early '30s. They spent their days writing, learning German, and giving English lessons. As both men were gay, they also took advantage of the sexual freedom that has become associated with the Weimar years. The various people Isherwood befriended in Berlin were often the inspiration for his short fiction and novels of the period. For instance, British writer Jean Ross was the genesis of Sally Bowles,[9] Isherwood's most famous character and the protagonist of *Goodbye to Berlin*. The real-life Ross was a nightclub singer, chorus girl, and model in Weimar-era Berlin early in her life, but went on to become a war correspondent during the Spanish Civil War, a passionate political activist, and a film critic.

Sally, on the other hand, is presented as a mixture of brash sexuality and misguided innocence, concerned only with a free life of hedonism. For example, her garish makeup—green fingernails, heavily penciled black eyebrows, and a pale white face—is described alongside her childishly dirty hands. Like real-life Weimar cabaret presence and future Hollywood star Marlene Dietrich, Sally's magnetism largely stems from sexual charisma, her persistent desire to buck social conventions, and her apparent emotional unavailability. She is not explicitly a prostitute, but exchanges sex for wealth, affection, or even the promise of a good time.

In the somewhat autobiographical story, a struggling writer meets a number of colorful figures targeted by the Nazis, such as a Jewish heiress, his poor but understanding landlady, and a gay couple unsure of their future when the Nazis assume power. The promiscuous and manipulative Sally is the culmination of all these personalities, a figure who is at risk from fascism not because of her racial identity or lifestyle, but simply because of her naïve and optimistic determination to ignore hardship. Sally is a blend of alluring contradictions. This sense of denial, decadence, and contradiction can be found in many of the female characters in Italian World War II films from this era, including *The Damned*, *The Conformist*, and especially in the films of Liliana Cavani and Lina Wertmüller.

A line can be drawn directly from these '70s films and *Cabaret* back to the blueprint of decaying morals, personal failure, and cabaret life introduced in Josef von Sternberg's *Der blaue Engel* (*The Blue Angel*, 1930). One of the first important German sound films, this early classic rocketed star Marlene Dietrich to fame seemingly overnight. Lola Lola (Dietrich), a lovely singer in a traveling cabaret at a club called the Blue Angel, ensnares an upstanding local teacher (Emil Jannings). He quickly becomes involved in a whirlwind affair with Lola, grows obsessed with her, and convinces her to marry him. After they blow through his money, he is forced to take a job at the cabaret alongside her—as a clown—and the strong man (Hans Albers) replaces him as her new love interest. This drives him insane and after attempting to kill Lola, he dies of heartbreak.

The core plot of a man drawn to an overtly sexual cabaret singer, who becomes swept up in her world to his detriment, is one of the recurring narratives in pop culture depictions of World War II. Following this thread allows for an examination of changing moral and political attitudes about women and sex, as well as changing perceptions about Nazi Germany and the war itself. In *The Blue Angel*, Lola Lola is remote and unreal, a symbolic stand-in for the growing debauchery and despair in post–World War I Germany. Sally, on the other hand, is a figure that represents the end of an era. Her subtle nihilism and determination to ignore the Nazi onslaught is a product of late '20s and early '30s Europe. Sally is determined to stay frozen in a moment of performance, to party while the world ends, and to keep the merriment alive even when friends and lovers are being imprisoned, tortured, and murdered.

The characters of Sally and Lola Lola are both a product of '20s flapper culture that found its way from the American jazz scene across the Atlantic. Exemplified by scandalous attire (initially short skirts), cigarette smoking, alcohol drinking, seductive dancing, driving, dark makeup, a casual attitude towards sex, and a lack of concern about social impropriety, this figure was represented by both cinematic roles and real-life counterparts. Actresses like Frances Marion—who starred in 1920 film *The Flapper* and was arguably the first to portray the type—Clara Bow, Joan Crawford, and others found fame and popularity with this style. Meant to buck conservative Victorian values and Prohibition alike, the flapper was often found in private saloons, speakeasies, or cabarets. Writers like F. Scott Fitzgerald popularized flapper characters in his novels, while female writer and cynic Dorothy Parker became associated with the type herself due to her notorious affairs, venomous wit, and alcoholism. Women like Marlene Dietrich and Coco Chanel similarly helped pioneer the flapper as an international icon, though Louise Brooks, an American actress who travelled to Germany to portray a flapper-like character in *Die Büchse der Pandora* (*Pandora's Box*, 1929) and *Tagebuch einer Verlorenen* (*Diary of a Lost Girl*, 1929) for director G.W. Pabst, is perhaps its reigning queen.

For *Cabaret*, Vincente Minnelli allegedly advised his daughter Liza to study Brooks in particular for the role of Sally Bowles.[10] The factual Brooks—who was also know for her independence, casual attitude towards marriage, and occasional lesbian relationships—and the fictional Bowles provide a fascinating parallel between the underground sexual revolution of the '20s and '30s with the more blatant one experienced in the '60s and '70s, as represented by Minnelli's onscreen Bowles. Various versions of Sally appeared throughout the years to increasing acclaim. *Goodbye to Berlin* was published in 1939 and a decade later a play, *I Am a Camera*, was produced in New York starring Julie Harris as Sally. The 1955 film adaptation unfortunately presented a watered-down version of the story, stripping the plot of its sexual decadence and references to homosexuality and abortion. Fosse's adaptation emphasized the rising terror of Nazism and the increasingly tense atmosphere in Berlin, where Weimar debauchery and personal freedom are gradually replaced with restrictive fascist policies.

Though there are deviations from the novel, Fosse restored much missing from previous adaptations, and this was one of the first Hollywood films with a sympathetic, openly gay protagonist. The majority of the film takes place in the Kit Kat Klub, where Sally performs a number of suggestive songs alongside female dancers and the gender-bending Emcee. The songs ooze with innuendo and a casual attitude towards sex is certainly implied, along with prostitution, lesbianism, bisexuality, and rampant drug use. Insdorf writes,

> They goose-step about the stage, suggesting a perversity that underlines Nazism; indeed, the overt sexual decadence in the Kit Kat Klub consistently de-eroticizes and depersonalizes

(mutually dependent processes). The lewd jokes and abstract female flesh suggest that Nazism is predicated on a denial of love and sex, a display of flesh to be automatized into parade formation.[11]

In a song titled "If You Could See Her Through My Eyes," the Emcee sings about how the object of his love is wonderful to him, even though everyone else may disagree. He is joined by a dancer in a gorilla costume wearing a dress. During the final bar, he quietly sings, "I understand your objection/ I grant you the problem's not small/ But if you could see her through my eyes/ She wouldn't look Jewish at all…." The sense of playfulness—the scene appears to be mocking the Nazis—is disturbing because the parody is doubly subversive. The scene makes fun of the Nazis and their absurd insistence that Jews are subhuman, immoral, and criminal. But it does not attempt open rebellion or resistance and suggests that the Emcee knows his love is perverse—and perhaps enjoys it more for this reason.

In the world of *Cabaret* bodies are for sale, with an increasingly ominous implication—a theme shared with the Italian films to follow it. It seems that if an American director like Fosse was willing to depicted homosexual relationships and proudly promiscuous women in mainstream Hollywood cinema—particularly in a previously wholesome genre like the musical—European directors were determined to push the envelope further still. Director Liliana Cavani is one of the most notorious examples, particularly with *The Night Porter*, though much of her career has been concerned with cinematic explorations of World War II.

Cavani essentially got her start as a director making television documentaries for the Italian network RAI, namely *Storia del III Reich* (*History of the Third Reich*, 1962–63). Made up for four, 50-minute episodes, this brief series was "the first of its kind in Italy,"[12] according to Giorgio Bertellini. He writes, "Her reconstruction of the history of National Socialism draws from films she found in French, West German and American film archives, as well as from propaganda manifestos and George Grosz's grotesquely stylized cartoons."[13]

Cavani also went on to helm the similarly themed documentary *La donna nella Resistenza* (*Women of the Resistance*, 1965), perhaps the only film about the role of Italian women in the Resistance. Cavani interviewed a wide variety of women—from couriers to fighters—and reminds her likely conservative Italian viewers that their mothers, sisters, wives, and daughters took an active role: for example, she shares statistics that roughly 4,000 women were arrested and tortured for their participation in the Resistance, 600 were killed, and 6,000 were deported to camps and prisons in Germany.

The interviews seemed to have a profound effect on Cavani. She relates the story of a woman she interviewed who was transported to Dachau for her role in the Resistance, but managed to survive.[14] To Cavani's surprise, the woman returned to visit the area every single year. This theme of being unable to completely move on from past traumas is felt strongly in the documentary, as is the amoral aspect of the survival instinct that was experienced by many of the survivors during their wartime ordeal—also themes of *The Night Porter*. Though Cavani was born in 1933 and effectively grew up during the war years, the experience of making these two documentaries was perhaps the beginning of her fascination with fascist horrors as a filmmaker. She recounted her experience making the documentary series to writer Gaetana Marrone:

The Germans loved to record every event on film, and they did it well. Hitler and his entourage loved cinema. My editor and I saw rolls on the *Lager* and on the Russian campaign. One day we had to stop because we became sick. When the artists of the duecento attempted to paint the inferno, they were naive. Clearly, there has been a progress in cruelty, in fact a true escalation. For whom did those cameramen think they were leaving those images? For monsters?[15]

She set one of her first films, *I cannibali* (*The Year of the Cannibals*, 1970), in a fictionalized fascist country, though it is an adaptation of Sophocles' *Antigone*. A young woman (Britt Ekland) struggles to have her dead brother buried. Because he is considered an enemy of the state, the government won't allow it. The countryside is littered with many such disgraced bodies. Ultimately an experimental film with little in the way of a linear plot structure or dialogue, Cavani took the themes of *The Year of the Cannibals* and applied a more rigorous narrative structure for what is widely regarded as her masterpiece, *The Night Porter*.

This 1974 film straddles the border between exploitation and art cinema and, alongside Pasolini's *Salò*, is one of the most controversial works of Italian cinema. Beginning in the late '50s, the film follows former SS Officer Max Aldorfer (Dirk Bogarde), who works as the night porter of a hotel. He still maintains a connection to a Nazi sleeper cell attempting to carry on their old ways through strict rules and secret tribunals. Lucia (Charlotte Rampling), once a concentration camp prisoner and Max's victim, comes to stay at the hotel with her composer husband (Marino Masé). Max and Lucia recognize each other and almost immediately resume the sadomasochistic sexual relationship they had in the camp years ago.

Unfortunately, Lucia is recognized by the sleeper cell, who decide that she knows too much and must be executed. Max barricades Lucia and himself inside his apartment, consensually chaining her to the wall. The escalating violence of their sexual relationship climaxes in a mutual suicide pact. They begin starving to death and ultimately attempt to flee, only to be gunned down by Nazi bullets. The inability to escape the trauma of the

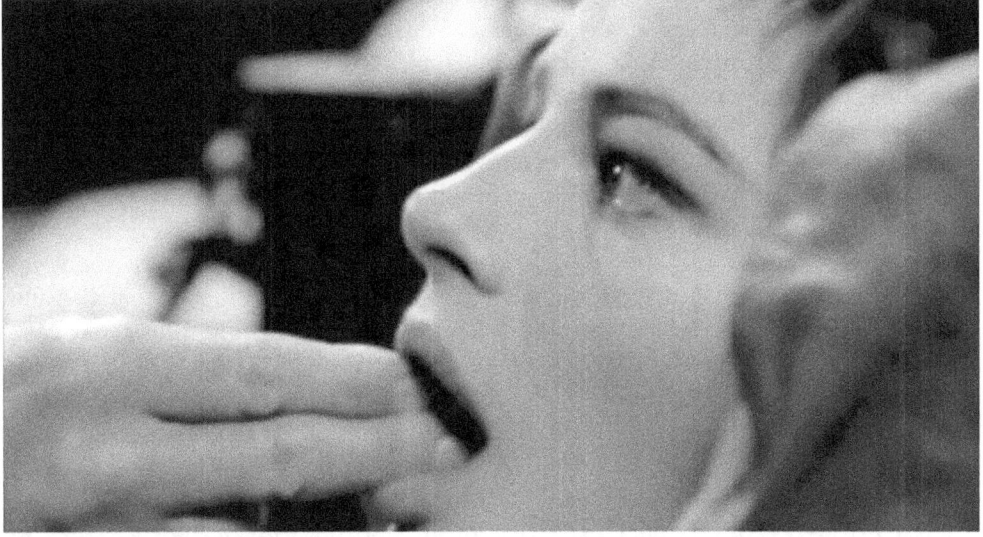

Max (Dirk Bogarde) and Lucia (Charlotte Rampling) enact their sadomasochistic relationship in *The Night Porter* (*Il portiere di notte*, Lotar Film Productions, 1974).

past sucks them into a loop where the lines between victim and perpetrator disappear. The only release is death, which they go to, if not willingly, fully aware.

This deeply subversive film wasn't overwhelmingly popular with critics upon its release—the majority of them viewed it as little more than tasteless, offensive smut—but it has come to be regarded as a challenging cult classic that examines the often-contradictory nature of desire, victimhood, and memory. Much of the controversy is related to the presentation of a sadomasochistic relationship between a Holocaust survivor and the former Nazi who both victimized and protected her while in a concentration camp. Rebecca Scherr writes, "In narrative accounts of Holocaust testimony, explicit discussions of sexuality and eroticism are almost nonexistent. If the theme does occur in eyewitness accounts, it is often the enforced lack of sexuality that is the object of commentary."[16]

Sexualizing the Holocaust and the experience of survivors remains taboo, particularly in fictional narratives, though the factual sexual experiences of Holocaust survivors also remains little explored in historical writing or documentary. Scherr writes,

> Trauma, displacement and incarceration, starvation and its consequent exhaustion, overwork, the segregation of men and women, the destruction of family units, the shaving of body hair, the cessation of menstruation, the constant presence and threat of death—all of these factors conspired to strip the individual of any means towards imagining oneself a being, human and sexual.[17]

During the same period, other films also began to examine the Holocaust in a sexual light, though most of these belong firmly in the exploitation genre and came to be known as Nazisploitation films. Arguably *The Night Porter* is an erotic arthouse drama that doesn't quite reach the full excesses of exploitation filmmaking.

Where *The Night Porter* begins to overlap with exploitation cinema is in its treatment of voyeurism, spectacle, and performance. Cavani sets up a number of set pieces that do little more than highlight the obscene theatricality of public eroticism: such as Max and Lucia engaging in theoretically consensual sex acts together before a group of emaciated camp prisoners; or Lucia's mock cabaret number, where she sings "Wenn ich mir was wünschen dürfte" ("If I could make a wish"), while topless, wearing only the hat, pants, and suspenders of a Nazi uniform. This song, popularized by Marlene Dietrich, seems like an obvious reference to *The Blue Angel* and *Cabaret*. In general, the cabaret scene has come to signify decadence, particularly in '70s and '80s cinema. Cavani pushes the connection between cabaret performance and decadence to its most transgressive limits.

The film is also rife with references to art, performance, and spectatorship. Lucia's husband is a conductor and she and Max have an anxiety-fueled run in at his production of Mozart's *Die Zauberflote*. In addition to Lucia's musical scene at the camp, a male ballet dancer performs for the Nazis, something he later privately resumes in the hotel for Max. Even the underground Nazi cell has an element of theatricality with their mock trials and codified appearances. Cavani proves that there are scant steps between play-acting, theater, ritual, and personal transformation, and even Max and Lucia change costumes as they revert to old roles.

Voyeurism is also of importance to Max and Lucia's relationship, which did not begin in private, as conventional sexual relationships do, but with an audience. They are surrounded by camp inhabitants whose appearance contrasts dramatically with Lucia's youthful loveliness: they are old, starving, dirty, and sick. Marrone writes,

Max is first identified while filming Lucia, naked, upon her arrival at the concentration camp. He focuses on a close up of her terrified stare, as she turns away from the bright light aimed at her. The viewer seems no longer to be watching a film but rather to be witnessing a horrific event as it unfolds. Here, as elsewhere in *The Night Porter*, the complicity of cinema with transgression and voyeuristic compulsion becomes a subject of the film itself.[18]

Cavani seems more interested in examining the often inherently transgressive nature of desire itself rather than the Holocaust in literal, historical terms. Marcus writes, "It could indeed be argued that the *Lager* setting serves as a mere pretext, a laboratory for Cavani to study the workings of human sexuality pushed to the breaking point."[19] The relationship between Max and Lucia is a complicated one that includes the dichotomies of sadist and masochist, older man and younger woman, perpetrator and victim, Nazi and Holocaust survivor. As Cavani first explored in *Women of the Resistance*, the act of survival often necessitates shedding conventional morals and values, which is a major factor here. It's perhaps intentionally difficult to discern if *The Night Porter* is an unusual love story or a perverse tale of Stockholm Syndrome. Cavani herself said the film is based on a "pseudo-masochistic story that is justified by the extreme situation in which both man and woman find themselves. It is the detonator that allows them to express themselves."[20]

And yet, this is also one of many '70s art house films about the dark underbelly of the '50s economic boom experienced in many European countries—for example, in West Germany, this is a subject that Rainer Werner Fassbinder would explore regularly. Only a few years after the war, it seemed like the world was struck with mass amnesia and a desire to forget the horrible events of the '40s. This was contrasted by the experiences of many survivors who were unable to move beyond the events of the past, a theme that marks many factual and fictional Holocaust narratives. *The Night Porter* presents a world populated by desperate, lost characters determined to skulk in the shadows and cling to a hellish past. Marrone writes that Cavani

> evokes an oneiric dimension, a kind of a sinister limbo that encloses all existential interrogations; identified with an event of the past, the present is reenacted to the extreme possibility: the "humoral" solution of psychological (and physical) suicide. At a structural level, Cavani constructs images that convey the magic, subterranean qualities of a ritualistic descent *ad inferos*.[21]

Perhaps coincidentally, the film's star, Dirk Bogarde, personally experienced this descent. During the war years, he was a Captain with the Queen's Royal Regiment in a military career that took him around Europe, to the Pacific theater, and involved intelligence work. He also claimed to be among the first to enter Bergen-Belsen after its liberation in April of 1945 in a joint mission by Britain and Canada, an event that deeply affected him. The liberating officers uncovered some 13,000 corpses and approximately 60,000 inmates, many of whom were barely alive thanks to disease, mistreatment, and starvation. Some 10,000 of these survivors died shortly after liberation. BBC broadcaster and journalist Richard Dimbleby, who was also present, described the scene in a radio announcement:

> Here over an acre of ground lay dead and dying people. You could not see which was which. The living lay with their heads against the corpses and around them moved the awful, ghostly procession of emaciated, aimless people, with nothing to do and with no hope of life, unable to move out of your way, unable to look at the terrible sights around them…. This day at Belsen was the most horrible of my life.[22]

It is interesting that in light of this traumatic experience, Bogarde played Germans several times throughout his career, most notably in *The Damned* and *The Night Porter*, though in a later chapter, I'll also examine his turn as a Russian businessman in Nazi Germany in Rainer Werner Fassbinder's *Despair* (1978). In a 1975 television interview with Mark Caldwell, he spoke highly of *The Night Porter*, describing it as, "A totally true film, it's a love story and a grave warning … about totalitarianism, about lack of control, and about lack of discipline."[23]

Like Bogarde, Cavani continued to return to the subject of the war and revisited it just a few years after *The Night Porter* with *La pelle* (*The Skin*, 1981), based on a book of short stories by Curzio Malaparte. An early supporter of fascism and a friend of Mussolini's, Malaparte became a staunch critic when the party took on more conservative values. He was exiled, imprisoned multiple times for his troubles, joined the Allied Army, and became one of Italy's most experienced war correspondents. He appears as a translator in the film (played by Marcello Mastroianni), but *The Skin* loosely follows the difficult lives of three women during the Allied liberation of Naples in 1943. Like *The Night Porter*—and Malaparte's similar book *Kaputt*, about Germany's violent exploitation of Europe—the overall theme of *The Skin* is about what people are willing to do in order to survive.

Like Rossellini's *Paisan*, *The Skin* is more a series of unconnected stories than it is a single cohesive narrative, and, like his *General Della Rovere*, it captures the sense of Italian ambivalence about the presence of both German and American invaders. In *The Skin*, the Americans bring with them the harshest, most exploitative kind of capitalism and there is the sense that Cavani is trying to go toe-to-toe with Pasolini when it comes to exploring the evils of postwar capitalist exploitation and man's commodification of man.

The Skin was criticized for being anti–American, as the soldiers are shown to be greedy and callous invaders—rather than heroic liberators—who are more than willing to take advantage of the Italians. In particular, Cavani shows the sexual subjugation of women by the conquering forces and her major alteration of Malaparte's material was to expand three of his female characters. Like *The Night Porter*, *The Skin* is an examination of sexual exploitation and the totalitarian impulse that lies at the heart of man, though here Cavani includes more comic and absurdist qualities and moves away from a personal story to take a communal view of the chaos and desperation of life in the '40s.

A decade after *The Night Porter*, Cavani revisited the war a third and final time with *The Berlin Affair* (1985). An adaptation of Jun'ichirō Tanizaki's erotic novel *Quicksand* (1930), this Italian-West German coproduction moves events to Berlin in 1938. A diplomat's wife, Louise von Hollendorf (Gudrun Landgrebe), begins an affair with Mitsuko Matsugae (Mio Takaki), the daughter of the Japanese ambassador. But when Louise's husband Heinz (Kevin McNally) tries to break them up, he falls for Mitsuko himself. When their relationship becomes an uneasy ménage à trois, it leads to the ruination of all three.

While *The Night Porter* uses something of a creative historical license to complicate its central love story, *The Berlin Affair* uses Nazi Germany as little more than a stylistic backdrop. The change of time period from the novel—which enraged many critics of the day—adds a heightened sense of repression and imminent violence, but the centerpiece is the chaotic central threesome. This complex relationship, where a manipulative, often cruel personality dominates a more submissive, dependent lover (or lovers, in this case), is a trademark of Cavani's and is a trope of equal importance to her career as her fascination with World War II-era history.

Perhaps the most direct parallel to Cavani's work can be found in her contemporary,

Lina Wertmüller, another Italian director fond of exploring both political and sexual themes, albeit with far more surreal humor and anarchism. After serving as assistant director to Fellini on *8½* (1963), Wertmüller received acclaim when she embarked on a productive collaboration with actor Giancarlo Giannini in the '70s with films like *Mimí metallurgico ferito nell'onore* (*The Seduction of Mimi*, 1972), *Film d'amore e d'anarchia, ovvero: stamattina alle 10, in via dei Fiori, nella nota casa di tolleranzaI*, (*Love and Anarchy*, 1973), and *Travolti da un'insolito destino nell'azzurro mare d'agosto* (*Swept Away*, 1974).

Love and Anarchy—whose original Italian title translates to *Film of Love and Anarchy, Or, "This Morning at 10 in Villa dei Fiori in the Well-Known Brothel..."*—may not be as concerned with sexual perversion as earlier films like *The Damned*, *The Conformist*, or *The Night Porter*, but it is certainly sexually explicit. Set during the '20s when the National Fascist Party took control of Italy, Tunin (Giancarlo Giannini) learns of the death of one of his friends who planned to assassinate Mussolini, and Tunin takes it upon himself to complete this task. He travels to Rome from his home in the countryside and meets Salomè (Mariangela Melato), the madam of a brothel who wants to help him. While Tunin and Salomè plan the assassination, Tunin falls in love with a young prostitute, Tripolina (Lina Polito).

It is ultimately Tripolina's love for Tunin that botches their plans and causes him to needlessly sacrifice himself. This comic tragedy was apparently based on the story of a real-life man from the countryside who attempted to assassinate Mussolini, failed, and was executed, but was given no attention by the government or press. The ending of the film—which shows a brief fascist report, which reads "This Morning at 10 in Villa dei Fiori in the Well-Known Brothel..."—is a direct reference to the fascist tendency to manipulate truth, media, and even history. Giorgio Bertellini writes,

> The unnamed Sardinian peasant is not the only historical source for Tunin's character. Anteo Zamboni, whom Tunin comes to replace in Salomè's affections, and who serves as the protagonist's double in the preamble of the story, was a real anarchist who was killed by a mob for allegedly firing on Mussolini during an official visit to Bologna in 1926. In remembering Zamboni, Wertmüller's film becomes doubly epitaphic in the neorealist sense, rescuing two anti–Fascist martyrs from the oblivion to which history had consigned them[24]

Like the early films of Pasolini such as *Accattone* (1961), *Mamma Roma* (1962), and *La ricotta* (1963), Wertmüller uses unconventional heroes who exist on the margins of society: peasants, criminals, and whores. She was harshly criticized for her confrontational, ribald depictions of sexuality, but this Rabelaisian surface layer provides a colorful contrast to the film's steadily building sense of anxiety and impending violence. Like Pasolini's tragic heroes, particularly those played by Franco Citti, Tunin is absurd and chaotic, destined to fail. Wertmüller's bitter message in the film is the sense that all political action is ineffectual and perhaps also thus irrational. Both Tunin and Salomè are not driven to kill Mussolini because of their moral convictions; rather they become involved in order to avenge dead friends or lovers.

Wertmüller tread even more controversial ground on her next film with Giannini, *Pasqualino Settebellezze* (*Seven Beauties*, 1975). If *Love and Anarchy* depicted unlikely heroes, *Seven Beauties* takes things to an entirely new extreme and is set a few years later, in the midst of war. Pasqualino (Giannini) starts out as a common criminal, but murders a pimp when the man turns Pasqualino's sister into a prostitute. He dismembers the body and attempts to get rid of it but is picked up by the police and sent to an asylum, where he rapes another patient. He joins the Army to escape, but deserts and is put in a concentration camp by the Germans, where he is willing to do anything to survive. The grotesque female commandant (Shirley Stoler) of the camp allows him to seduce her and he is given the status of kapo in exchange for sexual favors. He is also asked to make increasingly difficult decisions—such as selecting six prisoners to die so that the commandant doesn't have the entire barrack killed—while the camp sinks further into misery and depravity.

Despite its graphic nature and subject matter that includes genocide, rape, murder, suicide, sadomasochism, and sexual exploitation, *Seven Beauties* was, perhaps incredibly, nominated for several Academy Awards and received widespread critical acclaim. Wertmüller was the first woman ever nominated for Best Director. It is the grimmest of black comedies and makes light of everything from war—in its newsreel-style opening sequence, which takes a comic turn—to Italian machismo, as Pasqualino starts out on this path because he's an opportunistic bully who tries to control his seven sisters (and his mother).

Really Pasqualino is nothing more than a fool. Despite a variety of unlikable character traits, he somehow comes through the film possessing a strangely charismatic quality. Like some of the characters in *The Night Porter*, he's concerned with survival, above all, at the complete expense of morality—though it's clear that he wasn't a particularly moral person to begin with and Wertmüller seems to suggest that this is why he is able to survive. His main objectives are to uphold what he views as his honor as a man, which includes protecting the female members of his family as he sees fit, and to pursue all pleasures of the flesh.

Despite scenes of graphic sex, mass murder, and concentration camp horrors, it is actually Pasqualino's unchecked appetites and lack of a clear moral system that makes *Seven Beauties* so troubling. Psychologist, writer, and Holocaust survivor Bruno Bettelheim wrote an impassioned critique of the film for *The New Yorker*, "Surviving," in which

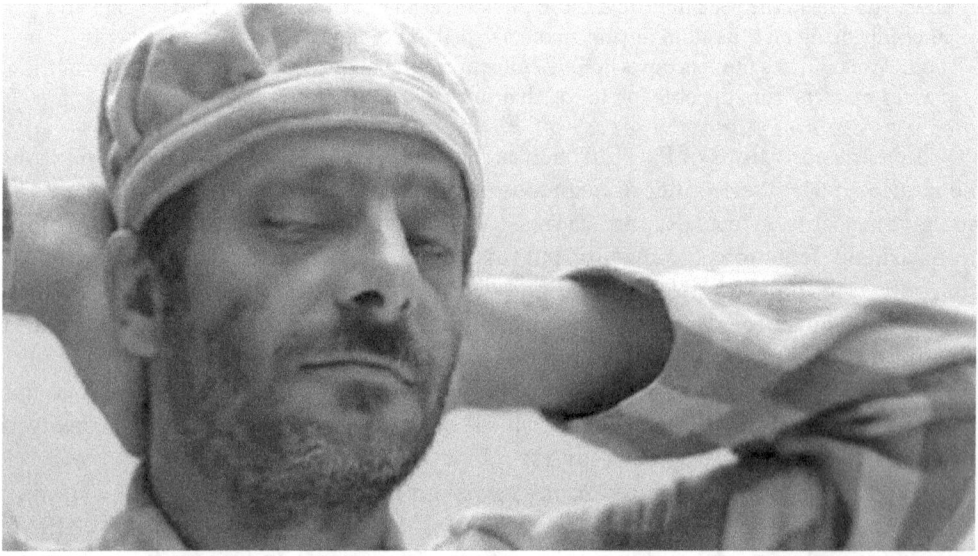

Pasqualino (Giancarlo Giannini) continues to leer at women, even after he's a concentration camp prisoner in *Seven Beauties* (*Pasqualino Settebellezze*, Medusa Distribuzione, 1975).

he argued that although *Seven Beauties* is undeniably a work of art, its cruel, amoral tone is a cause for real concern. He writes, "These audiences seem to accept the completely erroneous implication that to survive in the camps one had to act as if one were vermin, as Pasqualino does in the film."[25]

Bettelheim, like some critics from the period, had trouble separating a historically accurate depiction of the Holocaust with Wertmüller's blackly comic, nihilistic, and irreverent interpretation of events. Bettelheim writes,

> While the horrors of war, Fascism, and the concentration camp are clearly and overtly presented, covertly they are much more effectively denied, because what we watch is a farce played in a charnel house, and, furthermore, because to survive despite evil and survival through doing evil seem to be in the end all important, regardless of the form that either the evil or the survival takes.[26]

Unlike *The Damned* or *The Night Porter*, perverse sexuality is not the film's centerpiece, but merely a means to an end. It is this sense of cruelty that Bettelheim finds so discomfiting. He explains, "I believe that consciously Wertmüller rejects Fascism, machismo, and the world of the concentration camps but that unconsciously she is fascinated by their power, brutality, amorality—their rape of man."[27]

While Wertmüller would later return to a World War II setting with films like *Fatto di sangue fra due uomini per causa di una vedova. Si sospettano moventi politici* (*Blood Feud*, 1978) and *Ninfa plebea* (*The Nymph*, 1996), *Seven Beauties* and its exploration of the "rape of man" belongs in a rare category alongside such late '60s and '70s films as *The Damned*, *The Conformist*, and *The Night Porter*, which explore fascism alongside themes of survival, amorality, and sexuality. Marcus writes, "For Wertmüller, indeed, the *Lager* can give birth to no possible narrative of human redemption—only survival tales of the worst social Darwinist kind could ever be delivered from its horrid depths."[28]

A final film worth mentioning is director Ettore Scola's *Una giornata particolare* (*A Special Day*, 1977), which also uses sexuality as a lens through which to examine the effects of war and fascism, albeit with more subtlety. Scola's film takes place on the day of Hitler's visit to Rome, May 8, 1938. An overworked housewife, Antonietta (Sophia Loren), stays home to attend to chores while her husband and six children attend the celebration. She finds herself alone in the apartment complex with a neighbor, Gabriele (Marcello Mastroianni), a radio broadcaster who has just been fired on account of his homosexuality. He is not attending the rally, because he's quietly waiting for the authorities to pick him up and deport him. Despite their numerous differences, the two spend the day talking, which culminates in a sexual affair just before Gabriele is taken to prison and Antonietta's family returns.

With this film, Scola took two of Italy's biggest stars—Loren and Mastroianni, who were often paired together for onscreen romance—and used them against type to explore issues of gender within Italian society. Loren's uneducated housewife is homely and utterly unglamorous. She idolizes Mussolini and quietly accepts her domestic fate, even if it makes her unhappy. In turn, leading man Mastroianni's character is anti-fascist, intellectual, and gay, at least the last of which must have scandalized '70s filmgoers in Italy. The plot is also something of an attack on traditional Italian values, as Loren's Antonietta is clearly a figure to be pitied, a downtrodden woman whose primary function is to bear children and whose home life is misery.

Hitler's visit really only provides a backdrop for Antonietta and Gabriele's day together, but Scola's commentary on Italian fascism is one of the most subtle yet profound out of all his contemporaries. This is truly a look at fascism and oppression through the lives of ordinary citizens; instead of including staged scenes of Hitler and Mussolini's visit, Scola relied on historical newsreel footage and radio commentary used as propaganda by the fascist government. The enclosed set—the film was shot at the Palazzo Federici, a fascist-designed structure built in the '30s—captures the mounting sense of tension. With no overt scenes of violence or horror, and very little action to speak of, it nevertheless becomes clear that there is no freedom, no privacy to be had anywhere in such a climate.

Though sex plays a relatively small role in the film, Scola uses it in a layered, complex way. Essentially both Antonietta and Gabriele are home from the celebration because of an underlying sexual issue. Antonietta is exploited by her husband, who pressures her to attend to the household above all else and demands she become pregnant again in order to have their seventh child. Gabriele's life has been ruined because of the fascist attitude towards homosexuality. After being fired, he will be deported and exiled or, worse, sent to a concentration camp. Their affair may seem improbable—working class wife and gay intellectual—but it is surprisingly tender while also lacking sentimentality. No great romance is revealed at the end of the film, rather Antoinetta's family returns home and Gabriele is arrested and taken from the building.

The intersection of sexuality and fascism found in Italian arthouse films from Visconti's *The Damned*, Bertolucci's *The Conformist*, Cavani's *The Night Porter*, Wertmüller's *Seven Beauties*, and Scola's *A Special Day* helped paved the way for a new kind of war cinema. Not only did filmmakers find transgressive, confrontational ways to explore World War II themes, but the war itself often exceeded the bounds of history and came to symbolize of something more: where Nazism represents absolute evil, the Holocaust is an example of the depths of human perversion, and survival does not necessarily mean redemption or a happy ending.

6

The Punishment Begins

The Films of Rainer Werner Fassbinder

"Love is the best, most insidious, most effective instrument of social repression."—Rainer Werner Fassbinder[1]

The emergence of New German Cinema marked a turning point in the country's national film output—particularly in terms of how German filmmakers would begin to reflect on Germany's past and the legacy of fascism. While the majority of directors working under the umbrella of New German Cinema examined turmoil in contemporary Germany, Thomas Elsaesser notes that by the mid- to late '70s, "political questions, social issues, current affairs and historical topics began to be treated in fiction films and documentaries in a manner unknown before in the Federal Republic."[2] New German Cinema's *enfant terrible*, Rainer Werner Fassbinder, was responsible for the bulk of this.

Easily the most famous figure of the movement, this director, actor, and writer is generally remembered for his controversial life as much as his prolific and brilliant cinematic output. In less than 15 years, Fassbinder produced 40 feature films, a few short films, two television series, and numerous plays. In addition to his work as a director, he acted in dozens of films—including several of his own—was responsible for the design, editing, and cinematography for much of his output, and ran a theater group. His films often shocked or provoked, which kept him continually in the limelight, despite the fact that the German media did not take him seriously until after his premature death at age 37 in 1982.

Towards the second half of his career, Fassbinder examined the state of contemporary German life, in particular the impact of World War II and its lingering ghosts. Many of Fassbinder's films from this period explore the themes that caused so much terror and violence during the years of Hitler's reign: cruelty and indifference, racism, bigotry, and the effects of exploitation, particularly economic, sexual, and emotional. His protagonists often served as both victims and perpetrators, and they were generally caught in the mundane though horrifying web of daily life from which Fassbinder implies there is no escape. He attacked intolerance in all its forms, seeming to suggest that there is a rotten core to human nature. The same impulse that made the Holocaust possible was not expunged from humanity with the defeat of Nazi Germany; it merely submerged and changed forms.

Born in Bavaria in 1945, mere weeks after the Allies liberated the country, Fassbinder was born into a bourgeois family. As a child of divorce, he was shuttled around between relatives. He later claimed that the cinema was his only real family and he spent most of his childhood in movie theaters. He gravitated toward theater study in Munich and quickly took over directorship of the Munich Action Theater in 1967, where he met several of his key collaborators, such as the actress Hanna Schygulla, actor and designer Kurt Raab, and composer Peer Raben. Many of these relationships were allegedly often unhealthy and abusive. It complicated matters that his romantic partners—both male and female—were frequently cast in his films and that these relationships had a tendency to end badly.

His early films are nihilistic and experimental, combining the influences of American gangster movies, film noir, Godard's *Bande à part* (*Band of Outsiders*, 1964), and Bertolt Brecht's theories on theater. The apparent normalcy of cruelty and fascism—and its latent existence in all Germans—is a theme Fassbinder returned to constantly throughout his career. In Hannah Arendt's controversial treatise, *Eichmann in Jerusalem*, she writes, "The trouble with Eichmann was precisely that so many were like him, and that the many were neither perverted nor sadistic, that they were, and still are, terribly and terrifyingly normal."[3] This is Fassbinder's overarching thesis.

As early as his second film, *Katzelmacher* (1969), Fassbinder began exploring the effects of what he saw as deeply rooted fascism lingering in postwar German life. As with all his early efforts, the film focuses on a series of apparently emotionless twenty-something characters. They seem to be somnambulists in a state of inertia, unable to act or think independently, merely reacting to their environments. The boredom of daily life is repressive and claustrophobic and ultimately leads to routine acts of violence. Characters are emotionally or physically abusive to each other with no obvious consequences. When a Greek immigrant named Jorgos (played by Fassbinder himself) moves to town, he disrupts their lives, resulting in a physical attack. The scene of the men beating Jorgos is surprisingly pathetic, an act that is disturbing not because of the degree of violence, but because of Jorgos' innocence and ignorance, and the suddenness with which they explode. The act is not really premeditated, but the prejudice, xenophobia, and hatred have been there all the time, boiling under a surface of middle-class civility.

Katzelmacher introduced many of Fassbinder's important future themes: bourgeois repression, emotional exploitation and cruelty, and the implication that the impulse toward violence is inherent in society. Nearly all of his works suggest that the legacy of hatred and intolerance of World War II had not disappeared despite postwar peace and the prosperity of the '50s. This hatred is also reflected in individual characters with cruelty and manipulation as the defining factor in close relationships not only in *Katzelmacher*, but nearly all of Fassbinder's body of work. Elsaesser writes, "Loneliness, homelessness, isolation, fear and failure have often been identified as the main preoccupations of the New German Cinema."[4] These themes are central to every single one of Fassbinder's films.

Not long after *Katzelmacher*, he turned to the interwar period with *Pioniere in Ingolstadt* (*Pioneers in Ingolstadt*, 1971). Alma (Irm Hermann) and Berta (Hanna Schygulla), two young women in the village of Ingolstadt, are excited by the presence of handsome soldiers, who have arrived to build a bridge. The soldiers become bored and restless, as they would rather be fighting a war than assigned to construction detail, and they pursue affairs with the women of the town. The more practical Alma has sex with several of the soldiers, some just out of sympathy, while other affairs are in exchange for payment. The more idealistic Berta falls in love with the handsome, but illusive Karl (Harry Baer), and becomes agonized when he doesn't return her feelings.

Based on a play by Marieluise Fleisser, a protégé of Brecht's (who directed the original production), *Pioneers in Ingolstadt* was originally written in 1928, but was adapted several times over the years and revised in 1968. It was one of Fassbinder's few films not based on his own material, though it contains many of his favorite themes. In many ways, this can be seen as a precursor to Michael Haneke's *Das weiße Band* (*The White Ribbon*, 2009), a film also about cruelty and corruption in a small German town, which acts as a microcosm for a society on the brink of fascism and war. Fassbinder's made-for-TV film similarly depicts a world on the verge of Nazism. Like one of his other early made-for-TV films, *Die Niklashauser Fart* (*The Niklashausen Journey*, 1970), *Pioneers in Ingolstadt* is made up of a blend of time periods: 19th-century village life, the Weimar era, the Nazi state, and contemporary Germany.

Fassbinder's most frequent collaborator, Hanna Schygulla, appears in a role that she would repeat for the director several times throughout the years: an idealistic woman who falls in love with a man and pursues a committed relationship, only to have him discard her in favor of an intimate bond (occasionally homosexual) with another man. Her character here, Berta, also seems obsessed with victimization and she becomes a willing martyr, sacrificing herself for a romanticized ideal of love. Berta's would-be lover, the soldier played by Fassbinder-regular Harry Baer, is another similar character type found especially in Fassbinder's early films: an aloof man uncertain of his purpose in life and almost pathologically desired by a woman. Karl does not openly reject Berta, and perhaps cruelly encourages her feelings, but prefers the company of men. He and the majority of the film's characters sleepwalk through their love affairs, squabbles, and the act of bridge building. Fassbinder uses the bridge as a bit of black comedy, an ironic metaphor for alienation that serves as a symbol of the gaps rather than connections between characters.

Händler der vier Jahreszeiten (*The Merchant of the Four Seasons*, 1972) also skirts around the subject of war and follows a soldier's inability to adjust to life in the postwar years. Hans (Hans Hirschmueller), a fruit-peddler in 1950s West Germany, lives a life of quiet misery and hasn't quite recovered from a wartime stint in the French Foreign Legion. His mother (Gusti Kreissl) lamented his return and has actively obstructed his happiness, forcing him to take up a career that drove away the woman he loved (Ingrid Caven). His wife (Irm Hermann) despises and mocks him.

Though Fassbinder was incredibly prolific throughout his life, generally making four or five films per year plus theatrical productions, 1971 was strangely devoted to only *The Merchant of the Four Seasons*. This marks a major transitional phase in the director's career, where melodrama inspired by German director Douglas Sirk—who had relocated to Hollywood in the late '30s because of his Jewish wife—began to have a bigger influence on his output.

The Merchant of the Four Seasons shares a common theme with many of his nihilistic, mid-period melodramas, such as *Angst essen Seele auf* (*Ali: Fear Eats the Soul*, 1974), *Faustrecht der Freiheit* (*Fox and His Friends*, 1975), and *Angst vor der Angst* (*Fear of Fear*, 1975): the horror of suburban life in a postwar world. In these films, Fassbinder explored everyday cruelty while also critiquing German society. He examines the effects of the financial boom of the '50s and the class and racial prejudice buried within. Fittingly, *The Merchant of the Four Seasons* ends with its earliest chronological flashback, where Hans is saved from death during the war, but instead wishes that he could have died—a sentiment it is obvious he has felt ever since—and many of Fassbinder's films from this period imply that despite apparent prosperity, real life somehow stopped with the war.

Around this time, Fassbinder also caused a major controversy with the production of his play *Der Müll, die Stadt und der Tod* (*The Garbage, the City, and the Death*), in turn based loosely on Gerhard Zwerenz's novel *Die Erde ist unbewohnbar wie der Mond* (*The Earth is Uninhabitable Like the Moon*, 1973). It was also turned into a film in 1976, a Swiss-West German co-production retitled *Schatten der Engel* (*Shadow of Angels*). Fassbinder turned over directorial duties to his collaborator Daniel Schmid but co-starred in the film alongside much of his regular stock company.

The beautiful Lily Brest (Ingrid Caven) prostitutes herself to support her abusive, gambling-addicted boyfriend, Raoul (Fassbinder). She is soon hired by one of the city's most powerful men, known only as the Rich Jew (Klaus Löwitsch), who becomes devoted to her. Raoul becomes insanely jealous, while others around town ostracize her, including her wheelchair-bound mother (Annemarie Düringer) and ex-Nazi father (Adrian Hoven), a drag performer at a local cabaret. Consumed with despair, she hopes to end her life and thinks the Rich Jew may be her only way out.

The play and Schmid's film bear much in common with Fassbinder's deeply personal later works, *In einem Jahr mit 13 Monden* (*In a Year with 13 Moons*, 1978), the television series *Berlin Alexanderplatz* (1980), and *Die Sehnsucht der Veronika Voss* (1982). *Shadow of Angels* shares three main themes in common with these films: the commodification of human life, an exploration of post–Holocaust anti-Semitism, and a central character plunged into despair by the banality of daily life. Fassbinder strove, with many of his films, to show that the social impulses behind Nazism were not an exception, but the norm. Elsaesser writes,

> What the notion of Hitler as a uniquely aberrant individual and the Nazi elite as a gang of common criminals sanctioned was the screening out of political and economic factors that had made fascism part of the modernizing forces of industrialization and the crisis cycles of finance capitalism.[5]

The play was attacked for its exploration of anti-Semitism, thanks primarily to the fact that a character is named "the Rich Jew." Four separate performances were banned over the years, though it has finally been staged as far afield as New York and Israel. Fassbinder was deeply wounded by the backlash against the play and, in particular, accusations that he was anti-Semitic. He was also criticized around the same time for negative depictions of homosexuals in *Fox and His Friends*. In fact, Fassbinder's entire career revolved around depicting abused, marginalized characters, which included a wide range of social groups: Germans, foreigners, men, women, gay, straight, black, white, old, young, and so on. It is important to note that these types of marginalized characters were not only portrayed as victims or heroes, but also as antagonists. Fassbinder seemed to object to the idea that any particular group—whether economic, religious, or political—was sacred, inviolable, or above criticism in some way. The message of many of his films is that to be flawed and to struggle is to be authentically human.

His obsession with attacking the *Wirtschaftswunder* is largely an attempt to explore prejudice in a country that attempted to forget about its central role as perpetrators of the Holocaust. Fassbinder viewed the '50s in Germany as something akin to suburban bliss in the United States during the same decade: a surface layer of rosy sentimentality and financial success that hid an underbelly of corruption and exploitation. During this period in Germany, thousands—if not hundreds of thousands—of Nazis and Nazi collaborators avoided prosecution and were reintegrated into German society, with roles in business, politics, and law enforcement.

With *Shadow of Angels*, Fassbinder was attempting to show that anti–Semitism lingered on in Germany and had not abated since World War II, it just became a taboo subject. In Fassbinder's defense of the play, he said that he included an anti-Semitic character—Lily's father, the former Nazi, who admits that his role during the war was to kill Jews—because there were still people like this in Germany, whether the public felt comfortable acknowledging that or not. This situation had changed very little by the '70s and it would arguably not change until after the release of the American TV series *Holocaust* (1978) inspired a more varied, open discourse about genocide.

Admittedly, naming one of his characters "the Rich Jew" was provocative and Fassbinder seems to have been asking for trouble, which he often openly did. The character, played by Fassbinder regular Klaus Löwitsch, is described in dialogue—in both the film and the play—as old, fat, ugly, and horrible, but this strongly contrasted with how he is depicted. Löwitsch was one of Fassbinder's most classically handsome actors and his character is ultimately revealed as the film's only honest, sympathetic figure. He comes to be the one person who genuinely cares for Lily. It is possible that Fassbinder chose this unfortunate descriptor, because the other characters are unable to see past what they view as the defining traits of "the Rich Jew": his wealth and his Judaism.

In his essay *Anti-Semite and Jew*, Sartre writes (also perhaps misguidedly) that if the Jew did not exist, the anti-Semite would create him. He goes on to explain that the anti-Semite is primarily a conservative being stuck in the past, resisting a changing society, and that he has distilled his fears and hatred into the figure of the Jew, the ultimate scapegoat. But the scapegoat in *Shadow of Angels* is not the Rich Jew, it's Lily, who becomes hated by everyone—especially those close to her, such as her lover, her parents, and other prostitutes—except for the Rich Jew.

Fassbinder would explore this concept of the *pharmakos*, the ritual sacrifice of an exile or scapegoat, many times throughout his career, particularly in *Fox and His Friends*, *In a Year with 13 Moons*, *Berlin Alexanderplatz*, *Veronika Voss*, and many more, but Lily is serves as an early incarnation of this character type. Ingrid Caven, briefly Fassbinder's wife, is like a ghostly presence haunting the film. A mixture of tragic, alluring, and emotionally void, Lily is in the world, but not of it. Early in the film, she strangles a kitten out of quiet despair. This theme of choking and strangulation prevails until her death at the literal hands of the Rich Jew, who puts her out of her misery out of a sense of profound love—one that transcends conventional morality.

Lily is not Fassbinder's only protagonist complicit in their own exploitation and destruction. Another example of this theme can be found in *Bolwieser* (*The Stationmaster's Wife*, 1977), a tale of marital infidelity and the despair of a greedy small-town train station manager Bolwieser (Kurt Raab in one of his best performances for Fassbinder) in the interwar years. The masochistic Bolwieser is so consumed by his many insatiable appetites that he seems bent on self-eradication. On one hand, his overwhelming hunger for sex, food, alcohol, and his wife (Elisabeth Trissenaar) seem interchangeable. On the other hand, Bolwieser's determination to turn his head and remain blind to the truth of his wife's countless infidelities subtly links him to the German complicity in Nazi atrocities. This also is yet another film where Fassbinder examined German society's obsession with rules, rituals, and authority. Bolwieser's transition from pompous bureaucrat to dejected prisoner is finally complete with his replacement in the train station by a snide, fastidious member of the Nazi party.

Around the same time as *Shadow of Angels* and *Bolwieser*, another of Fassbinder's close collaborators, actor and director Ulli Lommel, also explored World War II themes with the Chaplinesque *Adolf und Marlene* (1977), an all but forgotten comedy that explores Hitler's (Kurt Raab) obsessive, unrequited love for actress Marlene Dietrich (Fassbinder regular Margit Carstensen). He persuades her to return to Germany—which Dietrich refused to do in real life—and the actress's continual torments drive him further into sexual frenzy and madness. Hitler's alleged real-life practice of falling into such a psychotic frenzy that he would lay on the ground and chew on the carpet is the culmination of the film.

The cast includes several members of Fassbinder's acting troupe, including Lommel, who wrote, directed, and co-starred as Goebbels, as well as actors Harry Baer, Volker Spengler, Armin Meier, and Fassbinder himself (who also produced). Lommel would loosely return to this satirical exploration of Nazi themes with *Strangers in Paradise* (1984), a U.S.-produced musical comedy about a man (played by Lommel, who also wrote and directed) who cryogenically freezes himself to escape from Nazi Germany but is revived in modern day by a group of neo-fascists who want him to help them recreate the Third Reich.

Fassbinder returned to a World War II theme with *Despair* (1978), an adaptation of Vladimir Nabokov's 1934 novel of the same name. Hermann Hermann (Dirk Bogarde), a successful Russian businessman and chocolate factory owner living in Germany, becomes increasingly paranoid during the Nazi Party's rise to power. He is convinced that he won't be able to leave the country and, after seeing a film, decides to commit the perfect crime: he will find a physical double of himself and kill that man, so that he can escape to a simple blue collar life of freedom and anonymity in Switzerland. He finds a homeless man named Felix (Klaus Löwitsch) that he believes could be his twin—although Hermann is obviously mistaken as the two look nothing alike—and sets about his plan while descending into madness.

Fassbinder's only English-language film and the only one to feature an international star in the form of Bogarde is an oddly neglected work. Based on one of Nabokov's last novels written in his native Russian, the book was adapted for the screen by celebrated British playwright Tom Stoppard. The set reflects that this film was also Fassbinder's most expensive: Hermann obsessively celebrates bourgeois culture, and his elaborate home is like a museum to it. Filled with sculptures, glass, mirrors, and reflective works of art—some of Fassbinder's most common recurring visual themes throughout his career—this extravagant-looking film was shot by one of his regular collaborators, Michael Ballhaus, who transformed Hermann's beautiful home into an ornate prison where comfort and claustrophobia are inseparable.

Nabokov wrote the novel while he was living in Germany in the early '30s and the sense of paranoia he undoubtedly felt is palpable in his protagonist. Hermann is a foreigner constantly judged by his neighbors and there is something innately comical and absurd about him. Nabokov allegedly intended to spoof Dostoyevsky's tormented, hysterical protagonists and as a result, Hermann is intentionally flawed, gloomy, nervous, and constantly deceives himself. He is actually a false narrator; he believes he has planned the perfect crime (*a la* Raskolnikov of *Crime and Punishment*) and believes Felix looks exactly like him, though the two men are dramatically physically different.

6. The Punishment Begins

Despair is full of mirrors, glass, and reflections that hint at Hermann's (Dirk Bogarde) fracturing identity (*Despair*, Bavaria Atelier/Bavaria Film/Filmverlag der Autoren, 1978).

There is some sexual content in the film, including S&M-fueled scenes between Hermann and his wife (Spanish actress Andréa Ferréol), as well as her flimsy attempts to cover up an affair with her "cousin" (Volker Spengler) when Hermann finds them in compromising positions. But the only truly erotic moments in the film occur when Hermann is psychologically and physically attempting to transform Felix into himself.

Hermann first sees his own double while having sex with his wife, and it is a source of equal anxiety and fascination. It is telling that he believes the more handsome Felix—who is muscular, unlike Hermann, with lighter hair and eyes, and seems to even be a different height—to be his double. There is are several homoerotic moments in the film, including scenes where he has Felix strip off his clothes and another where he gives him a haircut and manicure. Oddly, Felix seems to understand some of Hermann's self-deception and goes along with it as long as Hermann continues to tell him a semblance of the truth.

Hermann optimistically—and ignorantly, Fassbinder points out—thinks that he will find freedom by abandoning his wealthy lifestyle in favor of a simpler blue-collar existence, but *Despair* shows that there is no escape from societal constraints; this works as sort of an inversion of similar economic themes in *Fox and His Friends* and *The Marriage of Maria Braun*. Like many of Fassbinder's characters, Hermann believes that his life would be better if it were different—if he could change geographical location or economic status. He fondly if improbably reminisces about Russia, even though he was forced to fight several wars there, and idealizes Switzerland, where he hopes to live out his days. This portrayal of Hermann's self-deception serves as a precursor to Fassbinder's later World War II-themed masterpieces like *Berlin Alexanderplatz*, *The Marriage of Maria Braun*, and *Veronika Voss*.

While *Despair* examines the horror of Nazism's rise, this blackly comic film is also concerned with one of Fassbinder's deeply held beliefs: that bourgeois society results in oppression every bit as much as totalitarianism. Hermann himself explains the lack of difference between black shirts, brown shirts, and white and red armies. There is the collusion of power, money, and violence. For example, attention is called to the fact that the brown uniforms of the SA are the same color as the candy bars Hermann sells in his chocolate factory. In another scene, the word "merger" is confused with "murder." Next to the later *Lili Marleen*, this is perhaps Fassbinder's most transparent use of the Third Reich, though it seems he tried to move away from Nazi kitsch, so prevalent in '70s cinema, suggesting instead that fascism is only possible in the first place because everyday life is already so cruel, violent, and alienating.

Curiously, there were two other relatively big budget, West German, English-language productions made around the same time, also set during World War II, though both suffer from poor reputations. The first is essentially Ingmar Bergman's parallel to *Despair*: *Das Schlangenei* (*The Serpent's Egg*, 1977), a U.S.-West German coproduction that remains the director's sole dalliance with Hollywood. Considered one of Bergman's most divisive films, this was made at a time when Bergman fled Sweden for tax evasion and lived in exile in Germany. It follows the rise of Nazism in '20s Berlin through the character of Abel Rosenberg (David Carradine), a Jewish-American trapeze artist stuck living in Berlin with his sister-in-law, Manuela (Liv Ullmann), a cabaret singer and prostitute, after his brother/her husband commits suicide.

The film essentially charts Abel's descent into madness—which coincides with his realization that the onslaught of fascism is inevitable—and its plot is largely composed of scenes of paranoia, voyeurism, and surveillance. Suicide is another key theme: the two main events of the film are the suicide of Abel's brother and the later suicide of his brother's wife. Perhaps the best that can be said about *The Serpent's Egg* is that it's a nebulous arthouse take on *Cabaret*, with a discomfitingly shallow approach to fascism and an odd mystery subplot, some horror genre elements, and even a mad scientist (Heinz Bennent of *The Tin Drum*, who would go on to star in Bergman's German follow up in 1980, *From the Life of the Marionettes*). The film's most effective moments actually involve Bennent's role as the scientist, where, in the concluding moments of the film, he explains to Abel the series of disturbing psychological human experiments he has undertaken, which involve a personal link to Abel himself.

In some ways similar is David Hemmings' curious misfire, *Schöner Gigolo, armer Gigolo* (*Just a Gigolo*, 1978), also set during the interwar period, helmed by a foreign (as in non-German) director and featuring an English-speaking star. David Bowie appears as a young officer, Paul, who returns home to Berlin after World War I. Through a series of misadventures, he finds work as a gigolo in a brothel run by a countess (played by an aged Marlene Dietrich, in the first film she made in fifteen years, which was to also be her final role). He is killed in a violent skirmish between Nazis and Communists and, like Fassbinder's later *Lili Marleen*, this focuses on the fallacious Nazi appropriation of an individual's legacy.

Meant to be satirical, *Just a Gigolo* is also connected to *The Serpent's Egg* in the sense that it borrows much from *Cabaret*'s sexual (and musical) themes. Like Sally Bowles from *Cabaret* and Hermann from *Despair*, Bowie's Paul wanders through the world as a sort of innocent, seemingly unaware of the consequences of his actions or the impact of his behavior on those around him. Through sheer accident, Paul cheats death from a shell blast at the beginning of the film, but is not so lucky at its conclusion. There is the sense—shared by titles from the period as far afield as *The Damned, Cabaret, Despair, The Serpent's Egg, Lili Marleen*, and even *The Marriage of Maria Braun*—that the protagonists of these films are simply waiting around for their time to die, often lost in a haze of drugs, alcohol, sexual excess, or just plain boredom. A phrase of the film's titular song, sung by Dietrich, captures the mood perfectly: "There will come a day when youth will pass away, then what will they say about me? When the end comes, I know, they'll say, 'Just a gigolo,' and life goes on without me."

Fassbinder wouldn't fully address the war itself until *The Marriage of Maria Braun*, though he does make an allusion to it in the follow up to *Despair, In einem Jahr mit 13 Monden* (*In a Year with 13 Moons*, 1978). One of his most heartbreaking and personal films, it is only briefly worth mentioning here. The film follows a transsexual prostitute, Elvira (Volker Spengler), once known as Erwin, whose life has been in shambles since she transitioned from male to female. Her operation was inspired by the remarks of an unrequited love, Anton Saitz (Gottfried John), now a feared local gangster. Though Elvira's friend Red Zora (Ingrid Caven), another prostitute, attempts to care for her, Elvira is determined to confront her past regardless of the cost.

Not only is this Fassbinder's most personal film, but it is one of his greatest masterpieces and is the culmination of all his themes: the trauma of German history, the search for identity, love, and family, and an individual's masochistic self-sacrifice at the hands of a cruel loved one. Erwin/Elvira—played by Volker Spengler in one of the best performances in any Fassbinder film—is a figure that intersects all borders: male and female, past and present, wounded child and absent parent, erotic and repulsive, living and dead. Elvira is Fassbinder's ultimate sacrificial figure, a being whose martyrdom takes on almost religious connotations. She has no true identity of her own, but instead reflects those around her.

In a tableau-like reimagining of the death of a Catholic saint, her friends and family gather around her after her suicide. Despite the bleak tone of the film, its seemingly inevitable conclusion is somehow hopeful, as if Elvira has successfully managed atonement and somehow solidified, through sacrifice, her message of absolute love. Elsaesser writes,

> *In a Year of Thirteen Moons* allegorizes German-Jewish relations in a form already familiar from Fassbinder's other films: as a matter of love, which is to say, as an inherently impossible and yet necessary exchange.[6]

The film—on which Fassbinder served as director, writer, producer, cinematographer, set designer, and editor—stands not only as a treatise on the impossible nature of love, but as a final love letter to his long-time boyfriend and sometimes actor, Armin Meier, who committed suicide earlier in 1978.

In addition, the identity dilemma present in all of Fassbinder's films is part of an increasing dialogue that developed throughout his work and led to themes of the double in *Despair* and *Berlin Alexanderplatz*. That also culminates in *In a Year with 13 Moons*, not only between Erwin and Elvira, but between Elvira and Anton Saitz (Gottfried John, who would return for a similar role in *Berlin Alexanderplatz*). The first time Saitz is introduced, he wears a skimpy tennis outfit and forces Elvira and his goons to reenact a scene from a Jerry Lewis musical. Saitz, as a symbol of corrupt post-war Germany, sits at the crossroads between the industrial factory, the slaughterhouse (Elvira's former place of employment), and the concentration camp. Elsaesser writes,

Fassbinder refuses to assume that there has to be a natural solidarity between victims. Instead, one finds an almost Bunuelian vision of the right of outcasts and underdogs to be as mean, inhuman and evil as anyone else.⁷

Saitz is a key example of this theme. He is a survivor of the Bergen Belsen concentration camp—where he spent his childhood—but is also a violent gangster who has taken control of much of industrial Frankfort. At one point Fassbinder explains Saitz as an acronym: S is for Saltz (salt), A is for Auschwitz, I is for Ich (I), T is for Tod (death), and Z is for Zeit (time).

Fassbinder's next film, *Die Ehe der Maria Braun* (*The Marriage of Maria Braun*, 1979), returns to wartime themes and is the first in a trilogy of films set in the immediate postwar years known as the BRD (*Bundesrepublik Deutschland* or the Federal Republic of Germany) Trilogy. One of Fassbinder's most difficult and expensive productions beset by going over budget (allegedly due to the director's costly cocaine habit that enabled him to work all hours of the day and night) and legal trouble with his long-time producer who oversold shares of the film, *The Marriage of Maria Braun* was also his most popular film at that time. It struck a balance between arthouse style and accessibility, which led to international appeal and acclaim from German audiences and critics.

Maria (Hanna Schygulla) and Hermann Braun (Klaus Löwitsch) are married as bombs fall on Berlin. They have barely any time together before he must return to the front. Though she is devoted to Hermann, Maria is told he has been killed in the war and tries to find a way to survive on her own. She works as a hostess in a club for American soldiers and begins an affair with one of them (George Byrd), while also learning English. Hermann comes home to find she and the soldier undressing and provokes a fight. Maria

The marriage of Maria (Hanna Schygulla) and Hermann (Klaus Löwitsch) is officiated in the rubble as bombs fall on Berlin, a destructive omen for their relationship (*Die Ehe der Maria Braun*, Albatros Filmproduktion, 1979).

accidentally kills the man, trying to break it up, but Hermann takes responsibility and goes to prison. Meanwhile, she begins working for a wealthy industrialist (Ivan Desny) who falls in love with her.

While *The Marriage of Maria Braun* is essentially a tale of one woman's attempts to gain her independence, in a broader sense, it's also a story of the very real struggle to survive during the war years. Maria is not ashamed to use her sexuality as a resource or a weapon. She essentially sells fantasies and illusions, and though she is not a prostitute, she trades sex for things of increasing value throughout the film: cigarettes, stockings, a secretarial job, a respected position in the company, expensive clothing, and a large house.

But through her struggle to pursue increasingly lofty, romanticized goals, fantasy leads to tragedy as Maria persists in self-delusion. She is obsessed with Hermann, despite barely knowing him, and holds him as her ideal of pure, unspoiled love. On the other hand, she treats Oswald cruelly and makes it clear that she is using him for money, social advancement, sex, and even entertainment—but never love. Her success results in increasingly cruel behavior on her part, sort of an insidious, personalized form of fascism, and she treats Oswald, the office secretaries, the accountant, and even some of their clients abysmally. She essentially becomes like a stereotype of the professional "dragon lady," a corporate femme fatale that will go to any ends to achieve financial and personal success.

Fassbinder does present her as inherently sympathetic and implies that she is ultimately unable to succeed in life—returning yet again to this theme—because of the inherently corrupt nature of society. It is revealed that Hermann, the love of her life, accepted a deal from Oswald where he essentially sold Maria; Hermann agreed that he would leave the country until Oswald's death, at which point Hermann and Maria would become the sole heirs of Oswald's considerable estate. When Maria discovers this, she kills them both, blowing up her house by leaving the gas on and lighting a cigarette. Even before she learns this news, Hermann's homecoming is awkward and disappointing. He wants to kiss her and finally consummate their marriage, but she insists that he eat or bathe, that she change her clothes first, seemingly desperate to avoid a moment of real intimacy. In the film, their deaths are ambiguous and don't occur on screen, but in the original script, she intentionally drove them both off of a cliff.

This original ending was lifted from Otto Preminger's film noir *Angel Face* (1953)—also the tale of an individual's struggle to survive in the immediate postwar years—though Fassbinder's primary inspiration for the film was *Mildred Pierce* (1945). That film noir classic follows Joan Crawford's titular character, a woman who becomes financially successful in the postwar years—to her detriment. In *The Marriage of Maria Braun*, which begins and ends with explosions, the axis rotates around Hermann and Maria's obsession with him. His enigmatic figure symbolizes her dreams for a better, brighter future, but when he is shown to echo her own greed and ambition, her fantasies inevitably, violently collapse.

Fassbinder stayed with similar themes for his next project, *Berlin Alexanderplatz* (1980), possibly the greatest masterpiece of a prolific, brilliant career. This fourteen-part made-for-television miniseries was based on Alfred Döblin's novel of the same name, a book Fassbinder considered one of his favorites. Its influence can be felt throughout his career and his life; for instance, its protagonist's name, Franz Biberkopft, or even just "Franz," is a recurring character name through Fassbinder's films. His adaptation of the novel is relatively faithful and, clocking in at over fifteen hours, lengthy, feels more like an epic film than a TV show.

In 1930s Berlin, Franz Biberkopf (Günter Lamprecht) is released from prison after serving a few years for killing his girlfriend. He's sent back into society without many hopeful prospects, but he meets up with a loyal friend, Meck (Franz Buchrieser), and takes his old apartment. Women come in and out of his life and he works a series of odd jobs: selling neckties, Nazi newspapers, and shoelaces. He has trouble adjusting to life outside of prison and has breakdowns and alcoholic binges. His old girlfriend, Eva (Hanna Schygulla), who he used to pimp out, still has great affection for him and tries to support him financially and emotionally. She introduces him to Mieze (Barbara Sukowa), a young woman who becomes the love of his life, but their happiness is troubled by Reinhold (Gottfried John), a local criminal who fascinates Franz.

The suggestion of the first episode title, "The Punishment Begins," is that Franz's real suffering is not to be found in prison, but in daily life. Franz's attempts to leave behind pimping, theft, and criminality are met with constant setbacks. For example, the only consistent, well-paying job he is able to find is selling Nazi newspapers. Even though he doesn't share their beliefs, he is forced to wear a swastika armband. He is soon ostracized by some of his Jewish and communist friends and eventually quits. This attempted journey towards expiation and goodness is consistently met with resistance, hostility, and ultimately failure.

Throughout the course of *Berlin Alexanderplatz*, Franz's story essentially becomes

Franz (Günter Lamprecht) leaves prison, which is when the punishment really begins in this episode one title card of *Berlin Alexanderplatz* (*Berlin Alexanderplatz*, Bavaria Film, Westdeutscher Rundfunk [WDR], 1980).

a spiritual allegory of sorts. He is bound up between two figures: the angelic Mieze and the diabolical Reinhold. The latter represents a sense of destructive passion that marks many of Fassbinder's antagonists. Franz and Reinhold's perhaps inexplicable love for one another is physically enacted by their sexual sharing of women. Reinhold has a desperate need not to be alone, but tires of women quickly. Until Mieze arrives on the scene, he turns his abandoned sexual partners over to Franz. This love-by-proxy has a violent underbelly and results in Reinhold murdering Mieze when she refuses to become part of the exchange.

She does agree to prostitution to support herself and Franz when he loses an arm, thanks to Reinhold's involvement during a heist gone wrong. This loss of flesh, which soon includes the murder of Mieze at the hands of Reinhold and the loss of Reinhold thanks to his prison sentence, results in Franz's ultimate descent into a sort of internal hell. In what is perhaps Fassbinder's most visionary work, the epilogue of *Berlin Alexanderplatz* deviates the most from the novel, and is an inspired blend of existentialist angst, absurdist humor, surrealism, and expressionism. While there are some of these elements throughout the series, particularly in Fassbinder's voice overs, where he reads sections of the novel in quiet monotone, the epilogue is an *Inferno*-like descent into both Franz's subconscious and the zeitgeist of 1930s Germany.

Much of this takes place in Franz's dream world, where the car accident that took his arm and his various crimes are repeated over and over, mixed with charnel house scenes that dissolve into orgy. It's easy to compare the pile of naked, sometimes bloodied limbs with historical photographs of concentration camps or cinematic reproductions of the Holocaust. These final scenes are also the culmination of the novel's religious themes, as Franz is eventually crucified and accompanied by angels that appear to have stepped out of a Derek Jarman film. The baby Jesus, of course, wears a vivid swastika armband.

What *Berlin Alexanderplatz* perhaps does most elegantly is to chart the movement from freedom to totalitarianism experienced by the Germans of the 1930s, such as by Döblin himself. He was forced to flee Germany when the Nazis burned his books in 1933, which led him on a decade-long nomadic lifestyle, as he traversed Europe, England, and America trying to find employment as a writer. He eventually returned to Germany, where he died in a sanatorium. Both his masterwork and Fassbinder's adaptation explore the degeneration and disintegration of society, one that Döblin personally experienced and Fassbinder also felt he was living through in postwar Germany.

Fassbinder stayed with similar subject matter for *Lili Marleen* (1981), a loose companion piece to his BRD Trilogy. Willie (Schygulla again), a German singer, is involved in a passionate affair with a Swiss Jewish composer, Robert (Giancarlo Giannini). They plan to get married, though this is prevented by the rise of Nazism and the objections of Robert's wealthy family. Though they are safely hiding out in Switzerland, Robert regularly sneaks back into Germany to aid the Resistance. Willie, wanting to be a bigger part of his life, helps him, but is barred from Switzerland thanks to the machinations of Robert's family. Forlorn, she takes a job in a cabaret and sings one of Robert's songs, "Lili Marleen," which is an overnight success. To her delight, she becomes a sought-after Nazi icon, but risks her life to carry on a secret affair with Robert.

Based on the autobiography of German singer Lale Andersen, *Lili Marleen* is largely a product of the success of *The Marriage of Maria Braun*. The latter was lauded for its blend of art house style and accessibility, which *Lili Marleen* shares, though it is based more firmly in historical fact, as Andersen skyrocketed to fame for her war-time performance of the film's titular song. The Nazis banned her from performing for nearly a year thanks to her friendship with a number of Swiss-Jewish artists and her attempted suicide.

Fassbinder adds other historical elements as well, such as the name of his own character, Günther Weisenborn, the head of the resistance in *Lili Marleen*. The real Weisenborn was a writer, actor, and member of the infamous German Resistance faction, the Red Orchestra. He escaped to the U.S. in the '30s but returned to Germany in 1937 under a false identity. He was arrested and sentenced to death, though this was commuted to a lengthy prison sentence, much of which he served at Gestapo headquarters in Berlin. After the war, he wrote frequently about his experiences, including script contributions to Falk Harnack's film *The Plot to Assassinate Hitler* (1955).

But Fassbinder's fictional "Lili Marleen" singer, Willie, is more a product of Hollywood melodrama than of history. With this film Fassbinder clearly attempted to harken back to the days of Technicolor splendor, while also exploring what was so appealing about the pomp of National Socialism. Willie's Nazi handler is even named Henkel, after the Hitler character in Chaplin's *The Great Dictator*. While Maria Braun's life paralleled the transition from wartime poverty to the German economic "miracle" of the '50s, Willie's life brushes against the height of Nazi power. Unlike Maria Braun, Willie is not fundamentally changed by this encounter. When she becomes famous enough to warrant a meeting with Hitler, his office doors open to reveal a blinding white light. Willie should have emerged from it altered—many of Fassbinder's other protagonists experience a defining moment of personal transformation—but she does not. Perhaps what makes Willie and *Lili Marleen* so fascinating, yet narratively frustrating, is that she remains untouched by and seemingly unaware of the monumental events unfolding around her—even more incredible considering the fact that her lover is Jewish, and she is helping him smuggle photographic evidence of concentration camps.

Like "Lili Marleen" and Willie's fictionalized association with it, the real-life Nazi anthem, the "Horst Wessel Lied," was also built on a lie. Horst Wessel, an SA officer and the author of the song named for him, was martyred by the Party after he was shot, likely over a financial dispute. Willie's fame is similarly a tool of Nazi propaganda, a convenient fairytale briefly marred by an inconvenient love affair. But it is through this affair that Fassbinder subverts the Hollywood melodrama: the great tragic love story between Robert and Willie is revealed to have little real substance and as romantic heroes Robert and Willie more or less fail. Willie does attempt to commit suicide when her fame is snatched from her and Robert's life is threatened by the SS, but she soon reconciles with her Nazi handler.

Robert is an even more troubling figure. He allows his prestigious family to ostracize Willie because she is neither wealthy nor Jewish. After he is freed by the SS—his father exchanges Robert's freedom for the film footage of the concentration camp—he distances himself from his wartime experiences, marries a woman his family approves of, and becomes a famous composer. Willie eventually finds him and is devastated to learn how he has so casually abandoned her.

Lili Marleen is yet another example of Fassbinder showing how humanity is stripped away in favor of survival and self-preservation, a theme often found in Holocaust memoirs like Primo Levi's *If This Is a Man* (1947) or documentaries like Claude Lanzmann's epic *Shoah* (1985). *Lili Marleen*'s most subversive element—its insistence on presenting the world in a moral grayscale—is in direct contrast with the multitude of conventional war-themed films that depict Holocaust survivors as fundamentally heroic or worse, and more commonly, as helpless victims. In the '70s and early '80s, when World War II again became a popular subject for filmmakers, it was—and largely still is—taboo to suggest that perpetrators could be anything other than the embodiment of evil and survivors could be more than innocent victims. It is no wonder then that Fassbinder tread lightly with this theme after the controversy of *Der Müll, die Stadt und der Tod*.

He would explore this in quite a different way in *Lola* (1981), the third part of his BRD trilogy. This candy-colored, yet acerbic melodrama is set during the late '50s and directly addresses Fassbiner's recurring theme that the rift caused by World War II never healed but was happily glossed over during the postwar American occupation and the subsequent economic miracle. He portrays West Germany as a fundamentally corrupt place where most Nazis and collaborators were never prosecuted, but simply reintegrated into German society alongside Holocaust survivors. This sense of greed, murky morality, and a desire to forget the past is at the heart of *Lola*.

In *Lola*'s direct precursors—*Berlin Alexanderplatz*, *Despair*, and *The Marriage of Maria Braun*—Fassbinder suggests that a decent person is unable to survive in society. *Lola* examines this idea in the Technicolor light of Hollywood melodrama and romantic comedy, as an upstanding building commissioner Von Bohm (Armin Mueller-Stahl) repeatedly struggles against popular demands that he should give up his lofty ideals and just conform like everyone else. His good-hearted but ridiculous character was inspired by *Professor Unrat*, Heinrich Mann's novel that was also the basis for Sternberg's *The Blue Angel* (1930).

Where the protagonists differ is the key to *Lola*. In *The Blue Angel*, Professor Rath (Emil Jannings) is a respected member of the community and staunchly opposed to the local cabaret until he meets the singer Lola-Lola (Marlene Dietrich). Obsessed, he marries her, effectively becomes her slave, and is forced to work as a clown in the cabaret. This humiliating new life combined with Lola's promiscuity drive him to madness and violence. Von Bohm begins with the same rigid morality. But where Professor Rath is driven mad by love, von Bohm eventually surrenders his convictions in what is perhaps Fassbinder's most cynical conclusion.

The concepts of rationalization and willful amnesia are at their brightest and boldest here with *Lola*'s elaborate visual world. The pastel-colored lighting and set pieces have an artificial, Disney World vibe and continually—even during scenes set in nature—evokes the unreal, the staged, and the performed. Much like Lola (Barbara Sukowa) herself. Though von Bohm appears to be the protagonist, she is the film's most commanding presence. Sukowa's marvelously energetic, physical performance is full of an abandon unequaled by any of Fassbinder's other female stars. *Lola* has much in common with *The Marriage of Maria Braun*: both films are ultimately concerned with a marriage, a love triangle, a business arrangement, and an assured woman who negotiates her own financial independence. But they are drastically different in tone thanks to the female leads.

Another of Fassbinder's most memorable female characters comes in the middle entry of the BRD trilogy, *Die Sehnsucht der Veronika Voss* (1982). Filmed in black and white, it was inspired by *Sunset Boulevard* (1950)—where an aged star (Gloria Swanson) spiraling into madness attracts a middle-aged writer (William Holden) and keeps him prisoner in her house, eventually killing him. *Veronika Voss* is based loosely on the life of Nazi actress Sybille Schmitz. In addition to appearing in some of the best films of the '20s and early '30s including Pabst's *Tagebuch einer Verlorenen* (*Diary of a Lost Girl*, 1929) and Dreyer's *Vampyr* (1932), she continued working during the Nazi reign, despite the fact that Goebbels allegedly disliked her. After the war, she was shunned and only worked intermittently while succumbing to depression and drug and alcohol abuse. She committed suicide in 1955, which was facilitated by a female doctor who lived with her, prescribed her morphine, and stole her fortune.

In Fassbinder's interpretation, Veronika Voss (Rosel Zech), a former Nazi starlet, has lapsed into reclusively and paranoia by the mid-'50s. No film studio will hire her and she is utterly dependent on Dr. Katz (Annemarie Düringer), a greedy neurologist who drains Veronika's bank account and keeps her addicted to drugs. But Veronika soon meets a reporter, Robert (Hilmar Thate), and they begin an affair despite the fact that he already has a girlfriend (Cornelia Froboess). Hoping to free Veronika from Dr. Katz' obsessive clutches, Robert and his girlfriend team up to investigate the doctor.

At its heart, *Veronika Voss* is a film about the loss of fame, artistic relevance, and creative power, something Fassbinder possibly feared at this point of his life. He struggled with drug addiction and depended on cocaine to ensure his staggering creative output. It was, of course, his undoing, and he died the following year from an overdose, reportedly just as he planned to quit cold turkey. While it's easy to interpret *Veronika Voss* as a statement about the Third Reich, war trauma, and forgetting, Fassbinder was a master of equating the historical with the personal, of which the addiction themes of *Veronika Voss* are a key example. At the same time that he developed this film, he was also planning to adapt Pitigrilli's 1921 novel *Cocaine*, another tale of drug use with a fascist history. It was banned in Italy in the '30s by both the Catholic church and the government, thanks to anti-Semitic laws (Pitigrilli was Jewish).

Tied to its themes of addiction, *Veronika Voss* is also a film about obsession. Like plenty of Fassbinder's earlier works and the other two films in the BRD trilogy, *Veronika Voss* is focused on a protagonist obsessed with an enigmatic second character. In some ways, this is framed as a detective story with the basic outline that a man (typically a writer, detective, or reporter in film noir) meets a mysterious, alluring woman who is in trouble. He seeks both emotional and sexual intimacy with her, as well as a solution to her problems. In this case, Robert (and through him, his girlfriend) seeks to solve the puzzle of Veronika Voss. Fassbinder turns the genre on its head somewhat, because there is no ultimate revelation. Veronika dies and her story simply fades away; there is no book written or criminal investigation undertaken, and it is even someone other than Robert who writes about her death for the newspaper.

In addition to Voss's inability to transcend her Nazi past, the film's emphasis on World War II trauma is highlighted by an old Jewish couple, antique dealers and Holocaust survivors also being treated by Dr. Katz for "nervous disorders." They are survivors of the Nazi death camp Treblinka and welcome the relief of morphine from constant emotional pain. This suggestion that trauma is a wound healed only by death is constant throughout the film and Fassbinder's other works—particularly *Fox and His Friends* and *In a Year with 13 Moons*—share this abiding sense of personal misery and the desire for oblivion.

It is also worth questioning if Fassbinder's selection of Treblinka was intentional. *In a Year with 13 Moons* introduces Saitz as a survivor of Bergen-Belsen, a concentration camp located near Hanover (about three hours east of Berlin). It was used primarily for labor or transit and lacked gas chambers or gas vans; yet of the roughly 120,000 people who passed through the camp, around 50,000 were killed. Despite this staggering statistic, it

The elegant, tragic Veronika Voss (Rosel Zech) hovers like a spectral presence throughout the film (*Die Sehnsucht der Veronika Voss*, Laura Film/Tango Film/Rialto Film, 1982).

maintained the reputation of being one of the easier camps to survive. Treblinka, on the other hand, located in Nazi-occupied Poland, was the site of mass exterminations organized by Operation Reinhard, the Nazi code name for the planned annihilation of Jews in the *Generalgouvernement* (a large territory in occupied Poland and Ukraine). Organized by Reinhard Heydrich, this elaborate plan included the construction of previously mentioned death camps Belzec, Sobibor, and Treblinka, and later, Majdanek.

In the three years that it was open, nearly a million people were killed at Treblinka, making this the location of the second highest number of Holocaust deaths next to Auschwitz. But unlike Auschwitz, the Germans were prepared for the arrival of Soviet soldiers and the camp was destroyed. An attempt was made to hide all evidence of genocide. Treblinka was one of the camps to experience an uprising and as a result, roughly 70 people—out of nearly a million—survived. Only a few of those made it past the war years and many devoted the rest of their lives to telling their story to the world. Examples include survivor Hershl Sperling, who gave testimony but eventually committed suicide, as did another survivor, author Richard Glazar. Sculptor Samuel Willenberg, is the rare example of a Treblinka survivor who also took part in the Warsaw Uprising, lived into his 90s and passed away in 2016.

This intersection between drug overdose, survivor guilt, depression, loneliness, and suicide that can be found in *Veronika Voss*—as well as *Fox and His Friends* and *In a Year with 13 Moons*—encompasses main characters who are all tired, in pain, and, above all, ready to die. Before *Veronika Voss*, Fassbinder's most spectacular image of death was the eerie, blue subway station where Fox lays down to die in *Fox and His Friends*. Here, it is surpassed by the image of Veronika's own farewell party—seemingly held hours before her suicide—where she looks glamorous and sings the Dean Martin song, "Memories are Made of This"; and later by Dr. Katz's brilliant-white office, a waiting room that is a place of absence, forgetting, and death.

7

Pasolini's *Salò* and Nazisploitation

"Sade had to make up his theater of punishment and delight from scratch, improvising the decor and costumes and blasphemous rites. Now there is a master scenario available to everyone. The color is black, the material is leather, the seduction is beauty, the justification is honesty, the aim is ecstasy, the fantasy is death."—Susan Sontag, *Fascinating Fascism*[1]

In 1975, Pier Paolo Pasolini executed the final blow of his long career as an artist, intellectual, journalist, philosopher, poet, and filmmaker before being brutally murdered: *Salò o le 120 giornate di Sodoma* (*Salò, or the 120 Days of Sodom*). Nearly 40 years later, *Salò* remains one of the most loathed and banned films in history. A loose adaptation of the Marquis de Sade's seemingly inadaptable 18th-century novel *Les 120 journées de Sodome*, *Salò* is set in a fictionalized fascist Italy, in a version of Mussolini's Republic of Salò populated by libertines and Nazis, clouded by an unmistakable aura of the Holocaust. Immediately following his bawdy, erotic *Trilogy of Life*, *Salò* is the first film in an intended, but never completed *Trilogy of Death*. While Pasolini's three previous films, *Il Decameron* (*The Decameron*, 1971), *I racconti di Canterbury* (*The Canterbury Tales*, 1972), and *Il fiore delle mille e una notte* (*Arabian Nights*, 1974), are all celebrations of life and sexuality, *Salò* utterly and bitterly rejects these themes.

Also inspired by Dante's *Inferno*, the film is split into four segments. In the first, *Ante-inferno*, four powerful men in the Republic of Salò make a strange and debauched pact. A Duke (Paolo Bonacelli), President (Aldo Valetti), Magistrate (Umberto P. Quintavalle), and Bishop (Giorgio Cataldi) all marry each other's daughters. They hire a number of guards and a handful of male "studs," who are chosen solely because they have large penises. Then they kidnap nine male and nine female teenagers, forcing them all to an isolated palace. With them are four aged prostitutes, hired to supervise the teenagers and tell perverse, erotic stories. Between tales, the teenagers are subjected to a number of tortures and humiliations.

The film's second section, *Circle of Mania*, concerns further adventures at the villa. One of the prostitutes tells detailed stories directly from *Les 120 journées de Sodome*. More debauchery ensues, including rape, anal sex, and a forced marriage between two of the captives. The grotesque wedding ceremony involves more rape—none of the captives are allowed to have pleasurable, consensual sex—and the Duke and Magistrate have anal sex with each other. The next day, they force the boys and girls to act like

A forced ritual marriage in *Salò* is just one of the horrific rituals depicted on screen (*Salò o le 120 giornate di Sodoma*, Produzioni Europee Associate [PEA]/Les Productions Artistes Associés, 1975).

dogs and one of them is whipped to death when he refuses. Nails are hidden in their food.

The Circle of Shit, the film's third segment, is fairly self-explanatory, as it largely involves coprophagia, or shit eating. Another prostitute tells a story about killing her own mother that excites the President and he begins sexually abusing some of the captives. When one of the girls resists, the Duke has the guards strip her naked and he defecates in front of everyone, then forces her to eat it. This is so arousing to the four men that they later serve giant plates of excrement to everyone for dinner.

The film's conclusion, the bleak *Circle of Blood*, begins with a sinister group wedding between the four men and the well-endowed studs. Morale is at an all-time low for the captives, several of whom have died. Those remaining turn on one another, desperate to survive, but they are brought out into the courtyard for hours of torture—scalping, eye-gouging, tongue removal, branding, and more—culminating in systematic murder, while the four men greedily look on.

Considered a masterpiece by many critics and filmmakers, *Salò* was banned in several countries because of its explicit subject matter, which includes kidnapping, torture, rape, anal sex, coprophilia, murder, suicide, and child abuse. Released during an unprecedented wave of films with Holocaust themes, namely mainstream movies that treated Nazi atrocities as the subject of melodrama, Pasolini certainly intended *Salò* to be alienating and uncomfortably graphic, the ultimate challenge for filmgoers.

Salò was not the first or last film of its decade to explore themes of Nazism and fascism in conjunction with erotica. One of the earliest, *Love Camp 7* (1969), and its more famous cousin, *Ilsa: She Wolf of the SS* (1975), spawned ten years of mainly Italian produced Nazi-themed exploitation films that flooded the European grindhouse market. In some ways, *Salò* is a response to these films. Though *Salò* both borrowed from and influenced the disreputable genre of Nazisploitation, its inherent intellectualism and powerful anti-eroticism set it widely apart—so while many of these Nazisploitation titles are not generally considered to be arthouse films, I have decided to discuss them in relation to *Salò*. Unlike other exploitation films or Pasolini's earlier works, *Salò* allows for no release or resolution, whether physical or narrative. Amid a faded, detested sub-genre and related pornographic films, it stands as a cinematic howl of rage and anguish that is, according to critic Marcal Martin, "as glacial and opaque as marble, as pure and cutting as diamond."[2]

Much like *Salò*'s origins in 18th century French literature, Nazi exploitation cinema—or Nazisploitation as it became known—also took inspiration from literature, albeit a more contemporary source. As mentioned in previous chapters, this is related to the trial of Adolf Eichmann, which began in Israel in April of 1961. With it, the silence that had settled around the subject of the Holocaust finally burst. Eichmann was effectively responsible for the deportation of millions of Jews and political prisoners to ghettos and concentration camps all around Europe. With hundreds of new testimonies and evidence exhibits, death camps were back in the news and, soon after, found their way into entertainment periodicals. Oddly beginning in Israel, a series of pornographic pulp novels known as stalag fiction birthed the Nazi exploitation genre. Stalag is the German abbreviation for prisoner of war camps, called *stammlager*. These are commonly depicted in post–World War II film and fiction, most famously in films like *The Great Escape* (1963) and TV shows such as *Hogan's Heroes* (1965–1971).

Stalag fiction was read primarily by Israeli teenagers, many of whom were likely the children of camp survivors. The most famous of these, *I Was Colonel Schultz's Private Bitch*, is a classic example of the subgenre: sexually aggressive, female SS officers brutalize camp prisoners until they eventually revolt, in turn raping and torturing their buxom captors. Though they disappeared or were ignored for several decades, a recent documentary from Ari Libsker, *Stalags: Holocaust and Pornography in Israel*, was produced in 2008. Libsker explained that the first Holocaust pictures he saw, even as someone who grew up in Israel, were often of naked women.[3] Curiously, stalag fiction was some of the only available pornography in the newly settled Israel of the '60s.

Stalag fiction has a strange parallel with early Nazi propaganda, in the sense that odd references to sex and sadism popped up in both Hitler's speeches and even Nazi newspapers. Eminent World War II historian William Shirer writes,

> There is a great deal of morbid sexuality in Hitler's ravings about the Jews. This was characteristic of Vienna's anti–Semitic press of the time, as it later was to be of the obscene Nuremberg weekly *Der Stürmer*, published by one of Hitler's favorite cronies, Julius Streicher, Nazi boss of Franconia, a noted pervert and one of the most unsavory characters in the Third Reich. *Mein Kampf* is sprinkled with lurid allusions to uncouth Jews seducing innocent Christian girls and thus adulterating their blood.[4]

Shirer, who had met Streicher and seemed to have a particular loathing for him, writes that *Der Stürmer*, "thrived on lurid tales of Jewish sexual crimes and Jewish 'ritual murders'; its obscenity was nauseating, even to many Nazis. Streicher was also a noted pornographist."[5] Shirer notes that he never went anywhere without a "whip in his hand or belt," making Streicher seem very much like a sadistic caricature from stalag fiction.

Part of what made the stalag subgenre so controversial was its occasional veracity; stalag fiction was at times inspired by real memoirs from camp survivors. This first-person narrative technique was inspired by Yehiel De-Nur, known only as the writer

Ka-Tsetnik 135633 until he testified at the Eichmann trial under his real name. De-Nur was one of the first survivors to write about the Holocaust in Israel and though his works contain factual elements and were based on his experiences in the camps, they were combined with elements of often shocking fiction. De-Nur's pen name comes from his name in Auschwitz, made up of his concentration camp number and "ka-tzetnik," meaning "concentration camp" in Yiddish. His books, such as *Salamandra* and *House of Dolls*, are lurid tales of sexual slavery, child abuse, and cannibalism. *House of Dolls* in particular discusses the *Freudenabteilungen* (or "Joy Division"), brothels where women were forced to serve German soldiers. This book is likely the direct origin of stalag fiction, as it includes detailed, often pornographic descriptions of sex and violence.

The stalags reached their popularity during the early '60s—coinciding with the Eichmann trial—but were banned soon after their creation. Instead of dying out, the genre relocated to the pulp novels of Italy. Known as *gialli*, these books began as cheap works of mystery and crime fiction that rose in popularity in the late '20s. These eventually became more violent and sexual in nature, until they bled over into the film market with Mario Bava's seminal *La ragazza che sapeva troppo* (*The Girl Who Knew Too Much*, 1963), which created a popular and prolific film genre in its own right.

During this period, thanks to temporarily relaxed censorship and a boom in the European film market, the exploitation genre grew by leaps and bounds. As a result, producers constantly sought new material to test the boundaries of decency, eroticism, and violence. Thanks to European art cinema efforts in the late '60s and early '70s that forged a link between Nazism, decadence, and sexual perversion, such as those discussed in the previous chapter, exploitation producers were soon attracted to the same themes.

Really the first World War II film of the decade to explicitly combine fascism with sexual perversion and specifically sadomasochism was Roger Vadim's Italian-French production *Le Vice et la Vertu* (*Vice and Virtue*, 1963), which loosely adapted the Marquis de Sade's novels *Justine* (1791) and *Juliette* (1797) and updated them to World War II. Serving as something of a precursor to *Salò* or Tinto Brass's *Salon Kitty* (1976), *Vice and Virtue* follows the innocent Justine (Catherine Deneuve in her first major film role), whose fiancé (Jean-Pierre Honoré) is arrested by the Gestapo for his role in the French resistance. She pleads with her corrupt, perverse sister, Juliette (Annie Girardot), to intervene on her fiancé's behalf, as Juliette is the mistress of a Nazi general (O.E. Hasse). Their lives are further disrupted when the highest-ranking Nazi in Paris, SS Colonel Erik Schörndorf (Robert Hossein), forces Juliette to become his mistress, while Justine is sent to an isolated castle and trained to become a Nazi concubine.

Vice and Virtue is essentially a costume drama with transgressive ambitions that wouldn't be fully realized on screen until the World War II films of the '70s like *The Night Porter*. While much is implied—such as Juliette's sexual promiscuity and the virginal Justine's enforced prostitution—very little is depicted overtly. Despite its nods to sadomasochism, there are really only two implied sex scenes in the whole film: one where Schörndorf and Juliette kiss in bed, with an implied fade to a sex scene, and another where Justine is forced into a bedroom with a prospective client.

Strangely, the film lacks the bold, steamy subject matter of Vadim's early masterpiece, *Et Dieu ... créa la femme* (*And God Created Woman*, 1956). Its protagonist, also named Juliete (Vadim's wife and first muse, Brigitte Bardot), revels in her own sexuality and takes genuine pleasure from it, while *Vice and Virtue*'s Juliette is only shown to be protected and insulated by the power that comes from bedding senior Nazi officials. As

The castle of sex slaves in *Virtue and Vice* is more closely related to gothic fantasy than it is to historical reality (*Le vice et la vertu*, S.N.E (Gaumont/Trianon Productions/Ultra Film, 1963).

with Rossellini's early films, the Nazis are shown to be obsessed with opulence—amassing wealth, artwork, fine food and wine, and even architecture, as exemplified by the picturesque castle transformed into a sexual playground—though they never seem to be satisfied by this gluttony.

There is also the confluence of fascism and depravity. Schörndorf is clearly aroused by torture and has an elaborately outfitted room where he extracts confessions. Juliette's relationship with him essentially begins after she is forced to witness him extensively torturing a Resistance member from inside a private booth tucked behind a false mirror. After the torture session is over, it is implied that their affair begins. Similarly, it's implied that Justine and the other female prisoners of the chateau are required to perform unusual sex acts and there is an undeniably fetishistic element to their incarceration.

And though the high melodrama of *Vice and Virtue* is enhanced by lush costumes, stylish set pieces, and pleasing black and white cinematography, the war themes are manipulated into the narrative and the World War II stock footage used repeatedly by Vadim is awkwardly placed. Though Vadim survived the war in the French Alps—helping his mother to run a hostel that reputedly assisted exiles fleeing the Nazis—French audiences were apparently aghast at his appropriation of history and the film is one of his most ignored works, remaining unavailable for decades. Known for sexually explicit work that frequently wandered into the realm of exploitation cinema, Vadim dipped his toe into those waters here with an opening statement that acts as both explanation of and apology for the World War II setting—alongside early shots of stock footage of planes dropping bombs—a technique that would uncomfortably be aped by Nazi exploitation films a decade later.

A far more explicit example of this comes with the first Nazisploitation film: in 1969, American sleaze producer Bob Cresse teamed up with exploitation director Lee Frost to create *Love Camp 7*, the first official entry in the genre and—alongside Jess Franco's *99 Women* from the same year—the first women in prison film, one of the most beloved exploitation subgenres. Hollywood began making films about female prisoners in the '30s, with *Caged* (1950) as the first really controversial effort. Interestingly, there are even a few World War II-era female prisoner films, including *Two Thousand Women* (1944) and *Three Came Home* (1950), both relatively subdued, melodramatic tales of women in internment camps, respectively set in France and Borneo. These early mainstream efforts are understandably tame in nature compared to the exploitation films of the '70s, which generally contained frequent nudity, sadistic guards, lesbianism, shower fights, and sexualized torture.

In *Love Camp 7*, two British agents (Maria Lease and Kathy Williams) go undercover and infiltrate a Nazi camp to gain information and rescue a prisoner with important information. They discover that the female prisoners are forced to serve as prostitutes for officers of the Reich and are tortured, humiliated, and raped. In order to retrieve a woman from solitary confinement, one of the agents is forced to subject herself to extreme torture and punishment before they can stage their rescue mission, which results in a violent battle.

Love Camp 7 includes a number of characteristics that would appear throughout the Italian Nazisploitation films of the '70s. In addition to soft-core sex—both consensual and rape—there are a number of perversions on display, including bondage, bootlicking, graphic torture, prisoners used as sex slaves, and almost constant female frontal nudity. The perverse camp commandant, played by none other than the film's producer, Bob Cresse, plans a full-scale orgy for his soldiers, which transforms into a bloody battle to the death. This sort of conclusion would become commonplace within the genre, along with the film's brazen opening claims that the events are historically accurate.

Though otherwise unremarkable, *Love Camp 7* is an early if fairly typical example of both the Nazisploitation and women in prison subgenres. Though it's described as "a one-stop supermarket for all your misogynistic needs" by cult movie label Something Weird Video, within a few years it spawned another American-produced follow up film that would far surpass it in terms of sex, violence, and moral depravity: *Ilsa, She Wolf of the SS* (1974). It remains one of the most infamous exploitation films of all time. With graphic scenes of humiliation, torture, nudity, and violence—including a castration—coupled with moments of soft-core sex, it is easily the most notorious film of its genre.

Dyanne Thorne stars as Ilsa, the commandant of a mixed-gender stalag. She uses her status as darling of the SS to delve deeply into medical experimentation, attempting to prove her theory that women can withstand much higher degrees of physical pain than men and should be allowed on the front lines to defend the *Vaterland*. In addition, Ilsa attempts to quell her insatiable sexual appetite with male prisoners. When they inevitably fail her, she has them castrated or executed, until a captured American soldier (Gregory Knoph) manages to pass the test and exploit her weakness, bringing her carefully controlled dominion to an end.

Unlike later women in prison films or other exploitation subgenres, which are based almost entirely in the realm of fantasy, early Nazisploitation, *Ilsa, She Wolf of the SS* included, take key elements from historical events. These films primarily explored three subjects inspired by factual parallels in the Third Reich: the repulsive medical experimentation undertaken at concentration camps like Auschwitz-Birkenau and Dachau, sexual slavery, including military brothels, forced prostitution in the camps, and rape, and, finally, the role of women in the SS. All of these elements appear in Nazisploitation films and while some are exaggerated—such as the role of women as commanders—others barely scratch the surface of real Nazi horrors.

The medical experimentation depicted in *Ilsa, She Wolf of the SS* and other Nazisploitation films was heavily documented in the Nuremberg trials and includes a wide range of horrors, such as testing human aptitudes for poison, gas, explosives, malaria, sterilization, transplants, temperature, and altitude. These tests were primarily performed on adult Jews, but children, Romani, prisoners of war, political dissidents, and others were also unwilling subjects.

While it is common knowledge that these experiments took place at Auschwitz, they were widespread throughout the camp systems. For example, at Mauthausen, one of the most brutal labor camps of Nazi Germany, located in occupied northern Austria, Aribert Heim—known as Dr. Death or the Butcher of Mauthausen—injected prisoners with various toxins, removed organs without anesthesia, performed unnecessary surgery, and even used an unfortunate prisoner's skull as a paperweight.[6] Another doctor, Karl Gross, killed hundreds by injecting them with typhus and cholera.

At Block 10 of Auschwitz, doctors Eduard Wirths, Josef Mengele, and others performed similar experiments and also included caustic methods of sterilization on women—such as attempts at X-ray sterilization resulting in radiation burns—and horrific tests on pairs of twins. Similar sterilization experiments were performed at Ravensbrück, the women's camp in northern Germany. The experiments of these notorious doctors, which resulted in thousands of deaths, have forever changed medical ethics. During the war, Nazis claimed that the experiments were undertaken to help German soldiers on the front lines, but it is difficult to see them as anything but torture. Modern scientists and medical experts have argued, from an objective standpoint, whether or not the experiments can be considered valid science on account of the numerous scientific and methodological inconsistencies.

The United States Holocaust Memorial Museum explains that the research occurred primarily for three reasons: attempting to prolong the survival of Axis soldiers (such as altitude, pressure, and temperature tests), experimenting with pharmaceuticals to treat injuries and contagious diseases (immunization tests, mustard gas exposure, surgeries), and the third, perhaps most unpleasant aspect was eugenics, advancing the Nazi racial ideology.[7]

The notorious medical testing grew out of the Weimar-era notions of eugenics and "racial hygiene" that became such a critical aspect of Nazi ideology. This essentially began with moral imperatives, such as encouraging "Aryan" specimens to marry and breed. As funding and support grew, a law was passed in 1933, the Law for the Prevention of Genetically Diseased Offspring, which allowed the sterilization of "men and women who 'suffered' from any of nine conditions assumed to be hereditary: feeblemindedness, schizophrenia, manic-depressive disorder, genetic epilepsy, Huntington's chorea (a fatal form of dementia), genetic blindness, genetic deafness, severe physical deformity, and chronic alcoholism."[8] It is believed that 400,000 Germans were sterilized as a result of this. A law criminalizing intercourse and marriage between Jews and non-Jews followed two years later in 1935.

By 1939, these two laws progressed to medical euthanasia for "undesirables," including deformed children and later children and adults considered incurable or "unproductive." Known as Operation T-4, this was mostly carried out in hospitals and institutions. It is believed that 200,000 people were killed by carbon monoxide poison in hospital showers converted to gas chambers, by starvation, or with overdoses of medication.

This program was brought to occupied Poland, where Nazis began segregating Jewish communities into ghettos, which turned into mass killing by firing squad and later into forced marches to a growing number of death camps, such as Auschwitz-Birkenau, Treblinka, Chełmno, Sobibor, and Belzec. The latter four were designed primarily as killing centers, rather than concentration or work camps. Auschwitz, however, became the largest and most efficient killing center in World War II. The strong or moderately healthy were sent to work, while women, children, the elderly, and the sick were killed outright, abused, or used in medical experiments.

Though medical experimentation was widespread throughout the camps, it is only one horror out of many perpetrated on prisoners. While the men were often worked to infirmity or death, the women of the camps—Jewish, Roma, Polish, Soviet, and otherwise—faced a variety of unique problems, particularly sexual terrors. Military and civilian brothels were often staffed with camp inmates, generally non–Jewish women, rapes and sexual abuse occurred, and women who became pregnant were given involuntary abortions and sometimes sterilized.

The sexual slavery depicted in *Salò* and Nazisploitation films like *Ilsa, She Wolf of the SS* is based loosely in fact. Out of all Nazi sex crimes, the best documented and more well known are the *Lagerbordell* or military brothels—the previously mentioned Joy Division. At the height of Nazi occupation in Europe there were allegedly over five hundred of these across France and Eastern Europe. There were also camp brothels meant to reward compliant prisoners, usually prisoners of war or political enemies of the state. There is documented evidence of this at some camps, including Ravensbrück, Mauthausen, and Auschwitz's infamous Block 24, among others.

Joy Division women were forced into sexual slavery and raped, abused, and replaced by women of neighboring camps when they died or were killed. While it is explored in a fictional work like *House of Dolls*, there is also factual documentation such as in *Memory of the Camps*, a documentary produced by the British Ministry of Information. Alfred Hitchcock was famously so affected by the early footage from this film that he assisted as a producer and allegedly offered editing advice.[9] Robert Sommer's *Das KZ Bordell* (*The Concentration Camp Bordello*, 2009) is the first book solely dedicated to the subject, thanks to the taboo which still plagues the topic and related difficulty doing thorough research.

There were also several concentration camps solely for women. Ravensbrück, the largest of these, was opened as early as May of 1939, north of Berlin. Auschwitz-Birkenau in occupied Poland had a separate section known as Auschwitz II for women, opened in 1942. In 1944, Bergen-Belsen in northern Germany was expanded to include a women's camp and women were transferred there from other camps towards the end of the war. Women were particularly vulnerable in the camps, as pregnant women and mothers of babies or young children were deemed unfit for work and often killed in the gas chambers, experimented on, or given unsafe abortions.

Another taboo subject that plagued Holocaust survivors and is portrayed in Nazisploitation films is rape. While Jewish women were certainly raped in the camps, this is an aspect of the Holocaust that has been kept relatively silent over the years. Just as rape is one of the most unreported crimes around the world, it is also one of the most unreported, under-discussed subjects of the Holocaust. Historians have been attempting to sweep back the veil of silence in recent years, presumably before it is too late to interview survivors. The 2010 anthology, *Sexual Violence Against Women During the Holocaust*, edited by Sonja Hedgepeth and Rochelle Saidel, attempts to cover everything from rape, prostitution, sterilization, and more. It is the first publication of its kind and builds off of Leonore Weitzman's *Women in the Holocaust* (1998), the first book of Holocaust scholarship solely about women.

There has been more research done about the plight of non–Jewish concentration camp prisoners, such as the Polish, Russian, and other Eastern European women often forced to exchange sex for food, warmer clothes, and other necessities, as well as the civilians. There were countless rapes perpetrated outside the camps, by "friendly" soldiers and liberators, as well as by invaders. While there are reports of Nazis raping Polish and Soviet women during times of invasion and occupation, women in China, Japan, and Okinawa suffered similar fates.

And the Allied armies don't have a much better record: there are reports of British soldiers raping women and girls in Europe and French soldiers raping women in Africa and Germany. For example, an estimated 7,000 women and children were raped during the course of the Battle of Monte Cassino. Soviet soldiers also practiced this frequently during their invasions of Poland and Germany. It is estimated that two million women were raped, gang raped, raped repeatedly, and/or impregnated and denied abortions. American soldiers raped allegedly 14,000 French women from D-Day through the liberation, a disgusting epidemic that's the subject of Robert J. Lilly's *Taken by Force: Rape and American GIs in Europe During* World War II.

But as the Nazisploitation films reflect, women were not solely victims during the Holocaust. Though the title character of *Ilsa, She Wolf of the SS* is an exaggerated caricaturization, German women did serve in the concentration camps. Women did not serve in the Wehrmacht directly as soldiers or commanders, but as auxiliaries; there were supposedly 500,000 by the end of the war. Ravensbrück, the first female camp, staffed more than 100 female guards and was a training center for future *Aufseherinnen*, or female camp overseers. These women were notoriously sadistic and given nicknames like "The Beast of Ravensbrück" (Elfriede Muller), "The Blonde Angel of Auschwitz" (Irma Grese), and "The Bitch of Buchenwald" (Ilse Koch).

Medical camp Commandant Ilsa (Dyanne Thorne) may be loosely based on historical figures, but she is truly a creation of sadomasochistic fantasy (*Ilsa: She Wolf of the SS*, Aeteas Filmproduktions, 1975).

Ilsa, She Wolf of the SS was inspired by the latter two women, Irma Grese and Ilsa Koch. Grese was a lead *Aufseherin* at both Ravensbrück and Auschwitz. Like others in her field, she was blue collar and not particularly skilled or well educated; she found her way to the camps via the fanatic League of German Girls. Grese apparently set dogs on inmates, tortured, beat, and shot them, showing particular brutality towards women, and hand-selected individuals for the ovens. She supposedly beat prisoners to death with a whip she carried around at all times. She was accused of war crimes at the Belsen Trials and reputedly curled her hair before her execution.

Ilse Koch—wife of the commandant of Buchenwald and Majdanek—had a reputation for being particularly cruel and allegedly kept the tattooed skin of some of her victims. She and her husband were so repugnant that they were actually arrested and tried by Nazis in 1943 (primarily for extortion). While her husband was executed, she escaped punishment until she was later arrested by the U.S. army. Four witnesses claimed she had prisoners killed and then made lampshades from their skin, the likely source of a colorful rumor that has never been factually verified.

Grese and Koch are just the tip of a particularly sadistic iceberg that includes Elizabeth Volkenrath of Ravensbrück and Auschwitz, Hermine Braunsteiner—extradited to Germany from the U.S. in the '70s for crimes that included beating and kicking inmates with her jackboots and contributing to the murders of 100 children—and Maria Mandel, one of the most gruesome, who was the head female official at Auschwitz and led 500,000 women to their deaths.

Where these women differ from *Ilsa, She Wolf of the SS*'s female commandant or other *Aufseherinnen* depicted in Nazisploitation is in sex and glamour. Though they were known to have sexual relationships with members of the SS and camp commandants, there are no recorded sexual relationships between prisoners and female guards. They were certainly as brutal as their filmic counterparts, though their tortures were generally less exotic than grotesque medical experiments, castrations, and the like. Perhaps most importantly, they were not entirely equals with the male members of the SS and—unlike the titular character in *Ilsa, She Wolf of the SS*—no woman was ever in charge of an entire concentration camp.

And while early efforts like *Love Camp 7*, *Ilsa, She Wolf of the SS*, and arthouse films like *Salò* maintain a tenuous connection to historical fact, their predecessors would move further into the realms of violent fantasy. *Ilsa, She Wolf of the SS* kicked off the Nazisploitation subgenre full force, while creating a few sequels of its own: *Ilsa, Harem Keeper of the Oil Sheiks* (1976), *Ilsa, The Wicked Warden* (1977), which was a Swiss and West German coproduction, and *Ilsa, The Tigress of Siberia* (1977). These three films follow nearly the same plot as the first film, but with different locations and historical themes.

In general, the emerging Nazisploitation films either mimicked the plot of *Ilsa, She Wolf of the SS*, or borrowed from another film hot on its trail: Tinto Brass's blend of art house and exploitation, *Salon Kitty* (1976). Based on Peter Norden's novel of the same name, the film is concerned with the real-life events that occurred at Salon Kitty, a World War II-era Nazi brothel. Located in Berlin, the brothel opened in 1930 and was run by Kitty Schmidt. Schmidt tried to flee Germany, but the Nazis made her a bargain: cooperate or be sent to a concentration camp.

The SD or *Sicherheitsdienst*, the intelligence service infamously run by Reinhard Heydrich until has assassination in 1942, took over the brothel and used it for espionage, recording rich and powerful clients with hidden microphones and using hand-selected, highly trained prostitute-spies. Its customers included some of the highest-ranking Nazis, as well as diplomats and foreign dignitaries, who were encouraged to disclose state secrets. It was eventually infiltrated by British intelligence, who wiretapped the microphones for their own eavesdropping.

In Brass's film, SS Officer Helmut Wallenberg (Helmut Berger) is ordered to set up the brothel, hire the female staff, and secretly outfit the building with surveillance equipment. He selects and trains 20 beautiful young prostitutes, all fervent Nazis, led by Madam Kitty (Ingrid Thulin). With the success of the operation, Wallenberg becomes power mad and begins blackmailing high ranking officials to increase his own position in the Nazi Party. But when one of the girls, Marguerite (Teresa Ann Savoy), learns what is actually going on—and that Wallenburg has had her lover murdered—she vows revenge with Madam Kitty's help.

With a larger budget and a more robust sense of style than many Nazisploitation films, *Salon Kitty* is the love child of director Tinto Brass, known for his avant-garde, often erotic epics—such as *Caligula* (1979)—and this Italian-French-West German production is no exception. Boasting an X-rating and almost nonstop nudity, including full frontal shots of male and female characters and vaginal close-ups, *Salon Kitty* seems like little more than an attempt to catalogue as many perversions as possible. In addition to traditional Nazisploitation fare like whippings and sadomasochism, there are graphic scenes of masturbation, homosexuality, rape, sex with a dwarf and other "freaks," orgies, voyeurism, and even a bloody sex scene at a slaughterhouse. The girls are forced to endure a number of training exercises, including a scene of group sex with a full band accompanying the 20 women and their soldier companions.

The film reunites *The Damned*'s stars Helmut Berger—wearing some spectacularly campy fetish uniforms—and Ingmar Bergman regular Ingrid Thulin, the latter of whom has a number of improbable, Marlene Dietrich–like musical sequences. There is a scant amount of plot between the erotic scenes, but Brass does include several direct references to the horrors of life in the Third Reich. Before fleeing to Berlin, Marguerite has a dinner scene with her hypocritical industrialist parents, who are solely interested in being on the side of the "winners," regardless of their politics. There is also a tragic moment in an aquarium where a blonde German girl—one of Wallenberg's soon-to-be recruits—coldly crushes the toy of a young Jewish girl under foot.

For the most part though, *Salon Kitty* is confused about its politics and the heroes of the film become the apolitical madam and Marguerite, an avowed fascist who wants revenge on Wallenberg in the name of love, with her political motivations in the distant background. Unlike the majority of Nazisploitation films, *Salon Kitty* is more concerned with sex and sleaze than it is with graphic violence—in keeping with Brass's other sexploitation fare—and moves away from *Love Camp 7* and *Ilsa, She Wolf of the SS*'s concentration camp locations to the more glamorous world of the brothel.

Following *Salon Kitty*, primarily in 1976 and 1977, a slew of Italian Nazisploitation films, which came to be known as *il sadiconazista*, were released. Generally, these plots borrowed directly from *Ilsa, She Wolf of the SS* or *Salon Kitty* with surprisingly little deviation. Sergio Garrone's *Lager SSadis Kastrat Kommandantur* (*SS Experiment Camp*, 1976), for example, is essentially a rip off of *Ilsa, She Wolf of the SS* and was a notorious Video Nasty, banned in the UK. It concerns a medical experimentation camp where an emasculated Nazi officer (Giorgio Cerioni) gets revenge on young women. Thanks to the poster art—which depicts a nearly nude woman being crucified upside down while a swastika bracelet dangles from her wrist—it had a worse reputation than its actual contents reflect, a common issue with exploitation films during this period.

As the cycle continued on, each of these films sought to be gorier, more graphic, and more offensive than the last. For example, one of the most notorious of the *il sadiconazista* films is Luigi Batzella's *La bestia in calore* (*Beast in Heat*, 1977, a.k.a. *SS Hell Camp*). Like *Ilsa, She Wolf of the SS*, the central character is a villainous female Nazi officer (Macha Magall) who tortures and rapes the camp inmates. In a particularly outrageous twist, she has bred a half-man/half-beast hybrid (Salvatore Baccaro of *Salon Kitty*) that she uses to rape and torture prisoners.

Yet another Video Nasty banned in the UK, *Beast in Heat* doesn't deviate very far from the plot of *Ilsa, She Wolf of the SS*, and includes similar scenes of rape, torture, and partisans planning to violently resist against the camp. The film has a remarkably low budget, limited set pieces, and even includes footage from some of Batzella's other World War II-themed exploitation films, such as *Quando suona la campana* (*When the Bell Rings*, 1970). It is also one of many Nazisploitation films from the late '70s to include torture by rats (or in this case, some sad-looking guinea pigs standing in for rats).

Another entry, *L'ultima orgia del III Reich* (*Last Orgy of the Third Reich*, 1977, a.k.a. *Gestapo's Last Orgy*) is one of the most infamous, horrifying of these titles. It essentially presents an exaggerated version of the plot of *Ilsa, She Wolf of the SS*. Female prisoners of a death camp are used in an orgy that includes sodomy, incest, coprophagia, and torture. People are burnt alive and fed to dogs, and the orgy soon escalates to cannibalism and infanticide, when Nazi guards consume a stew made of Jewish fetuses. Unlike other films in the series, the Nazis are depicted as fervently anti–Jewish—in the sense that it names Jews as the victims of the horrors, while other exploitation films are a bit more vague on the subject—and goes absolutely over the top in its efforts to be offensive.

Gestapo's Last Orgy attempts a slightly more serious, less campy tone than much of its brethren. Possibly in an attempt to mimic *The Night Porter*, the film also relates

A horrific dinner sequence commences in *Gestapo's Last Orgy* (*L'ultima orgia del III Reich*, Cine Lu.Ce., 1977).

the doomed love story of a Nazi guard (Adriano Micantoni) and a female prisoner, Lise (Daniela Poggi), who reunite at the former death camp where he served as commandant and she as prisoner. The commandant was spared prison after the war thanks to Lise's testimony, though he and his Nazi mistress (Maristella Greco), an Ilsa-like figure, participated eagerly in the torture of countless women.

Other late Italian efforts began to include more elements of *Salon Kitty*, such as *Le lunghe notti della Gestapo* (*Red Nights of the Gestapo*, 1977), where a Nazi officer uses beautiful women to seduce and root out traitors to the Reich. Italian horror and exploitation director Bruno Mattei made *Casa privata per le SS* (*SS Girls*, 1977), with almost exactly the same plot, or Mattei's *KZ9: Lager di sterminio* (*Women's Camp 119*, 1977). Other such Italian offerings have dizzyingly similar names, such as *Le deportate della sezione speciale SS* (*Deported Women of the SS Special Section*, 1976) or *SS Lager 5: L'inferno delle donne* (*SS Camp 5: Women's Hell*, 1977).

The rest of Europe slowly caught on to the cycle, particularly France. *Fraulein Devil* (1977) and *Train spécial pour SS* (*Hitler's Last Train*, 1977) both concern a special train car filled with prostitutes meant to service the Führer or high-ranking members of the SS. *Helga, la louve de Stilberg* (*Helga, She Wolf of Stilberg*, 1977) is a blatant rip-off of *Ilsa, She Wolf of the SS*, while *Nathalie rescapée de l'enfer* (*Nathalie: Escape from Hell*, 1978) concerns a sexy Russian doctor (Patrizia Gori) who must escape from a Nazi brothel in yet another twist on *Salon Kitty*.

A rare German-language entry includes the Swiss-filmed *Ein Armee Gretchen* (*She Devils of the SS*, 1973), which is something of an early comic twist on the genre. It follows German women who prostitute themselves to the soldiers of the Reich and includes a notorious scene of naked women running through a battlefield as bombs explode around them. There are even a few hardcore Nazisploitation films, such as U.S. films *Hitler's Harlot* (1973) or *Nazi Love Island* (1980), or Mario Caiano's Italian entry, *La svastica nel ventre* (*Nazi Love Camp 27*, 1977), starring *The Beast*'s Sirpa Lane, and depicting scenes of graphic rape with a bull horn, among other atrocities.

Though these Nazisploitation films undoubtedly contain some historical elements, they ultimately present sexualized, deeply problematic caricatures of real figures, events, and atrocities. The powerful shadow of the Holocaust that falls over these films also casts a dark light over *Salò*, which is likewise filtered through this lens of fantasy. Though Pasolini took care to specifically name and place *Salò* within the historical location of Mussolini's Salò, the caricatures found in Nazisploitation films play an almost equally significant role in the visual and thematic context of *Salò*. Mira Liehm writes,

> Not only had Pasolini arrived at the conclusion that making sex the centerpiece of cinematic populism brings one closer to exploitation than to liberation, but he was also reacting to the exploitation of sex in the Nazi-porno films that were flooding the Italian market at that time. In *Saló*, the substitution of the Italian fascist establishment for the Nazi-porno caricatures of German war criminals became an important part of Pasolini's cultural commentary.[10]

Instead of responding directly to political fascism or the trauma of the Holocaust, Pasolini constructed his cinematic world around a visual language partly inherited from exploitation and erotica. Like his *Trilogy of Life* a few years before, *Salò* anticipated a new wave of cinematic sexual commodification. When Pasolini completed his *Trilogy of Life*, he was one of the first filmmakers to push explicit content farther than it had previously been allowed to go in Italian film. Perhaps inevitably, a series of pornographic and exploitation films followed in its wake. Such titles as *I racconti di Viterbury: Le più allegre storie del '300* (*The Sexbury Tales*, 1973), *I racconti di Canterbury N. 2* (*The Lusty Wives of Canterbury*, 1973), *Il Decamerone proibito* (*Forbidden Decameron*, 1972), and *Le calde notti del Decameron* (*Hot Nights of Decameron*, 1972) flooded the market. Immediately after *Salò*'s completion and release, this trend was echoed with Nazisploitation films.

But *Salò*, despite its connection to this disreputable genre, rises above its exploitative brethren—it is an arthouse classic. With an icy, intellectual beauty, it manipulated the commodification of fascism, or what Susan Sontag called the "master scenario." Saul Friedländer described a "new discourse" of Nazism, one where the Third Reich is no longer a symbol of pervasive, all-corrupting evil. Instead, it exists with a contradictory, dual function. Partly it is the kitschy shadow of a horror that is no longer possible in the current social and economic climate, a once indescribable trauma that is now explained over and over again, pinned down by language. Conversely, it lingers as a recurrent psychological hold for "a particular kind of bondage nourished by the simultaneous desires for absolute submission and total freedom."[11]

With *Salò*, Pasolini responded to this new interpretation of fascism. His recreation of Mussolini's Salò, like any good fantasy, is replete with accurate details, but is otherwise removed from factual historical context. From 1943 to 1945, Salò was the seat of Mussolini's Italian Social Republic or Republic of Salò, a puppet government run by the Nazis in the northern half of Italy. Fascist Italy had a historical reputation for being lenient on the Jews and Italy had one of the highest survival rates for Jews in Europe after the war (topped only by Denmark and Bulgaria).

This idea of a rosy Italian defense of Jewish people has been challenged recently, particularly in terms of the period of 1943 to 1945 when the Nazi government put its machine of hatred and mass extermination to work. Of course, anti–Semitic actions began before the German occupation. Joshua Zimmerman writes,

> During the years 1938–43, prior to the loss of Italian sovereignty, Fascist Italy waged a debilitating campaign against its Jewish population. The passage of anti–Jewish laws, introduced primarily before the Second World War and without German interference, dealt a sharp blow to the Italian Jewish community.[12]

By decree of King Victor Emmanuel III's "Laws for the Defense of Race," Jews were removed from schools, both as students and instructors, military service, state employment, from owning medium to large businesses and valuable land, etc. It only got worse from there: roughly one-fourth of the Jewish population was forced to convert or emigrate by 1943. By 1944, Italian soldiers had arrested thousands of Jews on Mussolini's orders. Friedländer writes,

> Throughout the country the roundups continued until the end of 1944: The Jews were usually transferred to an assembly camp at Fossoli (later to Risiera di San Sabba, near Trieste) and, from there, sent to Auschwitz. Thousands managed to hide among a generally friendly population or in religious institutions; some managed to flee across the Swiss border or to the areas liberated by the Allies. Nonetheless, throughout Italy about 7,000 Jews, some 20 percent of the Jewish population, were caught and murdered.[13]

While Italian concentration camps are generally not considered as gruesome or cruel as their Nazi counterparts, the fact remains that they did exist. Risiera di San Sabba was an Italian camp mostly used as a prison or killing center for political prisoners, but it was also a transit center that transported Jews and other "undesirables" to Auschwitz and occasionally other locations. Jews from not only Italy, but also neighboring countries Croatia and Slovenia were sent to their deaths through San Sabba. Other camps include the more lenient Campagna, where prisoners were allowed to receive mail and food, and visit sick relatives. In 1943, locals helped the inmates escape before Germans flooded the area. They were hidden underground, in cellars, on farms, and in churches and convents, sometimes disguised as priests and nuns.

Friedländer related an anecdote about the brutal torture practices that Jews and partisans sometimes experienced at the hands of Italians themselves, by men like the soldier and secret police commander Pietro Koch:

> In Milan a gang of Italian fascists outperformed the Germans in feats of bestiality; this was an uncommon achievement by all accounts, and an atypical one. Pietro Koch's men had established their headquarters in a villa soon known as Villa Triste ("sad villa"), where they tortured and executed their victims, Jews and non–Jews. Koch's thugs were assisted by two famous Italian actors, Luisa Ferida and Osvaldo Valenti, known as "the Fred Astaire and Ginger Rogers of torture," who lent a macabre, surreal quality to Villa Triste that has made it a symbol of the decadent twilight of fascism.[14]

The "Villa Triste" was actually a name used for a number of such torture centers throughout fascist Italy. In addition to the Milan headquarters, similar institutions could be found in Florence, Rome, Trieste, Genoa, and others.

Pasolini's formative years occurred during the war. In 1939, he began attending the University of Bologna. He joined a cinema club, published some of his poetry, learned Friulan—a rural Italian language that would become one of the great loves of his life—and had his first affair with a male student. His experiences with Italian and German fascism were long lasting and escalated between 1940 and 1945. He was fired from a magazine by its fascist-leaning chief editor and a fateful trip to Germany pushed him towards Communism. Though he spent most of this time in a sheltered part of the Italian countryside, he was eventually drafted. He was soon imprisoned by the Wehrmacht, though he managed to escape by pretending to be a peasant. His brother was not so lucky and died during a skirmish.

The effects of the war on Pasolini's life are incalculable. In many ways, *Salò* is the culmination of all these themes. It does not reflect a single wartime memory but is the sum of Pasolini's ideas about the futility and toxicity of capitalism, consumerism, and fascism which began during the war and developed throughout this life. He writes, "the reality of innocent bodies has now also been stained, manipulated, and destroyed by the power of the consumer society."[15] *Salò* is not a specific film about the treatment of Italians during the war, but a brilliant examination of the total European experience: imprisonment, surveillance, control, torture, death.

And while *Salò* begins as a fantasy, this notion is quickly dashed against the rocks of intellectualism by Pasolini. He destroys any idea that we are simply viewing a catalog of perversions, monstrosities, or erotic curios. He is quick to ensure that *Salò* is, if not an outright intellectual exercise, at least steeped in a rich tradition of literary scholarship and philosophy. Astoundingly, he provides a *bibliografia essenziale* or reading list following the opening credits, which includes such thinkers as Roland Barthes, Maurice Blanchot, Simone De Beauvoir, Pierre Klossowski, and Phillipe Sollers as his co-conspirators, giving book and article titles as well as specific published editions. Though this indicates

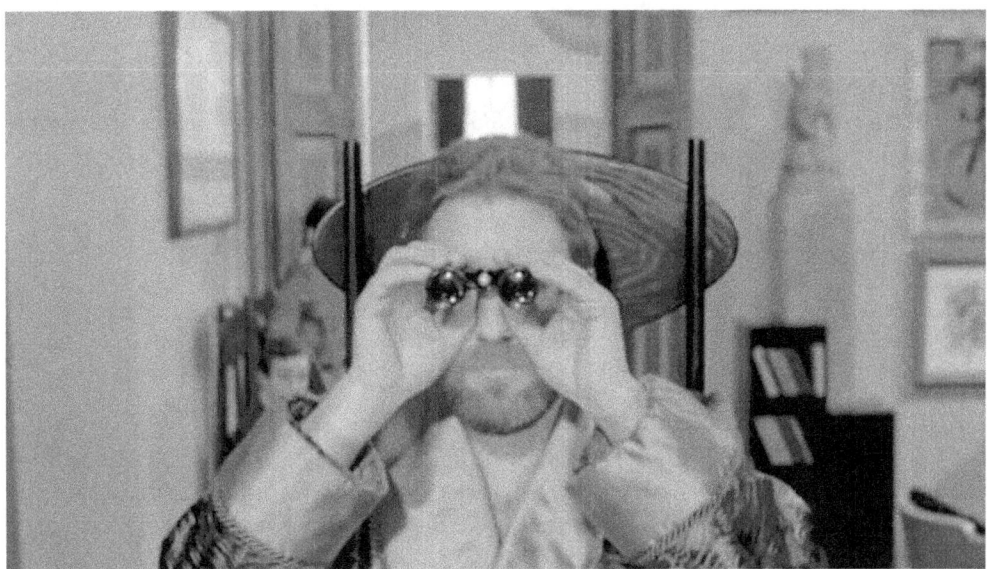

The Duke (Paolo Bonacelli) is an eager spectator of the orgy of torture unfolding in the courtyard in *Salò* (*Salò o le 120 giornate di Sodoma*, Produzioni Europee Associate [PEA]/Les Productions Artistes Associés, 1975).

some sort of explanation or possible warning for what we are about to experience, it makes an indigestible film even more difficult to process. The lengthy scenes to come are difficult enough without Pasolini's challenge to understand them in an isolated, intellectual context.

Notably, *Ilsa, She Wolf of the SS*, also opens with a written address to the viewer that attempts to explain or apologize for the following hour and a half. Like the "white coat" sex films of the '60s and '70s, it was likely an attempt to avoid censorship laws. The most famous of these are Vilgot Sjömans *Jag är nyfiken—en film i gult* (*I Am Curious: Yellow*, 1967) and Dusan Makavejev's *Misterije organizma, W.R.* (*WR: Mysteries of the Organism*, 1971), the latter of which also depicts the struggle to cope with sexual desire and personal agency in a post–Holocaust world. The opening of *Ilsa, She Wolf of the SS* reads:

> The film you are about to see is based upon documented fact. The atrocities shown were conducted as "medical experiments" in special concentration camps throughout Hitler's Third Reich. Although these crimes against humanity are historically accurate, the characters depicted are composites of notorious Nazi personalities; and the events portrayed, have been condensed into one locality for dramatic purposes. Because of its shocking subject matter, this film is restricted to adult audiences only. We dedicate this film with the hope that these heinous crimes will never occur again.

This preposterous message at the opening of *Ilsa* is presented by the producer, rather than its director. David Friedman, whose entire career was built on producing exploitation and sex films, used a pseudonym unique to *Ilsa, She Wolf of the SS*: Herman Traeger. Whether or not his introduction was an attempt to slide past censorship and explain its offenses before they have even begun, it also smacks of gratuitously false advertising. Claiming that *Ilsa, She Wolf of the SS* is in some way a factual representation of camp atrocities is ridiculous at best and the attempt to dedicate the film to Holocaust victims is flagrantly offensive. The "hope that these heinous crimes will never occur again" dissolves the instant the film begins to roll.

In a fetishized, fictionalized way, *Ilsa, She Wolf of the SS* repeats history every time the film plays. Friedländer discusses this desire for repetition in connection with his concept of an evolved understanding of Nazism that can only exist in a post-war world. He states that Nazism as a symbol of death and destruction must be exorcised in order for it to be mastered in the collective social consciousness. He writes,

> An exorcism, finally, whose total endeavor, in the past and the present, is—in the face of Nazi criminality and extermination policies—to maintain distance by means of language, to affirm the existence of another reality by inverting the signs of this one, and finally to appease by showing that all the chaos and horror is, after all, coherent and explainable.[16]

The Nazisploitation films of the decade exemplify this need to exorcise the demon of fascism. Like a carefully conscripted ritual, these films contain a specific set of elements that allow them to rhythmically reenact and finally purge the psychological fascination of fascism, as well as the remembered historical reality. Most of the films in this genre—along with arthouse efforts like *The Damned* and *The Night Porter*—end with operatic orgies of group violence, usually camp revolt. Most of the characters, especially the perpetrators, die painful, bloody deaths; only in rare instances are characters able to escape and attain liberation. It is only *Salò* that dispels any such notion that release will be found in death.

What Susan Sontag called the fantasy of death is critical to all violent exploitation films, particularly those fixated with fascism. In these efforts, death is frequently a stand in for orgasm, and though orgasms occur, none are as dramatic or eroticized as moments of death. For example, at the end of *Ilsa, She Wolf of the SS*, the titular character is gagged and tied to her bed in black lace lingerie with the horribly disfigured corpse of her most extreme torture victim draped over her, oozing blood and pus. A portrait of Hitler looks over the room and a German radio station plays loudly enough that no one can hear her muffled cries for help.

Unbeknownst to Ilsa, the prisoners have revolted and are engaged in a shootout with the camp guards. At the last moment, German troops sent from headquarters arrive with the secret mission to exterminate Ilsa's stalag and burn it to the ground, erasing the horrible evidence of her unsanctioned medical experiments and sexual depravity. The commanding officer enters Ilsa's bedroom and removes her gag. As she begins to thank him and explain herself, he pulls out a pistol and shoots her in the head, then radios in to confirm that his mission is complete.

While sex, sadism, and death are the primary motivators in Nazisploitation films, in *Salò*, sex is nearly devoid of value and pushed to such extremes that the inherent eroticism of intercourse is stripped away. The only actions that have any real value to the libertines in *Salò* are the carefully conscripted rules and rituals that separate public from private. As the Duke states in the beginning of the film, any perversion is accepted, if not encouraged. The unspoken implication is that sex, as well as any normally private, personal act—including defecation—is only acceptable in the performative sphere of the orgy room. This disavowal of personal space and identity is one of the elements that sets *Salò* apart from other Nazi exploitation films.

Michel Foucault illustrates the growing importance of sexuality on the development of personal identity in *The History of Human Sexuality*, a theme that is repeatedly rejected in *Salò*. Foucault states,

> We have arrived at a point where we expect our intelligibility to come from what was for many centuries thought of as madness; the plenitude of our body from what was long considered its stigma and likened to a wound; our identity from what was perceived as an obscure and nameless urge. Hence the importance we ascribe to it, the care we take to know it. Hence the fact that over the centuries it has become more important than our soul, more important almost than our life.... Sex is worth dying for.[17]

Salò, on the other hand, asserts that sex is not worth dying for; in fact, nothing is, because death has no power in a world that rejects individual personality or social norms. Towards the end of the film, several characters are brutally punished or casually killed for their sexual relationships. A girl is added to the blacklist for concealing her boyfriend's picture under her pillow. A pair of girls are almost executed for engaging in a sexual tryst; they are only spared because they show the libertines the location of a guard and maid mid-coitus. This last sexual relationship, which apparently has occurred for some time, breaks the ultimate law of *Salò*. Whether they are expressing love or attraction for one another, the enacting of sex in private is met with only one response: immediate execution.

Though frequently intended to be disturbing, uncomfortable, and exploitative, sexuality in Nazisploitation is generally meant to be inherently erotic. But *Salò*'s intellectual rejection and repeated denial of eroticism provides no release from its world of torment, humiliation, and ugliness. In his theoretical work, "The Cinema of Poetry," Pasolini states that a director

> chooses a series of objects, or things, or landscapes, or persons as syntagmas (signs of a symbolic language) which, while they have a grammatical history invented in that moment ... do, however, have an already lengthy and intense pregrammatical history.[18]

He purposefully chose a series of acts, sexual and perverse, that have direct origin in Sade and are explored in '70s exploitation cinema. The concept of humanity as a crushing, churning machine, devoid of individual identity, began with Sade and found its fullest expression under Germany's Third Reich. Pasolini united these themes in the ultimate rejection of sex and disavowal that death is an escape from the cruelty of life.

Death in *Salò* is an entirely different animal, divorced from eroticism. Murder and suicide are casual acts separated from the ritual torture and degradation that is the daily menu of the villa in *Salò*. There are a number of murders that punctuate the cyclical rhythm of the film, subverting and breaking the building loop of intensity that would otherwise end in climax, whether violent or sexual. In fact, the film begins with a murder that is cruel, casual, and separate from the libertines' program of perversion and torture. It indicates to us, early on, the worth of human life and dramatic importance of extinguishing one: null.

A group of male and female children and teenagers are rounded up and examined by the four libertines. Once approved, they are shipped off to the villa at Salò in covered trucks, much like the trucks carrying prisoners of war in *Ilsa, She Wolf of the SS*. A young boy leaps out of the truck and escapes to the side of the road, running along the scenic riverside. The libertines laugh, barely notice, and joke about the number of boys in their possession, turning it into a word game. Once nine, now eight, like the fr"eight" in the trucks. The soldiers don't bother to chase him but stand at the overpass and shoot him with their machine guns until he falls down, riddled with bullets. No further attention is given to his departure, whether by ritual celebration or physical attempt to conceal the crime. It simply has no impact, and the entire scene takes up less than a minute of screen time in the lengthy, almost two hour long film.

The second death occurs about half an hour into the film, just before the second story told by one of the aged prostitutes. A young girl who cried for her mother earlier in the film and feebly tried to escape has locked herself into a small devotional closet with a fresco of the Virgin and Child. When the doors are broken open, she collapses backwards to the ground and it is obvious her throat has been cut. One of the libertines laughs and again tells a numerical joke. They all laugh and resume the music and storytelling. They don't bother to move her body and the prostitute stands in front of her, her full-skirted dress and dramatic arm movements blocking the corpse from view.

The final death of some importance is the suicide of the piano player, one of the few adult staff working at the villa. She acts as musical entertainment, assistant, and accomplice to the libertines for the duration of the film. At the conclusion, when a series of final atrocities are being committed in the yard, she snaps. Initially, she is doing what she does in almost every other scene of the film that takes place in the "orgy room" or main parlor: playing the piano. In this last scene, she stops, crosses the room, and looks out the window, where she can presumably see the yard. She gets a look of horror on her face, leaves the room, and runs up a dark flight of stairs. She reaches another window, stands up on the ledge, and flings herself down two stories onto the well-manicured lawn. The camera briefly shows us her bent, limp body before moving back to the atrocities.

This complete disregard for death gives *Salò* one of its nastiest and most chilling elements. While the libertines will kill to punish, as can be seen with the boy in the beginning of the film as well as a guard and servant having an illicit relationship later on, they really ascribe no value to human life. Suicide, which Michel Foucault describes as having a certain power of its own, is also lost on them:

> It is not surprising that suicide—once a crime, since it was a way to usurp the power of death which the sovereign alone, whether the one here or the Lord above, had the right to exercise—became, in the course of the nineteenth century, one of the first conducts to enter into the sphere of sociological analysis; it testified to the individual and private right to die, at the borders and in the interstices of power that was exercised over life.[19]

The libertines give suicide no power of its own. Their callous jokes about numbers are more important than the sudden loss of bodies or the problem of what to do with those bodies. No one is buried during the film and no funeral rites or rituals of mourning are enacted. Though the two characters who kill themselves are permanently freeing themselves from the circle of Hell at Salò, it is clear that this is not an act of freedom or liberation. It is a meaningless exercise that only serves to illustrate that there is no inherent value to human life.

Pasolini intentionally and uncomfortably pushed his final film into new territory. The taboo, but familiar world of perverse sexuality is stripped of its erotic content, resulting in what critics have called the "funeral dirge" of eroticism, what Gilles Deleuze described as a "theorem of death." There is no escape from this *Inferno*-like realm of torment. *Salò* never ends. It forces us to constantly relive past and present horrors without placing that trauma inside a specific historical framework. The specter of fascism is named, but never exorcised as it is in other Nazisploitation films of the era. Though the end of the film culminates in an orgy of violence, Pasolini simply focuses on the different libertines watching the scene through a window and binoculars, reminding us of our own voyeuristic complicity in the horror of sexual commodification.

In a 1967 interview, Paolini said, "It is only at our moment of death that our life, to that point undecipherable, ambiguous, suspended, acquires a meaning."[20] And there is, of course, another layer of death associated with *Salò*: Pasolini's own. Several months after the film's release in 1975, the director was run over with his own car by a young male prostitute in Ostia, a picturesque beach town in Rome. Nearly thirty years later, the man— Pino Pelosi—claimed that he was forced to make a false confession and a conspiracy has developed involving potential blackmailers who supposedly stole rolls of the film. Pasolini had long been the object of scandal in Italy due to his hardline communist beliefs, insistence on unconventionality, and somewhat open homosexual lifestyle.

> The murder was brutal. [...] The corpse was severely mutilated, the thorax was crushed and the liver lacerated. Half an ear had been ripped away from the head.... Was it really credible that a fit athlete like Pasolini would be overcome by one rather skinny boy? Could Pelosi really have inflicted such serious lesions with no more than his fists and a wet piece of wood? How come Pelosi had only a couple of small stains on his clothes, when all indications pointed to a furious struggle in a muddy field?[21]

These later doubts were further problematized by shoddy police work, a lack of forensic evidence, and other questionable elements. His death has left a frustrating legacy, one that is inextricably bound up with his crowning achievement, *Saló*, which remains one of the most visceral, challenging, and taboo works of cinema.

8

Innocent Children and Kafkaesque Doubles

Jewish Identity in French Cinema

"From the 1970s, the French were increasingly reminded in films, books, and newspapers that millions of people had revered Marshal Pétain; that Vichy laws, not German ones, had represented the 'true' France and discriminated against French Jews and French Freemasons; that French policemen, not German ones, had arrested Jews and Communists; that the resisters had been a small minority; and that most people had been attentistes not heroes. The myth was turned on its head. [...] Vichy, not de Gaulle or the Resistance, now seemed to represent the 'true' France."—Julian Jackson, *France: The Dark Years, 1940-1944*[1]

Despite the many films about World War II made between 1945 and 1965, not many of them directly addressed the fact that Jews were the primary victims of the Holocaust; or that the Nazi aim for systemic annihilation was encouraged by deeply engrained anti-Semitism throughout Europe. France is an interesting example of this situation. While occupied France was home to many Jews—approximately 350,000, roughly half of which were French, while the remainder had recently emigrated from Central and Eastern European countries—and a smaller percentage of them perished than in countries like Poland, strongly rooted anti-Semitism can still be found throughout the nation's history. As the United States Holocaust Memorial Museum states, "Vichy administrators promulgated antisemitic legislation, 'Aryanized' Jewish property, interned thousands, and periodically rounded up thousands of foreign and French Jews to transport to transit camps and, later, usually to Auschwitz, where most were murdered."[2]

Part of Vichy's legacy—and the truth about the actual size and impact of the French Resistance, as I have discussed in earlier chapters—is the French government's role in furthering Nazi policy. In many cases, French citizens were not just content to pay attention to their own affairs in an attempt to survive the war unscathed. Many of them actively participated in the murder of Jews, communists, and other resistors. Julian Jackson writes,

> The Vichy government liquidated France's democratic institutions, persecuted Freemasons, Jews, and Communists, and embarked on a policy of collaboration with Germany. Eventually 650,000 civilian French workers were compulsorily drafted to work in German factories; 75,000 Jews from France perished in Auschwitz; 30,000 French civilians were shot as

8. Innocent Children and Kafkaesque Doubles

hostages or members of the Resistance; another 60,000 were deported to German concentration camps.[3]

It is perhaps not surprising that French audiences didn't want to be confronted with their own role in the Holocaust. France is not unique in this regard; there were few films from any country to directly address the role of Jews in the Holocaust for decades after the war. France is also a particularly interesting case to consider, because of their degree of complicity with Nazi occupying forces. Leah Hewitt writes,

> On the whole, collaboration with the Nazis had been less widespread in Belgium, Holland, Denmark, and Norway than in France. Paradoxically, in the former, the number of individuals sent to prison for collaboration was comparatively high, as public rage fueled judicial proceedings. In France, on the other hand, where collaboration had been more extensive, the process was incomplete, as relatively few went to jail or were executed.[4]

As mentioned in an earlier chapter, formative documentaries like *Night and Fog* sidestepped this issue and it wasn't really until the wake of the Eichmann trial—in the late '60s and into the '70s—that filmmakers from any country began to focus on this topic more openly. Interestingly, many of those films to first feature Jewish characters defer to two stock roles: as innocent children or as two-dimensional side characters that essentially exist on screen so the film's non–Jewish protagonists can respond and react to them—and often rescue them.

It is worth briefly mentioning a few early American examples, which provide an interesting point of comparison to the later French films. Orson Welles, ever an iconoclast and provocateur, was one of the very first directors to depict the Holocaust in a feature film. His thriller *The Stranger* (1946) was released very shortly after the war ended. Though generally forgotten beside his celebrated masterpieces like *Citizen Kane* (1942) and *The Magnificent Ambersons* (1942), it's a gripping look at post-war paranoia in small town America that builds off of film noir tropes.

In *The Stranger*, Mr. Wilson (Edward G. Robinson), from the United Nations War Crimes Commission, is hunting Franz Kindler (Welles), a high-ranking Nazi official who escaped to the U.S. to begin a new life. Kindler changed his name to Charles Rankin, began working as a professor in smalltown Connecticut, and married local girl Mary (Loretta Young). Mr. Wilson's arrival heralds a number of strange events, including the poisoning of Mary's beloved dog and the discovery of a body in the woods. Wilson realizes that he needs Mary's testimony to arrest Kindler, who uses her love for him to manipulate her. When Wilson makes her watch concentration camp footage, she is pushed to the edge of hysteria.

Written, directed by, and starring Welles, *The Stranger* is notable because it was the first film released after the war to include real footage from concentration camps. Taken from *Death Mills* (1945), Billy Wilder's short documentary film produced for the United States Department of War, the clip includes graphic footage of liberated camps Belsen and Auschwitz. Originally intended to be shown to American audiences, *Death Mills* was deemed too graphic, but Welles, concerned that fascism would find a new way to rear its ugly head, was insistent that the footage would make an appearance in his film. Loretta Young's Mary stands in for the average American, reluctant to believe the worst of humanity until she is literally unable to look away from the evidence.

A later, more overt example—and one of the first films to explore the trauma of Holocaust survivors—is *The Juggler* (1953), starring then up-and-coming actor Kirk

Douglas, who was born Issur Danielovitch to poor, Jewish immigrants from Russia. Douglas portrays Hans Müller, a former entertainer and the survivor of a concentration camp, who has recently arrived at a displaced persons camp in Israel. Unlike many of his fellow émigrés, Müller is unable to settle in his new country, as he is suffering from survivor's guilt and what is now known as post-traumatic stress disorder. He confuses a family for his dead wife and children, runs away from the camp, and accidentally attacks a policeman. Believing the policeman dead, Müller flees deep into Israel with an orphaned teen, Yehoshua (Joseph Walsh), as his only companion. They come across a welcoming kibbutz in northern Israel, where Müller meets the beautiful Ya'El (Milly Vitale) and contemplates settling down, though he believes the police are on his trail.

While *The Juggler* may seem overly simplified to modern-day audiences, it introduced moviegoers to the often painful reality of life for Holocaust survivors and how that coincided with the establishment of Israel as a nation of its own. It touches upon key elements of the experience of a camp survivor, such as poverty, homelessness, and the inevitability for many of staying within a camp structure, as hundreds of thousands of survivors had literally nothing left after the war. References are made to the fact that Müller was in a death camp, not just an internment camp, as he states that his family went to the ovens while he was in solitary confinement—shocking dialogue for 1953. He fears small spaces and authority figures, especially those in uniform, and has become cynical, angry, and paranoid. *The Juggler* is utterly unlike a film such as *The House on Telegraph Hill* (1951), an American film noir about a Holocaust survivor who assumes a dead woman's identity and takes up her life after the war in the U.S., which focused on melodrama, romance, and crime, and primarily used the war narrative as a backdrop. *The Juggler*, on the other hand, is constantly informed by Müller's Holocaust experiences.

The Juggler was a complicated production thanks to political issues. This was the first Hollywood film to be shot on location in Israel, but its director, Edward Dmytryk, was also targeted by McCarthyism. Several years earlier, Dmytryk was named one of the Hollywood Ten, a group of cinema professionals blacklisted for their refusal to testify in front of HUAC about potential communists within Hollywood. He fled to Britain for a time but was prosecuted and imprisoned when he returned to the U.S. Dmytryk eventually consented and testified, which allowed his career to continue, and producer Stanley Kramer—remembered for overtly political works known as "message movies" like *On the Beach* (1959) and *Guess Who's Coming to Dinner* (1967)—gave him a steady stream of low budget films to direct. But most of Dmytryk's career—which spans genres as far afield as drama, romance, film noir, westerns, and more—was concerned with the war.

Examples include spy-comedy *Counter-Espionage* (1942); *Seven Miles from Alcatraz* (1942), where escaped American prisoners encounter German spies; Asian-themed films *Behind the Rising Sun* (1943) and *Back to Bataan* (1945); *Tender Comrade* (1943) about life on the home front; *Cornered* (1945), a film noir about a POW who returns to France to discover the murderer of his French Resistance-member wife; *Till the End of Time* (1946) and *Where Love Has Gone* (1964), about former soldiers adjusting to home life; *So Well Remembered* (1947) and *The End of the Affair* (1955), set in England; and later war films like *Eight Iron Men* (1952), *The Caine Mutiny* (1954), *The Young Lions* (1958), and *Anzio* (1968).

In addition to *The Juggler*, Dmytryk made three earlier, highly political films with war themes: *Hitler's Children* (1943), *Crossfire* (1947), and *The Sniper* (1952). *Hitler's*

Children was a propaganda piece that presented the awful reality of the Hitler Youth organization and depicted some surprisingly graphic situations. The American protagonist (the innocent-looking Bonita Granville of *The Children's Hour* and *Nancy Drew*) is a young woman who lives and works in Germany, until she is imprisoned in a concentration camp, threatened with sterilization, whipped, and eventually shot to death. The less propagandistic and more complex *Crossfire* follows an anti–Semitic soldier, Montgomery (Robert Ryan), who kills a Jewish man (Sam Levene) while on leave from the war. A detective (Robert Young) and a sergeant (Robert Mitchum) work together to solve the murder.

The film is based on Richard Brooks' 1945 novel *The Brick Foxhole*. Brooks was a Marine sergeant and worked at Quantico, giving him realistic insight into the lives of career soldiers. Allegedly Robert Ryan, a fellow soldier at the time, helped with the novel's transition into film—and in turn it helped launch his career. A major alteration was that in Brooks' novel, the murder is committed because of homophobia, not anti–Semitism, but the Production Code had a boycott on gay characters. In Dmytryk's autobiography, he explained,

> What is the murder was the main spine of the story and what if the victim was a heterosexual Jew? We could then tell the story of bigotry as it relates to anti–Semitism and, by analogy and implication, the story of all racial hatred as well. Nothing like this had ever been attempted in Hollywood before.[5]

Though this is similar to Elia Kazan's *Gentleman's Agreement* (1947), where a journalist (Gregory Peck) goes undercover as a Jew to write about his experiences, *Crossfire* benefits from its film noir sensibilities. Dmytryk writes, "We had a lot of serious things to say, but how were we going to get people to listen? Simple. Our message was buried within a murder mystery to make it palatable."[6] This tactic of enfolding war themes within genre trappings—which would continue in European films in the '70s—was certainly not limited to film noir. Another early film to follow on the heels of *The Juggler* (1953) was the tragicomedy *Singing in the Dark* (1956), which also highlights the issue of how Judaism and Jewishness functions within the film. This would continue to be a complicated subjection in the European films of the '70s, which were undoubtedly inspired by these early representations of Judaism.

Russian-born Yiddish actor Moishe Oysher starred in *Singing in the Dark*, in his only English-language appearance as Leo, an amnesiac newly arrived in America. After he has a drink of alcohol, he discovers that he can sing and soon finds a job performing in nightclubs. But his memories of Europe begin to return. He remembers that his father was a renowned cantor, and his parents were killed in the Holocaust. Unlike *The Juggler*, which examined trauma and healing within the context of a Jewish community in Israel, *Singing in the Dark* is a strangely comic film about Jewish assimilation into American culture. Oysher speaks English for the first time on screen, Yiddish songs are duly translated, and his Jewish identity is not directly discussed. Instead of relying on the community for healing, his memory is jarred by physical trauma—a gangster-type mugs him—and he seeks the assistance of a psychiatrist.

But the assimilation of *Singing in the Dark* is not about cultural death, or about forgetting, it is concerned with the hope of a new beginning. Lost for years, the film was recently restored by the National Center for Jewish Film and its obscurity—along with that of *The Juggler*—stands as a reminder that Jewish characters and Holocaust themes were largely ignored for decades. Patricia Erens explains that in 1950s cinema "few films featuring Jewish characters are made and in those works appropriated from the Broadway stage, the Jewish characters are so changed they are almost unrecognizable"[7] (228). *The Juggler*, *Singing in the Dark*, and a comic film like *The Goldbergs* (1950), which was adapted from a popular TV show and radio program, represents cinema audiences' limited interactions with Holocaust survivors on screen, but all that changed with the arrest and trial of Adolf Eichmann in 1960.

In American cinema, this would be followed by films like Sidney Lumet's *The Pawnbroker* (1964), about a pawn shop worker, Sol (Rod Steiger), who has survived the Holocaust and is living in New York in utter misery. He is unable to repress the memories of his dead family or his experiences in a concentration camp, and he remains frozen in time. He bitterly rejects attempts at friendship from a co-worker (Jaime Sanchez) and a local woman (Geraldine Fitzgerald). When he learns that his boss (Brock Peters) is using the shop as a front for more illicit businesses, such as prostitution, he begins slowly getting revenge by practically giving money away—setting in motion tragic events that force him to confront his repressed, tragic memories.

But in French cinema, directors were slower to confront anti-Semitism and the legacy of the Holocaust with quite as much trangressiveness. One of the first to do so was the young Claude Berri—born Claude Langmann—with his debut feature as a director and screenwriter, *La vieil homme et l'enfant* (*The Two of Us*, 1967). This tender, affecting film meditates on the relationship between a young Jewish boy, Claude (Alain Cohen), and his adoptive grandfather (Michel Simon), a surly but sweet Frenchman; the film's title literally translates to "the old man and the child." Though more of a conventional drama than a transgressive art film, *The Two of Us* is worth discussing because it began a wave of films to explore similar themes.

Director Claude Berri was born in Paris in 1934 to Jewish immigrants from Romania and Poland and the film is meant to be a loosely autobiographical reflection of his own experiences as a boy during the occupation. *The Two of Us* follows the young Claude's removal from Paris by his parents, who fear that despite frequently relocating and laying low, they will be discovered and deported. Claude is sent to the rural home of a sympathetic friend's aging parents who have no idea he is Jewish. They believe he is merely seeking refuge from dangerous city life. The grandfatherly Pépé is good-natured and comes to love Claude intensely, but he is also representative of the average rural Frenchman of his generation: politically conservative, he worships Marshal Pétain, believes that Jews and communists are responsible for the war, and is anti-Semitic even though he has never actually known as a Jewish person.

The Two of Us is a film that depicts an intense, physically enacted sort of domestic love—not only between the young Claude and his parents, but between Claude and his adoptive grandparents. While physical and verbal affection is relatively rare between fathers and sons in English-language films, here it is abundant, and it serves three purposes. First, it offers a wordless explanation for why Claude's parents want to send him away without much additional exposition: their love for him causes them to fear constantly for his life. He's a young enough child that he can't understand that the family has to hide their identity and he can't comprehend the risks that come from him acting and playing like a normal boy. The love all around him is also a subtle reminder of the fundamental injustice of prejudice; Claude is an innocent and genuinely lovable child. He cannot help being Jewish and Berri demonstrates repeatedly throughout the film that he often isn't sure what being Jewish even means. He becomes afraid that it means he is bad or monstrous.

Finally, the love Pépé feels for Claude serves as a way to redeem an anti-Semitic character and to make him relatable. He claims to hate Jews and—ironically—blames the war on them, but it becomes clear that he's merely regurgitating accepted local views. In other words, he's full of hot air and these beliefs don't seem to hold a lot of personal weight. He, and the many Frenchmen he is meant to symbolize, represent an older, conservative generation largely removed from urban life and political events. Pépé and his ilk live safe, comfortable lives in the country, where they are sheltered from the suffering of Nazi persecution. He proudly hangs a photograph of Marshal Pétain in his living room but comes to admit that maybe the time for his way of life, his way of thinking, has passed.

Countries like Holland, Denmark, and even Hungary sought to protect their Jewish citizens, where France was not so kind. Proportionally, compared to Eastern European countries like Poland, a larger percentage of Jewish citizens survived; but the Vichy government enacted its own anti-Semitic laws and directly aided in the deaths of over 75,000 French Jews. Despite incidents of anti-Semitism, in the interwar period it was known as a place of tolerance, resulting in thousands of Jews immigrating to the country from Eastern and Central Europe, who thought they would be safe there. But by the '30s, a strain of anti-Semitism took hold in more conservative groups, like the Catholic Church, right wing political parties, and the military. Some, as in the United States, feared Jewish immigrants more out of a sense of xenophobia and the belief that anyone relocating from a foreign country could be a spy.

While it may seem incomprehensible that some blamed World War II on any Jews,

Claude (Alain Cohen) comforts Pépé (Michel Simon) in *The Two of Us* (*Le vieil homme et l'enfant*, Production Artistique et Cinématographique [PAC]/Renn Productions/Valoria Films, 1967).

the French people Pépé represents were often caught up in public opinion and were reacting to the memory of political leaders like Prime Minister Léon Blum, who was both Jewish and socialist. For his troubles, the Vichy government Blum so opposed arrested him and had him sent to the Buchenwald concentration camp, though against the odds, he survived and continued to be a force for good in French politics. The leader of the Vichy government, Marshal Pétain, who so many like Pépé idolized, was a celebrated World War I military hero. He was 84 when he took office and those scrambling to find a strong leader followed his example. Taking up a collaborationist policy with the Nazi occupying forces would have been bad enough, but Pétain and the Vichy government were actively anti-Semitic in many of their policies.

The Jews who sought safety in "free" France were stripped of their professions, possessions, and finances in many cases. Pétain's government greedily set up organizations like the Commission for Jewish Affairs to ensure stolen Jewish property would go to the French government, rather than the Nazi occupiers. Thousands of Jews, including young children, were rounded up, arrested, and sent to French internment camps like those at Drancy, Gurs, and Le Vernet—where many of them were then sent on to their deaths at Auschwitz. Fortunately, public opinion began to change by 1944 and French citizens intervened to help to hide their Jewish countrymen and immigrants alike.

The practice of hiding Jews and particularly Jewish children in the French countryside became commonplace. Some of these children were hidden in the northern, occupied zone, while the majority of them were concealed in the south. This was often a highly secret operation, with concealed records of the children's original names, their new names, and the location of their new homes. An example of this can be found in the life story of one of France's most popular musicians and a filmmaker in his own right, Serge Gainsbourg. His parents were Jewish Russian immigrants who had relocated to Paris after the Russian Revolution, but who fled the city for the French countryside thanks to forged papers. This is one example out of thousands. The Jewish Telegraphic Agency archive reports:

> After July, 1942, when the Germans suddenly swooped down on the Jewish quarter of Paris and arrested 20,000 women and children, the remaining Jews began the underground task of hiding youngsters. While many families managed, individually, to place their children with French families, three organizations undertook mass placement. They were the OSE the Jewish Health Society—the Federation of Jewish Societies and the Zionist Youth Organization.[8]

Children were certainly not the only people attempting to escape into the countryside during the war. More French filmmakers would explore this subject into the '70s, particularly in the wake of what is possibly the most important French World War II film of the period: Marcel Ophuls' *Le chagrin et la pitié* (*The Sorrow and the Pity*, 1969). Ophuls' explosive documentary was commissioned for French television but was rejected when Ophuls unveiled his final work. Running at over four hours, a combination of dozens of interviews and archival footage explore the extent of French collaboration during the Nazi occupation and possible reasons for why it occurred. The two parts of the film focus on opposing figures: part one on Pierre Mendès France, a leftist Jewish fighter with the Free French Air Force and briefly Prime Minister of France; part two on Christian de la Mazière, a fascist journalist and aristocrat who served in the Vichy military and joined the Waffen-SS.

The Sorrow and the Pity wasn't shown in France until 1981, over a decade after its completion, and presents a scathing view of French anti-Semitism. Like Claude Lanzmann's later documentary, *Shoah*, critics of Ophuls' film said that *The Sorrow and the Pity* was too one-sided and twisted facts to fit his narrative, but in the decades since its release, it has come to be regarded as one of the greatest documentaries made about France's role in the war. The German-French Ophuls was the son of celebrated director Max Ophüls. Though born in Frankfurt, the young Ophuls and his Jewish family fled Germany in 1933 and resettled in France. They hid out in the free zone before escaping to Spain and eventually the U.S., where they lived out the war. By 1950, Ophuls returned to France and became a filmmaker. Though he first focused on more mainstream fictional films, the majority of his career has been focused on war crimes and war-related social injustice.

Ophuls direct, precise method of interviewing doesn't lack humor or empathy, but does rip away the veil of myth and fantasy covering the collective French memory about the country's role in the Holocaust. A sense that runs throughout the film is not that France was inherently evil or anti-Semitic, but that people—especially rural Frenchmen—were the product of their environments. Many were trying to do their best to survive the war, but fell prey to ignorance and prejudice, particularly related to Jews taking over their society or invasion by the Soviets. The true theme of *The Sorrow and the Pity* is the banality of collaboration; Ophuls suggests that it was a regular, everyday occurrence often without deeper philosophical or moral motivations. For many, it was just the obvious thing to do. As a result, Ophuls shows that the individuals who joined the Resistance and fought for their lives—especially in the early years of the war—were a minority in a hostile environment.

This overarching theme began to appear more frequently in French cinema in the

Archival footage of Hitler in Paris from *The Sorrow and the Pity* (*Le chagrin et la pitié*, Télévision Rencontre/Société Suisse de Radiodiffusion et Télévision [SSR]/Norddeutscher Rundfunk [NDR], 1969).

wake of *The Sorrow and the Pity*. In the '70s, in particular, was a wave of films that focused romantic plots but examined how collaboration and resistance affected French life. An early example of this is Pierre Granier-Deferre's *Le train* (*The Last Train*, 1973). Julien (Jean-Louis Trintignant), a radio repairman living in a village near the Belgian border, is forced to flee home with his pregnant wife (Nike Arrighi) and young child—and the rest of their community—when the Germans invade. They board a crowded train and Julien is separated from his family; women, children, and the elderly are allowed in the more comfortable first cars, while everyone else is jammed into cattle cars. It is there that Julian meets Anna (Romy Schneider), who comes to rely on him for protection. They soon begin a romantic relationship, and it is ultimately revealed that Anna is a German Jew on the run for her life.

Both Julian and Anna are aware there is a time limit to their love; Anna knows Julian's pregnant wife is on the train and later has been removed safely to a village hospital. But that doesn't prevent them from taking solace in each other. Anna's Jewishness is barely addressed and it really only serves two purposes: first, to give an explanation for why she is traveling alone despite the obvious danger. For example, on the train ride, she is threatened with sexual violence from another passenger. It also establishes that she and Julian are opposites. He is from a small village, has never traveled, and seems quiet and naive, though good-hearted. Anna reveals herself to be well-educated, sophisticated, and has traveled the world.

The Last Train doesn't go in depth on the complexities of their relationship or their differences, rather it uses the war as a way of bringing disparate people together for a passionate and somewhat melodramatic romantic encounter. When they finally arrive at the village where Julian's wife is recovering from childbirth, they know they must part. As a last act of love, Julian accompanies Anna to the local police station and claims that she is his wife but has lost her papers, meaning she can get new, false papers asserting that she is French, not German Jewish. Years later, just at the end of the war, they run into each other in a Gestapo-run interrogation, where Anna has been detained for her role in the Resistance. Julian is called in to ask about her identity papers and pretends not to know her, until he finally gives in to his feelings and betrays himself. The film ends ambiguously, but with the implication that both Anna and Julian will be punished.

There are other romantic films from the same period with a similar theme: that love or at least sexual desire can inspire people to overcome differences or prejudices, to abandon principles, and to risk their own lives. For example, in *Le sauveur* (*The Savior*, 1971) a teenage girl (Muriel Catalá) in the countryside secretly rescues a stranded British officer (Horst Buchholz), despite the fact that she and her family worship Marshal Pétain and respect the Germans. She falls in love with him but comes to learn that he's actually a Nazi and is quite cruel, which causes her to rethink her views.

A particularly important example is Louis Malle's groundbreaking *Lacombe, Lucien* (1974). A 17-year-old Lucien (Pierre Blaise) tries to join the local Resistance branch in rural Normandy but is turned away with the excuse that he's too young and inexperienced. One evening he accidentally winds up at the nearby headquarters of the Carlingue, French police who worked for the Gestapo and other Nazi branches like the SS. Out of anger, Lucien points them towards the Resistance leader who rejected him, and they decide to offer Lucien employment. His position includes newfound power, an outlet for violence, a sense of purpose in his life for the first time, and something of a de facto family—including father figures which he lacked as his own father is missing as a prisoner of war. This is disrupted when he falls in love with France (Aurore Clément), the sophisticated Jewish daughter of a tailor (Holger Löwenadler) hired by the Carlingue. Lucien decides to save France and her family, who are trying to escape to Spain.

After *The Sorrow and the Pity*, *Lacombe, Lucien* was one of the first films to present such an overt depiction of collaboration in France. Lucien is not a particularly likable figure, but he is sympathetic because of his youth, because he lacks education or a solid understanding of the overall political situation, and because he has no clear parental guidance or purpose in life. Malle makes it seem inevitable that the Carlingue would offer him a place in the world. Leah Hewitt writes,

> It can be argued that, for the general public in the 1970s, *Lacombe Lucien* had a greater impact in changing the understanding/memory of the past than *The Sorrow and the Pity*. Malle's film was seen by more spectators, and as a feature film, captured the public's imagination through the highly provocative story of a rough adolescent peasant, Lucien Lacombe, who, more by accident than by conscious choice, ends up on the wrong side, as a thug working for the German police in 1944. Although Ophüls's use of numerous interwoven interviews from the present, and actual film clips from the Occupation, was no doubt highly effective as a political critique of collaboration and Pétainism, the controversial allure of Malle's storytelling goes a step further.[9]

It should be stressed that Lucien's relationship with France is a fundamentally problematic one; it is not the innocent, wistful longing found in so many tales of teenage romance. Lucien essentially forces himself on France and while their sexual relationship seems consensual, there is a coercive, invasive quality to his courtship. He first enters her household when a Carlingue leader brings him there to have the tailor make Lucien a suit, on the grounds that it is more appropriate attire than his farm boy clothes. During his fitting, Lucien spies France and if it is not love at first sight, it is at least attraction.

His attempted courtship is forceful but naive; he brings her flowers and calls her "chérie." He shows up unannounced and assumes he will be given a dinner invitation and that he will later be allowed to take her to a party. His romantic pursuit can be chalked up to inexperience and immaturity, though he does use his position with the Carlingue to get her attention. She gives in to his advances, against her father's wishes, but Lucien does genuinely seem to care for her. At the end of the film, when a Resistance attack on the town results in a massacre, his first thought is to run away with her deeper into the countryside where she can be safe. Despite this good deed, the closing credits announce that at the end of the war, he was executed for collaborating with the Nazis.

Not much is made of France's Jewishess within the film. As in *The Last Train*, it is expressed merely as a contrast to the protagonist: the male lead is awkward, uneducated, and rural, while his Jewish love interest is sophisticated, well educated, and urban. In other words, the purpose of both of these films is not to explore Jewishness, but to examine the non–Jewish, French motivations for either collaboration with the Germans or sympathy with their victims. As Hewitt writes, "*Lacombe, Lucien*'s power lies in a dramatic fiction that seems opaque on moral issues, and as such, makes it a lightning rod for political discussions dealing with commitment, free choice, and collaboration."[10]

Michel Drach's *Les violons du bal* (*Violins at the Ball*, 1974) is an inversion of these themes, but is far more conventional and less transgressive. The highly autobiographical film cuts between Drach's childhood during World War II with his present (where he is played by actor Jean-Louis Trintignant) as a director trying to make a movie about his own life. Unlike *Lacombe, Lucien*, which highlights collaboration and explains how and

Lucien (Pierre Blaise) watches France (Aurore Clément) bathe nymph-like in a forest stream as they flee fascist violence in *Lacombe, Lucien* (Nouvelles Éditions de Films [NEF])/Universal Pictures/Vides-Film, Rome/Hallelujah Films, 1974).

why it could happen, particularly to young men, *Violins at the Ball* casts a rosy, nostalgic view of the war. In the film, Drach's family goes into hiding and then escapes to Switzerland, but the focus is more on the beautiful landscape than any emotional tension. A certain fairy tale-like quality removes the tone of violence and dread that always lingers in *Lacombe, Lucien*.

A similar theme is dealt with more subtly in *Les Guichets du Louvre* (*Black Thursday*, 1974), where a student (Christian Rist) learns that Jews in Paris are going to be arrested and tries to save a series of strangers, but no one will believe him. This film from Bulgarian-born director Michel Mitrani is reminiscent of *Lacombe, Lucien* in the sense that it focuses on a gentile French boy as its protagonist—played by first-time actors in both films—with Jewish characters in the background. *Black Thursday* is a fairly conventional drama, but it is worth mentioning because of the outrage it caused upon its release; it was the first film to depict a mass arrest of Jews in Paris perpetrated not by the Nazis, but by the French themselves.

This tragic event is known as the Rafle du Vel d'Hiv. On July 16 and 17 of 1942, the French police assisted the Nazis in a roundup of more than 13,000 Jews, including thousands of children and even babies, who were left without food or water in overcrowded, unsanitary conditions in the Vélodrome d'Hiver (or "Winter stadium"). They were shipped to Auschwitz along with other Jews from Nazi internment camps in France, such as Drancy and Pithiviers, were they were murdered. Out of the more than 40,000 Jews sent to Auschwitz, less than a thousand would return after the war.

French police and government employees were actively involved in this attempt to wipe out France's Jews, despite the fact that many were deeply integrated into French society—in fact, most of the French Jews killed during the Holocaust were foreigners who had resettled in France to escape the initial years of Nazism. Though no religious register had been kept since the mid–19th century, French police enthusiastically complied with Nazi requests and began forcing Jews to register. Though there were smaller prior deportations, Adolf Eichmann himself collaborated on the plan for Vel d'Hiv.

This event is primarily important because it speaks to the reality faced by French Jews but especially foreign Jews seeking asylum in France during the war years. This contrasts with the stories adopted by France during and after the war, of *fraternité*, widespread revolt, and Resistance membership. Julian Jackson writes, "Vichy shed no tears over the fate of the foreign Jews in France, who were seen as a nuisance, 'dregs (*déchets*)' in Laval's words. He told an American diplomat that he was 'happy' to have a chance to get rid of them."[11] This wasn't depicted in French films really until the '70s, after *The Sorrow and the Pity* (1969), in films like Joseph Losey's *Mr. Klein* (1976).

Robert Klein (Alain Delon) is a well-off art dealer in wartime Paris. By 1942, his profits had been bountiful because he profited off of Jews fleeing the country, selling off valuable art for much less than what it is actually worth. The Catholic-identifying Klein says he pities his clients, but becomes enraged when a Jewish newspaper—addressed to Robert Klein—shows up on his doorstep. He contacts the local police to convince them that he is not Jewish and realizes that another man named Robert Klein, who is Jewish, is targeting him for some reason. His hunt for the other Klein becomes increasingly obsessive, while the police begin to suspect that he himself is actually Jewish. When Klein and his lawyer (Michael Lonsdale) fail to immediately produce proof that Klein is Catholic and Alsatian, he begins to quietly sell off his property and prepare to escape—while continuing his search for the second Klein. It leads him right into a Nazi roundup where Jews are being loaded into boxcars heading for Auschwitz, in a loose reenactment of the Rafle du Vel d'Hiv.

Though Robert begins the film as a collaborator with no clear moral code, content to profit off of the misery of others, he soon learns that he can't trust anyone, not even his lawyer, his lovers, or his previously unshakable family line. Losey, responsible for controversial films like *The Boy with the Green Hair* (1948), *The Prowler* (1951), and *The Servant* (1963), had studied with Brecht in Germany and made *Mr. Klein* while he was blacklisted from Hollywood and in many way, *Mr. Klein* is the story of a hunted outsider wrongly accused. In David Caute's Joseph Losey biography, he writes,

> Losey's life embraces a major crisis in political commitment (the 1930s) and public tolerance (the blacklist); his career; his *oeuvre*, spans the most fundamental cultural confrontation of the century—between Marxism and Modernism, between progressive "realism" and the avant-garde subversion of optimism.[12]

Allegedly inheriting the project from French-Greek director Costa-Gavras, Losey made *Mr. Klein* while waiting for a Proust collaboration with Harold Pinter to materialize. Though the latter remains sadly un-filmed, *Mr. Klein* is one of Losey's enduring masterpieces, a surreal, absurd, and occasionally humorous work of great visual beauty, existential terror, and a sense of dread that does not fade with the closing credits. While the film could easily be read as an allegory for Losey's own encounters with American fascism in the guise of McCarthyism and his lengthy exile from his home country, it is also an effective thriller and a frank exploration of persecution in World War II France.

This was Losey's second collaboration with French actor Alain Delon after *The Assassination of Trotsky* (1972). The handsome Delon made a name for himself outside

Robert Klein (Alain Delon) searches for another Robert Klein in *Mr. Klein* (Lira Films/Adel Productions/Nova Films, 1976).

of the usual leading man romantic roles with frequent appearances in art house films like *Rocco e i suoi fratelli* (*Rocco and His Brothers*, 1960), *L'Eclisse* (1962), *La piscine* (*The Swimming Pool*, 1969), and *La prima notte di quiete* (*Indian Summer*, 1972), and especially crime films, such as *Le cercle rouge* (1970), *Un flic* (1972), and many more. In his key roles—such as *Plein soleil* (*Purple Noon*, 1960) and *Le samouraï* (1967)—he was cast as a murderer. With his aloof, icy stare, Delon often played morally ambiguous characters on both sides of the law—perfect qualities for the charismatic yet dubious Klein.

Coincidentally, a few years before *Mr. Klein*, Delon was cast as tormented man and his diabolical double in *Histoires extraordinaires* (*Spirits of the Dead*, 1968), an art house anthology that adapted three of Edgar Allen Poe's tales. Director Louis Malle chose Poe's "William Wilson" about a student and his doppelgänger. Published in *Tales of the Grotesque and Arabesque* in 1839, it prefigures much of *Mr. Klein*'s plot. While the titular William Wilson meets his double in his youth, it is implied that the second Wilson exists to remind the first that his wealthy and aristocratic pretensions will be his downfall. Much of the story surrounds issues of class and morality. Like the characters in Poe's "Masque of the Red Death," Wilson is a privileged man who uses his advantages in life to become increasingly debauched. The double returns when he begins acting immorally—cheating at cards, seducing a married woman—and his persistent interventions incite the frustrated Wilson to murder his double, only to realize that he has also slaughtered himself.

Mr. Klein takes many aspects of this, for example, Klein's double as psychic retribution for his war profiteering. The second Klein first appears when he cheats a victimized Jew fleeing the country, giving him a low price for 17th century Dutch painter Adriaen van Ostade's "Portrait of a Gentleman." It is this portrait—itself a sort of double—that acts as a paradigm shift for Klein. Like Alice's descent into a bizarre, illogical world in Lewis Carroll's *Alice's Adventures in Wonderland*, the painting of a "gentleman" tilts

Klein's world. His aristocratic body—not unlike that of the painting—becomes a site of anxiety, existential horror, and asserts that identity itself is mutable, unstable.

The film's opening foreshadows this terror. An anonymous middle-aged woman is being examined by a cold, unfriendly doctor who handles her body roughly. He forces her to strip naked and performs a surprisingly brutal examination to decide whether or not she is Jewish—and the unspoken implication is that this examination will decide her fate. The results are inconclusive, though she hides this from her husband, who she meets after the invasive appointment. When the film cuts to Klein's purchase of the painting, it is impossible to avoid drawing a parallel between the two. Jennifer Lynde Barker writes,

> He soon begins to feel a powerful connection to the painting he buys at the beginning of the film, a portrait by Adriaen van Ostade brought from Holland by the seller's family. The Dutch "portrait of a gentleman" gazes out at the world, holding a magnifying glass, seeming to invite us to look more closely, though we are denied any close-ups of the painting.[13]

This painting is not the only symbolic figure in the film. Klein's apartment is full of mirrors, portraits, and sculptures. He is both defined and haunted by these artifacts, which he uses to assert his sense of taste, wealth, and class. Even art objects shown elsewhere in the film begin to symbolize him. Christopher Weedman writes, "Losey visually implies Klein's dual identity as a predator and a victim in the recurring image of a tapestry depicting a vulture pierced through the heart by an arrow."[14]

His body also becomes confused with the elusive second Robert Klein. Barker writes, "Their bodies become interchangeable throughout the course of the film; others remark on their likeness and they even share possessions—the razor and the dog."[15] In a telling scene, Klein is summoned at a restaurant by his double. He is told the second man greatly resembles him and he is disoriented after seeing his own reflection in a mirror and confuses himself for the second Klein. Set up like a thriller or murder mystery, Klein's quest becomes not just about physically locating the second man but unraveling the mystery about his own identity. His allegedly stable life has been thrown into chaos by the mere delivery of a newspaper.

This absurdist element evokes Kafka, and the film can be seen as a bridge between Poe's "William Wilson" and Kafka's unfinished novel *Das Schloß* (*The Castle*, 1926). The novel follows K., a land surveyor who arrives in a village—because he has been hired—and learns he needs permission to live and work there. He seeks out the unseen authorities residing in a nearby castle, but is never able to reach them. It's believed that Kafka intended to end the novel with K's death coinciding with receipt of a letter from the Castle giving him special permission to stay in the village.

The Castle's influence on *Mr. Klein* has been noted by many film scholars. Annette Insdorf writes, "*Mr. Klein* enters a truly Kafkaesque realm, more hallucinatory than historical. It seems no coincidence that the title brings to mind 'Mr. K.,' for Losey depicts an absurd universe of paranoia where the antagonists remain nameless and faceless."[16] While Poe's Wilson is essentially his own worst enemy, Klein—like Kafka's K.—becomes sympathetic because he is also a victim of the bureaucratic machine, where guilt is assumed and innocence must be proven against seemingly insurmountable odds. For Klein, ironically, his innocence (his non-Jewishness) is only clearly established by the state once he has accepted death, as in the presumed ending of *The Castle*.

In Hannah Arendt's *The Jew as Pariah*, she reads *The Castle* as a modern interpretation of the tale of the Wandering Jew, the "despised pariah Jew, dismissed by contemporary society as a nobody."[17] Like Jews under Nazi rule, K. is stripped of legal residence—the fundamental right to live, work, and own property—by the totalitarian powers at work in the Castle. This state reflected the life of thousands of refugees wandering the world between World War I and World War II—many of them Jews. As Isak Winkel Holm explains,

> According to Arendt, the masses of allegedly superfluous persons—refugees, expatriates, deported aliens, stateless persons and displaced persons—spelled out the need for a basic human right, namely the right to live as a rights bearing member of society and not, as K., to live in a normative vacuum outside the bounds of law.[18]

As is evident in *Mr. Klein*, Kafka's writing seems uniquely prescient, despite the fact that he passed away in 1924 of complications from tuberculosis. In a letter to Jewish historian Gershom Scholem, Walter Benjamin writes that Kafka's typical protagonist was a "modern citizen who realizes that his fate is being determined by an impenetrable bureaucratic apparatus whose operation is controlled by procedures which remain shadowy even to those carrying out its orders and *a fortiori* to those being manipulated by it."[19] Holocaust survivor Primo Levi writes, "Kafka understands the world (his, and even better, ours of today) with a clairvoyance that astonishes and wounds."[20] But Kafka is only one out of a long-standing tradition of European absurdist writers whose work provides context for many of the 20th century's atrocities: World War I, World War II, the Holocaust, Soviet oppression, and atomic terror. Absurdist literature became a way to deal with totalitarian repression—under both Nazi and Soviet rule—and in the '70s, it found an odd resurgence in films directly or obliquely about the war and the Holocaust, such as *Mr. Klein*.

Precursors to this loose movement can be found in 19th century Russia in such works as Nikolai Gogol's short story "The Nose" (1836) and Dostoyevsky's novella *The Double* (1866). The later Polish writer Bruno Schulz wrote in this vein with short story collections like *The Cinnamon Shops* (1934) and *The Hourglass Sanatorium* (1937); he also helped translate *The Trial* into Polish for the first time. Many of his works were destroyed during the Holocaust and Schulz himself was shot to death by a Nazi while returning to a ghetto in 1942. The concept of the absurd began to gain critical, philosophical ground in that same year when Albert Camus published *The Myth of Sisyphus*, about man's choice to survive or commit suicide in the face of an ultimately meaningless and absurd world.

Kafka and Schulz were by no means the only Eastern Europeans writing in this vein to have died before the worst years of the war. Other examples include Czech writer and artist Karel Čapek, who introduced the word "robot" in his science fiction, and writer, artist, and philosopher Stanisław Ignacy Witkiewicz. Russian surrealist writer Daniil Kharms rebelled against Soviet realism and would have had his work destroyed if it had not been hidden by friends. He died in a psychiatric hospital in 1942 during the Nazi's siege of Leningrad. It is the world of these men and others like them that began to be associated with anti-fascist, anti-totalitarian sentiments through the use of the absurd—a mix of satire, black humor, and existential horror.

It was also bound up with Jewish culture, as many of these writers were Jewish, which inevitably also made its way into the United States during the wartime and postwar migrations. Avner Ziv writes, "Black humor, coming to the American canon of letters after World War II, may have some of its deepest roots not in our literary traditions but rather in a tradition we think of as Eastern European … the fool-as-protagonist; and more precisely, the *shtetl* tradition of the *schlemiel* and the *schlimazel*."[21] *Shtetl* refers to small, self-reliant, and deeply insular Jewish communities. These were spread all over Europe, particularly Eastern Europe, until they were eradicated by the Nazis. The *schlemiel*, on the other hand, is a Yiddish word describing a person who is unlucky, foolish, or occasionally destructive. *Schlimazel* has a similar meaning but refers specifically to a person who is unlucky, who fate appears to be conspiring against.

One of the most important postwar adaptations of Kafka to introduce some of these cultural themes came from American director and legend Orson Welles, with an adaptation of Kafka's *The Trial* (1962). This French-Italian-German co-production is certainly an indication of the fact that by this time, Welles was driven out of a Hollywood that refused to respect his insistence on creative freedom and his budgetary demands. He believed this was the best of all his films, though it unsurprisingly received a mixed reception and has only been widely viewed as a masterpiece in more recent years. Though it was filmed over a decade before many of the films discussed in this chapter, it is necessary to explore its influence.

Josef K. (Anthony Perkins), a bank employee, is startled one morning when police arrive at his home and declare him under arrest. They won't explain why and do not take him to prison but interrupt his life at random moments and continue to persecute him. Various women in his life suggest he seek advice from figures of authority—such as a lawyer (played by Welles himself)—but soon a priest (Michael Lonsdale) tells him that he's been condemned to death with no hope for appeal. He is brought to a quarry pit by guards, given a knife, and ordered to kill himself.

The Trial presents an evolution of film noir's sense of disorienting style and Dutch angles—which Welles himself helped bring about with *Citizen Kane* (1941)—that

Josef K (Anthony Perkins) is on the run in *The Trial* in a sequence reminiscent of Carol Reed's *The Third Man* (1949) (Le procès, Paris-Europa Productions/HISA-FILMS/Finanziaria Cinematografica Italiana, 1962).

transform the film's universe into a hostile prison slowly closing in on its protagonist for really no reason at all. This sense of the absurd is subtly emphasized by black comedy and sexual menace. Welles heightens the sexual anxiety of Kafka's novel and K. is the target of several women played by glamorous European starlets: Jeanne Moreau, Romy Schneider, and Elsa Martinelli. Welles also expertly cast *Psycho*'s Anthony Perkins. The actor's unique brand of nervous energy, deep emotional tension, and arrogance works perfectly here. K. is not just an unfortunate *schlimazel* and Perkins' inherent sense of disdain prevents the character from becoming truly downtrodden or pathetic.

While Kafka has been posthumously understood as a prophet of fascism and the horrors of war, Welles further manipulated this post-war interpretation of *The Trial*. Anne-Marie Scholz writes,

> After the end of World War Two and the Third Reich, during which time Kafka's works had been banned in Germany, those same works re-entered the Federal Republic (they continued to be banned in East Germany) essentially altered in their original meanings. They had become symbolic of what is still known as "the Kafkaesque," an atmosphere of "Angst," resignation and powerlessness linked with the anxieties of postwar life.[22]

The film's Holocaust and World War II themes are perhaps undeniable, because of both Kafka's text and Welles' postwar interpretation. This was so obvious that a mainstream film critic like Roger Ebert noted it in his review of the film: "Kafka published his novel in Prague in 1925; it reflected his own paranoia, but it was prophetic, foreseeing Stalin's gulag and Hitler's Holocaust, in which innocent people wake up one morning to discover they are guilty of being themselves."[23] Welles may have rearranged some of Kafka's book—adding a prologue and changing the ending—but it remains nightmarish, surreal, and blackly comic. The world of *The Trial* is a place of horrifying alienation.

Thanks to a last-minute stroke of luck, Welles shot significant portions of the film in Paris's Gare d'Orsay train station. Though he filmed all over Europe, he was ironically blocked from shooting in Prague, as the communist government had banned Kafka's work. Instead, Welles transformed the station into an absurdist playground, a place of bureaucratic oppression and physical terror. In an interview about *The Trial*, Welles said the train station

> is a very beautiful location, but it is full of sorrow, the kind of sorrow that only accumulates in a railway station where people wait. I know this sounds terribly mystical, but really a railway station is a haunted place. And the story is all about people waiting, waiting, waiting for their papers to be filled. It is full of the hopelessness of the struggle against bureaucracy. Waiting for a paper to be filled is like waiting for a train, and it's also a place of refugees. People were sent to Nazi prisons from there, Algerians were gathered there, so it's a place of great sorrow. Of course, my film has a lot of sorrow too, so the location infused a lot of realism into the film.[24]

This sorrow is slightly mitigated at the film's conclusion by Welles' alteration of the novel's ending. The K of the novel died "like a dog"; he was dragged to a pit and stabbed in the heart with a knife by guards. Welles' K is ultimately a figure of resistance, laughing in the faces of his would-be executioners and refusing to submit willingly to death. Welles felt that the original ending seemed wrong in a postwar world. He said, "To me that ending is a ballet written by a Jewish intellectual before the advent of Hitler. Kafka wouldn't have put that in after the death of six million Jews. It all seems very much pre–Auschwitz to me."[25]

Mr. Klein seems to have borrowed much from Welles' *The Trial*, including but not limited to the use of an isolated, morally ambiguous protagonist targeted for unknown reasons, the presence of several sexually predatory female characters, an absurdist plot with elements of violence, nihilism, and black comedy, and a striking visual style. *The Trial* also shares these themes with several other films from the '70s, such as director Roman Rolanski's *The Tenant* (1976). Though *The Tenant* is not overtly a film about World War II, it is worth briefly discussing because of its Holocaust subtext.

In *The Tenant*, a man named Trelkovsky (played by Polanski himself) inquires about moving into a newly vacated apartment in Paris. It seems the previous tenant, Simone, jumped from the window in an attempted suicide and badly injured herself. When she dies a few days later, Trelkovsky moves in to find the apartment full of her belongings. His odd neighbors, who are all obsessed with quiet, begin to wear on the passive Trelkovsky. He has a few friends over and receives a complaint about noise. As the days pass, they protest about seemingly any movement he makes, among other things, and he finds a human tooth hidden in his wall. He comes to believe that his neighbors are trying to transform him into Simone, as they increasingly pressure him to adapt her habits. This eventually drives the paranoid Trelkovsky to buy a wig and dress in her clothing. He tries to form a relationship with Simone's friend Stella (Isabelle Adjani), but comes to believe that she is part of his neighbors' conspiracy to drive him mad. Desperate to avoid becoming Simone, his life begins to unravel.

The Tenant is the last film in director Roman Polanski's so-called "Apartment Trilogy," which includes *Repulsion* (1965) and *Rosemary's Baby* (1968). While *Repulsion* is a psychosexual thriller and *Rosemary's Baby* is satanic horror, all three films focus on the growing madness and paranoia an individual experiences in a claustrophobic urban setting. With these films, Polanski explored the unnaturalness of living in a small space and the hazards of postwar city life, particularly the dissolution of identity and the encroachment of society upon the individual. Based on Roland Topor's novel *Le locataire chimerique* (1964), *The Tenant* is yet another film about an outsider contending with issues of identity, privacy, and individual rights. Trelkovsky is seen as a foreigner and constantly has to remind everyone that he is a French citizen, despite his Polish name and pronounced accent. His foreignness increases once he moves into the apartment, where he is ostracized by the other tenants, though it is unclear if this is in his mind or is really happening as he succumbs to insanity.

Though *The Tenant* is not overtly a horror film, it explores the same themes as the rest of Polanski's trilogy, albeit in an absurdist, darkly comic way. Trelkovsky's attempts to follow the rules his neighbors lay down for him are frequently ridiculous. Their obsession with noise becomes contagious, jarring, and invasive. The film could easily be interpreted as a critique against either the Nazi or Soviet governments, as both Polanski and Roland Topor are Holocaust survivors. Born in France in 1938, Topor was the child of Polish Jewish immigrants. Thanks to the French practice of hunting down foreign Jewish refugees—including children—he was hidden by his family in Savoy, near Lake Geneva and the Western Alps. In the postwar years, he went on to form the performance art and theater-based Panic Movement with Spanish writer Fernando Arrabal and Chilean surrealist Alejandro Jodorowsky. He also wrote absurdist novels, made short, animated films, and appeared in art house movies as far afield as Dušan Makavejev's radical *Sweet Movie* (1974) and Werner Herzog's *Nosferatu* (1979), among others.

Polanski was actually born five years earlier, in 1933, also in France to Polish parents. Tragically, the family relocated back to Kraków in 1936 and just a few years later they were forced to move into the Kraków Ghetto. Thanks to his father's efforts, young Roman escaped and fled to a dangerous, isolated existence in the countryside. Though he reunited with his father after the war, his pregnant mother was murdered in Auschwitz. Polanski later mined these terrible experiences in the ghetto for *The Pianist* (2002), the tale of a historical musician who hid in the ghetto and escaped liquidation, but became trapped into a desperate, solitary existence. *The Tenant* is the first reflection of some of these themes. While exploring the connection between the two, Christos Tsiolkas writes,

> Though set in contemporary Paris, the decaying apartment block hauntingly suggests an older Europe. And with a cast of stern and cold septuagenarians in supporting roles—Melvyn Douglas, Lila Kedrova and Jo Van Fleet—the tenants too seem to emerge from a past bourgeois age. Polanski plays Trelkovsky as a wide-eyed and slightly dull man, an innocent like Josef K in Kafka's *The Trial*. His ensuing madness seems to arise not so much from the spectral visions he glimpses through his apartment window at night, but from his inability to fathom his fellow tenants' contempt for him. [...] Trelkovsky's persecution, in its senselessness and cruel persistency, cannot help but suggest the European tragedies of World War II.[26]

And like *The Trial*, many of *The Tenant*'s scenes involve the protagonist's interactions with his neighbors. Neither man is able to afford an independent home and must live in a boarding house or apartment building with invasive, judgmental neighbors. But unlike *The Trial*, where K is told he is guilty of an unspoken crime, Trelkovsky is made to feel guilty simply because he is seen as an outsider. No police officers or magistrates haunt his steps, but his neighbors increasingly control his behavior, eventually forcing him to occupy the same figurative and physical space of the apartment's previous tenant.

This is the second feature where Polanski both starred and directed, including *The Fearless Vampire Killers* (1967), another of his films that played with absurd characters, black humor, and Jewish stereotypes. *The Tenant* is an overwhelmingly physical film and much of Trelkovsky's unease and discomfort are almost taken to the level of slapstick. In the novel, Topor writes, "He was perfectly conscious of the absurdity of his behavior, but he was incapable of changing it. This absurdity was an essential part of him. It was probably the most basic element of his personality."[27] These absurd physical elements transition violently between comedy and horror and the extreme physical elements are akin to body horror films of genre auteurs like David Cronenberg.

The apartment's former tenant, the woman that Trelkovsky's neighbors try to force him to become, is shown primarily as a rigid body in a full body cast. Trelkovsky finds a tooth hidden in a crack in his wall and he begins seeing doubles of himself. He dresses as a woman and speculates whether or not he's pregnant. His own attempted suicide, which mirrors hers directly, is a failed act with ludicrous, comic overtones, where he only breaks a few bones the first time he throws himself out the window and makes the agonizing crawl back up the stairs to finish the job. The relentless dissolution of his identity, his obvious sexual repression, and gender issues drove away conventional moviegoers and horror film fans.

This is certainly one of Polanski's most elusive, unsettling works and it forms odd parallels with *Mr. Klein*. Of *Mr. Klein*, Christopher Weedman writes, "Not only was the film a box office disappointment, but also, echoing the audience reception of the similarly-themed thriller *Le locataire*. [...] French audiences were unsettled by the film's unflattering depiction of French anti–Semitism and xenophobia."[28] In general, these absurdist-influenced films from the '70s used dark humor, farce, the preposterous

8. Innocent Children and Kafkaesque Doubles

situations often found in real-life wartime, and doubles, among other literary tropes. These often uncomfortable films challenge notions of the wartime narrative as a morally black and white playing field divided evenly into victims and perpetrators. They also work to expose the degree of complicity—and anti–Semitism—that spread throughout European society like a cancer, lingering long after 1945.

This trend would not continue into the '80s with the same vigor and while there were several French efforts from this period to depict the experience of Jews in France during World War II, they were generally relegated to the roles of children or secondary characters. Truffaut's *Le dernier métro* (*The Last Metro*, 1980) is a primary example of this. A celebrated Jewish theater owner and director, Lucas (Heinz Bennent), is forced to go in hiding in the basement of his own theater, while his actress wife Marion (Catherine Deneuve) runs the rehearsal of their upcoming play. Their new male lead (Gérard Depardieu) is secretly a member of the Resistance and Marion develops an attraction to him.

Though brilliant German actor Heinz Bennent is memorable as Lucas, the Jewish theater owner, he is a character literally relegated to the shadows and the film's focus is much more on Marion's experience. But Lucas going into hiding is less an exploration of the way Jewish identity was suppressed during the war and more of a plot device to allow a love triangle to develop. Truffaut does put more focus on anti-Semitism than earlier films mentioned in this chapter. The film's primary antagonist is influential theater critic Daxiat (Jean-Louis Richard), who claims to admire Lucas but is very vocal about his support of the Nazis and his hatred of Jews. He slams their latest play in a review and attempts to take the theater away from Marion. This reflects a much more mainstream approach to war narratives than many of the other films in the chapter. For example, the central characters may not be aware of each other's secrets, activities, or politics, but they are all essentially working in unison against the Nazis, who are uniformly presented as evil.

Comedies from this period tackled similar themes, like *L'As des as* (*Ace of Aces*, 1982). In the film, Jean-Paul Belmondo plays a champion boxer who rescues a Jewish boy and his entire family during the 1936 Olympics. This is essentially an action-comedy meant to highlight Belmondo's stunt work (mostly performed by the actor himself) and the function of the Jewish characters is to make Belmondo, the "regular" Frenchman, seem heroic—he is willing to sacrifice his life and his career to save a Jewish child. This is a film intended for mainstream audiences and as a comedy, the subject matter is handled in a fundamentally light-hearted manner where Frenchmen are heroes and Nazis are villains.

One final film worth mentioning is Louis Malle's *Au revoir les enfants* (*Goodbye, Children*, 1987), where the director returned to the early '40s and mined his own experiences as a boy. Malle went to a Catholic boarding school near Paris, where he befriended a Jewish student—one of a few at the school. Malle was forced to watch the Gestapo arrest his friend, other Jewish students, and a Jewish teacher, who were all deported to Auschwitz. The school's headmaster, active Resistance member Père Jacques, was arrested for trying to shelter the students and sent to Mauthausen, among other concentration camps. Because of the treatment he endured there, he died shortly after liberation.

This experience directly inspired *Goodbye, Children*, which follows a young student, Julien (Gaspard Manesse), who develops a reluctant friendship with Jean (Raphaël Fejtő), a new arrival at boarding school. Soon Julien learns that Jean is Jewish and, along with a few other students, is secretly being hidden by the school's headmaster (Philippe

Morier-Genoud). Eventually the boys are betrayed by a kitchen worker at the school and Julien is forced to watch the Gestapo take his friend and the other Jewish children away. The headmaster is arrested and the school is closed down.

This well-received and relatively mainstream affair is a marked departure from *Lacombe, Lucien*, in part because *Goodbye, Children* was released a decade later, after France had begun to accept its real role in the occupation. Like *The Two of Us*, dialogue throughout the film reveals that anyone who is anti-Semitic has this prejudice out of ignorance or because it is a popularly held opinion. While *Goodbye, Children* does depict some characters as being anti-Semitic—or at least willing to turn a blind eye to the Nazi treatment of Jews—it is mostly about innocence lost and the young protagonist learning the importance of judging people on their own merits. Jean becomes Julien's closest friend at school, for example. But Malle does not necessarily ask the audience to identify with Jean or any of the other Jewish characters and this is more of a somber coming of age film than a fully fledged war drama. As the years passed since the release of Ophuls' incendiary documentary, *The Sorrow and the Pity*, more films set during the war became similarly concerned with stirring the heartstrings and less about examining French identity and the legacy of its role in World War II.

9

Apocalyptic Visions
The Holocaust on Screen in Poland

"And when he had opened the fourth seal, I heard the voice of the fourth beast say, Come and see! And I looked, and behold a pale horse: and his name that sat on him was Death, and Hell followed with him. And power was given unto them over the fourth part of the earth, to kill with sword, and with hunger, and with death, and with the beasts of the earth."—*The Apocalypse of John*, Chapter 6 (7–8)

Polish cinema requires its own discussion separate from the films of the Soviet Union for several reasons: not only cultural and language differences, but because of Poland's key role in the war, which can be simplified into two major points. First, the invasion of the country by *both* Nazi and Soviet forces in September of 1939 marks the official beginning of World War II. Second, it was the site the Nazis chose to house their extermination camps, with the largest and most notorious of these, Auschwitz, as the enduring symbol of the horrors of the Holocaust. Polish Jews were nearly wiped out as a result of Nazi actions in their country—90 percent of their population was murdered—though the Nazi campaign of genocide was also extended to the Polish people in general. Nearly a quarter of the country's inhabitants were killed in the war, roughly six million people.

Hitler and Nazi leadership did not seek a policy of collaboration with Poland, as they did with many other occupied countries; they were determined to murder or enslave the majority of Poland's population in order to make room for German expansion, and because they believed that Poles were racially inferior. Poland was disbanded as a country and the Nazis established the *Generalgouvernement*, a zone in central Poland that was essentially a satellite of the Reich, to be run by Hans Frank. Poland was a major site of resistance, including the Polish government in exile which operated out of London, the partisan fighters of the underground *Armia Krajowa* or Home Army, and organized Jewish resistance. Poland was also the site of some of the worst violence of the war, some of which were in response to this widespread resistance. Next to Belarus, Poland was home to arguably the worst atrocities of the European theater. This began with Soviet executions and deportations in the '30s under Stalin and continued on with the systematic annihilation of higher levels of Polish society, the establishment of Jewish ghettos, concentration camps, and extermination camps, a mass starvation policy, the 1944 Warsaw Uprising—the largest resistance operation in all of Europe during the war—and its horrific aftermath.

The situation in Poland is unique compared to the other countries of Nazi-occupied Europe and includes the sort of horrors not typically taught in English-speaking classrooms. In *Bloodlands: Europe Between Hitler and Stalin*, Timothy Snyder argues that the death camps are a more recognizable but relatively small portion of the mass violence in Eastern Europe, particularly Poland. Though the majority of the country's Jewish population was killed, so were millions of non–Jewish Poles, who were targeted not only by the Nazis but also by Soviet Russian forces. For example, Snyder notes that "by a conservative estimate, some eighty-five thousand Poles were executed in 1937 and 1938"[1]—before the war had even broken out.

Unlike countries such as Austria or Czechoslovakia, who acquiesced to Nazi occupation, Polish forces fought back, resulting in violent reprisals from the early days of the war. Invading forces left brutality in their wake, including mass executions by firing squad, as well as more grisly actions. Snyder writes,

> German soldiers had been instructed that Poland was not a real country, and that its army was not a real army. Thus the men resisting the invasion could not be real soldiers. German officers instructed their troops that the death of Germans in battle was "murder." Since resisting the German master race was, in Hitler's terminology, "insolence," Polish soldiers had no right to be treated as prisoners of war. In the village of Urycz, Polish prisoners of war were gathered into a barn, where they were told they would spend the night. Then the Germans burned it down.[2]

The widespread rape, slaughter, and burning of Poland was largely carried out by Reinhard Heydrich, head of the *Sicherheitsdienst* or SD, the Nazi Security Service, and the *Einsatzgruppe*. These were largely non-military actions; in other words, trained soldiers attacked and massacred civilian populations, both Jewish and non–Jewish, razing entire communities to the ground. As Snyder states, "By the time the gas chamber and crematoria complexes at Birkenau came on line in spring 1943, more than three quarters of the Jews who would be killed in the Holocaust were already dead."[3] This included mass shootings in the east, more limited medical euthanasia programs and mobile gas vans, death from illness and overwork in concentration camps, and *then* the development of dedicated killing centers located within Nazi-occupied Poland: Auschwitz-Birkenau, Bełżec, Chełmno, Majdanek, Sobibór, and Treblinka. But as Snyder notes, "The gas chambers allowed the policy pursued in the occupied Soviet Union, the mass killing of Jews, to be continued west of the Molotov-Ribbentrop line. The vast majority of Jews killed in the Holocaust never saw a concentration camp."[4]

There are also key events that happened in Poland which resulted in thousands of deaths—of both of Christian and Jewish Poles. The example of the Warsaw Ghetto is an important illustration of this; it was the largest ghetto in all of Nazi-occupied Europe. It opened in 1940 and housed more than 450,000 people. In January of 1943, the ghetto was dissolved by order of Himmler. But the Jews living there resisted, resulting in a battle that lasted days and led to a thousand Jewish casualties; the remaining thousands were deported to camps. This is strictly counter to the stereotype of Jews going passively to their deaths. The Polish underground assisted the revolt, resulting in massive casualties. As Snyder writes, "More Poles were killed during the Warsaw Uprising alone than Japanese died in the atomic bombing of Hiroshima and Nagasaki."[5]

Outraged by this rebellion, Himmler ordered the destruction of the ghetto down to the very buildings. Horrifyingly, the remnants of the demolished ghetto were transformed into a concentration camp—an event not frequently discussed in more common accounts of Holocaust history. Known as the Warsaw concentration camp, it was a relatively small camp comparatively, but was intended for brutal slave labor meant to work its inhabitants to death. Many of its surviving inhabitants were sent on a death march when it seemed that the Soviet Army liberation was close at hand. Snyder describes the camp as "one of the ghastliest creations of Nazi rule."[6]

There is also the issue of Polish complicity. Historians have long debated the role of Polish anti-Semitism in the Holocaust. Did the Nazis choose Poland as the site of their death camps because the country had such a high concentration of Jews? Or because Poland had such ingrained anti-Semitism and the local population was unlikely to interfere in the extermination of their Jewish neighbors? A nation that once housed over 3 million Jews and was a focal point for Jewish culture was utterly transformed within a few years; now only a few thousand Polish Jews remain. Part of the problem in resolving this question of Polish complicity in the Holocaust lies in understanding the makeup of Poland prior to the war. When the Germans invaded in 1939, the country was not simply divided into Christian and Jewish Poles. Poland was home to a diverse population that included Germans, Ukranians, and other groups who were forced out of the country when territorial lines were redrawn in 1939 and again in 1945.

The issue is further complicated, particularly where Polish Holocaust films are concerned, by the situation in the '50s. After Stalin's death, Soviet leaders lashed out against Jewish communists, who were heavily represented in Party leadership and particularly in the secret police. This resulted in a wave of anti-Semitism that included show trials, expulsions, and executions. Marek Haltof writes, "Polish films about the Holocaust, and about Polish-Jewish relations in general, reflect the postwar political status quo and the changing historical and political circumstances more than historical truth."[7]

Unlike earlier chapters, I have chosen not to note all the biographical connections to the war of the filmmakers discussed in the interest in length; it is best to assume that every person mentioned who made Polish films about World War II was affected. As Antonin and Mira Liehm write,

> There wasn't a single Polish family that hadn't lost someone: on the battlefronts, in the concentration camps, during the Warsaw Uprising, during the Nazi reprisals, or in the civil struggles at the end of the war. Nazi Germany saw in the Poles, as in the nations of Yugoslavia, a people that dared to show defiance, and as such, ought to be exterminated. And Polish film, like Yugoslav film, found its greatest inspiration in the collectively experienced tragedy; it kept returning to this period, painfully and painstakingly examining it from all points of view.[8]

The postwar communist government, which formed into the Soviet satellite known as the Polish People's Republic, was essentially under the control of Stalin and then Nikita Khruschkev and Leonid Brezhnev, at least for the purposes of this chapter, and thus followed the general Soviet attitude towards cinema—namely an insistence on formulaic realism. A component necessary to understanding Polish cinema is related to the abrupt change in Polish culture that began in 1939 and continued under the Soviet occupation. For example, as Antonin and Mira Liehm write, in the '30s "Polish literature of the time was characterized by oppressive presentiments of impending tragedy, apocalyptic visions, futile struggles, and Kafka-like depictions of the absurdity of day-to-day life."[9] Examples can be found in writers like Bruno Schulz, Witold Gombrowicz, and Stanisław Ignacy Witkiewicz (known as Witkacy). But this was largely absent in the Polish World

War II films of the '50s and '60s due to Soviet censorship and the restrictions imposed on filmmakers.

Though World War II-themes would become overwhelmingly popular in Soviet and Eastern European cinema, an important early example of how this system represented the Holocaust can be found in Wanda Jakubowska's *Ostatni etap* (*The Last Stage*, 1948). It's more or less a conventional drama—though one with a documentary style and almost neorealist tone—but it was one of the first films ever made about the Holocaust and, importantly, was made by a survivor of Auschwitz. Nearly every mainstream Holocaust film to come after would follow its lead—particularly those set in concentration camps.

When Martha Weiss (Barbara Drapinska) and her family are sent to Auschwitz, she is spared at the last moment because of her ability to speak German and is recruited as a translator. She learns about the steadily smoking crematoria, where her family have been murdered in the gas chambers, and, alongside other women in the camp, tries to survive in time for the supposedly approaching Soviet Army to liberate the camp. She is also secretly helping the resistance movement. The film's cloying conclusion involves Martha's near execution by hanging for her minor resistance activities, but at the last moment another prisoner cuts the rope tying her wrists behind her back and slips her a razor. On the scaffold, she cuts a guard's face while announcing that the Soviets will arrive soon to liberate the camp, just as their planes fly overhead.

The Last Stage introduced a number of themes that would continue to play a

A defiant Martha (Barbara Drapinska) looks on as her execution is interrupted by the triumphant arrival of Soviet planes (*Ostatni etap*, Film Polski, 1948).

prominent role in Holocaust films: the prominence of female characters, a clear division between downtrodden but determined prisoners, sadistic guards, and selfish kapo. Despite a realism that was bold for the time, *The Last Stage* also universalized the experience of the Holocaust itself, taking the emphasis away from the Jewishness of the majority of the victims. Toby Haggith and Joanna Newman write, "Until the collapse of communism, Polish cinema, like Polish history in general, played down the significance of the Jews' extermination during the war."[10] They explained that primary reasons for this—in addition to ingrained Polish anti–Semitism—include a desire

> to represent the war as a conflict between fascism and communism [and to emphasize] Polish suffering at the expense of other nations, especially Jews, which was particularly the case of Andrzej Wajda's films; and to erase any doubts that during the war Poles did not help their Jewish neighbors as much as they could.[11]

And while there are some elements that were probably gruesome for the time—implied torture, train transport sequences, and the looming towers of the ovens—Jakubowska herself admitted to stripping much from the production. She says, "The camp's reality was human skeletons, piles of dead bodies, lice, rats, and various disgusting diseases. On the screen, this reality would certainly cause dread and repulsion. It was necessary to eliminate those elements which, although authentic and typical, were unbearable for the postwar viewer."[12]

The film was co-written by German Holocaust survivor Gerda Schneider and involved other survivors and German prisoners of war in the production; they were expected, at least for a time, to live on site in an odd reenactment of the horrors many of them had just recently escaped. Despite this, the characters in *The Last Stage* are portrayed as clean, healthy, and attractive. Their plight is certainly horrifying, but is far from a realistic depiction of the mass suffering and death of Auschwitz. Perhaps because of this, the film was a success and won several awards, and even contributed to Jakubowska's appointment as a professor at the famed National Film School in Łodz. *The Last Stage* is essentially the standard for mainstream Polish depictions of the Holocaust, an important counterexample I will be working against throughout this chapter.

As a result of *The Last Stage*'s success, the sanitized World War II films of the '50s follow a similar pattern in Polish cinema, namely Aleksander Ford's *Ulica Graniczna* (*Border Street*, 1948) and Andrzej Wajda's celebrated war trilogy, which includes *Pokolenie* (*A Generation*, 1955), *Kanał* (1956) and *Popiół i diament* (*Ashes and Diamonds*, 1958). All of these tow the Party line. As Snyder explains,

> The history of the Warsaw Ghetto Uprising of 1943 had to be rewritten. [...] In the politically acceptable history of the Second World War, the resistance in the ghetto had little to do with the mass murder of Jews, and much to do with the courage of communists. This fundamental shift of emphasis obscured the Jewish experience of the war, as the Holocaust became nothing more than an instance of fascism.[13]

Border Street is about the Warsaw Ghetto and the horrifically violent uprising in 1943, when Nazis attempted to purge the ghetto and send its remaining inhabitants to be murdered in death camps. Like so many of the Soviet films from this period, it presents heroic partisans and innocent victims versus evil Nazis and—like the French films to cover after it—focuses on children, showing the contrast between poor and bourgeois families. Though *Border Street* has elements of neorealism and does aim for some historical accuracy, it is fundamentally a melodrama. Ford focuses on innocence lost, sacrifice made out of love, and characters who start out as anti-Semitic but courageously learn the error of their ways. Like so many state-approved films made under Soviet communism, there is the strong flavor of propaganda. Haltof writes, "The importance of the Polish left-wing underground, largely organized and controlled by the Soviets, was exaggerated and elevated to suit the dominant ideology."[14]

Similarly, Wajda's war trilogy focuses on heroic Poles overcoming Nazi oppression to fight for their country. The first of these, *A Generation*, follows a young man (Tadeusz Łomnicki) who begins with small acts of rebellion against the Nazis in occupied Warsaw and soon joins the Resistance, ultimately participating in the Warsaw Uprising. *Kanał* is directly concerned with the Warsaw Uprising and *Ashes and Diamonds* focuses on the underground Polish Army and their struggles against the Nazis. This trilogy and *Ashes and Diamonds* in particular were well-received by Polish critics and have become considered classics of Polish cinema. But after 1989—and the revolutions in Poland—historians reevaluated the film and criticized it for misrepresenting Polish history and the role of the underground army. Wajda's slightly later film *Lotna* (1959) furthered these themes; it is a glorification of the role of the Polish Army during the war and depicts heroic events that didn't actually happen.

The up-and-coming directors of the Polish School, on the other hand, sought to free themselves from these formulaic Soviet plots. Haltof writes,

> The young emerging filmmakers, trained at the Łódź Film School, believed in a genuine depiction of vital national themes. [...] Unlike older filmmakers, including Aleksander Ford and Wanda Jakubowska, who opted for cinema imitating the Soviet epic models, the young filmmakers clearly favored the Italian neorealist approach, which offered them a chance to break with their predecessors and reflect the spirit of the de-Stalinization period.[15]

For example, director Jerzy Kawalerowicz expanded upon these themes somewhat with *Cień* (*Shadow*, 1956) and *Prawdziwy koniec wielkiej wojny* (*The Real End of the Great War*, 1957). *Shadow* focuses on a man's death during the war and captures several points of view, as in Akira Kurosawa's *Rashōman* (1950). While the film does depict a common Soviet-era sense of paranoia, it also suggests that the war, and memories of events that took place during those years, are subject to different interpretations and can be colored by memory, individual motivations, or political agendas. *The Real End of the Great War*, on the other hand, focuses on the relationship between a married couple, how it is interrupted by the war, and how they reunite and attempt to overcome war trauma. Other films in this general romantic melodrama subgenre include Wojciech Has's *Pożegnania* (*Lydia Ate the Apple*, 1958) and Tadeusz Konwicki's *Ostatni dzień lata* (*The Last Days of Summer*, 1958), which takes a more allegorical approach to the theme of Poland recovering from war trauma. Konwiki would go on to make the similarly themed if more conventional *Zaduszki* (*All Souls' Day*, 1962)—all examples of how popular World War II subject matter was at that time in Polish cinema.

Andrzej Munk, however, presented a more cynical take on the same material with *Eroica* (*Heroism*, 1958), which examines Polish ideas of heroic behavior during the war via two stories. The first follows a drunk who accidentally becomes a soldier in the Home Army during the Warsaw Uprising, while the second focuses on a POW who becomes a hero to his fellow prisoners when he escapes the camp, though in reality he never escaped at all and is hiding inside the camp. *Zezowate szczęście* (*Bad Luck*, 1959) follows a man whose life is shaped by a series of unfortunate incidents that overlap with the war. He is inherently selfish and small minded and his disastrous attempts to better his life shape him as something of a comic anti-hero, a regular person swept along by the tide of history who is attempting to ignore it.

Gradually, directors began to use approved and popular World War II themes to comment on life under Soviet rule. Antonin and Mira Liehm write,

> The first postwar films in Eastern Europe sought their inspiration for the most part from wartime experience and the Nazi occupation. Nor had this theme lost its power by the second half of the fifties, when it played an important role in the evolution of Polish, Soviet, and Yugoslav cinema. [...] The occupation and the war were used as a package to smuggle in contemporary themes: films about the recent past became a disguise for contemporary commitments.[16]

Many of the films of the '60s are concerned with the inability to escape the past and the lingering effects of war trauma on individuals as well as Polish society at large. Kazimierz Kutz's *Nikta nia woła* (*Nobody's Calling*, 1960) and Wojciech Has's *Jak byc kochana* (*How to Be Loved*, 1963) are key examples of this. Generally, these films can best be categorized as romantic melodrama and involve a protagonist looking back on the war. Haltof writes,

> Polish psychological war dramas usually narrate their stories with two planes of action. Set in the present, they stress the effects of the war: the inability to live normal life, to communicate, and to love as a result of traumatic war experiences. Memories of the war often return as nightmarish flashbacks, and prevent burned-out protagonists from completely returning to life.[17]

Other works that go against this expected grain are some of the experimental short films from the period, such as Janusz Morgenstern's *Ambulans* (*Ambulance*, 1962), about a group of children who are loaded into an ambulance—actually a gas van where they will be killed. These vans were used by the Nazis in Eastern Europe to kill groups of primarily women and children before the gas chambers were built in the death camps. The Jewish Morgenstern survived the Holocaust by hiding out and later joined the Polish Army, so this was a uniquely personal project for him.

Experimental filmmakers and animators like Jan Lenica and Walerian Borowczyk made more abstract interpretations of similar themes with their shorts from the early '60s. Lenica's *Labyrinth* (1962) is an obvious allegory of life under fascism. Daniel Bird describes it as "a self-consciously Kafka-esque tale of a winged lonely man literally devoured by totalitarian rule."[18] Borowczyk's *Les jeux des anges* (*The Game of the Angels*, 1964) similarly seems to describe life in a concentration camp. In the film, an angel is subjugated to what seems to be a factory of death. Borowczyk made the film in France after his departure from Poland, where he remained for the rest of his career; there he was able to make films more freely than under Soviet rule.

Munk's incomplete final film, *Pasażerka* (*Passenger*, 1963), based on a novel by an Auschwitz survivor, more explicitly confronts the idea of war trauma returning to haunt the present. While on board a cruise ship, Liza (Aleksandra Slaska) thinks she recognizes a fellow passenger (Anna Ciepelewska) as Marta, a prisoner at the concentration camp where Liza was a guard. Liza relates the story of how she tried to protect Marta on several occasions. This is contradicted by depictions of what really happened at the camp; in reality Liza was cruel and sadistic. Because Munk died before the film was complete, certain sequences involve documentary-style narration about the course of events that encourages us to try to understand what really happened in the film.

Munk's film is a poignant examination of the difference between memory, personal

In *Ambulance*, the van full of children drives off into the distance, where it is implied they will die of gas asphyxiation (*Ambulans*, Studio Malych Form Filmowych Se-Ma-For, 1961).

narrative, which applies as much to Polish memories of World War II as it does to Soviet rule. Antonin and Mira Liehm write, "the central idea is that the past can be mystified and closed off in history, but not in an individual conscience, which remains open to the past until the moment of death."[19] In his own perhaps subtle way, Munk was bucking the tradition of social realism imposed by Soviet censors by suggestion in *Passenger* and an earlier film like *Man on the Tracks*, that there are always multiple versions of the truth. Haltof explains that this is one of Munk's defining themes: "As in *Eroica* and *Bad Luck*, in *The Passenger* Munk also introduces the perspective of a character with whom the viewer cannot identify, an unreliable narrator."[20] This untrustworthy, complex figure is certainly a departure from the heroic communist protagonist in many of the more mainstream World War II films to come out of Soviet countries during this period.

Into the '60s, other films began to push harder against Soviet expectations. A particularly extreme example of this is Andrzej Brzozowski's *Przy torze kolejowym* (*By the Railway Track*, 1963), about an injured woman who has escaped from a transport train. She seeks assistance from passing villagers, but no one will help her, though they do wait around to find out what might happen to her. Eventually someone with compassion gives in to her pleas for death and shoots her. Brzozowski's bold film was banned and essentially disappeared for decades, because it paints Poles in such a negative light—as ambivalent bystanders unwilling to help a defenseless, dying woman in need.

Milder examples less offensive to Soviet leaders included Jerzy Hoffman's *Prawo i pięść* (*The Law and the Fist*, 1964), a loose take on the western genre where a former Resistance fighter joins a group of men immediately after the war to secure a town vacated by the Germans. But he learns that the men he is with—allegedly members of the government—are really there to loot the town for themselves. Claude Lanzmann's documentary *Shoah* touched on similar themes of Polish people exploiting their neighbors; in the case of that film, they moved into the abandoned homes of Jewish residents taken to the Nazi death camps. Tadeusz Konwicki's *Salto* (*Jump*, 1965) is a more Kafkaesque version of this, where a man goes back to a nearly abandoned town to confront his war memories, but no one claims to remember him. Wojciech Has's *Szyfry* (*Codes*, 1965) has similarly hallucinatory moments in a tale of a father's search for his son in the years after the war.

But in general, films about the war ground to a halt during this period because tightening censorship and new government restrictions, particularly around depictions of the Holocaust and Polish-Jewish relations. There was a relative dearth of confrontational films about World War II for over a decade. Haltof writes,

> The period between 1965 and 1980, despite some relaxation of censorship in the 1970s, may be called the time of organized forgetting about the Holocaust. This was an era characterized by projects that were rejected at the script stage, films that were unfinished or shelved, and by the imposition of state-controlled silence over sensitive issues.[21]

The most important film from this period to offer up a challenging depiction of war experience that went against Soviet expectations is undoubtedly Andrzej Żuławski's *Trzecia część nocy* (*The Third Part of the Night*, 1971). A young assistant to Wajda in the '60s, Żuławski's made his debut as a director with *The Third Part of the Night*. It presents a surreal interpretation of madness and violence a rural village during World War II. German soldiers murder the immediate family of Michał (Leszek Teleszynski, in his film debut, though he would work with Żuławski again), who survives by hiding in the forest with his father (Jerzy Golinski). He plans to join the Resistance, but is found out by the Gestapo, who chase him into an apartment building. A pregnant woman (Żuławski's first wife, Małgorzata Braunek)—who looks exactly like Michał's dead wife—agrees to hide him. In turn he helps her deliver her baby. He finds a job in a typhus lab, feeding disease-spreading lice with his own blood. He learns that the pregnant woman's husband, who has been mistaken for him by the Gestapo, has been arrested and tortured. Even though he has fallen in love with the woman, he realizes he must do something to intervene.

This eerie, terrifying film is undeniably effective as a parable of wartime violence, invasion, and genocide. But it also serves as a bold protest of the equal horrors of Soviet rule. As mentioned, Soviet World War II-themed films were expected to have a degree of realism mixed with nationalistic optimism. *The Third Part of the Night* is notably anything but and the young Żuławski's film has more than a little in common with the absurdist literary tradition so entrenched in Eastern European culture. Antonin and Mira Liehm write that Żuławski

> used expressionism and a wealth of naturalistic detail, stressing the overall atmosphere rather than the plot. His world, where the instinct of self-preservation makes man give his very blood to the lice, has all the attributes of the absurd, as it is known in the Polish literature of Gombrowicz, Bruno Schulz, Mrożek, and Witkiewicz. The story ends with madness and death.[22]

Here the notion of the absurd is taken to its most chaotic end. The film is grotesque body horror in anticipation of the genre, an apocalyptic time warp that introduces the sense of hysteria and disorientation that would reappear in the majority of Żuławski's films. Marta, the female protagonist, describes their existence as "sinking into a world

Małgorzata Braunek is an angelic if uncanny force in *The Third Part of the Night* (*Trzecia czesc nocy*, Polski State Film, 1971).

where all things have become alike." This is Żuławski's own brand of absurdism, where he follows few of the genre's established norms—such as the dizzying use of doubles throughout the film—and replaces comedy and satire with horror and abjection.

Absurdist literature played an important, but unstable role in Polish culture, as the communist government banned certain authors and then later relaxed censorship (at least compared to other Soviet states). Harold B. Segel explains,

> The impressive interwar Polish avant-garde exemplified by such writers as Stanisław Ignacy Witkiewicz (Witkacy), who committed suicide in 1939 shortly after the German invasion, and Witold Gombrowicz, who was in South America when hostilities erupted and spent the war years in Argentina, was put under a strict ban by the communists. [...] When the situation changed in the 1960s, younger Polish writers who had grown up in ignorance of this legacy embraced it with the fervor of zealots.[23]

Żuławski was undeniably influenced by this generation of writers, particularly Gombrowicz; his final film, *Cosmos* (2015), is an adaptation of the latter's novel of the same name. Like fellow Poles Roman Polanski, Walerian Borowczyk, and Jerzy Skolimowski, Żuławski's work has more of an international than strictly Polish flavor, thanks to the fact that all four directors were uprooted from Poland in the '60s or '70s and pursued work in France, England, and the U.S. Similarly, Gombrowicz happened to take a trip to Argentina in 1939, just before war broke out, so he was stranded in South America for its duration (which likely saved his life). The rejection of traditional Polish culture that informs his work can also be felt in Żuławski's films and it's no wonder that his follow up to *The Third Part of the Night*, *Diabeł* (*The Devil*, 1972)—about the 18th century Prussian invasion of Poland—was banned in Poland.

Like *The Devil*, which was made just after Żuławski's debut, *The Third Part of the Night* uses the themes of war and invasion primarily as a complex backdrop, which adds a rich sense of atmosphere, emotional chaos, and complex political themes. Michael Atkinson described the film as

> a wrenching nightmare about the Nazi occupation that is virtually divested of historical markers, instead focusing, in the director's particular manner, on paranoid panic and Theater of Cruelty catharsis. […] The movie's context is so abstracted and soaked with queasiness, so crowded with doppelgängers, raving lunacy, sudden corpses, secret signals, and intimations of plague, that the upshot is baldly Kafkaesque.[24]

The film also blends themes of biology—lice, typhus, the spread of disease, and attempts at immunization—with apocalyptic symbolism. The presence of the Book of Revelations looms large, giving the film its title, and the dialogue is peppered with quotes like, "And the third angel sounded the trumpet and a great star fell from heaven burning as it were a torch and it fell on the third part of the rivers and upon the fountains of waters. And the third part of the waters became wormwood. And many men died of the waters because they became bitter" (*Revelations* 8:10). But this apocalypse is personal rather than religious. Like many of Żuławski's later films, *The Third Part of the Night* is concerned with the breakdown of a romantic relationship and corrosive nature of a love triangle, as expressed in the nonlinear story of Michał, his wife, Helena, and her double Marta. Michał's search for redemption becomes an Orphic journey to the underworld with Lwów as a grey, putrid hell full of squirming lice and spurting, infected blood.

The Third Part of the Night was actually inspired by the wartime experiences of Żuławski's own father, Mirosław, who is credited as a co-writer. The film is set in Żuławski's birthplace, Lwów, now known as Lviv, in Ukraine, then the site of a large Jewish ghetto in Poland. The majority of ghetto inhabitants—some 120,000 people—were transported by the Nazis to either the Bełżec death camp or Janowska concentration camp. While several of Żuławski's relatives are remembered by Yad Vashem for their part in saving Jewish lives during the war, Mirosław represents the plight of many Polish intellectuals: in order to survive, he was forced to work as a lice feeder in the Weigl Institute.

In the film, Michał talks to his father about how to save their world. The older man replies, "The world has crumbled, has got smashed, has vanished." *The Third Part of the Night* reflects what many felt in postwar life, particularly in Soviet countries, that the world had never really been set right since those fateful years. Personal, political, and mythic all at once, *The Third Part of the Night* is an astounding debut film, where Żuławski effectively filmed his own birth, a gory, realistic sequence utterly devoid of hope.

Because of Soviet censorship, there were very few films like *The Third Part of the Night* in Poland in the '70s. The crack down after a relative period of freedom particularly repressed depictions of Polish or Soviet history that went against the official narrative. Haltof writes,

> The 1960 party resolution did not specifically mention films dealing with the Holocaust or Polish-Jewish relations, but the harsh criticism of the ideologically improper interpretations of the war and the occupation in Polish cinema could not go unnoticed. Polish filmmakers were criticized for their pessimistic portrayal of Polish reality.[25]

This was marked by a particularly anti-Semitic government campaign that essentially rewrote the war narrative and painted Polish Jews as the enemy and as outsiders in their own country. Several filmmakers, including actors and producers, left the country during this period to find work in the West. Despite this, in addition to *The Third Part of the Night*, a few surreal, dreamlike films were able to sneak through in the '70s, such as Konwicki's *Jak daleko stad, jak blisko* (*How Far from Here, How Near*, 1972). A man confronts his friend's suicide and his own past in what Haltof describes as a "dream-like film essay full of autobiographical, historical, and political references."[26] This includes many references to Jewish culture, the Holocaust, and World War II. It's likely that the film's surreal and stylized nature allowed it to slide past censors, because even though it is not the standard Soviet social realism of the '50s and early '60s, it also does not offer up an obvious critique of the Soviet regime.

Another important example is Wojciech Has's *Sanatorium pod klepsydrą* (*The Hourglass Sanatorium*, 1973). Józef (Jan Nowicki) goes to visit his ill father (Tadeusz Kondrat) in a sanitarium that seems to exist out of time, in a world that is deteriorating. Józef is repeatedly drawn into dreams and childhood memories. Though it is not overtly a war film, it is steeped in historical resonance and is based on the short stories of Bruno Schulz, from a collection of the same name. David Melville describes it as "a film that evoked the lost world of Polish Jewry became not only an escape into a mythical past, but also a challenge to a vicious and increasingly ugly present."[27]

Has meant it to be a spiritual rather than literal adaptation of Schulz's stories, which do not directly reference the Holocaust; Schulz was murdered in 1942 by a Nazi officer while on his way home to the Drohobycz Ghetto. Like other Eastern European Jewish writers from the period, beginning with Kafka, Schulz's tales are seen as an apocalyptic prophecy, foreshadowing the destruction of their entire world. The structure of the sanatorium itself, both in his writing and Has's film, can be seen as a foreboding symbol of oppression and death. Melville writes, "The limbo of the sanatorium (conceived in 1937) can even be read as an oblique prophecy of the ghettos and internment camps to which Poland's Jewish population would soon be confined."[28]

Has, whose father was Jewish, intentionally enhanced these elements of Schulz's stories at a time when it was politically risky for him to do so. This can be seen as Has's own autobiographical touch on the film, a memorial to his own boyhood; both men grew up in Galicia, a small former kingdom that once belonged to Austria-Hungary, was part of Poland before the war, and is now between Poland and Ukraine. Has was a teenager when war broke out. In this sense, *The Hourglass Sanatorium* can be seen as a fable, a dark fantasy about a place—the Jewish community of Galicia—that ceased to exist after 1945. Haltof writes that Has's film "deals with the theme of childhood recollections and offers a moody evocation of the lost Jewish world."[29]

The sanatorium as the site of a dying world and as the stand-in for Nazi camps was given a more literal interpretation later in the decade by Edward Żebrowski with *Szpital Przemienienia* (*Hospital of the Transfiguration*, 1979), an adaptation of Stanisław Lem's novel of the same name. Just after a young doctor (Piotr Dejmek) goes to work in a psychiatric hospital, it is invaded by Nazis who force the staff to choose between collaboration—meaning the slaughter of their own patients—or imprisonment or death for themselves. These themes of hospitalization and medicine as allegories for the war are common to *The Third Part of the Night*, *The Hourglass Sanatorium*, and *Hospital of the Transfiguration*, which also bear a stylistical similarity thanks to a shared cinematographer, the prolific Witold Sobociński, who would also work with Wajda and Polanski, among others. These three films can be thought of very loosely as a trilogy through their shared themes and visual style, and their directors' rare willingness to explore the Holocaust in a decade when that was particularly unpopular.

Some directors, like Żuławski, Borowczyk, Roman Polanski, and Jerzy Skolimowski would leave Poland permanently to make films elsewhere, while others left occasionally for productions in Western Europe. Such was the case with Andrzej Wajda, who directed *Eine Liebe in Deutschland* (*A Love in Germany*, 1983), a West German-French coproduction. Polish-born actress and Rainer Werner Fassbinder regular Hanna Schygulla stars as Paulina, a married grocery store owner whose husband is away fighting for the Wehrmacht. She begins an affair with a young Polish POW (Piotr Lysak), a relationship that becomes defined by mutual sexual obsession. The film uses flashbacks from the present day to tell its story, a convention frequently used in German World War II films from the late '70s and early '80s as well as several of Wajda's Polish films. *A Love in Germany* attempts to portray day-to-day German life in a rural village during the war years, but it is explicitly a conventional romance.

Wajda went to Germany to escape Soviet restrictions to attempt to tell a more radical story. He admitted that he continued to make films about the war because there were things he wanted to experience, but couldn't. In an interview, Wajda said, "My war experience was limited. I was in a concentration camp, so I couldn't take part in the Warsaw ghetto uprising, so it was natural for me to want to see it on the screen."[30] With *A Love in Germany*, the radical element is that Paulina's forbidden love for the Polish POW is entirely her own; it gives her a kind of freedom. One interpretation of the film is that she is persecuted because others envy this freedom, the private joy that is between her and her lover. This theme of jealousy, selfishness, and opportunism is a relatively common theme of conventional dramas set during the war and ultimately it is only the lovers who are punished for their transgressions. Wajda also addresses tensions between German and Polish society during the war years. *A Love in Germany* was written by Wajda's frequent collaborator, Agnieszka Holland, who would go on to make some of the most interesting Polish films about the Holocaust in the '80s and '90s, though she was forced to make some of these as non–Soviet European co-productions.

There were two important turning points in the Polish depiction of World War II on screen. The first of these came in 1985 with the release of Claude Lanzmann's French documentary *Shoah*. Running nearly ten hours long, it took Lanzmann over a decade to complete the film, which relates specific stories about the Jewish experience in Poland. Unlike Ophuls, Lanzmann chose not to rely on archival material and instead presents hours of interviews he conducted with survivors, bystanders, and even some perpetrators, about events in the Warsaw Ghetto and extermination camps Chełmno, Treblinka, and Auschwitz. It is a harrowing experience, particularly when Lanzmann interviews former Nazis (some of them recorded secretly), concentration camp guards, and prisoners forced to aid in the disposal of bodies. Lanzmann also speaks to a number of Poles living around the various camps who admit that they knew what was happening.

Shoah was met with some controversy, particularly in Poland, where it was felt that Lanzmann put a heavy spin on the material and painted Poland as deeply anti-Semitic. While his documentary is a breathtaking work, Lanzmann himself admitted a fictionalized component to the film, where he clearly focused on a particular angle—anti-Semitism in Poland—rather than trying to present a broad spectrum of historical facts. But gradually historians began to tell a similar story, from Jan Błoński's essay "The Poor Poles Look at the Ghetto" (1987) through to Jan Gross's *Neighbors the Destruction of the*

Claude Lanzmann serves as director and aggressive interviewer in *Shoah* (*Shoah*, BBC/Historia/Les Films Aleph/Ministère de la Culture de la Republique Française, 1985).

Jewish Community in Jedwabne (2001). The latter book described a 1941 pogrom in which Poles took part in the massacre of the Jews of their village; over 300 of them were locked in a barn and set on fire and dozens of Poles were found to have participated in the horror.

But these facts were slow to emerge in the '80s, when *Shoah* was released. In response, Polish filmmakers returned to the subject of the Holocaust, perhaps attempting to tell a more nuanced version of the story. In the '80s, directors like Kawalerowicz, Jerzy Hoffman, and Krzysztof Zanussi made World War II films, though as in earlier years, many of these continued to be melodramas and romances with the war as a backdrop—particularly those by Zanussi. Some of the most imaginative films from the period were the first to be made by Polish directors who did not experience the war personally. Haltof writes,

> Prior to 1989, films dealing with the Holocaust and Polish-Jewish relations were mostly made by filmmakers who were born before the war. Some of them experienced concentration camps, lived under the German or Soviet occupations, and survived the Holocaust hiding and changing their identities. Beginning in the 1980s, a new, "second generation" of filmmakers emerged who took up the subject of the Holocaust. They were born after the war but were affected by the war stories of their parents as well as by the films made by their mentors (Jakubowska, Munk, Wajda), and influenced by the torrent of literary and historical works.[31]

In the context of transgressive war films, the most important member of this group is Wajda-collaborator Agnieszka Holland. Like Wajda with *A Love in Germany*, Holland went to West Germany to make her first film about the Holocaust, *Bittere Ende* (*Angry Harvest*, 1985). Many of Holland's early films as a director were banned by the Soviet censors and *Angry Harvest* is perhaps predictably controversial. It is one of three films Holland made about World War II. Though she was born in 1948, after the war, it has been a major theme in her career; her father, an army captain, was Jewish and lost family during the war, but spent much of his life rejecting his own heritage. Holland's Catholic mother, on the other hand, was a Resistance fighter and participated in the Warsaw Uprising, among other acts of heroism. Throughout Holland's films, she resists depicting Jews as innocent victims and Poles as either heroic rescuers or anti–Semitic collaborators. In her cinematic universe, all individuals are flawed and everyone is capable of selfish, violent acts.

Angry Harvest not only explores women's bodies as the sites of political action, but uses sexual violence as a symbol for the widespread effects of war. Based on an autobiographical novel by Hermann Field and Stanisław Mierzenski, the film centers around Leon (Armin Mueller-Stahl), a Silesian farmer, and Rosa (Elisabeth Trissenaar), a married Jewish woman who has escaped from a train with her husband. Leon finds her and gives her shelter in the cellar of his house, but soon makes increasing demands of Rosa.

Leon is not immune to suffering—his own brother has been placed in a concentration camp—but becomes twisted by his obsession with Rosa, which grows out of loneliness and a need for companionship and sex. Though brought vividly and charismatically to life by the great Mueller-Stahl, Leon's character type is far from unique among cult films set during World War II. He represents a sort of antihero type loosely introduced by Rossellini in *Rome, Open City*, a character who is neither innocent victim nor sadistic perpetrator. He isn't even really a collaborator, but makes a series of sometimes unfortunate, but often selfish decisions that lead to tragic ends: the death of a woman, the failure of a Resistance mission, and so on. Gwendolyn Audrey Foster writes,

> Holland directly equates sexual relationships with fascistic manipulation and victimization in *Angry Harvest*. Once again conflating the personal with the political, Holland brings together the couple in a twisted, romantic entanglement, ending with the liberating figure of the farmer becoming a jealous, dominating, and brutalizing lover.[32]

If Lanzmann's *Shoah* was one turning point that changed the way Polish directors depicted the Holocaust on screen, the second, more explosive factor was the revolution of 1989 when Poland abandoned communism and transitioned to democracy. This led to an increase in production of Holocaust and war-themed films that has continued through the decades. Two examples out of many include stories of Auschwitz survival in Leszek Wosiewicz's musical *Kornblumenblau* (1989) and Jan Kolski's *Pogrzeb kartofla* (*The Burial of a Potato*, 1990), based on his grandfather's experiences surviving Auschwitz and returning home after the war to be greeted with hostility. In the film, Polish villagers are painted in an extremely unflattering light and are basically depicted as anti-Semitic brutes who view Jews, even Polish Jews, as outsiders.

Both Wajda and Holland returned to the subject in 1990: Wajda with the critically panned historical epic *Korczak*, about the famed teacher and director of an orphanage who went with his children to die in Treblinka when they were deported from the Warsaw Ghetto. Though Wajda dutifully returned to the theme of Jewish experience during the war throughout his career—a subject he thought was of vital importance even though it was inconvenient to the Polish communist government—his younger protégé Holland's *Hitlerjunge Salomon* (*Europa Europa*) is the more controversial film. Another coproduction for Holland between Germany, France, and Poland, *Europa Europa* follows a young Polish Jewish boy, Solek (Marco Hofschneider) whose attempts to survive the war drive him to various parts of Eastern Europe. Ultimately he is discovered by Nazi soldiers and steals a German student's identity; this saves his life, but he finds works as an army interpreter on the front. He is later adopted by a Nazi official who sends him back to Germany to attend a Hitler Youth academy. Holland's film highlights the importance of assimilation to survival, but the crux of the film is that the boy has been distancing himself from Jewish identity. He must embrace it to become whole. Ultimately he learns about the events of the Holocaust, which he had unwittingly escaped, and emigrates to Israel.

The subject would become even more popular into the 2000s and 2010s, with directors exploring wartime themes in more confrontational ways. Many of these films include elements of sexual transgressiveness and sexual violence, themes of moral ambivalence, and the idea that Poles and Jews are equally capable of selfish acts and of violence—as Holland presented in *Angry Harvest*. Roman Polanski's work often obliquely references the Holocaust and his experiences as a child surviving the war, but he wouldn't tackle this literally until *The Pianist* in 2002. Though it is a thoroughly conventional work—surprisingly so for Polanski—it's based on the memoirs of composer Władysław Szpilman (played by Adrian Brody in the film). He is ultimately able to escape certain death at Treblinka, where his family are headed, as well as slave labor and the violence of the Warsaw Uprising by hiding out in abandoned houses. He is eventually saved and protected by a Nazi officer.

In some ways, this is the most literal expression of Polanski's most frequently used theme, the lonely protagonist alienated by society. Antonin and Mira Liehm write that Polanski's early films "already revealed the strain of sarcastic sorrow that was to remain the most characteristic trait of Polanski's work. The plight of man living in an alienated society is expressed in Polanski's films, at one level, through the absurdity of common everyday experience and at a deeper level through the history of Polanski's homeland and the course of his own life."[33]

The Pianist also highlights two important themes that arises in many Holocaust

Solek (Marco Hofschneider) surveys the destruction in *Europa Europa* with a naive sense of enthusiasm that gradually turns to horror (*Europa Europa*, Central Cinema Company Film, 1990).

narratives: firstly the idea that survival means protecting oneself at the expense of others, secondly, the related survivor's guilt. This issue of comprising oneself in order to survive or to expose a horrific event shows up in various ways in films like Wajda's *Katyń* (2007), about the massacre of thousands of Polish soldiers by the Soviet NKVD, hidden by the Soviet authorities for decades; Holland's *W ciemności* (*In Darkness*, 2011), about Jews escaping the Lwów Ghetto through the sewer system with the help of maintenance workers; Władysław Pasikowski's *Pokłłosie* (Aftermath, 2012), about the Jedwabne pogrom where a village of Poles helped to murder their Jewish neighbors; Jan Kidawa-Blonski's *Wukryciu* (*In Hiding*, 2013), about a woman who hides a Jewish woman from the Nazis but keeps her imprisoned after the war ends; and Pawel Pawlikowski's *Ida* (2013), about an orphaned nun who goes to meet her real family in the years after the war when she learns her parents were Jews killed in the Holocaust. Like *The Pianist*, these films share an inherently conventional quality. They all rely on melodrama and essentially use the Holocaust as a way to manipulate the emotions of the audience. Though they were all made after the end of Soviet censorship, in many ways these later historical dramas fall prey to similar political restraints: in this case, the pressure to navigate how European Jews and non–Jewish Poles want to be portrayed on screen and how that may or may not contrast with historical fact.

10

The World Gone Mad
Czech and Slovak Cinema

"I cut myself off from the past entirely. Just like that."—*Ostře sledované vlaky* (*Closely Watched Trains*, 1965)

While the invasion of Poland on September 1, 1939, marked the official beginning of World War II, in reality it was a gradual process that started a year earlier and included the seemingly enthusiastic annexation of Austria and the Sudetenland region of Czechoslovakia. Hitler's excuse was that he wanted to unite all ethnic Germans and protect them from hostile foreign governments. But just a few months later, in March of 1939, Slovakia was pressured into declaring independence and became an ally of Nazi Germany, while the Czech territories were invaded and dissolved into the Nazi Protectorate of Bohemia and Moravia. Czechoslovakia was a particularly active site of resistance during the war, which included the assassination of Reichsprotector and early architect of the Holocaust, Reinhard Heydrich. Nearly 10,000 people were arrested in retaliation for his death and thousands were executed; the entire villages of Lidice and Ležáky were wiped out either because the citizens were executed (as in the case of all adult males) or because they were sent to death camps (primarily the women and children).

Despite this, and unlike Poland, the Czechs received somewhat better treatment by the Nazis. It is speculated that this is because they were viewed as being "ethnically" closer to the Germans than Slavic Poland and thus they were candidates for possible "Aryanization." Historically there were many Germans living in Czechoslovakia and many Czechs spoke at least passable German. There is also the more disturbing—and more likely—possibility that Czechs received better treatment because the Nazis were using their country as a personal workforce for the German military machine, in other words keeping the population strong and well fed to continue producing arms for the Nazis. However this isn't to say that they were treated kindly; it's estimated that roughly 50,000 Czechs were killed, in addition to over 70,000 Czech Jews murdered by the Nazis.

Czech and Slovak films made after the war reflect this trauma and, as with other countries under Soviet control, follow four primary aims: to bear witness to past trauma; to solidify national identity after the German occupation and Soviet restructuring of the country; to reflect Soviet propaganda; and/or as a means to criticize Soviet totalitarianism. The emergence of the Czech New Wave in the '60s, during a period of relative freedom, is particularly important in regards to the latter and will be the focus of this chapter. Unlike some other more carefully repressed national cinemas under the Soviet Union, an obvious line can be drawn between pre-war art and culture in Czechoslovakia and the New Wave films.

Partly this is due to the role Prague played as a cultural hub in Eastern Europe. As Antonín and Mira Liehm write, "Avant-garde art trends were carried rapidly from France to the countries of Central and Eastern Europe, surfacing most visibly in Czechoslovakia."[1] For example, in the '20s, Prague birthed Devětsil, an avant-garde movement later destroyed by the Nazis. It would go on to have an influence on Czech filmmakers in the '60s. The Czech capital became sort of the Paris of the East, home to avant-garde and surrealist art. Some of this is due to the influx of commerce and culture from the West, but pre–World War II Czechoslovakia was a diverse country. Peter Demetz writes that it was "a state made up of many nationalities, including Czechs, Slovaks, Germans, Jews, Magyars, Poles, Ruthenians, and Ukrainians."[2] And with the rise of Nazism, Prague became a haven for refugees from the Germanic countries, particularly for intellectuals and artists who were either actively anti–Nazi or found themselves hated by the Reich.

Thousands of refugees flooded the country after January 1933. For Germans and Austrians, Czechoslovakia was a natural choice, as many—particularly writers, journalists, teachers, and translators—could still get work in their native language. The sympathetic, leftist-leaning government also offered support organizations for refugees and anti–Nazi activists. But those very activists were suddenly in danger in 1939. Demetz writes,

> Prague had once been their haven and was now their hell—whether they were Jews who had sought rescue in Masaryk's republic, or non–Jewish intellectuals and writers whose books had been burned in the Third Reich, or functionaries of the German left, Communists, or Social Democrats (defeated Austrian Socialists came to Brno after 1934).[3]

The strong spirit of resistance that lived on in Czechoslovakia during the war is evident in many of the postwar films, where it also began to be directed against Soviet oppression. One of the earliest films to approach this subject matter was Frantisek Cáp's early Cannes festival winner *Muzi bez krídel* (*Men Without Wings*, 1946), essentially a revenge drama about the aftermath of Heydrich's assassination. Focusing on how the assassination and how the widescale Nazi retribution affected one family, *Men Without Wings* is basically a conventional drama. But even in these early years, there were directors willing to risk the ire of Soviet censors. Otakar Vávra, one of the founders of the famed FAMU Prague film school, began to explore some taboo subject matter, first with *Krakatit* (1948), an antinuclear science fiction thriller, and even moreso with *Němá barikáda* (*Silent Barricade*, 1948). With this film about civilians holding off the German military in the final days of the war, Vávra found himself briefly censured by the government. He resumed making films a few years later, but largely stuck to approved material in support of the communist government.

A particularly important early counterexample to *Men Without Wings* is Alfréd Radok's bold and expressionistic *Daleká cesta* (*Distant Journey*, 1949). *Distant Journey* was subject to Stalinist censorship and was prevented from having a full premier, though it was allowed some early screenings; soon it was banned outright and remained unavailable for decades. Like many Polish films to come in later decades, *Distant Journey* is essentially a Holocaust drama with a central romantic relationship as its focal point. The marriage between a Jewish eye doctor, Hana (Blanka Waleská), and her non–Jewish husband Toník (Otomar Krejca) is already complicated because their families don't approve,

172 The Legacy of World War II in European Arthouse Cinema

but is seemingly doomed by the Nazi occupation and waves of Jewish transports to concentration camps. Hana and her family are sent to the Theresienstadt camp, while Toník secretly joins the underground resistance.

But unlike many of the mainstream World War II melodramas that focus on tragic romance, the actual focus of *Distant Journey* is life in Theresienstadt. Radok attempts a degree of documentary-style realism, including the use of newsreel clips and footage from Leni Riefenstahl's *Triumph of the Will* (1935). Experimentally, Radok often juxtaposes these factual sequences with his film, shrinking them down within the frame to layer one image on top of another. Radok shows the realities of life in wartime Prague, like Jews being banned from public spaces and events, including the theater. Beginning in 1939, Jews were banned from many professions and from certain public places, which included entertainment, parks, museums, and even public transportation. At first a policy of segregation was enforced and Jews had to register their homes and identities. The public areas and government services available to them gradually dwindled. Then deportations began.

This is the environment at the beginning of *Distant Journey*. One of the opening sequences features the quiet suicide of an old Jewish man; though the violence occurs off-screen, it is clear what has occurred. Unlike the majority of films made under Soviet rule, including Jakobowska's *The Last Stage*, which depicts Auschwitz as a rather sanitized experience, *Distant Journey* does not shy away from the fact that Jews were the primary victims of the Holocaust, or the horrifying extent of Nazi crimes. Perhaps this is because

In *Distant Journey*, arrival at Terezin is chaotic and soon reveals that the camp is more than a benign retirement center (*Daleká cesta*, Ceskoslovensk? Státní Film, 1950).

10. The World Gone Mad

Radok was Jewish—though he had been baptized as Catholic just before the war in the hope of assimilation—and lost his father and grandfather in Terezín, the Czech name for Theresienstadt. Radok himself was interned in the Klettendorf labor camp in eastern Austria.

Theresienstadt or Terezín is a unique, repulsive example of Nazi machinations. It was not a traditional concentration camp, but a hybrid center established in 1941. Part ghetto, part concentration camp, and part transport center—a stopover before Jews were sent to the killing centers in the east. It was also built for propaganda: the camp was beautified for Red Cross examinations and the filming of a false "documentary," all meant to ensure that the Allies would think the concentration camps weren't so bad. The camp was advertised as a place where prominent Jews would go to retire in comfort. It appeared to have shops, plenty of food, and medical care, which was a deception. In reality however, it did have both official and underground schools, libraries, places of worship, and outlets for the arts including theater—all essentially unheard of in the other camps.

In reality, the majority of Czechoslovakia's Jewish population—as well as those of other countries—either died at Theresienstadt or because they were sent on to Auschwitz. Demetz writes,

> About 88,100 Jews lived in the protectorate (approximately half of them in Prague), yet Heydrich's SS transported to Theresienstadt 141,000 people, including Jews from Germany, Austria, Holland, and Denmark. Conditions in the small town, or rather in the eleven or twelve old military barracks, their damp casemates, and a few houses, were unspeakable; nourishment was insufficient, and disease rampant. While 88,000 people successively were transported farther east to the gas chambers, 33,500 died in the camp itself.[4]

Radok shows Theresienstadt as a place of contradictions, where Jewish culture and identity is able to thrive in the face of death. And unlike many later, more mainstream films about the Holocaust set primarily within concentration camps, *Distant Journey* features a wide range of Jewish characters who prove to be far more than limited stereotypes. In addition to setting a strong-minded woman as the film's protagonist, *Distant Journey* also includes a number of vignettes featuring characters of different ages, backgrounds, and attitudes. This goes far beyond conventional World War II cinema which often adopts the distasteful practice of painting Jews as little more than hapless victims. The only real exception to Radok's radical, honest depiction of events is the film's conclusion, in which a group of healthy concentration camp inmates rush into the street at liberation, cheering wildly. In reality, months before liberation, the camp was flooded with the Reich's intended final victims. The survivors were weak, starved, and often sick from various illnesses and many of them had recently survived death marches. An epidemic of typhoid spread through the camp, claiming more lives, partly because the new arrivals refused to be decontaminated; they were afraid the showers were actually gas chambers. A similarly horrific event is recreated in *Distant Journey*, where a transport of children arrives and refuses to enter the showers. This is based on a real occurrence, where a group of children was sent to Auschwitz to their deaths.

Like other territories occupied by the Nazis and then controlled by Soviet forces, Czechoslovakia suffered from its own internal anti-Semitism, which enabled the Holocaust at least to some extent. As Demetz writes,

> Hereditary Czech anti-Semitism has a long history reaching back to the first decades of the nineteenth century, and after the departure of President Beneš in October 1938, it emerged

with new force, not at first as a prejudice based on racial assumptions, as in Germany, but rather as an illiberal and narrow view of ethnicity defined by habits of living and, above all, by language shared or not.[5]

Language was a particular determinant of identity before, during, and after the war. While Germans living in Czechoslovakia were given special treatment by the Nazis, Germans after the war experienced the opposite under the Soviets. In general, unless they had married Czechs and had a record of antifascist activity, they had their property seized and they were expelled from the country. This is likewise true of Poland. Hungarians in Czechoslovakia experienced a similar fate.

These early films, such as Radok's, were made in the waning months of the democratic Third Czechoslovak Republic. But in 1948, the Communist Party of Czechoslovakia took over and the country was transformed. As already mentioned, *Distant Journey* was banned after limited screenings and the subject of the Holocaust did not fully reappear on Czech screens until the emergence of the Czech New Wave in roughly 1963. There was an April 1950 resolution that mirrored the Soviet model of the '40s, which meant fewer films and more thematic restrictions. Antonin and Mira Liehm write,

> Soon a wave of arrests and trials, first of non–Communists and later of Communists hit Czechoslovakia. [...] Most of the defendants and the condemned were Jews. At the same time, the campaign against "cosmopolitanism" reached its peak and Czechoslovak film settled on its own Stalinist style, "national in form, socialist in content."[6]

There was a period of violence in the '50s evocative of the Nazi occupation. Peter Hames writes, "The purges are calculated to have included some 136,000 victims through death, imprisonment, and internment."[7] As in Poland, the films from the '50s stuck closely to approved Soviet themes and can be read largely as works of propaganda. But by the middle of the decade, filmmakers began to gradually creep out from under the Party's fist by forming their own production companies, an example set down by Poland that was followed by other Eastern European countries including Czechoslovakia. This coincided with a period of relative freedom beginning in 1956, the "thaw" that I have discussed in other chapters, which seems to have had a particularly liberating effect on Czech cinema. Hames writes, "The year 1956 saw not only the denunciation of Stalinism but also the 'Polish October' and the Hungarian Revolution. For much of Eastern Europe, the period from the mid-fifties to the early sixties was to present a scene of cultural 'thaw' followed by reaction."[8]

This led to Czech directors at the end of the decade returning to World War II themes more openly. Antonin and Mira Liehm write that war themes

> gradually became a safe refuge in moments of repression for cinema as a whole as well as for individual filmmakers. The distinctions in these stories were precise: good was white and ultimately victorious, evil was black and safely vanquished. [...] But there was a third dimension of wartime subject matter, one that came to the forefront in the difficult period at the end of the fifties and in the early sixties. The occupation and the war were used as a package to smuggle in contemporary themes.[9]

Director Jiří Weiss's Shakespeare-inspired *Romeo, Juliet a tma* (*Romeo, Juliet and Darkness*, 1959) is an important precursor to the New Wave in this respect. A Jewish woman (Daniela Smutná, Weiss's then wife) is rescued and hidden by a young man (Ivan Mistrík) and the two fall in love. But when his mother (Jiřina Šejbalová) discovers this, she forces the residents of their building to collectively decide if the girl should be allowed to stay. Things come to a head in the aftermath of Operation Anthropoid, the assassination of Heydrich by two agents sent from England by the Czech government in exile. In the ensuing chaos, the girl is killed.

This was a personal project for the Jewish Weiss; he escaped the war by emigrating to England, where he made a documentary about his country's invasion, *The Rape of Czechoslovakia* (1939). He later made documentaries for the British Army, which allowed him to be present for the liberation of Buchenwald, among other triumphant moments for the Allies. But he returned to Czechoslovakia to find that his family had died in the Holocaust. It is likely that Weiss's seeming political savvy helped him survive not only World War II, but the communist purges and show trials of the '50s. After the repressive Warsaw Pact Invasion in 1968—a subject to which I will return—he fled west and lived out his life as a playwright and professor.

Romeo, Juliet and Darkness is somewhat of a variation on Weiss's previous film, *Vlčí jáma* (*Wolf Trap*, 1957), where an orphan girl comes to stay with a couple and the man of the house falls in love with her. Some of his later films, like British coproduction *Ninety Degrees in the Shade* (1965) also concern the idea of a love triangle in close quarters. But these films, particularly *Romeo, Juliet and Darkness*, imply the hopelessness of love in the face of political oppression. Heydrich's assassination and its aftermath serves to raise the dramatic stakes—a mother disliking his son's romantic partner becomes an issue of life and death. It was a particularly grisly time in Czechoslovakia. Heydrich's death was an excuse to push ideology to its extremes and to pursue a carefully thought out plan for the mass extermination of Jews, as well as non–Jewish Poles, and some Czechs. Timothy Snyder explains,

> Heydrich's assassination meant the loss of a planner of the Final Solution, but the gain of a martyr. Hitler and Himmler met and spoke on June 3rd, 4th, and 5th 1942. Himmler gave the eulogy: "Ours is the holy duty to avenge his death, to take up his labor, and to destroy the enemies of our people without mercy or weakness." One Czech village, Lidice, would be totally destroyed as retribution for the assassination of Heydrich. Its men were shot on the spot, its women sent to the German concentration camp at Ravensbrück, and the children gassed at Chełmno. The Nazi policy of the complete elimination of Polish Jews in the General Government now took the name "Operation Reinhard," as a tribute to Heydrich.[10]

In the case of *Romeo, Juliet and Darkness*, an intimate story becomes a stand in for Czech and Jewish relations during the occupation. The Gestapo raids and executions that occurred in response to Heydrich's assassination can also be seen as subtly symbolic of Soviet terror in the '50s, a subject Weiss could never have approached literally. Weiss was also not the only director to explore this event. Jiří Krejčík's *Vyšší princip* (*Higher Principle*, 1960) follows the arrest of three high school boys after Heydrich's assassination and their professor's attempts to intervene on their behalf. In this incredibly downbeat film, the three boys are arrested by the Gestapo for playing a prank—drawing a mustache on a memorial photo of Heydrich—and despite attempts to save them and a Nazi official's promise to do say, they are scheduled to be executed.

The senselessness of such violence is a common theme among the few World War II films from this period, beginning with *Romeo, Juliet and Darkness* up through the beginning of the New Wave in 1963. For example, Krejčík would continue to explore similar subject matter with *Polnočná omša* (*Midnight Mass*, 1962) about a town that agrees to hide partisan fighters despite the obvious danger. Melancholic films followed, such as

Vojtěch Jasný Přežil *jsem svou smrt* (*I Survived Certain Death*, 1960) and Slovakian director Stanislav Barabáš's *Pieseň o sivom holubovi* (*The Song of the Gray Dove*, 1960), which focuses on a group of school children during the war. *The Song of the Gray Dove* also marks the first real beginning of an independent Slovakian cinema. Weiss's *Zbabelec* (*The Coward*, 1962) is likewise set in a Slovakian village at the end of the war, when a married couple are divided because the wife wants to help antifascists while the husband continues to support the Germans.

The Czech New Wave began shortly after with the 1963 debut films of several young directors, though this period of brief freedom was not solely the purvey of a younger generation—many of the more seasoned directors had waited years to be able to freely explore their own creative visions. Many of the films of the Czech New Wave did not take a literal approach to war themes but included elements of expressionism, horror, fantasy, and the surreal. Hames writes, "In the 1960s, Holocaust films became a significant strand in Czech cinema, ranging in style from realist to expressionist, intimate to experimental, to tragi-comedy, black comedy and horror."[11]

Somewhat like French cinema under the Nazi occupation, themes of fantasy and folklore were an avenue for creative expression in Czech cinema of the '60s, which connected back to prewar Czech literature. Antonin and Mira Liehm explain, "In any consideration of the 'experimental' or 'fantastic' films of the Czechoslovak New Wave, the influence of prewar literature is readily apparent. There are fairly obvious links with the work of Kafka, Vančura, Nezval, and the poetist/surrealist tradition."[12] This literary revival is also directly related to the 1963 Liblice Conference on Kafka, in which the Czech writer was finally unrestricted by Soviet authorities and, for really the first time, celebrated by his home country. Kafka had been banned by the Nazis and remained so for nearly 20 years of Soviet control. For the next five years, many Czech films, particularly those set during World War II, would take on Kafkaesque elements including black comedy, absurdity, and a grim tone not able to be scrubbed out by socialist realism.

An early example of this is Slovakian director Peter Solan's *Boxer a smrt* (*The Boxer and Death*, 1963), about a concentration camp prisoner (Stefan Kvietik) who is able to escape execution by agreeing to box with a Nazi officer (Manfred Krug). It's a bitter and somewhat hopeless look into what a desperate man is willing to do to survive, what compromises he is willing to swallow. In order to avoid instant death, Jan agrees to train—which includes better treatment than the average camp inmate—to become a worthy opponent for Sturmbannführer Kraft, which means he amounts to little more than a plaything. Jan must constantly swallow his pride to prolong his survival and his life essentially becomes dependent on the whims of a bored sadist. The story is based on real fighting rings at Auschwitz, organized to entertain Nazi guards. Solan draws attention to the ironic and fundamentally absurd seriousness of an amateur boxing match inside a mass killing center.

Another important example is Ján Kadár and Elmar Klos's *Smrt si říká Engelchen* (*Death Is Called Engelchen*, 1963), which follows an injured resistance fighter (Jan Kacer) in the last days of the war as he meditates on his experiences. Kadár and Klos were an effective pair and their film is almost flagrantly anti-realist with its grim tone and non-linear narrative that challenge the Soviet understanding of partisan fighting as inherently heroic. Antonin and Mira Liehm write that *Death Is Called Engelchen* raises the point that "it is no longer a question of the 'good guys' and the 'bad guys' but of war itself, war as an evil, destroying moral values on all sides and scarring the victors as profoundly as the vanquished."[13]

Death Is Called Engelchen brutally exposes the hopelessness and messiness of war. Despite the partisan's brave fighting and many sacrifices, his effort seems pointless; he is shot in the spine immediately after peace is declared. Being a resistance fighter is shown to be a thankless task and anyone who collaborated to save lives or steal information will now likely become a target after the war. The resistance fighter is even shown to struggle with killing a German and feels clear sympathy for the soldier he has been ordered to kill. Ewa Mazierska writes, "Jan uses introspection not to indulge in his heroism but to rebuild his inner unity that was shattered by the war. However, by pondering on his past, he transforms what is already a history into an everlasting nightmare."[14]

Zbyněk Brynych's *Transport z ráje* (*Transport from Paradise*, 1963) is even bleaker and returns to explore the themes of *Distant Journey*: life in Terezin. Like *Distant Journey*, *Transport from Paradise* focuses on the horrifying double nature of Terezin as part ghetto, part concentration camp, part transport center, and part masquerade. The script is based on *Night and Hope*, written by Holocaust survivor Arnošt Lustig, who spent time in Terezin, Auschwitz, and Buchenwald, and whose writings also inspired Jan Němec's film *Démanty noci* (*Diamonds of the Night*, 1964). *Transport from Paradise* is, at least in part, a highly stylized exploration of *Theresienstadt: Ein Dokumentarfilm aus dem jüdischen Siedlungsgebiet* (*Terezin: A Documentary Film of the Jewish Resettlement*). This is the fake documentary Nazis forced actor Kurt Gerron to shoot in the camp to make it seem like a pleasant vacation resort. Brynych folds these staged moments into *Transport from Paradise* and includes documentary-style footage that appears to be behind-the-scenes shots.

The ghetto streets have been recently cleaned for beautification in *Transport from Paradise* (*Transport z ráje*, Československá Filmexport/Československá Státní Film/Filmové studio Barrandov, 1963).

Like Radok, Brynych focused on the cruelty and hopelessness of life under totalitarian oppression. Unlike many American or western European films, a full range of Jewish characters are shown heroically attempting to survive their ordeal; including members of the camp underground who print "Death to the Fascists!" posters. Because the culprits are not found, Nazi officials declare they will send thousands to Auschwitz, but the leader of the Jewish council must decide personally on who will be transported to their deaths. This was a relatively typical experience. A Jewish council known as a Judenrat was required to form in ghettos and certain concentration camps. This was a particularly sadistic form of bureaucracy; the Judenrat leaders were expected to "govern" their communities and were given limited power in exchange for cooperating with the Nazis. Some historians have interpreted their function as collaborationist. There are also stories, as Hannah Arendt discusses in *Eichmann in Jerusalem: A Report on the Banality of Evil* (1964), of the Judenrat taking advantage of their power.

Essentially though, as can be seen in *Transport from Paradise*, they served as something of an intermediary between the Nazi overseers of ghettos and concentration camps and their own people. While some Judenrat members were more manipulative and sought to help only themselves or their own family members, others selflessly worked with the underground resistance. It can be clearly seen in *Transport from Paradise* that Nazi decision-making was not impacted by Judenrat actions in any substantial way, but was just another cruel attempt to make their Jewish prisoners suffer. When the leader in *Transport from Paradise* refuses to hand over a list of names, he is promptly replaced and added to the transport list himself. The Nazis within the film are not presented as evil because they are sadistic and bloodthirsty; rather because they are utterly indifferent, bureaucrats concerned with counting roll calls and measuring stolen property. There is even something tragic about a Nazi leader's driver (Jiří Vršťala), who speaks Czech and seems miserable yet resigned to his fate. His small acts of resistance include shooting a Jewish woman to prevent her further torture and torment.

Brynych immediately followed *Transport to Paradise* with *A pátý jezdec je strach* (*The Fifth Horseman Is Fear*, 1964). Though it's set in an innocuous apartment building rather than a concentration camp, the tone is similar. Even more than *Transport from Paradise*, *The Fifth Horsemen Is Fear* subtly focuses on communal guilt and complicity. The film follows Dr. Braun (Miroslav Macháček), a Jewish doctor who has been forbidden from practicing medicine by the Nazis and is now employed to sort and catalog stolen Jewish property. When Braun agrees to tend to a wounded resistance fighter, he winds up going on a surreal journey through the city to find morphine for the man's pain. This doubles as Braun's journey to find himself again and to redeem himself.

Though the Holocaust is not literally depicted in the film, Brynych evokes by showing Prague in the grip of apocalyptic fear—Braun wanders through a whorehouse, a wild club fittingly called the Desperation Bar, and a madhouse—a Kafkaesque cityscape that is also an obvious allegory for Soviet totalitarianism. Šárka Sladovníková argues that many Holocaust films from this period, like *The Fifth Horseman Is Fear*, are concerned primarily with the theme of fear, and fear as a reaction to evil. She writes,

> The main characters in the films of the 1960s deal with ethical dilemmas and are confronted with evil, sometimes collaborating with it (*The Shop on Main Street*) and other times taking a stand against it (*The Fifth Horseman Is Fear*). An important theme is the evil within people (*Transport from Paradise*, *The Shop on Main Street*, *The Cremator*), portrayed primarily through ordinary "little" people and run-of-the-mill citizens.[15]

It's important to note that the film was co-written by Ester Krumbachová—adapted from a novel by Hana Bělohradská—whose involvement in the Czech New Wave was pervasive but still hasn't been as widely acknowledged as she deserves. At the time, she was generally credited as a costume designer, as she is on *The Fifth Horseman Is Fear*, but she worked regularly as a scriptwriter, which included collaborations with some of the most important directors of the period: Brynych, her then-husband Jan Němec, and Věra Chytilová, among others. Krumbachová's influence on the New Wave cannot be understated; her "costume design" credits often mask input on style and production, while her scripts contain themes that occur throughout her career, making her something of a background auteur.

Alice Němcová Tejkalová writes that "fundamentally, Krumbachová is concerned with the issue of freedom and the complex ways in which pleasure cannot be an easy index of value."[16] Her scripts for *The Fifth Horseman Is Fear* and Němec's radical *O slavnosti a hostech* (*A Report on the Party and the Guests*, 1965) are concerned with subjects like the evils of totalitarianism and power's ability to corrupt. Brynych and Krumbachová intentionally kept the film vague in terms of historical references. Hames writes that they

> deprived it of its topical references, including the Nazi insignia, in order to represent fascism as "an international disease" whose symptoms were to be found in many countries. A world of fear and of informing is evoked.[17]

The Fifth Horseman Is Fear is not the last of Brynych's films to explore these themes. He would go on to make *Ja, Spravedlnost* (*I, Justice*, 1968), a sci-fi-tinged thriller effort that follows another doctor charged to treat a mystery patient during the Nuremberg trials: Hitler, whose suicide was faked and who is now being held in a sanatorium. A shadowy organization that includes former Nazis have decided Hitler must be punished for Germany's defeat. They pretend the war is still on and reenact his capture, trial, and near execution over and over again, until the doctor decides to be merciful. *Transport from Paradise*, *The Fifth Horseman Is Fear*, and *I, Justice* are all concerned with how totalitarianism impacts a community and the ways in which individuals are responsible for and complicit in their own destruction. Brynych asserts that it is an individual's duty to stand up and do what is right, to resist—as with the Jewish leader in *Transport from Paradise* and the respective doctors in *The Fifth Horseman Is Fear* and *I, Justice*. But his films also end on hopelessly grim notes, which suggest that resistance only leads to death.

A more literal interpretation of the Holocaust can be found in Němec's feature debut, the surreal and nightmarish *Démanty noci* (*Diamonds of the Night*, 1964), which follows two Jewish boys (Ladislav Jánský and Antonín Kumbera) running from a train transport meant to take them to a concentration camp. Their Grimm fairytale-like flight through a forest is intersected with memories, dreams, and hallucinations—such as sequences where the boys contemplate violence and imagine its outcomes. Based on another autobiographical work by Arnošt Lustig and cast with non-professional actors, *Diamonds of the Night* was a unique experiment in Czech cinema at the time of its release. Liehm writes, "What Němec is striving for can best be described as psychological truth. […] The flashbacks of *Diamonds of the Night* are incomplete and almost subliminal in quality, flashing in and out of consciousness in accordance with the physical and psychological demands of the present."[18]

Diamonds of the Night is actually Němec's second attempt at such material. While a student at the famed FAMU Film School, he made a short film, *Sousto* (*A Loaf of Bread*,

1960), another Lustig adaptation about two men who steal bread from a train guarded by the SS. The importance of objects is central to many Czech Holocaust films from *Transport from Paradise* through to later in the decade like *The Cremator*. A loaf of bread is key not only to *A Loaf of Bread* but also to *Diamonds in the Night*. Hames writes,

> The film's main narrative device centres on a pair of boots which has been exchanged for bread on the train. It is because of the ill-fitting boots that they will be captured. A close-up of the mud-caked boots leads to an immediate flashback to them in the railcar among emaciated camp members. It is the first of a series of close-ups that provide a potent evocation of increasing lameness. In repeated images, we see boots painfully eased off, the bruised feet painfully unwrapped or prodded.[19]

Instead of conveying information through dialogue or some expository sequence, objects are often the key to unlocking the subconscious mind: either unraveling a memory or fantasy that gets to the heart of the experience of survival. *Diamonds of the Night* in particular stresses that this attempt to survive either twists good people to become violent or merely brings out the latent violence that exists in everyone; it is certainly a departure from the mainstream Holocaust narrative of evil Nazis and their innocent victims. Němec is able to put the audience in the shoes (literally and figuratively in this case) of Holocaust survivors. Hames writes, "He is not interested in telling a story or explaining the actions of his characters, but in making a close identification with their mental state."[20]

Like many other Czech World War II films in the '60s, it's also a comment on life under a totalitarian system—and not a particularly subtle one as Němec was blacklisted soon after thanks to the double whammy of *Diamonds of the Night* and *A Report on the Party and the Guests*. Antonin and Mira Liehm write that *Diamonds of the Night* ultimately depicts an "abstract vision of young people persecuted by a hostile world with which they strive in vain to establish contact—a world that is most tellingly represented by a group of impotent old men in a position of power."[21] The film's ambiguous ending, where the boys are caught and it is suggested they will be executed, is intentionally vague. Němec leaves the burden of deciding the likely outcome to the viewer, in a way making his audience complicit with the townspeople who turn in the two boys.

It was not only Czech directors who began to explore this parallel between Nazis fascism and Soviet totalitarianism; Slovakian filmmakers soon turned to these themes. Perhaps the most famous Slovakian film ever made, at least on an international level, remains Ján Kadár and Elmar Klos's *Obchod na korze* (*The Shop on Main Street*, 1965).[22] It has long been lumped in with the Czech New Wave but it is important to remember that this was largely a Slovakian production and was shot (and set) in a Slovakian village. While it certainly belongs to the tradition of other Czechoslovak World War II-themed films like *Distant Journey*, *The Boxer and Death*, *The Fifth Horseman Is Fear*, and *Diamonds in the Night*, it's necessary to discuss *The Shop on Main Street* as a distinctly Slovakian film because of the somewhat unique participation of Slovakia not only in World War II, but particularly in the Holocaust.

In 1942, Tóno (Jozef Kroner), a carpenter who has had trouble finding work and is constantly nagged by his wife (Hana Slivkova), is given a surprise promotion from his high-ranking fascist brother-in-law (Markus Kolkocký): he's ordered to take over a sewing shop owned by an elderly, Jewish widow, Mrs. Lautmannová (Ida Kamińska). The local Jewish businesses are all being gifted to Aryan "protectors" as part of the Nazi policy of Aryanization. But she's almost deaf and has no idea what has been going on in the world; a protective neighbor convinces her that Tóno is a distant relative who has come to serve as her assistant. Feeling sorry for her and won over by her naive sweetness, Tóno agrees to this ruse, even though he learns the shop isn't profitable and his brother-in-law has (unintentionally?) duped him. The local Jewish council offers him a regular stipend to remain the old lady's protector and as he stays on, he grows quite close to Mrs. Lautmannová. But to his horror, he learns that transport trains have arrived and a round up of the town's Jews is imminent.

Shown at Cannes and the recipient of the 1965 Academy Award for Best Foreign Language Film, *The Shop on Main Street* holds an interesting position in that it is a celebrated Holocaust film while also avoiding the trappings of conventional films like Wanda Jakubowska's *The Last Stage*. Hames writes, "Despite its grim and ironic theme, the film is played primarily as a comedy, observing the human qualities and failings of its protagonists. It is conventional in its narrative approach while including subjective and fantasy sequence scenes within its framework."[23] Like Jakubowska, Kadár was a survivor whose family died in Auschwitz. In an essay on the film, he writes,

> I am not thinking of the fate of all the six million tortured Jews, but that my work is shaped by the fate of my father, my friends' fathers, mothers of those near to me and by people whom I have known. I am not interested in the outer trappings—figures, statements, generalizations. I want to make emotive films.[24]

Kadár explains that Klos, his longtime collaborator, gave him relative creative freedom for the film, which was based on a novel from Ladislaw Grosman, who also wrote

An eager Tóno (Jozef Kroner) meets Mrs (Lautmannová (Ida Kamińska) in *The Shop on Main Street*, unaware that he will soon become her protector (*Obchod na korze*, Filmové studio Barrandov, 1965).

the script. Their loose theme was "fascism from within" and—bucking the expectations of traditional Soviet cinema—Kadár and Klos sought to make a film about the experiences of an ordinary individual. Kadár writes,

> Ladislav Mnacko wrote in connection with the Eichmann trial that he found the key to understanding the fate of the Jews he had known personally, not in the sum total of those indirectly killed by Eichmann. [...] The most perfect reconstruction of a situation—and this brings us to *The Shop on Main Street*—cannot outdo a picture of fascism concentrated in the tragedy of a single human being.[25]

Tóno is an absurd, even comic figure with a tolerable, if seemingly satisfying life, but he is a powerful symbol of the film's themes of greed and opportunism versus moral purity. Unlike many other European nations who suffered under Nazi occupation, Slovakia was technically independent, though it was really a satellite state (much like Croatia). Part of the Austro-Hungarian Empire for centuries and then part of Czechoslovakia thanks to the redrawing of borders in 1918 as a result of World War I, it is likely that the nation's desire for independence—and the prominence of fascist factions within the country, like the Hlinka guard—led to this bargain with the Nazis. Though not required to, they participated in the Nazi invasion of Poland that led to the start of World War II and later, the invasion of the Soviet Union. Slovakia was enthusiastic in aiding the Nazi destruction of the country's Jewish population. For example, in the case of Slovakian Jews being sent to Auschwitz, Timothy Snyder writes,

> Because Auschwitz was well supplied with water and well connected by rail, Himmler saw it, as did the upper management of IG Farben, as an ideal site for the production of artificial rubber. Himmler sought Jewish laborers in Slovakia, whose leaders were happy to be rid of them. Himmler made the case in October 1941; within a year Slovakia had deported 57,628 of its Jewish citizens. Almost all of them would die.[26]

The Shop on Main Street, then, is concerned directly with this issue of willing collaboration and the enthusiasm of local populations to participate in anti–Semitism violence at worst, opportunism at best. A character in the film references the German saying, "Feed the wolf and keep the sheep," and many of the film's characters, including Tóno's wife, are either unable or unwilling to see the evil they are causing because of a sense of greed and entitlement. The "us versus them" mentality includes the notion that "a Jew lover is worse than a Jew," as if empathy is the ultimate crime. Tóno's fundamental decency drives him to madness and (some very unexpected) violence and the downbeat ending flies in the face of communist cinematic conventions.

As discussed, the communist-controlled government took film seriously as a medium, primarily to disseminate its message. Socialist realism was the expected norm and *The Shop on Main Street*'s brittle, biting comedy is an attack against that—it is the tragic story of one individual trying to figure out how to do the right thing in a society of people who don't care what is or is not right moral action. Martin Votruba writes that in Soviet film

> The topics were to emphasize the need to work for the good of "the collective"—that is, communist society. Topics focusing on the individual and his or her personal feelings and concerns were deemed harmful, as was depicting anything negative about society. Tóno's community is not necessarily a fundamentally poisoned, corrupt place—there are several non–Jews who are sympathetic to Mrs. Lautmannová and their other neighbors—but none who are willing to act, save Tóno.[27]

The heart of the film lies in the two lead performances from Jozef Kroner and Polish actress Ida Kamińska. Kroner portrays Tóno as a fundamentally decent, if somewhat absurd, even flawed everyman; and the film's tragedy is that these good intentions are nowhere near enough to confront such consuming evil. But Kadár and Klos issue a challenge that such actions are necessary even if they are guaranteed to fail—a similar message that Brynych imparts in films like *The Fifth Horseman Is Fear*. It's impossible to fathom that any individual could focus on the rewards of local prosperity—as symbolized by the gradually growing wooden tower, a monument to the lure of fascism—when confronted with the look on Mrs. Lautmannová's face when she finally understands what is happening in her town. She asks, "am I going mad or has the world gone mad?" And in a devastating moment mumbles a word that speaks to not only World War II-era anti-Semitism, but to the historical plight of Jews in Eastern Europe: "pogrom."

Slovakian directors like Štefan Uher continued to explore the horrors of fascism as a parallel for totalitarianism with films like *Organ* (*The Organ*, 1965), where a Polish deserter (Alexander Březina) hides out in a Franciscan monastery. He happens to be a talented organist whose playing is encouraged by the monastery head (Kamil Marek), but he soon finds himself at odds with the choirmaster (František Bubík), who is going through a sort of moral crisis. The choirmaster's sense of superiority and his desperation to feel important drives him to become an informer. Religion—either in practice or as a cinematic theme—was particularly frowned upon by the Soviet authorities and Uher's film was banned not long after its release. Slovakian director Stanislav Barabáš explored similar moral conundrums in *Zvony pre bosých* (*The Bells Toll for the Barefooted*, 1965), about two partisans who take a young German soldier prisoner with the intention of turning him in, but they become lost in the wilderness.

But perhaps the most important film from this period—at least on an international level—is Jiří Menzel's debut feature film *Ostře sledované vlaky* (*Closely Watched Trains*, 1965). Based on a novel by Bohumil Hrabal, whose work Menzel repeatedly adapted, *Closely Watched Trains* is a return to the sort of Kafkaesque comedy that Czech filmmakers became known for in this period. The young and awkward Miloš (Václav Neckář) becomes a guard at a small train station during the occupation. He is mostly concerned with avoiding work and advancing his relationships with women, which includes losing his virginity. When this doesn't go well, he unsuccessfully tries to kill himself. Meanwhile the trains are being attacked by Resistance fighters and a Nazi collaborator has started spending time at the station. An experienced Resistance agent (Naďa Urbánková) delivers a bomb to the local underground and has sex with Miloš. When the intended agent is unable to blow up the station, a newly confident Miloš steps in and sacrifices himself for the Resistance.

Much of *Closely Watched Trains* plays out like an unexpected sex comedy—the more conservative figures are embarrassed by sex, while it is the central concern of the young Miloš's life. He associates virginity loss with both masculinity and maturity and when he prematurely ejaculates during his first attempt to have sex, he is filled with a genuine (if comedic) shame that leads to his attempted suicide. Liehm argues that this ribald humor actually has a subversive political edge. He writes, "This association of sex with the theme of national liberation as one of the most politically 'subversive' qualities of the film, undercutting the traditional (and inhuman) convention of the noble resistance fighter."[28] Miloš is ultimately heroic, but is also shown to be ridiculous, a type of protagonist found somewhat often throughout Czech films of this period, where audiences are asked to identify with antiheroes, absurd everyday figures, or young people caught up in dreams and fantasy. Several historians have discussed this in the context of Jaroslav Hašek's satirical World War I novel *The Good Soldier Švejk* (1921), about the fundamental absurdity of war and violence with a protagonist, Švejk, whose own stupidity and incompetence becomes a form of resistance.

But Czech films about violence as resistance were not always comedic, as in the case of the dark psychological thriller *Kočár do Vídně* (*Coach to Vienna*, 1966), about a young widow (Iva Janzurová) who is forced to drive Austrian soldiers to the border in her wagon. She has recently lost her husband, who was executed over a trivial theft, and plans to get revenge against the two soldiers—though they are young, injured, and seemingly innocent—on their long, lonely ride through the woods. However she succumbs to her own humanity and begins to sympathize with them. Ultimately she doesn't kill them when she has the chance. But the film takes an even darker turn; the carriage is set upon by partisans—Resistance fighters who are typically shown as heroic in Soviet cinema—who kill the soldiers and rape the widow. Several of these films in the mid-'60s explore how regular Czech citizens are pushed to violence by the war itself; there is also an increase in decent German characters and villainous Czechs—themes that made the Soviet censors increasingly uncomfortable.

But in 1968, a watershed year for Czechoslovakia, everything was to change, including the national cinema. Under the auspices of leader Alexander Dubček, Czechoslovakia went through a series of liberal reforms beginning in January of 1968. Unfortunately this

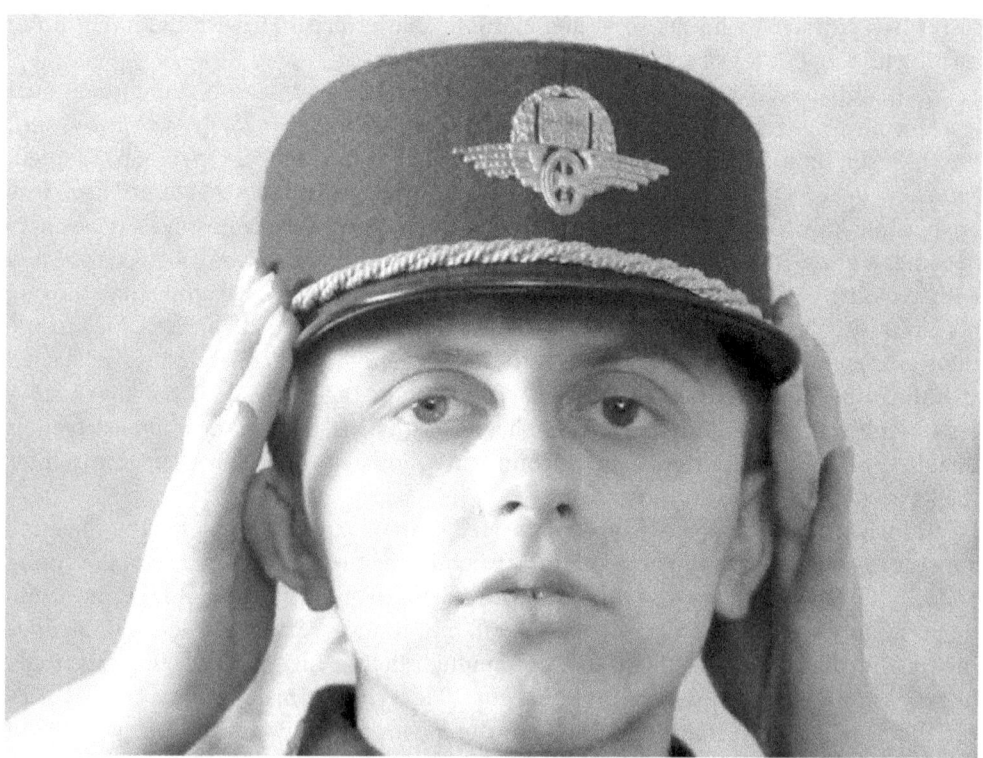

Miloš (Václav Neckář) prepares for his first day at the train station with a uniform that's too big for him (*Ostre sledované vlaky*, Filmové studio Barrandov, 1966).

only lasted about halfway through the year; by August, the country was invaded by the Soviet Union and the reforms were repressed, introducing a wave of even tighter restrictions. The so-called Prague Spring and the backlash it inspired effectively brought an end to the Czech New Wave and the cinema that flourished because of its motley band of directors, many of whom were banished, blacklisted from making films, or severely curtailed. Hames writes,

> After the 1968 invasion, film production remained unaffected until the reorganization of the industry in 1969–70, which led to the banning or stopping of some ten new features, a third of the annual output. The blacklist was subsequently extended backward to include many of the most important films of the 1960s.[29]

There was, however, a brief window where business carried on as usual, resulting in one of the most important World War II films of the period: Slovakian director Juraj Herz's *Spalovač mrtvol* (*The Cremator*, 1969). Jonathan Owen writes that "during late 1968 and 1969 Czechoslovak culture peaked in both achievement and audacity, with the Surrealists openly pursuing their activities and with many of the most aesthetically radical and politically provocative New Wave films being made."[30] *The Cremator* is both surreal and audacious, focusing on the deranged Karl Kopfrkingl (Rudolf Hrušínský), a crematorium worker in Prague in 1939, who becomes a Nazi collaborator. Kopfrkingl is delusional and increasingly dangerous. He believes that cremating dead bodies will release the souls trapped within and soon kills his Jewish wife and son. He thinks the Nazi suggestion of killing via gas chambers is revolutionary and will free souls—potentially all souls in the entire world.

Herz wasn't directly a member of the Czech New Wave; his preference for historical settings put him at odds with some of the more politically radical directors, but in this case Herz makes obvious parallels between Czechoslovakia in the '40s and in the

The world is distorted and turned upside down by the madness of fascism in *The Cremator* (*Spalovac mrtvol*, Filmové studio Barrandov/Sebor See, 1969).

'60s. Like other directors from the period adopting war stories, *The Cremator* has autobiographical connections. It was based on a novel by Ladislav Fuks, who also worked on the script; Fuks grew up during the Nazi occupation. Herz himself was Holocaust survivor and returned to the subject multiple times throughout his career. For example, for his later film *Zastihla me noc* (*Night Over Takes Me*, 1986), a more conventional Holocaust drama, he filmed one of his own experiences. He said,

> The first day I came into the concentration camp they undressed us and sent us into the showers. There were only a few children and the rest were men who started a terrible panic. At that time, it was already known what the showers meant. I was there looking at the panic-stricken adults and I knew there was no gas in the tubes because there were glass windows in the room. It would be easy to break them and let the gas out. So I knew it couldn't be a gas chamber. After a while, water started to come out from the tubes, and all the men were screaming that it was just water and not gas.[31, 32]

Though such horrific autobiographical moments don't appear in *The Cremator* in the same literal sense, it is as close to a horror film as you could find in Czechoslovakia at the time and was obviously indebted to German expressionism. The film's dreamlike script conflates Kopfrkingl's growing madness with the increased Nazi terror. Their presence in his country begins to warp his understanding of the world. The implication here is that to collude with fascist or totalitarian forces and to truly believe their political agenda is utopian, one must be delusional, even mad or psychotic. Hames writes,

> The fim is permeated by a sense of insanity. In selecting a madman as their hero, Herz and Fuks are able to generate an additional horror that provides a fresh response to the familiar and mundane qualities of Nazi logic and the collaborationist ethic.[33]

Like *Closely Watched Trains*, *The Cremator* draws an unsettling parallel between comedy and horror, Kafkaesque absurdism and emotional realism. Bodies and human sexuality itself are subjugated to the all-consuming maw of fascism in a literal sense as Kopfrkingl's crematoria becomes a death factory. Though he is not exactly a sympathetic figure, Kopfrkingl is tragic in his madness and is yet another Czechoslovakian protagonist from the period who is in some way absurd, ridiculous, or deeply flawed. As many Holocaust films assert, collaboration can often guarantee survival, but at what cost? Daniel Bird writes, "Herz's film offers a perverse, cynical twist, equating survival with conformity. The timing of the release of *Spalovač mrtvol* was uncanny, less than a year after the invasion of another regime in which conformists were also most required."[34]

The government was unsurprisingly not thrilled about this depiction of collaboration with totalitarian powers and the film was banned for decades, essentially sounding the death knell of subversive cinema in Czechoslovakia. Though there were a few films to come at the end of this period or somewhat later in the '70s, there is no body of work in Czechoslovak cinema to equal the vibrant period of the '60s and the New Wave. Certain films like Slovakian director Juraj Jakubisco's *Zbehovia a pútnici* (*The Deserter and the Nomads*, 1968)—an anthology with one segment set during the end of World War II—focuses on senseless violence and the absurdity of war, but neither Jakubisco nor his films would reach the same level of international fame as *The Cremator*. Examples include other films to come in the wake of the New Wave like František Vláčil's *Adelheid* (1970), which is really a romantic melodrama with the war as a backdrop to provide subtext about German and Czech relations.

Despite these few exceptions, the power of the New Wave was scattered to the winds along with its core group of directors. The majority of the movements major directed left the country and those who remained were unable to make further films. But over fifty years later, these Czechoslovakian films remain vital works—especially in terms of Holocaust cinema, particularly considering that both Hollywood and European studios continue to mine the themes of World War II and the Holocaust with predictable results, despite the unnerving modern political parallels.

11

Ordinary Fascism
World War II Films Behind the Iron Curtain

"The key planners worked under the watchful eye of Heinrich Himmler, and under the direct command of Reinhard Heydrich. Under the general heading of 'Generalplan Ost,' SS Standartenführer Professor Konrad Meyer drafted a series of plans for a vast eastern colony. [...] The general design was consistent throughout: Germans would deport, kill, assimilate, or enslave the native populations, and bring order and prosperity to a humbled frontier. Depending upon the demographic estimates, between thirty-one and forty-five million people, mostly Slavs, were to disappear."—Timothy Snyder, *Bloodlands: Europe Between Hitler and Stalin*[1]

Perhaps more so than any other territory on earth, the devastating effects of World War II have had an intimate, complicated, and continuing impact on the culture of Eastern Europe, and so, for a variety of reasons, I have chosen to examine these films as a loose group, with the exceptions of Polish and Czechoslovakian cinema, which have already been explored separately. In some ways, I find this frustrating; too often, the many nations that fall under the umbrella of Eastern Europe—or more correctly, Central and Eastern Europe—are lumped together by English language historians and cultural critics when the reality is that many of these nations don't share the same language and have wide cultural differences. But it makes sense for my purposes, for several reasons, to examine these films as a group, mainly because the films made in Central and Eastern Europe from 1945 to 1991 were made under the all-encompassing umbrella of Soviet censorship—a condition different to how films were made in other European countries.

Perhaps ironically, this is a direct result of World War II, of the way in which the boundaries of Central and Eastern Europe were redrawn at the end of the war. The Molotov-Ribbentrop Pact, signed in August of 1939, vowed mutual non-aggression between Nazi Germany and Soviet Russia and effectively split the territories between the two in half, beginning with the mutual invasion of Poland a mere month later. When the Soviet Army later pushed their way into Berlin at the end of the war, the territories they occupied would become part of the larger network of Soviet states known as the Eastern Bloc: this included the Soviet Union itself, a massive territory made up of contemporary Russia, Ukraine, Belarus, Estonia, Latvia, Lithuania, and numerous Asian countries south of Russia, as well as Soviet satellite states like Romania, Bulgaria, Poland, Czechoslovakia,

11. Ordinary Fascism

Hungary, Albania, and, to a different degree, Yugoslavia. This new map—and the ensuing political alliances it suggested—was then cemented by the Cold War.

But exploring the concept of World War II-themed films in these countries is a tricky undertaking, for a variety of reasons. First, because of the sheer wealth of World War II-themed films produced. The war was an overwhelmingly popular, officially sanctioned subject for Soviet cinema, though many of the films produced on this topic are still unavailable to an English speaking audience. Secondly, the territory between western Russia and the western border of Nazi occupied Poland was home to the worst horrors of the war, perpetuated by both Stalin and Hitler, including horrific prisoner-of-war camps, mass shootings on a scale unprecedented in human history, and mass starvations. But because of the communist censors, there are a serious lack of films that deal frankly and honestly with the atrocities committed before and during the war years.

The Soviet tendency to rewrite history further complicates matters. In general, mainstream war narratives remained symbolic of tragedy and perseverance, hardship overcome, a struggle against the ultimate evil; often it was an excuse to tell straightforward tales of politicized injustice, painted in stark black and white: moral absolutes that exalted the fight of heroic Soviets over fascist tyrants. It doesn't help matters that the majority of atrocities committed by Nazis or Soviets never became a part of official public record, the memory of these events lived on through the accounts of survivors (both alive and dead), many of whom had fled west or to Israel in the immediate postwar years. Finally, there is a shortage of what I would describe as arthouse cinema, at least in comparison with English-language, Western European, and East Asian films. If one is focusing on transgressive, cult, or non-mainstream films, this is almost non-existent in Soviet-controlled cinema; for instance, there is no Eastern European equivalent of the Nazisploitation subgenre or any similar type of exploitation movies. While science fiction movies exist, there are almost no horror films. Certainly, some genre films exist. There is a consistent absurdist, even surrealist literary influence that winds its way through Central and Eastern European cinema. This is largely thanks to a handful of key directors: wayward, determined individuals who were generally ejected from their home countries, forced to leave if they wanted to find work, or had their films banned. Their work was often possible because of periods of general tolerance, such as the thaw in the '50s in some countries.

The focus of this chapter will primarily be on the films of the Soviet Union, Romania, Bulgaria, and Hungary. I will also briefly discuss Yugoslavian cinema, which has some parallels but must be regarded as separate because of the complicated political history. The Socialist Federal Republic of Yugoslavia was recognized by the Soviet Union in 1945—it included modern day countries Bosnia and Herzegovina, Croatia, Macedonia, Montenegro, Serbia, and Slovenia. But its outspoken leader Josip Broz Tito parted ways with Stalin in 1948. Though Yugoslavia cannot be thought of as part of the Soviet Union, it adopted a similar policy to cinema, and as such can be explored alongside Soviet-produced films.

In 1945, there was already a system in place of what the Soviet Union and Stalin in particular had in mind for the path of Soviet cinema to come thanks to one Andrei Zhdanov, one of the Party leaders and effectively the government's chief propagandist. He believed that all art and culture should promote Soviet ideals and approved Party "morals." The perceived imperialistic influence of American culture was rejected and Zhdanov wanted any foreign influence excised. His ideal cinema presented the world in black and white terms and promoted socialism above all else. Antonin and Mira Liehm explain that the "Zhdanov resolution showed little concern for esthetics or the relationship between art and reality. All that was asked of art was that it be a weapon of day-to-day political work."[2]

Any films viewed as being bourgeois, avant-garde, realist, or modernist were blacklisted, and the rich pre–World War II film tradition all but disappeared with the death of cinema master Sergei Eisenstein in 1948. Artists that deviated from this expected standard were punished in various ways: having their work censored or banned, having their career interrupted or terminated, arrest, banishment, and so on. Antonin and Mira Liehm argue that while many Soviet artists and intellectuals understood the need for Party totalitarianism in the '20s and '30s, when the government was fighting to survive, by 1945 they expected more tolerance. They write,

> After years of purges, terrorism, and the apocalypse of war, Soviet intellectuals and artists once again began to speak out—as an act expressing their faith that a victorious regime need no longer fear enemies from within, and that it would now be willing to become a true government of the people.[3]

It's also important to understand that with the consolidation of the Soviet Union, the Party found themselves in control of more than just Russian cinema. The Soviet Union itself comprised Russia as well as Armenia, Azerbaijan, Belarus, Estonia, Georgia, Kazakhstan, Kyrgyzstan, Latvia, Lithuania, Moldova, Turkmenistan, Tajikistan, Ukraine, and Uzbekistan. Though the countries in the Eastern Bloc[4] were not all directly governed by the Soviet Union, they worked closely together thanks to the Warsaw Pact and Comecon arrangements. Many of their governments were closely modeled on the Soviet Union and are generally considered to be satellite states: the People's Republic of Bulgaria and the People's Republic of Albania were formed in 1946, the Polish People's Republic and the Socialist Republic of Romania in 1947, the Czechoslovak Socialist Republic in 1948, and the German Democratic Republic and the Hungarian People's Republic in 1949.

The Soviet films made in the years immediately following the war establish the model that other cinemas were expected to duplicate. A film like *Встреча на Эльбе* (*Encounter at the Elbe*, 1949) from the great Mosfilm studio is an important example of this. Focused on Elbe Day, in April 1945, the historical moment when Allied and Soviet troops met at the Elbe River in Germany, the film paints the Soviet soldiers as heroes and the Americans as villainous. Antonin and Mira Liehm write that it takes place in "the divided city of Altenstadt, with Americans looting while the Soviet Army aids its section of the town in rebuilding itself; the Soviets support the antifascists while the American administration seeks the aid of notorious Nazis."[5]

Films of this type, which dominated Soviet cinema for more than fifty years, became known as socialist realism—really little more than propaganda meant to rewrite history to the liking of Stalin and later Party leaders. A notable title is *Молодая гвардия* (*The Young Guard*, 1948), a two-part serial about young Russian students who bravely form an anti-fascist resistance organization in response to the German Army's arrival in their town. Though Soviet military forces have moved out, they take up combat themselves. Another key early example is *Падение Берлина* (*The Fall of Berlin*, 1949), another serial that follows an ordinary steel factory worker-turned soldier (Boris Andreyev) during World War II, which primarily exists to illustrate the magnificence of Stalin and the Party. Socialist realism demanded a focus on everyday people, especially workers, who were generally cast as protagonists. They were required to limit their narratives to events from mundane life, were expected to be "realistic" and optimistic, and most of all were required to support the Party and its ideology.

An early example of how these requirements clashed with realistic World War II narratives can be found in East Germany—the German Democratic Republic or GDR (Deutsche Demokratische Republik or DDR in German). Early East German cinema came from the state-run DEFA (Deutsche Film Aktiengesellschaft) studio and was initially inspired by socialist German artists, writers, and filmmakers like Bertolt Brecht, though many of them were soon alienated by the new government. There was a brief period of flexibility, where the main focus of the national cinema was to educate Germans living in the GDR about socialist values, but in general the DEFA and the GDR followed the Soviet cinema model from their earliest days.

I have already discussed the *Trümmerfilm* or rubble film in the context of West German cinema in an earlier chapter, but it is worth mentioning again as the genre began several years before the country was divided in two in 1949. Rubble films can be seen as foundational for the way both East and West Germany portrayed World War II on screen in the first decade or two after the war ended. *Murderers Among Us*, released in 1946, and one of the standards of the rubble film, was actually produced by DEFA before it became an expressly East German studio three years later. Its message of casting aside personal revenge and turning towards a hopeful future was reproduced for many rubble films. The GDR, like so many of the Soviet-occupied states, was quick to use the subject of fascist injustice as popular cinematic material.

Both before and after the foundation of the new government, DEFA made films addressing the Nazi persecution of Jews. Among the first of these was director Kurt Maetzig's *Ehe im Schatten* (*Marriage in the Shadows*, 1947), about the relationship between a German actor (Paul Klinger) and his Jewish wife (Ilse Steppat). Refusing to leave or divorce her, despite orders from the Nazi command, he kills himself alongside his wife. Maetzig, one of East Germany's most prominent directors, made the film as a memorial. It was based on the life of actor Joachim Gottschalk, who committed suicide with his Jewish wife and son rather than abandon them to a concentration camp. Maetzig said that elements of the film also reflect his own experiences, particularly the loss of his mother, who committed suicide during the war.[6]

Unbelievably popular, *Marriage in the Shadows* was the only film to be released throughout all of occupied Berlin and attracted more than 12 million viewers. It inspired similarly themed films like *Lang ist der Weg* (*Long is the Road*, 1948), which concerned Polish Jews who escaped during deportation to a concentration camp. *Long is the Road* takes the action away from German home life and into a ghetto, concentration camp, and displaced persons camp. Allegedly the first feature film told from the perspective of a Holocaust survivor—and cast with many non-professional actors who were actually displaced people wandering after the war—*Long is the Road*'s underlying message was the belief that refugees should be helped to emigrate to a promising new life in Palestine. Though these fit within a larger framework of the rubble film genre—*Long is the Road* is not a DEFA film, for example—they also stand as early adopters of the Soviet model and focus on heroic acts of bravery and survival and an ultimately optimistic tone about building life anew in a brighter future.

Moralizing was also popular. For example, a film like *Straßenbekanntschaft* (*Street Acquaintances*, 1948), focuses on destitution and poverty in postwar Berlin, where many

Kurt (Alfred Balthoff) consoles Elisabeth (Ilse Steppat) in the melodramatic *Marriage in the Shadows* (*Ehe im Schatten*, Deutsche Film [DEFA], 1947).

women were forced to turn to prostitution to survive. The film is surprisingly frank about the living conditions in German cities in the first few years after the war ended, when starvation, homelessness, and joblessness were paramount. It is essentially an anti-sex film, suggesting that thousands upon thousands of German women who were forced into prostitution as a last resort, who thought their husbands died at war and moved on, or who were simply having fun to alleviate the crushing misery of daily life are destined to get syphilis—which they will then pass on to morally upstanding men who have returned from war.

There were a handful of similar films from other Soviet-controlled countries, such as Hungary's first film produced after the war, *Valahol Európában* (*Somewhere in Europe*, 1948), sort of a Hungarian take on the rubble film. Géza von Radványi's tale of starving children in postwar Hungary driven to crime and exploitation is sometimes compared to Italian neorealism, with the major exception being that the children change their ways and shed their criminal impulses when they are properly educated in socialist values. One reason these sentimentalist propaganda films began to flood the Eastern European market is that in those early years getting script approval was a long and complicated process. This explains why there were relatively few films made and why the finished films resembled each other so closely. In the case of East Germany, Antonin and Mira Liehm explain,

> All scripts and finished films had to be approved both by the Soviet military administration and by Sovexportfilm, the Soviet distribution agency for the Soviet zone. In addition, the films

were presented for final approval to a commission consisting of members of the Soviet military administration and members of SED (Socialist Unity Party of Germany).[7]

With Stalin's death in 1953, the situation began to change somewhat and the Communist Party sought to increase annual film production, so by necessity, censorship had to be lightened—though it was still carefully implemented, script approval at least no longer required the signatures of dozens of Soviet officials. This period in the '50s is known as the thaw, where there was a slight liberalization and Soviet culture was more relaxed. Soviet leaders sought to overturn Stalin's cult of personality and give the Party a somewhat friendlier face. This had mixed results, as we will see, but it did lead to the production of more diverse films, particularly from the mid-'50s through the '60s.

There was also some recognition from within the Party that the communist world compared poorly with Western society and that its economy was collapsing. A restructuring of daily life and a reappraisal of Soviet values was in order. Lida Oukaderova writes, "Throughout the 1960s, the Soviet Union would focus on dramatically increasing economic production and improving standards of living."[8] The Soviet Union wished to be seen as a serious global force, which they could not do with a failing economy. Under Nikita Khrushchev, the Soviet Union became relatively kinder and gentler than under Stalin in the '30s and '40s. In addition to the relaxing of censorship and political repression, millions of prisoners were released and Khrushchev did not follow Stalin's model of mass starvation, mass arrests, imprisonments, and executions. If Stalin governed the Soviet Union as if it was still in the midst of a civil war—attacking its own citizens and its close neighbors like Ukraine—Khrushchev was more focused on the Cold War.

A film that changed everything for Soviet cinema for audiences within and without the Soviet Union was Mikhail Kalatozov's *Летят журавли* (*The Cranes Are Flying*, 1957), which follows ordinary people and the brutal impact of war on their lives. A young couple, Veronika (Tatiana Samoilova) and Boris (Aleksey Batalov), are living in Moscow with their families when the Nazis invade. Boris volunteers to serve at the front, despite how dangerous it is, and he ultimately dies. Veronika's parents are killed and she takes shelter with Boris's family, but his cousin (Aleksandr Shvorin) falls in love with her. When she refuses to betray Boris's memory, his cousin rapes Veronika and basically forces her to marry him. The family relocates to a life of misery in Siberia and Veronika attempts suicide, though she survives and is eventually redeemed in the eyes of Boris's family.

The Cranes Are Flying was the first Soviet film to present a realistic depiction of the war and to focus on emotional protagonists who are driven by love and misery—rather than motivated by a worship of the Soviet state. Masha Shpolberg writes,

> Domestically, the film liberated viewers with its honest and unheroic depiction of World War II—the first ever of its kind. Internationally, it surprised moviegoers with the seeming "unsovietness" of both its content and its form. The film's protagonists were not heroes of labour or paragons of socialist civic virtue, but rather ordinary people caught up in the maelstrom of World War II.[9]

This is an unremarkable romantic melodrama at its core: an ordinary young man and an ordinary young woman fall in love. But the presentation of this type of story within Soviet cinema was unimaginable at the time. And it didn't stop there; *The Cranes Are Flying* effectively suggests that in trying to do the right thing, in trying to be good Soviet citizens, Boris and Veronika bring tragedy and death into their lives. Boris's sin is being patriotic, joining the Army, and then dying in battle. Because his family is

Veronika (Tatiana Samoilova) and Boris (Aleksey Batalov) are presented as an ordinary if idyllic young couple in *The Cranes Are Flying* (*Letyat zhuravli*, Mosfilm, 1957).

incorrectly notified that he is missing in action—and not dead—Veronika's life is transformed. Through no misdeeds of her own, she is taken advantage of and raped by his cousin. Because she agrees to marry Boris's cousin, she is seen as a whore and a traitor; Boris's family think that he will return someday soon to find that Veronika has left him for another man.

Masha Shpolberg notes the illusions to Russian literature, specifically *Anna Karenina* with its female protagonist who betrays her husband with another man and then commits suicide.[10] Part of why *The Cranes Are Flying* was so influential at the time, particularly within Soviet cinema, was because it followed a complex female character—not a heroic, virginal comrade whose only motivation was helping her country, as in earlier war films centered on women. The audience is meant to identify with Veronika, whose life is shown to be terrible because of the war, but also because of the repressive society she lives in. Importantly, the expectation is also that the audience will not judge her behavior, but attempt to sympathize with her suffering: the loss of her love and her home, the death of her parents, surviving rape by a trusted friend, agreeing to an unhappy marriage, relocation to Siberia, and so on.

After *The Cranes Are Flying*, the focus of more Soviet films shifted from centering on two-dimensional protagonists meant to represent the whole of the Soviet Union to more rounded, emotional individuals. Anna Lawnton writes,

> Films about World War II have been the staple of Soviet cinema since the early forties. So many pictures have been made on this theme that they soon constituted a genre with its own peculiar conventions. [...] The turning point came at the beginning of the sixties when there developed a new sensibility for the personal lives of human beings caught in the war

catastrophe. Nevertheless, dozens of conventional and insufferably flat war movies continued to be made throughout the seventies.[11]

Despite the Soviet assertion that they heroically won World War II and defeated the Nazis, the reality was mass suffering for much of the Soviet Union and the citizens of its satellite countries. In Timothy Snyder's seminal *Bloodlands: Europe Between Hitler and Stalin*, on the slaughter perpetrated in Central and Eastern Europe in the '30s and '40s, he notes that the Soviet population had the highest number of losses, but that this came from *both* Nazi and Soviet action. Snyder writes,

> Between them, the Nazi and Stalinist regimes murdered more than fourteen million people in the bloodlands. The killing began with a political famine that Stalin directed at Soviet Ukraine, which claimed more than three million lives. It continued with Stalin's Great Terror of 1937 and 1938, in which some seven hundred thousand people were shot, most of them peasants or members of national minorities. The Soviets and the Germans then cooperated in the destruction of Poland and of its educated classes, killing some two hundred thousand people between 1939 and 1941.[12]

This monumental number of deaths only includes the first few years of the war, when the Nazis and the Soviets were allies. Events after 1941 included mass starvations on both sides, the sieges of Leningrad, Warsaw, and Belarus, millions shot by both Nazis and Soviet, and millions killed by gas in Nazi death camps. The numbers are staggering, so from an outside perspective, it's particularly baffling that early Soviet war films are presented with such optimism. *The Cranes Are Flying* was one of the first to reflect some of the suffering that regular citizens faced during those years.

It soon inspired other films that addressed the war in a more honest way, such as *Баллада о солдате* (*Ballad of a Soldier*, 1959). A young soldier, Alyosha (Vladimir Ivashov), is granted leave from the Eastern front as a reward for successfully destroying German tanks. He travels to visit his mother through a devastated Russia. On his way, he encounters a number of people caught up in their relationships: namely husbands and wives who want to send gifts and messages to each other. Alyosha also meets Shura (Zhanna Prokhorenko), who claims to be on her way to visit her fiancé, a pilot in the war. Later, he learns she is really going to see family and there is no such fiancé; the two fall in love though their relationship is never realized. Though he is able to finally see his mother, Alyosha is forced to return to the front, where it is revealed that he dies.

Like *The Cranes Are Flying*, *Ballad of a Soldier* is essentially the tale of an average young couple who are prevented from realizing their dreams by war. Boris and Alyosha do their patriotic duty—fighting Nazis—but die young anyway, and both films suggest that they could have done much more good in the world if they had not been prematurely killed. *Ballad of a Soldier* was, fittingly, directed by a young soldier: Grigory Chukhray. He was just 18 when he was drafted into the Army in 1939 and his extensive service certainly shaped his filmmaking career. Several of his films dealt with the subject of war, such as his debut, *Сорок первый* (*The Forty-First*, 1956), about the forbidden love between a female Red Army soldier and a male White Army officer. His follow up to *Ballad of a Soldier*, *Чистое небо* (*Clear Skies*, 1961), also followed a soldier, a pilot named Aleksei (Yevgeni Urbansky), who heroically survives but is accused of spying by Stalin's government. Eventually his honor is regained—coinciding with a love story—though tragically Aleksei's tale was commonplace in the late '40s when prisoners of war were dubbed traitors if they survived and returned home.

A common theme among Chukhray's films, which can also be found in *The Cranes Are Flying*, is how sexuality plays a role in the characters' lives. Julia Levin notes that the films of this period, particularly Chukhray's, began to explore sexuality, however hesitantly. Levin writes,

> The "Thaw" poetics are particularly evident in the treatment of Alyosha's sexual longing, something that would have never been represented during Stalin's era. Human sexuality, and its most subtle and most expressive manifestations, had been a forbidden subject for Soviet cinema.[13]

Love and sexual attraction could be found in other Soviet-made films of the period, for example East German director Konrad Wolf's *Sterne* (*Stars*, 1959). This East German-Bulgarian coproduction follows a Nazi transport taking Jews through Bulgaria to a concentration camp. A Nazi officer, Walter (Jürgen Frohriep), falls in love with one of the prisoners, a Jewish girl (Sasha Krusharska) from Greece. While their relationship amounts to little more than a series of philosophical conversations, *Stars* was one of the first films to cast a Nazi character as a sensitive protagonist and to attempt to humanize National Socialists in a more general sense. The film questions how Walter came to be in Bulgaria, how he lives his life, what he believes in. As Ruth has Walter questioning these things himself, the two wonder if people can really change. In this case, Wolf suggests that people can and that love can act as a powerful catalyst. Despite this positive message, *Stars* has both a downbeat tone and ending, similar to Russian films from that time like *The Cranes Are Flying*.

As with *Stars*, both *The Cranes Are Flying* and *Battle of a Soldier* revolve around two young people and their romance—however frustrated—which gives a more personal, intimate aspect to the larger war narrative. This focus on psychological conflict had not been regarded as an appropriate subject matter for Soviet cinema under Stalin, so while it may seem like an average melodramatic plot to English language audiences, it was a major step forward for Soviet film. Before the release of *The Cranes Are Flying* in 1957, Soviet World War II films were concerned with the collective experience and tended to ignore individual narratives. Chukhray's films for example, and especially *Battle of a Soldier*, use the suffering of one protagonist to show how pain and misery bind people together and create a sense of communal experience. Levin writes, "the ties of misfortune that keeps them together. At times, their commiseration is almost larger than life: no matter what hardships Alexei has to endure, he keeps the word he has given to his fellow soldiers, his mother, and even people he meets through incidental, fleeting encounters."[14]

This theme would continue throughout the decade in films like Sergei Bondarchuk's *Судьба человека* (*Fate of a Man*, 1959). This tragic, somewhat epic tale follows Andrei (Bondarchuk himself) as he tells his young son the story of his life, beginning in 1922 and ending in 1946. Andrei's happy home life is shattered when World War II breaks out and he is hired to be a truck driver for the Army. He is caught in the middle of a battle and is taken prisoner by the Nazis, who first sent him to a brutal POW camp and later to a concentration camp for hard labor. Though Andrei survives against the odds—including a scene where he is spared execution because he can drink an entire bottle of vodka (!)—and is ultimately named a war hero, he learns his family has been killed. The child he has been telling the story to is his newly adopted son, a war orphan whose parents were killed.

Bondarchuk became known for these sweeping psychological melodramas, several

11. Ordinary Fascism

adapted from classic works of literature such as Tolstoy's *War and Peace*, which coincided with this type of film becoming a normalized part of Soviet film culture into the '60s. *Fate of a Man* does also have a particular political importance. It was common practice for Soviet POWs and sometimes even concentration camp survivors to be branded as cowards or even traitors by the government after the war; it seems ironic that some survived years in Nazi camps or prisons only to be imprisoned or executed by the Soviets after liberation. *Fate of a Man* boldly shows its protagonist as someone captured and imprisoned by the Nazis who is also capable of heroic deeds.

An even more radical, if much darker interpretation of the themes of *Fate of a Man* can be found in Иваново дётство (*Ivan's Childhood*, 1962), the debut feature of the great Andrei Tarkovsky. A virulently anti-war film, it follows the framework of *The Cranes Are Flying* and *Battle of a Soldier*, and can be seen as a sort of inverse of *Fate of a Man*. Instead of following the father's journey through war, *Ivan's Childhood* instead focuses on the child (Nikolai Burlyaev). Tarkovsky's non-linear film, which includes dream sequences and flashbacks, focuses on the young orphan, Ivan, who has joined a partisan group after his family was murdered by Nazis. Despite his young age, Ivan wants revenge for his family and others killed at the Maly Trostenets killing site. Ivan wants to fight on the front line and does, for a time, successfully join an Army regiment, where he is used for reconnaissance missions. An epilogue reveals that Ivan was captured and hanged to death by the Germans.

This poetic, affecting work is one of the most accessible—and commercially

The expressionistic, harrowing beauty of *Ivan's Childhood* (*Ivanovo detstvo*, Mosfilm/Trete Tvorcheskoe Obedinenie, 1962).

successful—of Tarkovsky's films, and is notably far less melodramatic than *The Cranes Are Flying* or *Battle of a Soldier*. While it is surprisingly expressionistic and experimental, it is not surprising that the war served as subject matter for the young Tarkovsky's first film, considering how popular such material was both at home and on an international level. Dina Iordanova writes,

> At the time, much of the official discourse on Soviet identity was still largely shaped by the shadow of World War II. Closely observed by the powers that be, war movies were the most likely type of film to be shown at international festivals and get proper distribution. But the new wave of war films differed from earlier socialist realist efforts, which mostly featured glorious Homo sovieticus fighting the Nazis under Stalin's bright guidance.[15]

These later films, as Iordanova notes, focus on human suffering as the only possible outcome of war—regardless of the perceived Soviet victory. Though Nazis were understandably perceived as monsters, open discussion of specific atrocities was discouraged; the Soviet government was keen to avoid responsibility for the mass atrocities of their own doing, such as the massacre at Katyn. In 1940, the NKVD, the Soviet secret police, shot 22,000 Polish officers to death in the Katyn forest, but the Soviet government didn't take responsibility for the mass executions—or the decades of cover up that followed—until 1990. As I have mentioned earlier, the modern perception of the Holocaust is generally that most of its victims died in concentration camps and death camps—death by disease, overwork, or in the gas chambers. But the reality is the vast numbers were killed in massacres similar to Katyn, where whole communities were rounded up and shot and then dumped in mass graves.

Timothy Snyder notes that in the early years of the war, when the Soviets and the Nazis were allies, Eastern Europe was essentially fair game—particularly Poland, Belarus, and Ukraine. The deaths in these countries are often factored into the astronomical Soviet losses for the war as a whole, but many of their number were killed by the Soviets themselves. Snyder writes, "Particularly important are the lands that the Soviet Union occupied in 1939: eastern Poland, the Baltic States, northeastern Romania. People died there in horribly high proportions—and many of the victims were killed not by the German but by the Soviet invader."[16]

While *Ivan's Childhood* does not mention such atrocities, Ivan does reference Maly Trostenets, a site where thousands of Jews were killed by firing squad or in gas vans. It's estimated that at minimum 65,000 but likely closer to 100,000 Jews were killed there from various parts of Europe, including Germany, Austria, Ukraine, and Poland, with possible additional deaths of up to 200,000. Directly discussing the focus on Jewish victims was another touchy subject in the Soviet Union and its satellite states at this time. Thanks to the recent wave of Party sponsored anti-Semitism that resulted in show trials and executions, the government didn't want to emphasize that their Jewish population had suffered more—they also didn't want to admit to Soviet complicity in the Holocaust and as such, the Holocaust was not to become part of the official Soviet record of World War II. Snyder writes,

> "The number of Jews killed by the Germans in the Soviet Union was a state secret. The Germans killed about a million native Soviet Jews, plus about 1.6 million more Polish, Lithuanian, and Latvian Jews brought into the USSR by the Soviet annexations of 1939 and 1940. […] The shootings east of the Molotov-Ribbentrop line had implicated, in one way or another, hundreds of thousands of Soviet citizens. (For that matter, much of the crucial work at the death

facilities west of the Molotov-Ribbentrop line in occupied Poland had been performed by Soviet citizens. It was unmentionable that Soviet citizens had staffed Treblinka, Sobibór, and Bełżec.)"[17]

Many of the other Soviet films World War II of the '60s did not follow in the bleak footsteps of *Ivan's Childhood*, though more honest depictions of the war came to be somewhat normalized, as exemplified by films like Aleksandr Stolper's Живые и мёртвые (*The Alive and the Dead*, 1964), about a war correspondent witnessing brutal events in 1941 or the Georgian film ჯარისკაცის მამა (*Father of a Soldier*, 1964), about a father who follows his son into battle. Despite the thaw and a relative increase in artistic freedom, this was not the case across all Soviet territories, for several reasons. Firstly, in several countries, such as Hungary, Bulgaria, and Romania, a robust national cinema was slow to begin and production output was not prolific in the early years of the Cold War, which were spent trying to recover and rebuild after the devastation of World War II. By the late '50s, there was also a backlash in Hungary and other countries thanks to the failed Hungarian revolution of 1956—the first open threat to Soviet rule.

It is important to understand that World War II films were still a popular subject at this time and exploring every World War II-themed made in the Eastern bloc could be the focus of several volumes; for the Party, historical subject matter was favored above contemporary stories because it was considered safer and less likely to provide unwanted commentary on Soviet life. Aside from the aforementioned exceptions, these conventional Soviet World War II films from the late '50s and throughout the '60s continued to rely on socialist realism and favored nationalistic plots about heroic partisans, meant to instill Soviet values. In Bulgaria for instance, war films were very popular if propagandistic. Antonin and Mira Liehm write, "The antifascist resistance movement as a major life experience was a theme that reappeared again and again in Bulgarian cinematography. In these films, the war was not seen as a national tragedy, but as an initiation into life, as a test of adulthood."[18]

A common feature of this period is that directors with any kind of individual vision, such as Bulgarian director Binka Zhelyazkova, were generally silenced or forced to make more compromising films. An example is Zhelyazkova's А бяхме млади (*We Were Young*, 1961), about a small group of underground resistance fighters who are plagued by a traitor in their midst. Like many of the Russian films mentioned, it focuses on a central doomed romance, psychological tension, and has a downbeat ending which implies that resistance often amounts to nothing more than death—but is still a necessary endeavor. Zhelyazkova was one of very few active female directors in the world in the '50s but many of her films were banned by the Soviets and remained unavailable for decades. In a strange parallel with Nazi censorship, the Party—in Bulgaria and more generally throughout the Eastern Bloc—typically viewed younger artists' attempts to focus on poetic, experimental, or psychological material as aping western "decadence."

Many Soviet films in the '60s examined partisan resistance and other antifascist revolts, but there is a real lack of more controversial examples from this decade. Censorship was repressive in Hungary, Bulgaria, and conservative Romania during this time—likely a backlash of the purges of the '50s—and the majority of World War II films from these countries stuck to the expected socialist realism model. It is also important to remember the role these three countries played in World War II and how that was—or was not—reflected in their films. Hungary was a member of the Axis powers and helped the Nazis invade both Yugoslavia and the Soviet Union, as well as taking territory from its neighbors with Nazi approval. The country was home to nearly 450,000 Jews, 90 percent of whom died at Auschwitz. Though the government did eventually push back against deportations, it was too little too late. And though there was some underground resistance, it was repeatedly crippled by the Gestapo and was ultimately not as effective as the resistance movements in other Central European countries like Poland.

Similarly, Romania began the war as a neutral country, but had a strong fascist presence of their own, namely the Iron Guard. When the more liberal government was weakened, the fascists staged a coup and Romania joined the Axis powers in November of 1940. Like Hungary, they helped the Nazis invade the Soviet Union, but Romania was a much more enthusiastic ally, to say the least; they sent a massive amount of troops to the Eastern Front. The Romanian king eventually reclaimed the country and formed an alliance with the Allied powers, but not before over 300,000 of the country's Jews were killed, along with thousands of Romani. These pogroms were carried out by shooting squad, by transporting them to death camps like Auschwitz, or in a series of the country's own poorly organized concentration camps at Transnistria, which had abysmal living conditions. Though a greater percentage of Romania's Jewish population survived than many other countries in Eastern Europe, Romania took a more active role in the Holocaust than any country other than Germany.

Bulgaria, likewise, began the war as neutral, but joined the Axis powers in 1941, though their role in the war is perhaps more complicated. They pushed back against a lot of pressure from Nazi Germany to take a more active role in the war; they refused to invade the Soviet Union and changed sides in 1944, becoming an Allied power. Bulgaria did subject their Jewish citizens to the same repressive laws ordered by Nazi Germany and transported Macedonian Jews to their deaths at Treblinka. But there was more push back; they had agreed to roundup Bulgaria's Jewish population but then refused to transport them outside the country to Nazi death camps. This legacy can be felt in the films of the period, though almost none of which directly addressed the issue of Eastern European participation in the Holocaust—by the Soviet Union or any of the Axis countries.

Still, later in the decade some filmmakers began to rebel, however subtly. Bulgarian director Georgi Stoyanov echoed some of the tropes of the Czech New Wave with his use of irony and satire in *Птици и хрътки* (*Birds and Greyhounds*, 1969), which follows a group of young student activists who unexpectedly find themselves in trouble with the local authorities during World War II, leading to their torture and death. It is a film that seeks to explore the dynamics of power, while also attacking totalitarianism in all its forms—whether Nazi or Soviet. Partisan films from the period typically focused on sequences of action and Soviet heroism and stuck to stock characters. Antonin and Mira Liehm name the villains as "the bestial policeman, the drunken capitalist, and the mustachioed foreign agent" opposed by "the golden-haired angelic young girl, the unbending strikers, and the idea 'positive hero.'"[19]

The radical Hungarian director Miklós Jancsó turned to war themes early in his career with his debut feature, *A harangok Rómába mentek* (*The Bells Have Gone to Rome*, 1959), a relatively conventional film about children from a village who refuse to aid the Nazis. He would progress to the poetic antiwar film *Így jöttem* (*My Way Home*, 1965), about a boy wandering the countryside at the end of the war, his way home interrupted by encounters with soldiers and peasants, and seemingly random outbursts of violence.

As a young man Jancsó served in World War II and was held for a time in a POW camp. The majority of his experimental, highly stylized films are concerned with war, protests, and political conflict; while this focused on World War II in the early years of his career, it came to include the Russian Revolution of 1919, the failed Hungarian revolution of 1956, as well as political turmoil further back in Hungary's history.

It was also during this time that Russian director Mikhail Romm made a documentary about fascism, Обыкновенный фашизм (*Ordinary Fascism*, 1965), particularly focused on Nazi Germany. Though known as *Triumph Over Violence* to American audiences, its title actually translates to "Ordinary Fascism" and Romm does draw subtle parallels between the Nazis and Soviet totalitarianism. Despite the subject matter, his documentary was well-received, and it is an important example of how World War II films from 1965 on generally went in one of two directions. The majority of films continued to use historical war films as safe subject matter to reinforce Soviet socialist realism, while some began to use the war as a way to criticize Soviet totalitarianism and to explore the ways in which ordinary citizens of the Eastern Bloc participated in violence, genocide, and their own oppression.

In a similar vein, one of the most important Soviet World War II films of the '60s, András Kovács's *Hideg napok* (*Cold Days*, 1966), explores the Hungarian participation in genocide. It specifically focuses on the aftermath of the Novi Sad massacre, when Hungarian soldiers killed approximately 4,000 Yugoslavians. Though the claim was that they were trying to quash partisan fighting, it is more likely that they just wanted to expand Hungary's territory. The film focuses on a trial where several men believed to be responsible for the massacre await their fates. *Cold Days* becomes something of a philosophical debate about personality responsibility—an issue that surrounds all World War II related war crime trials, where most who claimed to be following orders were found not guilty of the crimes they helped perpetrate. *Cold Days* also looks at the subjective nature of memory and at each man's different perspective on what happened and why. Films like *Imposztorok* (*Imposters*, 1969), followed suit and began to address Hungarian dalliances with fascism.

Cold Days and the films that followed mark a transition in the way Soviets saw the war. For years, the only acceptable way to discuss World War II was in terms of fascists as villains and communists as heroes or victims. By the mid-'60s however, more of Soviet society began to acknowledge that Jews were victimized more so than any other group. As in countries like France and Italy, the Eastern Bloc began to try to come to terms with the events of the war; not only attempting to process the war trauma they suffered as individuals or communities, but larger issues of guilt and responsibility as well. John Cunningham also notes that the Soviet countries were not immune to the kind of rewriting of history and mythologizing that happened in western Europe. In the case of Hungary in particular, Cunningham writes, "the history portrayed in these films dispelled myths, but there is a danger that they also, at the same time, created another myth—that of the perpetual historical victim."[20]

Other notable examples from this period include Binka Zhelyazkova's satire Привързаният балон (*The Tied Up Balloon*, 1967), about a large balloon that arrives in a Bulgarian village in the midst of the war. It inspires a sense of wonder in the townspeople, which is soon quashed by a policeman's interference. It was another film by Zhelyazkova that would be banned, but also resulted in her career being put on hold for several years, during which she was not allowed to make films. When she was able to direct again, she returned promptly to the subject of resistance against fascism with *The Last Word* (Bulgarian: Последната дума (*The Last Word*, 1972), which follows several women—all political prisoners—who are in prison awaiting their executions.

Other Bulgarian directors would also explore the war in more comedic or satirical ways, such as Zako Heskiya's *Тримата от запаса* (*Three Reservists*, 1971), about three inept soldiers who don't want to fight in the war at all, but who are transformed into heroes by the horrors they witness. But despite its comedic beginning, *Three Reservists* becomes somewhat of a standard war film for the period: the war itself serves as a process by which the clumsily protagonists become respectable men. The same can be said of Georgi Djulgerov's *И дойде денят* (*And the Day Came*, 1973), about a young partisan fighter who matures during the war and his thoughts about violence begin to change. As Antonin and Mira Liehm write,

> The antifascist resistance movement as a major life experience was a theme that reappeared again and again in Bulgarian cinema. In these films, the war was not seen as a national tragedy but rather as an initiation into life, as a test of adulthood, the premature discovery of the tragic aspects of life, but a discovery that always breathed the soft breath of hope.[21]

Counterexamples to this include the work of another director necessary to mention, the confrontational Aleksey German, whose war films like *Проверка на дорогах* (*Trial on the Road*, 1971) and *Двадцать дней без войны* (*Twenty Days Without War*, 1976), presented unconventional, more honest views of life during wartime. *Trial on the Road* turned a traitor into a hero and was banned for showing partisans as anything other than heroic. Likewise, an example from East German cinema can be found in Frank Beyer's coproduction with Czechoslovakia, *Jakob der Lügner* (*Jakob the Liar*, 1975). While in a Nazi office in Poland, Jakob (Vlastimil Brodsky) overhears a radio report that the Soviet Army is advancing; when he returns to the ghetto, he tells the other residents this joyful news. No one believes him so he lies and says he secretly owns a clandestine radio. Soon, everyone begins asking him for information and because he doesn't know what else to do, he begins making things up. He delivers more false reports and weaves grander tales about the ghetto's imminent liberation. The community is given a renewed sense of hope, until they are abruptly transported to a death camp. Though they are lies, Jakob's stories effectively change the world around him, ostensibly for the better.

Jakob the Liar is based on a novel by Polish writer and dissident Jurek Becker, who survived his childhood years in the Łódź Ghetto and Ravensbrück and Sachsenhausen concentration camps. This story is allegedly based on a man Becker's father knew in the ghetto who risked owning a radio to share precious news of the outside world. Becker intended to make *Jakob the Liar* into a film in 1965—with Polish co-financing and filming locations in the Krakow Ghetto—but was delayed an entire decade thanks to issues with Soviet censorship and Polish reluctance to explore such sensitive territory. Becker was even banned from filmmaking for a period.

Instead of succumbing to defeat, he transformed the story into a prize-winning novel, which ironically allowed for the resurgence of his film project as an adaptation. Internationally successful, it was the only East German film to ever be nominated for an Academy Award. With sensitivity, pathos, and the deft use of comedy, *Jakob the Liar* is somewhat similar to other Soviet films from the early '70s in its use of satire and comedy as resistance. Despite the fact that World War II was common subject matter for East German studio DEFA well into the '70s, *Jakob the Liar* is an unusual example of Jews as resisters—compounded by the bold assertion that fantasy and even lies can change the world for the better, however temporarily.

Even more critical to discuss is Larisa Shepitko's agonizing swansong, *Восхождение* (*The Ascent*, 1977) about two partisan fighters, Sotnikov (Boris Plotnikov) and Rybak (Vladimir Gostyukhin) fleeing through Belarus trying to survive. Sotnikov is wounded during a fight and they are soon taken prisoner, then interrogated by Soviet police collaborating with the Germans. Under torture, Rybak agrees to collaborate, though he tells the police no more than what they already know; he is offered an official position with them while his friend is executed. Once Rybak realizes what he has done, he tries to kill himself. A deeply personal and important film for Shepitko, *The Ascent*'s release was a protracted battle with the censors, who attempted to cut as much from it as they possibly could. Shepitko was known as a difficult director (i.e., someone who insisted upon following her own vision) and the film was regarded as being too religious and too mystical.

Filmed in the extreme cold, the production of *The Ascent* took a dramatic toll on Shepitko's health and as a result, both the narrative of the film itself and the story of its creation have taken on a quality of spiritual sacrifice. Michael Koresky writes,

> From the film's opening images of telephone poles haphazardly jutting out of snowdrifts like bent crosses, Shepitko, with cinematographer Vladimir Chukhnov, plunges us into a nightmarishly blinding whiteness, a physical and moral winter that envelops everything in its path—except, ultimately, the victimized and beatific Sotnikov, whose slow journey toward death brings a strange enlightenment.[22]

Boris Plotnikov and Vladimir Gostyukhin futilely attempt to hide from the Nazis pursuing them in *The Ascent* (*Voskhozhdenie*, Trete Tvorcheskoe Obedinenie/Mosfilm, 1977).

The religious subtext is surprisingly bold for the time and, according to Shepitko's husband, director Elem Klimov, the only reason the film wasn't banned outright was because of the intervention of a Soviet official who was a partisan fighter during the war and was deeply moved by the film at its premier. Completely abandoning socialist realism, *The Ascent* is a wholly psychological film about one man's transformation in the face of violence and collaboration. It is a film of unrelenting despair and also lacks the trademark optimism and focus on heroic Soviet partisans generally required of war films made in the Soviet Union in any decade.

Before moving on to two major Soviet films of the '80s, I should address the state of Romanian and Yugoslavian cinema at the time. In terms of Romanian cinema, there was little in the way of controversial or transgressive films, particularly where World War II subject matter is concerned. Unlike Hungary or even Bulgaria to some degree, Romania chose not to explore its own history with fascism or its role in the Holocaust. Antonin and Mira Liehm write,

> From the beginning of the sixties on, there was an overall emphasis not only on the distant past, but also on the national aspect of contemporary Romanian history, on the "Romanisation of Romanian Communism." Native historians were called upon to revise past views on the history of Romania's liberation from fascism, emphasizing the native resistance.[23]

The cinema of Yugoslavia—modern day Serbia, Kosovo, Vojvodina, Croatia, Bosnia and Herzegovina, Slovenia, Montenegro, and Macedonia—has a similar dearth of controversial World War II films. As mentioned earlier, Yugoslavia was an exception for several reasons; the leader of the Socialist Federal Republic of Yugoslavia, Josip Broz Tito, broke with Stalin in 1948 and thus the territory was not just another satellite state of the Soviet Union. Though there were similar issues of censorship and control as in the Soviet Union, it is not exactly the same. Cinema took off in a major way in the '60s, with a parallel to the Czech New Wave known as the Yugoslav Black Wave, where rebellious young directors explored satire, black comedy, and surrealism within their often very experimental films. Yugoslavia was also the site of numerous western film productions and coproductions.

It is important to understand that partisan films were a staple of early Yugoslavian cinema; an entire book could be written on this subgenre. But in general, these followed a series of specific tropes, in which heroic partisans fought against Axis occupiers. As in the case of Soviet partisan films, they do not explore Yugoslavian participation in the Holocaust. Tito was the leader of the partisan resistance movement in Yugoslavia and the notion of Yugoslavians as resistors to the Nazis and the Axis powers was an important part of national identity for the burgeoning socialist republic. In addition to the world war raging outside Yugoslavian territories, there was also a civil war between partisan and fascist forces, resulting in the estimated deaths of a million victims, including the Yugoslavian Jewish community killed in the Holocaust.

Genocide was pursued enthusiastically by several different groups and can be seen as a precursor to the Bosnian War decades later. A particularly brutal aspect of this was the Nazi satellite state in Croatia, run by the fascist Ustaša regime, which targeted Jews, Roma, and anti-fascists. They had their own Croatian concentration camps which were notoriously awful, even by Nazi standards, including their an extermination camp, Jasenovac. This makes Yugoslavia the only country during World War II to have an extermination camp independent of the Nazis. Croatian fascists sought to "purify" Croatia from any Romani, Jewish, or especially Serbian influence, which involved both deportations and mass extermination. The Ustaša were particularly known for torture, one-on-one killings like stabbing and beating their victims to death, dismemberment, and other horrific behaviors. German officers submitted official complaints about the barbaric nature of their concentration camps.

It is perhaps understandable that the majority of the postwar socialist films would not question overall Yugoslavian involvement in these horrors, but instead set heroic partisans against barbaric fascists. This genre was a major force in Yugoslavian cinema from the '60s well into the '80s; key examples include Helmut Käutner's Austrian coproduction *Die Letzte Brücke* (*The Last Bridge*, 1954), *Orlovi rano lete* (*Eagles Fly Early*, 1966), international coproduction *Bitka na Neretvi* (*Battle of Neretva*, 1969), *Kad čuješ zvona* (*When You Hear the Bells*, 1969), and *Valter brani Sarajevo* (*Walter Defends Sarajevo*, 1972). Counterexamples include films by directors like Dušan Makaveyev, who peripherally referenced the war in his experimental, controversial films. Examples include *Nevinost bez zastite* (*Innocence Unprotected*, 1968), a strange but fascinating project where Makavejev took an unfinished film from 1941—made by the athlete Dragoljub Aleksić—and expanded it with newsreel footage from the period, so it doubles as part documentary and part experimental film.

Makavejev's work was essentially banned by his home government, so he went on to make coproductions with other countries in Europe. This includes *Sweet Movie* (1974), which is not explicitly about World War II or the Holocaust, but opens with a quotation from a letter written by the British Ambassador to Poland, Owen O'Malley, to British Foreign Minister Anthony Eden about the Katyn Massacre: "Let us think of these things always and speak of them never." Footage from the mass grave exhumation is also included. Later movies that would explore the partisan film in a different light include Slobodon Šijan's *Ko to tamo peva* (*Who's Singin' Over There?*, 1980), about a busload of strangers traveling through Serbia just before the Axis occupation begins. Essentially a dark comedy, it examines the way in which different types of Yugoslavian citizens interact with each other on the eve of chaos and violence erupting.

Overall, political changes in the early '80s led to a decline in World War II-themed films in both the Eastern Bloc and Yugoslavia. In general, films from this period were escapist or sentimental, or dealt with contemporary themes like the divide between rural and urban life and the changing state of the Soviet Union—which would only survive for a few more years. Regardless, some directors—such as the Polish Agnieszka Holland, who was discussed in an earlier chapter—were still forced to go west and pursue coproduction with other European countries to make World War II films. This is also the case with Hungarian director István Szabó, whose 1981 film *Mephisto* is one of the most important examples of controversial war films from the '80s, but was a coproduction between West Germany, Austria, and Hungary. Though it is not quite the same type of experimental cinema coming out of Yugoslavia or similar to the dizzying, surreal works from Hungarian director Jancso, *Mephisto* uses theater and elements of magical realism to explore the ways collaboration impacts individual identity.

Like *The Tin Drum*, *Mephisto* was based on an antifascist novel (itself based on historical events and real people), one hailing from a member of one of the most influential families in both 19th and 20th century German culture: the Manns. Though writer and patriarch Thomas Mann remains the most well-known member of his family, his children made names for themselves during the war years thanks to their prolific artistic output and often heroic anti–Nazi activities. *Mephisto*'s author, Klaus Mann, represented much of what the Nazis hated, particularly in conjunction with his sister Erika. The half-Jewish siblings both identified as homosexual; they made early strides as artists, writers, reporters, and world travelers, often appearing as a creative pair. They founded *Die Pfeffermühle* (*The Peppermill*), a revolutionary theater that openly protested the growing Nazi regime and acted as a rallying point for other figures of political and artistic resistance.

Erika and Klaus were also involved in the Emergency Rescue Committee (ERC). Organized by American writer and journalist Varian Fry, the Committee was designed to act where governments failed, by rescuing Jews and anti–Nazi artists and intellectuals stranded in Europe. Ultimately, the ERC managed to rescue somewhere between 2,000 and 4,000 Europeans, including such artists and intellectuals as Hannah Arendt, Jean Arp, Andre Breton, Marc Chagall, Marcel Duchamp, Max Ernst, Leo Feuchtwanger, Siegfried Kracauer, Claude Levi-Strauss, and Andre Masson, among many more. Klaus had worked as a playwright, journalist, magazine editor, and fiction author in Europe before their emigration to the United States. He also created a magazine, *Die Sammlung*, published in 1933 in Amsterdam, which featured artists in exile like Brecht, Max Brod, Ernst Bloch, Bruno Frank, Albert Einstein, and Lion Feuchtwanger, as well as Jean Cocteau, Andre Gide, Ernest Hemingway, and Aldous Huxley. He revived this concept in New York in 1940 with *Decision: A Review of Free Culture*, which essentially became a sounding board for the voices of exiles and émigrés.

His sixth and most famous novel, *Mephisto*, was written during his exile in the mid-'30s. Though it was published in 1936 in Amsterdam, it was banned in Germany off and on until 1981. Inspired by Goethe's *Faust* and the career of Erika's former husband, actor Gustaf Gründgens, both the novel and the film follow the rise of a young actor, Hendrik Höfgen (Klaus Maria Brandauer), and his rise to fame thanks to his willingness to work with the Nazis. Höfgen gets his start performing with a group of left-wing radicals who are soon arrested and exiled. Due to some convenient connections, he is pardoned from the Nazi blacklist and eventually attracts the attention of a general (Rolf Hoppe as a character meant to be Göring), who becomes his patron. Though he remains removed from politics as much as he is able, it is this friendship with the Nazi leader that allows him to soar to fame and become Germany's most beloved actor and theater manager with his signature role as Mephistofeles in *Faust*.

While the real-life Gründgens was homosexual—he allegedly had an affair with Klaus and he and Erika had a marriage of convenience to provide them both with some political protection—Höfgen is portrayed as having a masochistic sexual relationship with a black woman (Karin Boyd). He eventually abandons her, first hiding her in an apartment in Berlin, and later making a deal that if he cuts off contact, she will be safely deposited in France. Like Gründgens, Höfgen does not openly betray his friends or loved ones, but only makes minor efforts to help provided it doesn't interfere with his career. Höfgen is also briefly married to a leftist named Barbara (Krystyna Janda), but refuses to follow her into exile and does not protest the divorce, as he is eager to distance himself from any political dissident. He is passive, self-absorbed, and vain. Ironically, he essentially sells his soul for the role of Mephisto but realizes too late that he is more of a Faust figure, damning himself to win the favor of the Nazi general.

The charismatic Brandauer gives the character a sense of innocence. He is at once sympathetic and pathetic. This Höfgen is somewhat less satirical than the novel's version

Klaus Maria Brandauer as Hendrik Höfgen as Mephistopheles in *Mephisto*, where identity is little more than a performance (*Mephisto*, Mafilm/Objektív Film/Manfred Durniok Filmproduktion, 1981).

and it is frighteningly easy to see how such a man could be colluded by the Third Reich—or a totalitarian government such as the Soviet Union. *Mephisto* points out the importance of acting and performance during such times of censorship and violence. Just as the Third Reich itself was essentially an elaborate show complete with detailed costumes and scripted rituals, life in such an environment also requires constant performances from its citizens. It seems that out of all the characters, it is only Höfgen that lacks a hidden interior or a true personality and acting is his natural state. Even more so than Klaus Mann's novel, Szabó's *Mephisto* revolves around illusions: the deceptions people follow and lies they tell themselves and others to maintain the illusion of personal freedom. As Mephistopheles, Höfgen is an otherworldly being, an alien creature of power that manipulates and shapes the world. But out of his makeup, he's a conspirator at worst, a passive bystander at best.

Mephisto is not simply a film about historical events; it is a subtle commentary on life under Soviet control and has autobiographical elements for Szabó as well. Perhaps the most famous Hungarian director of the period—thanks to more international attention than directors like Jancso—Szabó has a way of blending together historical, psychological, and personal themes. David Paul writes, "Throughout his career, Istvan Szabó has been obsessed by history: history as understood in a Central European way—history as an intruder in human affairs, a destroyer of families, a brutish and impersonal antagonist locked in combat with the individual."[24] His family were of Jewish descent and had to hide out during World War II. Szabó lived in an orphanage during this period and his father died shortly after the war ended. Several of his early films dealt with these experiences, particularly his relationship with his father through films like *Apa* (*Father*, 1966) and *Tűzoltó Utca 25* (*25 Fireman Street*, 1973).

But it goes even further than this; in the '00s, there was a lot of controversy in

Hungary, because it came to light that as a young man he collaborated with the secret police. While he was a student, he submitted reports on his fellow classmates. Most of this came to nothing and he was considered largely cleared of wrongdoing. *Mephisto* is all about compromises, particularly those that seem harmless or at least ambivalent. Höfgen at first argues that he is working with the Nazis in order to protect his friends; it becomes clear that this is really in the service of vanity. But in an interview, Szabó said, "I don't think that life is possible without making compromises. The question is only one of limits: how far to go."[25] On a related note, the ending of *Mephisto* becomes more experimental, more fantastical, as Hofgen's identity fully slips away from him and he becomes little more than a voice for the state, his soul fully claimed by Mephistofeles, who is of course the general. *Mephisto* is a film about the steps with which we allow our morals, our freedom, and even our identity to be eroded when we are willing to sacrifice everything for the illusion of safety.

Other Soviet films from the early '80s began to explore these themes of complicity and collaboration more openly—films like Borislav Punchev's *Kravta ostava* (1980), about a man torn between police and partisans. After somewhat of a drop off, World War II became a major theme again because 1985 was the 40th anniversary of the end of the war. This resulted in what is perhaps the finest Soviet war film ever made: Elem Klimov's surreal, visceral *Иди и смотри* (*Come and See*, 1985). Co-written by Ales Adamovich, who was a partisan fighter in Belarus during the war, the film follows young Flyora (Aleksey Kravchenko), who decides to join the partisan resistance fighters. They only half-heartedly accept him and then abandon him. He teams up with a young girl, Glasha (Olga Mironova), who accompanies him on his journey home, but they discover that his entire village has been massacred. The two children find themselves lost in an apocalyptic countryside teeming with Nazi atrocities.

It took Klimov nearly a decade to be granted permission to make the film; much of this is because of the sheer brutality of the screenplay, which presents a record of largely true events. While the concentration camps remain an infamous symbol of Nazis atrocities, in particular Auschwitz, far less seems to be known about the horrors that occurred in Belarus—specifically during the period of 1941–1942. This particular territory was overrun with Waffen-SS Einsatzgruppen units who targeted Jews, partisans, and dissenters, but who also indiscriminately killed Belarusian civilians. They were rounded up and often killed in mass shootings or imprisoned. Snyder writes, "Belarus was the center of the confrontation between Nazi Germany and the Soviet Union. After the German invasion of June 1941, its inhabitants observed, if they survived, the escalation of both German and Soviet violence."[26]

It is estimated that throughout 1941 alone, 50,000 Jews were killed by killing squads; Einsatzgruppe B, led by Nazi Chief of Criminal Police Artur Nebe, operated in Belarus and were considered to be particularly ruthless. They were assisted by the notorious SS Special Commando Dirlewanger: a brigade made up largely of sadistic criminals. It was run by Oskar Dirlewanger, who had previously been kicked out the Nazi Party and had served prison time for raping a 13-year-old girl, among other sexual assault charges. The Dirlewanger Brigade specialized in killing unarmed civilians in Poland and Belarus and were known for mass rapes and sickening massacres, both of which are pictured in *Come and See*; the Nazi unit featured in the most horrifying sequences of the film are meant to be Dirlewanger and his men. Snyder writes, "Dirlewanger's preferred method was to herd the local population inside a barn, set the barn on fire, and then shoot with machine guns

Elem Klimov recreates a typically horrific Einsatzgruppen massacre in *Come and See* (*Idi i smotri*, Belarusfilm/Mosfilm, 1985).

anyone who tried to escape. The SS Special Commando Dirlewanger killed at least thirty thousand civilians in its Belarusian tour of duty."[27]

Entire villages were killed in this manner. Often anyone who could be described as a partisan would be executed, their entire community with them. This sense of personal responsibility and communal guilt is a major feature of *Come and See*. Though Jews were ostensibly the main target of Nazi atrocities, in Belarus lines were blurred between Jews, partisans, and non–Jewish civilians. It is also reportedly the area with the most aggressive Jewish resistance and in this somewhat unique case it seems that the Nazis did not make a real distinction between the two groups; usually and horrifyingly, they were obsessed with making quotas and keeping track of the number of those murdered. Here Belarusian Jews and partisans often overlapped and were thus generally regarded as one group. In any case, this resulted in massive losses. Snyder writes, "By the end of the war, half the population of Belarus had either been killed or moved. This cannot be said of any other European country."[28]

In addition to the constant guerrilla warfare between Nazis and Soviet partisans breaking out across the countryside—with civilians always caught in the middle—Belarus was home to some of the worst prisoner-of-war camps in all of World War II, where hundreds of thousands of captured soldiers and partisan fighters were tortured and killed. It was also here that the Nazis experimented with the techniques they would later transport to the death camps, namely poisoned gas. Survivors from these camps reported things like cannibalism—prisoners were starved and left out in the extreme cold—as well as prisoners packed so tightly together that no one could sit or lie down;

men were accidentally stampeded to death or even buried alive under corpses. For a sense of scale, Snyder explains, "As many Soviet prisoners of war died on a single given day in autumn 1941 as did British and American prisoners of war over the course of the entire Second World War."[29]

Unlike in France or Italy, it is far more complicated to explain the degree of collaboration between native Soviet populations and Nazi occupiers, particularly in these killing fields of Belarus, Poland, and Ukraine. A common practice was to "recruit" prisoners from the camps to work as auxiliaries to the police or military. Allegedly a million such men were taken from the camps and pressed into Nazi service; had they refused and stayed in the camps, they would almost certainly have died horrible deaths. They became concentration camp guards and particularly guards of the Operation Reinhard death camps, they dug ditches where bodies from mass shootings were dumped, and they assisted the Einsatzgruppen hunting down Jews and partisans. In many ways, this can be interpreted as the symbol of absolute evil: starving, beating, and psychologically tearing down men to the point where they agree to willingly participate in genocide.

Come and See remains a monument to such evil, a reminder of the sheer level of devastation and depravity experienced in much of the world between 1939 and 1945. Klimov makes it quite clear through Florya's brief evolution from innocent child to traumatized partisan that the impact of these events are not limited to their time but lingered on for decades. It was also a personal project for the director; he lived through the war as a child. Mark Le Fanu writes,

> He himself had been a witness as a child, in 1942, to the catastrophic destruction of Stalingrad, a turning point in the Second World War. He later spoke of escaping the city in a barge together with his family, and witnessing the entire Volga River—nearly a mile in breadth—engulfed in flames that had been caused by the emptying of an oil depot blown up by the Germans.[30]

Klimov's vision of the apocalypse is one of the most powerful films of the 20th century. It brings to life a radical depiction of the horrors visited upon Belarus that remains timeless despite the fact that the film was made 40 years after the war and, as of this writing, was released nearly 35 years ago. Though Klimov includes nightmarish and surreal sequences, even some that seem to come from out of a fairytale or fantasy film, *Come and See* feels more like a documentary than anything else. With experimental camera and audio techniques, Flyora's experiences become visceral and highly sensory; *Come and See* is the closest you can get to living through such terrors yourself. It offers no answers about how to survive or overcome such horrors, but serves as a reminder that such violence leaves behind a permanent stain—on the people who experienced such atrocities and on the very land itself.

Conclusion
The Trauma of Remembrance

Though I have chosen to end this book with Elem Klimov's 1985 film *Come and See*, it was far from the last European film made about World War II; a subject that will perhaps always be popular for directors to return to throughout the years. More recent acclaimed examples include films like László Nemes' *Saul fia* (*Son of Saul*, 2015), about the life of a Sonderkommando in Auschwitz. Like *Come and See*, it is visceral and experimental. But unlike *Come and See*, it is not particularly radical and tells a story that is still horrifying, but somehow familiar. Unlike the films mentioned in this book, it does not seek to challenge our interpretation of war or genocide, or to challenge national myths about individual responsibility and communal involvement in the war. This raises the question of whether or not it is still possible to make transgressive World War II films when the war ended 75 years ago, and when hundreds of films have already been made exploring this subject matter.

Arguably the type of film represented in this book, exemplified from the '40s with *Rome, Open City* through to the mid-'80s with *Come and See*, no longer exist, perhaps not since the fall of the Berlin Wall in 1989. Largely, this has to do with the passing of time and the gradual death of a generation; though some artists and filmmakers who survived the war are still active, such as Roman Polanski, they were children during the war years. It is also no longer the case that the majority of filmgoers are people who were alive during the war or who actively took part in it; most now are so far removed that they learn about the Holocaust in history class as teenagers or through the legacies of their own families. Survivors who have generously shared their stories are dying out.

Films about the war, particularly films made by major directors, have become increasingly mainstream and abstract, little more than parables about heroism in the face of absolute evil. This is particularly troubling in the current political climate, where right wing leaders are winning elections in a variety of countries. In America, children are being held in concentration camps under the logic that they are foreigners who don't belong. There is rioting in the streets and police are revealed to be thugs and are no longer trusted to uphold justice. Anti-Semitic violence is at a frightening high around the world and disliked political leaders are increasingly compared to Hitler.

It seems to me that the last films to effectively and confrontationally confront the Holocaust are those of Belgian director Chantal Akerman. Though Akerman was not explored in these chapters, it is because she is not someone who directly addressed the war very often in her experimental works; but it always looms like a specter in the background. The daughter of Auschwitz survivors, Akerman had a very close but seemingly intense relationship with her mother. This relationship was the abstract focus of several of her films, including *News from Home* (1977), *Les Rendez-vous d'Anna* (1978), and most importantly *No Home Movie* (2015), which was completed just before her mother's death. Akerman herself committed suicide just after it was released. Perhaps no other director has been able to capture the effects of trauma on families, the ways in which it is passed down through generations. Her mother's war trauma is one of the defining features of Akerman's life and work; though it is not addressed openly until *No Home Movies*, it hovers in the background like a festering wound that will never heal.

Akerman's masterpiece, *Jeanne Dielman, 23, quai du Commerce, 1080 Bruxelles* (1975) focuses on the banality, even the agony, of daily life as it follows a woman attempting to provide for her son, who is driven to violence by the injustice of survival. As many of the films in this book suggest, surviving trauma—particularly surviving war and genocide—is not an experience that can be understood in black and white terms. Survival often requires dehumanizing compromises, acts of indignity and injustice. Those we expect to protect or rescue us are revealed to be perpetrators, collaborators, or uncaring bystanders. Because of what it reveals to us about our communities, it is difficult to view the world in normal terms when we experience violent trauma, even after the incident has concluded.

As many trauma specialists now suggest, the traumatic event ends, but the trauma victim remains somehow crystalized, stuck in time. Though this is a largely psychological experience, it plays out again and again in the body, in the chemicals of the brain. While this has been well-documented in veterans of war, more researchers have begun to explore the issue, particularly in the wake of books like Judith Herman's *Trauma and Recovery* (1992).

There is effectively no way to resume "normal" life even after the trauma seems to be over and the individual—or the community—is safe. At this point it is beyond cliché to say that those who forget the past are doomed to repeat it. The legacy of the Holocaust—particularly as we experience it through art and culture—also suggests the importance of remembering and processing traumatic events, for individuals, for families, and for entire communities. And as the often controversial, transgressive films in this book underline, trauma may seem to be an individual experience, but violence does not exist in a vacuum. It affects the way we understand ourselves and our communities, sexuality and bodies, national identity and government responsibility, and broader issues like justice and morality. Films like *Germany Year Zero*, *Le silence de la mer*, *Hiroshima mon amour*, *The Night Porter*, *The Conformist*, *Salò*, *The Tin Drum*, *The Sorrow and the Pity*, *Ivan's Childhood*, and many others serve to remind us that we are all complicit.

Chapter Notes

Introduction

1. Liel Leibovitz, "Listless," *Tablet Magazine* (December 13, 2011), https://www.tabletmag.com/sections/arts-letters/articles/listless.
2. Liel Leibovitz, "Listless."

Chapter 1

1. Peter Bondanella, *The Films of Roberto Rossellini* (Cambridge University Press, 1993), 3.
2. Peter Bondanella, *The Films of Roberto Rossellini*, 5.
3. Peter Bondanella, *The Films of Roberto Rossellini*, 8.
4. Carlo Celli and Marga Cottino-Jones, *A New Guide to Italian Cinema* (Palgrave Macmillan, 2007), 47.
5. Michi's career effectively came full circle, as her last film before retirement was Tinto Brass's *Salon Kitty* (1976), which will be explored in a later chapter but, like *Rome, Open City*, is based on historical fact and set in a Nazi brothel.
6. Peter Bondanella, *Rome, Open City* commentary track (Criterion Collection DVD, 2012).
7. Carlo Celli and Marga Cottino-Jones, *A New Guide to Italian Cinema*, 12.
8. Peter Bondanella, *The Films of Roberto Rossellini*, 33–34.
9. Carlo Celli and Marga Cottino-Jones, *A New Guide to Italian Cinema*, 41.
10. Peter Bondanella, *The Films of Roberto Rossellini*, 65.
11. Carlo Celli and Marga Cottino-Jones, *A New Guide to Italian Cinema*, 44.
12. Roberto Rossellini, "Dix ans de cinema," *Cahiers du cinéma* 50 (August-September 1955).
13. Robert Shandley, *Rubble Films: German Cinema In the Shadow of the Third Reich* (Temple University Press, 2001), 14.
14. Robert Shandley, *Rubble Films: German Cinema In the Shadow of the Third Reich*, 1.
15. More fully explored in later chapters.
16. Robert Shandley, *Rubble Films: German Cinema In the Shadow of the Third Reich*, 24.
17. Millicent Marcus, *Italian Film in the Light of Neorealism* (Princeton University Press, 1987), 285.
18. Peter Bondanella, *The Films of Roberto Rossellini*, 111.
19. *Ibid.*
20. Peter Bondanella, *The Films of Roberto Rossellini*, 117.
21. Peter Bondanella, *The Films of Roberto Rossellini*, 121.
22. Robert Gordon, *The Holocaust in Italian Culture, 1944–2010* (Stanford University Press, 2012), 58.
23. Peter Brunette, *Roberto Rossellini* (University of California Press, 1996), 211.
24. Peter Brunette, *Roberto Rossellini*, 211.
25. Peter Brunette, *Roberto Rossellini*, 212.
26. Slavoj Žižek, *Organs Without Bodies: On Deleuze and Consequences* (Routledge, 2004), 140.
27. Mira Liehm, *Passion and Defiance: Italian Films from 1942 to the Present* (University of California Press, 1986), 165.
28. Quoted in Jacques Lezra, *Wild Materialism: The Ethic of Terror and the Modern Republic* (Fordham University Press, 2010), 194.
29. Jacques Lezra, *Wild Materialism: The Ethic of Terror and the Modern Republic*, 195.
30. Annette Insdorf, *Indelible Shadows: Film and the Holocaust* (Cambridge University Press, 2003), 180.
31. Millicent Marcus, *Italian Film in the Light of Neorealism*, 3.
32. Ingeborg Bachmann, *Wir müssen wahre Sätze finden: Gespräche und Interviews* (Piper, 1983), 144.
33. Annette Insdorf, *Indelible Shadows: Film and the Holocaust*, 95.
34. Millicent Marcus, *Italian Film in the Light of Neorealism*, 43.
35. Millicent Marcus, *Italian Film in the Light of Neorealism*, 47.

Chapter 2

1. François Truffaut, "André Bazin, the Occupation and I," in André Bazin (Ed.), *French Cinema of the Occupation and Resistance: The Birth of a Critical Esthetic* (Ungar, 1981), 18.
2. Wheeler Winston Dixon, "The Power of Resistance: *Les Dames du Bois de Boulogne*," *Senses of Cinema* (March 2008), http://sensesofcinema.

com/2008/feature-articles/dames-du-bois-de-boulogne/.
3. Wheeler Winston Dixon, "The Power of Resistance: *Les Dames du Bois de Boulogne.*"
4. Adrian Danks, "Border Crossings: Placing René Clément's *La Bataille du rail,*" *Senses of Cinema,* http://sensesofcinema.com/2003/cteq/la_bataille_du_rail/.
5. Fiona Watson, "Clouzot, Henri-Georges," *Senses of Cinema,* http://sensesofcinema.com/2005/great-directors/clouzot/.
6. Edward Baron Turk, *Child of Paradise: Marcel Carne and the Golden Age of French Cinema* (Harvard Film Studies, 1989), 204–205.
7. Christopher Lloyd, *Henri-Georges Clouzot: French Film Directors* (Manchester University Press, 2016), 76.
8. François Truffaut, *The Films in My Life* (De Capo Press, 1994), 3.
9. Christopher Lloyd, *Henri-Georges Clouzot: French Film Directors,* 78.
10. Christopher Lloyd, *Henri-Georges Clouzot: French Film Directors,* 83.
11. Susan Hayward, *Les Diaboliques* (University of Illinois Press, 2005), 11.
12. Tim Palmer, "An Amateur of Quality: Postwar French Cinema and Jean-Pierre Melville's *Le Silence de la mer," Journal of Film and Video* (Vol. 59, No. 4, WINTER 2007, 3–19), 8.
13. Claude Lanzmann, *The Patagonian Hare: A Memoir* (Farrar, Straus and Giroux, 2013), 512.
14. Annette Insdorf, *Indelible Shadows: Film and the Holocaust,* xix.
15. Phillip Lopate, "Night and Fog," Criterion Collection (June 23, 2003), https://www.criterion.com/current/posts/288-night-and-fog.
16. Annette Insdorf, *Indelible Shadows: Film and the Holocaust,* 29.
17. Peter Cowrie, *Hiroshima mon amour* commentary track (Criterion Collection DVD, 2010).
18. James Lord, *Six Exceptional Women: Further Memoirs* (Farrar, Straus and Giroux, 1994), 47.
19. Peter Cowrie, *Hiroshima mon amour* commentary track.
20. Kent Jones, "*Hiroshima mon amour:* Time Indefinite," Criterion Collection (July 13, 2013), https://www.criterion.com/current/posts/291-hiroshima-mon-amour-time-indefinite.
21. Kate Kennelly, "Re-envisioning the Postwar Documentary, Alain Resnais's *Night and Fog* and *Hiroshima mon amour," Bright Lights Film Journal* (March 6, 2015), https://brightlightsfilm.com/re-envisioning-the-postwar-documentary-alain-resnaiss-night-and-fog-and-hiroshima-mon-amour/#.XyeFG_hKjVo.
22. Robert Bresson, *Bresson on Bresson: Interviews, 1943–1983* (New York Review Books, 2016), 47–48.
23. Tony Pipolo, "*A Man Escaped*: Quintessential Bresson," Criterion Collection (March 25, 2013), https://www.criterion.com/current/posts/2628-a-man-escaped-quintessential-bresson.

Chapter 3

1. The films of East Germany will be discussed alongside Soviet cinema in a later chapter.
2. Thomas Elsaesser, *New German Cinema: A History* (Rutgers University Press, 1989), 13.
3. Eric Rentschler, "The Place of Rubble in the Trümmerfilm," *New German Critique* (No. 110, COLD WAR CULTURE, Summer 2020, 9–30), 9.
4. Eric Rentschler, "The Place of Rubble in the Trümmerfilm," 9.
5. Robert Shandley, *Rubble Films: German Cinema in the Shadow of the Third Reich* (Temple University Press, 2001), 3.
6. Eric Rentschler, "The Place of Rubble in the Trümmerfilm," 11.
7. Also notable because it was the first film of actor Klaus Kinski.
8. William Boston, "Burying the Past," *Time* (1 October 2003), http://content.time.com/time/magazine/article/0,9171,491731,00.html.
9. Quoted in Boston, "Burying the Past."
10. "Nightmares."
11. "Alpine dreams of a beautiful Germany."
12. Eric Rentschler, "The Place of Rubble in the Trümmerfilm," 20.
13. Peter Gay, *Weimar Culture: The Insider as Outsider* (W.W. Norton & Company, 2001), 110.
14. Peter Gay, *Weimar Culture: The Insider as Outsider,* 140.
15. Andrew Pulver, "The Brotherhood of Mann," *The Guardian* (August 13, 2004), http://www.theguardian.com/books/2004/aug/14/featuresreviews.guardianreview7.
16. Christian Goeschel, *Suicide in Nazi Germany* (Oxford University Press, 2009), 151.
17. Adam Kirsch, "Primo Levy's Unlikely Suicide Haunts His Lasting Work," *Tablet Magazine* (September 21, 2015), http://www.tabletmag.com/jewish-arts-and-culture/books/193650/primo-levis-complete-works.
18. Bernard Hemingway, "*The Devil Strikes at Night," Senses of Cinema* (December 2003), http://sensesofcinema.com/2003/cteq/devil_strikes_at_night/.
19. Thomas Elsaesser, *New German Cinema: A History,* 8.
20. Eric Rentschler, "The Place of Rubble in the Trümmerfilm," 25.
21. Timothy Corrigan, "*Young Törless,*" Criterion Collection (March 14, 2005), https://www.criterion.com/current/posts/669-young-torless.
22. Timothy Corrigan, "*Young Törless.*"
23. Timothy Corrigan, "*Young Törless.*"
24. Quoted in Peter Gay, *Weimar Culture: The Insider as Outsider,* 58.
25. Magdalena Saryusz-Wolska, "New German Cinema's Forgotten Film: Hansjürgen Pohland's *Katz und Maus," German Life and Letters* (66:1 January 2013), 113.
26. Magdalena Saryusz-Wolska, "New German Cinema's Forgotten Film: Hansjürgen Pohland's *Katz und Maus,*" 116.
27. Carrie Smith-Prei, "'Their Adam's Apple Put

Them on Screen': Hansjürgen Pohland's *Cat and Mouse* and the Narrative of the Male Body," in *Processes of Transposition: German Literature and Film*, edited by Christiane Schönfeld (Editions Rodopi, 2007), 191.
  28. Carrie Smith-Prei, "'Their Adam's Apple Put Them on Screen': Hansjürgen Pohland's *Cat and Mouse* and the Narrative of the Male Body," 195.
  29. Carson McCullers, *Reflections in a Golden Eye* (First Mariner Books, 2001), 1.
  30. Michelle Langford, *Allegorical Images: Tableau, Time and Gesture in the Cinema of Werner Schroeter* (Intellect Ltd, 2006), 146.
  31. Michelle Langford, *Allegorical Images: Tableau, Time and Gesture in the Cinema of Werner Schroeter*, 146.
  32. Michelle Langford, *Allegorical Images: Tableau, Time and Gesture in the Cinema of Werner Schroeter*, 147.
  33. Thomas Elsaesser, *New German Cinema: A History*, 34.
  34. Susan Sontag, *Under the Sign of Saturn* (Farrar, Straus, Giroux, 1980), 138–139.
  35. Walter Benjamin, "Theses on the Philosophy of History," *Illuminations: Essays and Reflections* (Schocken Books, 2007), 254.
  36. Susan Sontag, "Syberberg's Hitler," 144.
  37. Annette Insdorf, *Indelible Shadows: Film and the Holocaust*, xvii.
  38. Thomas Elaesser, *Fassbinder's Germany: History, Identity, Subject* (Amsterdam University Press, 1996), 130.
  39. Erik Rentschler, "The Tin Drum: Schlöndorff's German Fresco," Criterion Collection (May 9, 2004), https://www.criterion.com/current/posts/321-the-tin-drum-schl-ndorff-s-german-fresco.
  40. Erik Rentschler, "The Tin Drum: Schlöndorff's German Fresco."
  41. Elizabeth Gaffney, "Günter Grass, The Art of Fiction, No. 124," *The Paris Review* (Issue 119, Summer 1991), https://www.theparisreview.org/interviews/2191/the-art-of-fiction-no-124-gunter-grass.
  42. Erik Rentschler, "The Tin Drum: Schlöndorff's German Fresco."
  43. Both *The Marriage of Maria Braun* and *The Third Part of the Night* will be discussed more fully in later chapters.
  44. Thomas Elsaesser, *New German Cinema: A History*, 189.
  45. George Dietz and Nora Reinhardt, "Resurrecting Schlingensief at the Biennale," *Der Spiegel* (June 3, 2011), http://www.spiegel.de/international/zeitgeist/death-in-venice-resurrecting-schlingensief-at-the-biennale-a-766151.html.
  46. George Dietz and Nora Reinhardt, "Resurrecting Schlingensief at the Biennale."

Chapter 4

  1. André Bazin, "Le réalisme cinématographique et l'école italienne de la libération," *Esprit* (January 1948, 61–62), 61.
  2. Ginette Vincendeau, *Jean-Pierre Melville: An American in Paris* (British Film Institute, 2003), 50.
  3. Ginette Vincendeau, *Jean-Pierre Melville: An American in Paris*, 67.
  4. Michael Sragow, "Deep Focus: Leon Morin, Priest," *Film Comment* (May 11, 2017), https://www.filmcomment.com/blog/deep-focus-leon-morin-priest/.
  5. Gary Indiana, "*Léon Morin, Priest*: Life During Wartime," Criterion Collection (July 26, 2011), https://www.criterion.com/current/posts/1935-l-on-morin-priest-life-during-wartime.
  6. Ginette Vincendeau, *Jean-Pierre Melville: An American in Paris*, 68.
  7. James Monaco, *The New Wave: Truffaut, Godard, Chabrol, Rohmer, Rivette* (Harbor Electronic Publishing, 2004), 60.
  8. Michael Coates-Smith and Garry McGee, *The Films of Jean Seberg* (McFarland & Company, 2012), 107.
  9. Michael Coates-Smith and Garry McGee, *The Films of Jean Seberg*, 107.
  10. Darragh O'Donoghue, "*Story of Women* (*Une affaire de femmes*, 1988)," Senses of Cinema (February 2017), http://sensesofcinema.com/2017/cteq/story-of-women/.
  11. Quoted in Celestine Bohlen, "Chabrol Offers a Cool-Eyed Look at a Stormy Issue," *New York Times* (October 15, 1989), https://www.nytimes.com/1989/10/15/movies/film-chabrol-offers-a-cool-eyed-look-at-a-stormy-issue.html.
  12. Jonathan Kirschner, "Dark Undercurrents: Claude Chabrol's Second Wave from *Les Biches* (1968) to *Innocents with Dirty Hands* (1975)," *Bright Lights Film Journal* (March 25, 2018), https://brightlightsfilm.com/claude-chabrol-second-wave-les-biches-1968-innocents-dirty-hands-1975/#.XuKWM55KjVo.
  13. T. Jefferson Kline, "Double Projection," *Art Forum* (July 14, 2008), https://www.artforum.com/film/t-jefferson-kline-on-the-films-of-alain-robbe-grillet-20742.
  14. Toby McKibbin, "Alain Robbe-Grillet: Teasing the Real," *Senses of Cinema* (October 2014), http://sensesofcinema.com/2014/feature-articles/alain-robbe-grilletteasing-the-real/.
  15. Shusha Guppy, "Alain Robbe-Grillet, The Art of Fiction No. 91," *The Paris Review* (Issue 99, Spring 1986), https://www.theparisreview.org/interviews/2819/the-art-of-fiction-no-91-alain-robbe-grillet.
  16. Shusha Guppy, "Alain Robbe-Grillet, The Art of Fiction No. 91."
  17. Shusha Guppy, "Alain Robbe-Grillet, The Art of Fiction No. 91."
  18. Which will be discussed in later chapters.
  19. Robert O. Paxton, "Meville's French Resistance," Criterion Collection (January 11, 2011), https://www.criterion.com/current/posts/1711-melville-s-french-resistance.
  20. Robert O. Paxton, "Meville's French Resistance."
  21. To be discussed in a later chapter.
  22. Anthony Lane, "Jean-Pierre Melville's

Cinema of Resistance," *The New Yorker* (April 24, 2017), https://www.newyorker.com/magazine/2017/05/01/jean-pierre-melvilles-cinema-of-resistance.
  23. Adam Schatz, "Who does that for anyone?" *London Review of Books* (Vol. 41, No. 12, June 20, 2019), https://www.lrb.co.uk/the-paper/v41/n12/adam-shatz/who-does-that-for-anyone.
  24. Albert Camus, *Resistance, Rebellion, Death: Essays* (Vintage International, 1995), 258.
  25. Albert Camus, *Resistance, Rebellion, Death: Essays*, 62.

Chapter 5

  1. Peter Bondanella, *Italian Cinema: From Neorealism to the Present* (Continuum, 2001), 203.
  2. Millicent Marcus, *Italian Film in the Light of Neorealism*, 287.
  3. Millicent Marcus, *Italian Film in the Light of Neorealism*, 287.
  4. Millicent Marcus, *Italian Film in the Light of Neorealism*, 307.
  5. Sigmund Freud, *On Metapsychology* (Gardners Books, 1991), 380.
  6. Claude Lanzmann, *The Patagonian Hare: A Memoir*, 91.
  7. Ben Johnson and Anna Maria de Dominicis, "Alberto Moravia, The Art of Fiction No. 6," The Paris Review (Issue 6, Summer 1954), http://www.theparisreview.org/interviews/5093/the-art-of-fiction-no-6-alberto-moravia.
  8. Sherill Tippins, *February House: The Story of W.H. Auden, Carson McCullers, Jane and Paul Bowles, Benjamin Britten, and Gypsy Rose Lee, Under One Roof in Brooklyn* (Mariner Books, 2006), 45.
  9. Her name was inspired by the composer, music historian, and then soon to be writer Paul Bowles, who would go on to rent a house with Auden in New York during WWII.
  10. Liza Minnelli related this story during an interview on *Inside the Actors Studio*.
  11. Annette Insdorf, *Indelible Shadows: Film and the Holocaust*, 52.
  12. Giorgio Bertellini, *The Cinema of Italy* (Wallflower Press, 2005), 204.
  13. Giorgio Bertellini, *The Cinema of Italy*, 204.
  14. In her introduction to the documentary for Criterion's Blu-ray release of *The Night Porter*.
  15. Gaetana Marrone, *The Gaze and the Labyrinth: The Cinema of Liliana Cavani* (Princeton University Press, 2000), 84.
  16. Rebecca Sherr, "The Uses of Memory and the Abuses of Fiction: Sexuality in Holocaust Fiction and Memoir," *Other Voices* (v.2, n.1, February 2000), http://www.othervoices.org/2.1/scherr/sexuality.php.
  17. Rebecca Sherr, "The Uses of Memory and the Abuses of Fiction: Sexuality in Holocaust Fiction and Memoir."
  18. Gaetana Marrone, "*The Night Porter*: Power, Spectacle, and Desire," Criterion Collection (December 9, 2014), https://www.criterion.com/current/posts/3393-the-night-porter-power-spectacle-and-desire.
  19. Millicent Marcus, *Italian Film in the Light of Neorealism*, 52.
  20. Gaetana Marrone, *The Gaze and the Labyrinth: The Cinema of Liliana Cavani*, 82.
  21. Gaetana Marrone, *The Gaze and the Labyrinth: The Cinema of Liliana Cavani*, 81.
  22. Richard Dimbleby, "Audio Slideshow: Liberation of Belsen," BBC News (April 15, 1945), http://news.bbc.co.uk/2/hi/in_depth/4445811.stm.
  23. Mark Caldwell and Dirk Bogarde, *Film Talk* (1975), https://www.youtube.com/watch?v=Kx6D5FjbpyU.
  24. Giorgio Bertellini, *The Cinema of Italy*, 185.
  25. Bruno Bettelheim, "Surviving," *The New Yorker* (August 2, 1976), 32.
  26. Bruno Bettelheim, "Surviving," 33.
  27. Bruno Bettelheim, "Surviving," 32.
  28. Millicent Marcus, *Italian Film in the Light of Neorealism*, 59.

Chapter 6

  1. Ralph Tyler, "The Savage World of Rainer Werner Fassbinder," *New York Times* (March 27, 1977), https://www.nytimes.com/1977/03/27/archives/the-savage-world-of-rainer-werner-fassbinder-fassbinders-world.html
  2. Thomas Elsaesser, *Fassbinder's Germany: History, Identity, Subject*, 34.
  3. Hannah Arendt, *Eichmann in Jerusalem: A Report on the Banality of Evil* (Penguin Classics, 2006), 276.
  4. Thomas Elsaesser, *Fassbinder's Germany: History, Identity, Subject*, 211.
  5. Thomas Elsaesser, *Fassbinder's Germany: History, Identity, Subject*, 139.
  6. Thomas Elsaesser, *Fassbinder's Germany: History, Identity, Subject*, 210.
  7. Thomas Elsaesser, *Fassbinder's Germany: History, Identity, Subject*, 30.

Chapter 7

  1. Susan Sontag, *Under the Sign of Saturn*, 79.
  2. Quoted in Naomi Greene, "*Salò*: Breaking the Rules," Criterion Collection (October 4, 2011), https://www.criterion.com/current/posts/511-sal-breaking-the-rules.
  3. Laura Kern, "Eyeing Pornography That Uses the Holocaust as Titillation," *New York Times* (April 9, 2008), https://www.nytimes.com/2008/04/09/movies/09stal.html.
  4. William Shirer, *The Rise and Fall of the Third Reich* (Simon & Schuster, 2011), 26.
  5. William Shirer, *The Rise and Fall of the Third Reich*, 50.
  6. David Wroe, "Son of 'Dr Death' Aribert Heim to escape charges for concealing Nazi father's

existence," *The Telegraph* (February 5, 2009), http://www.telegraph.co.uk/news/worldnews/europe/germany/4524580/Son-of-Dr-Death-Aribert-Heim-to-escape-charges-for-concealing-Nazi-fathers-existence.html.

7. United States Holocaust Museum, "Nazi Medical Experiments," *Holocaust Encyclopedia*, http://www.ushmm.org/wlc/en/article.php?ModuleId=10005168.

8. United States Holocaust Museum, "The Biologcal State: Nazi Racial Hygeine, 1933–1939," *Holocaust Encyclopedia*, http://www.ushmm.org/wlc/en/article.php?ModuleId=10007057.

9. Richard Brody, "Hitchcock and the Holocaust," *The New Yorker* (January 9, 2014), http://www.newyorker.com/online/blogs/movies/2014/01/hitchcock-and-the-holocaust.html.

10. Mira Liehm, *Passion and Defiance: Film in Italy from 1942 to the Present*, 291.

11. Saul Friedländer, *Reflections on Nazism: An Essay on Kitsch and Death* (Indiana University Press, 2000), 19.

12. Joshua D. Zimmerman, *Jews in Italy Under Fascist and Nazi Rule, 1922–1945* (Cambridge University Press, 2009), 4.

13. Saul Friedländer, *Nazi Germany and the Jews, 1939–1945: The Years of Extermination* (Harper Perennial, 2008), 561.

14. Saul Friedländer, *Nazi Germany and the Jews, 1939–1945: The Years of Extermination*, 612.

15. Quoted in Mira Liehm, *Passion and Defiance: Film in Italy from 1942 to the Present*, 290.

16. Saul Friedländer, *Reflections on Nazism: An Essay on Kitsch and Death*, 19.

17. Michel Foucault, *The History of Human Sexuality, Vol. 1: An Introduction* (Vintage, 1990), 156.

18. Pier Paolo Pasolini, *Heretical Empiricism* (New Academia Publishing, 2005), 171.

19. Michel Foucault, *The History of Human Sexuality, Vol. 1: An Introduction*, 138–139.

20. Dennis Lim, "Pasolini's Legacy: A Sprawl of Brutality," *New York Times* (December 26, 2012), https://www.nytimes.com/2012/12/27/movies/pasolinis-legacy-a-sprawl-of-brutality.html.

21. Andrew Gumbel, "Who Killed Pasolini?" *The Independent* (September 23, 1995), http://www.independent.co.uk/arts-entertainment/who-killed-pasolini-1602381.html.

Chapter 8

1. Julian Jackson, *France: The Dark Years, 1940–1944* (Oxford University Press, 2003), 23.

2. United States Holocaust Museum, "France," *Holocaust Encyclopedia*, https://encyclopedia.ushmm.org/content/en/article/france.

3. Julian Jackson, *France: The Dark Years, 1940–1944*, 22.

4. Leah D. Hewitt, *Remembering the Occupation in French Film: National Identity in Postwar Europe* (Palgrave Macmillan, 2008), 2.

5. Edward Dmytryk, *Odd Man Out: A Memoir of the Hollywood Ten* (Southern Illinois University Press, 1996), 30.

6. Edward Dmytryk, *Odd Man Out: A Memoir of the Hollywood Ten*, 31.

7. Patricia Erens, *The Jew in American Cinema* (Indiana University Press, 1984), 228.

8. Jewish Telegraphic Agency, "Hidden Jewish Children Being Reunited with Parents in France; Many Others Orphaned" (October 5, 1944), https://www.jta.org/1944/10/05/archive/hidden-jewish-children-being-reunited-with-parents-in-france-many-others-orphaned.

9. Leah D. Hewitt, *Remembering the Occupation in French Film: National Identity in Postwar Europe*, 68.

10. Leah D. Hewitt, *Remembering the Occupation in French Film: National Identity in Postwar Europe*, 68.

11. Julian Jackson, *France: The Dark Years 1940–1944*, 217.

12. David Caute, *Joseph Losey: A Revenge on Life* (Oxford University Press, 1994), xiii.

13. Jennifer Lynde Barker, *The Aesthetics of Antifascist Film: Radical Projection* (Routledge, 2012), 180.

14. Christopher Weedman, "*Mr. Klein*," *Senses of Cinema* (July 2010), http://sensesofcinema.com/2010/cteq/mr-klein/.

15. Jennifer Lynde Barker, *The Aesthetics of Antifascist Film: Radical Projection*, 179.

16. Annette Insdorf, *Indelible Shadows: Film and the Holocaust*, 177.

17. Hannah Arendt, *The Jew as Pariah: Jewish Identity and Politics in the Modern Age* (Grove Press, 1978), 83.

18. Isak Winkel Holm, "The Calamity of the Rightless: Hannah Arendt and Franz Kafka on Monsters and Members," in (Eds.) Brendan Moran and Carlo Salzi, *Philosophy and Kafka* (Lexington Books, 2015), 160.

19. Walter Benjamin, *The Correspondence of Walter Benjamin: 1910–1940* (University of Chicago Press, 1994), 248.

20. Primo Levi, "On Translating Kafka," *La Stampa* (5 June 1983).

21. Avner Ziv and Anat Zajdman, *Semites and Stereotypes: Characteristics of Jewish Humor* (Praeger, 1993), 4.

22. Anne-Marie Scholz, "'Josef K von 1963...': Orson Welles' 'Americanized' Version of *The Trial* and the changing functions of the Kafkaesque in Postwar West Germany," *European Journal of American Studies* (4–1, 2009: Spring 2009), http://ejas.revues.org/7610.

23. Roger Ebert, "The Trial," RogerEbert.com (February 25, 2000), http://www.rogerebert.com/reviews/the-trial-1963.

24. Orson Welles and Nicholas Fry, *The Trial: A Film By Orson Welles* (Lorrimer Publishing, 1970), 11.

25. Orson Welles and Nicholas Fry, *The Trial: A Film By Orson Welles*, 9.

26. Christos Tsiolkas, "The Atheist's

Shoah—Roman Polanski's *The Pianist*," *Senses of Cinema* (May 2003), http://sensesofcinema.com/2003/feature-articles/pianist/.
27. Roland Topor, *The Tenant* (Centipede Press, 2006), 54.
28. Christopher Weedman, "*Mr. Klein*."

Chapter 9

1. Timothy Snyder, *Bloodlands: Europe Between Hitler and Stalin* (Basic Books 2012), 104.
2. Timothy Snyder, *Bloodlands: Europe Between Hitler and Stalin*, 120.
3. Timothy Snyder, *Bloodlands: Europe Between Hitler and Stalin*, 384.
4. Timothy Snyder, *Bloodlands: Europe Between Hitler and Stalin*, 382.
5. Timothy Snyder, *Bloodlands: Europe Between Hitler and Stalin*, 406.
6. Timothy Snyder, *Bloodlands: Europe Between Hitler and Stalin*, 295.
7. Mirek Halftof, *Polish Film and the Holocaust: Politcs and Memory* (Berghahn Books, 2014), 4.
8. Antonin and Mira Liehm, *The Most Important Art: Soviet and East European Film After 1945* (University of California Press, 1984), 112.
9. Antonin and Mira Liehm, *The Most Important Art: Soviet and East European Film After 1945*, 29.
10. Toby Haggith and Joanna Newman, *Holocaust and the Moving Image: Representations of Film and Television Since 1933* (Wallflower Press, 2005), 226.
11. Toby Haggith and Joanna Newman, *Holocaust and the Moving Image: Representations of Film and Television Since 1933*, 226.
12. Marek Haltof, *Polish Film and the Holocaust: Politics and Memory*, 32.
13. Timothy Snyder, *Bloodlands: Europe Between Hitler and Stalin*, 355.
14. Marek Haltof, *Polish Film and the Holocaust: Politics and Memory*, 2.
15. Marek Haltof, *Polish Film and the Holocaust: Politics and Memory*, 76.
16. Antonin and Mira Liehm, *The Most Important Art: Soviet and East European Film After 1945*, 228.
17. Marek Haltof, *Polish Film and the Holocaust: Politics and Memory*, 76.
18. Daniel Bird, "Only the Images: A Profile of the Late Jan Lenica," *Kinoeye* (November 12, 2001), https://www.kinoeye.org/01/06/bird06.php.
19. Antonin and Mira Liehm, *The Most Important Art: Soviet and East European Film After 1945*, 191.
20. Marek Haltof, *Polish Film and the Holocaust: Politics and Memory*, 104.
21. Marek Haltof, *Polish Film and the Holocaust: Politics and Memory*, 118.
22. Antonin and Mira Liehm, *The Most Important Art: Soviet and East European Film After 1945*, 378.
23. Harold B. Segel, *The Columbia Guide to the Literatures of Eastern Europe Since 1945* (Columbia University Press, 2008), 17.
24. Michael Atkinson, "Blunt Force Trauma: Andrzej Żuławski," *Exile Cinema: Filmmakers at Work Beyond Hollywood* (State University of New York Press, 2008), edited by Michael Atkinson, 81–82.
25. Marek Haltof, *Polish Film and the Holocaust: Politics and Memory*, 109.
26. Marek Haltof, *Polish Film and the Holocaust: Politics and Memory*, 125.
27. David Melville, "'The Fiery Beauty of the World': Wojciech Has and *The Hourglass Sanatorium*," *Senses of Cinema* (August 2012), http://sensesofcinema.com/2012/cteq/the-fiery-beauty-of-the-world-wojciech-has-and-the-hourglass-sanatorium/.
28. David Melville, "'The Fiery Beauty of the World': Wojciech Has and *The Hourglass Sanatorium*."
29. Marek Haltof, *Polish Film and the Holocaust: Politics and Memory*, 124.
30. Dan Yakir, "An Interview: Andrzej Wajda," *Film Comment* (November-December 1984), https://www.filmcomment.com/article/interview-andrzej-wajda/.
31. Marek Haltof, *Polish Film and the Holocaust: Politics and Memory*, 153.
32. Gwendolyn Audrey Foster, *Women Film Directors: An International Bio-Critical Dictionary* (Greenwood, 1995), 187.
33. Antonin and Mira Liehm, *The Most Important Art: Soviet and Eastern European Film After 1945*, 195.

Chapter 10

1. Antonin and Mira Liehm, *The Most Important Art: Soviet and Eastern European Film After 1945*, 22.
2. Peter Demetz, *Prague in Danger* (FSG Adult, 2009), 68.
3. Peter Demetz, *Prague in Danger*, 37.
4. Peter Demetz, *Prague in Danger*, 154.
5. Peter Demetz, *Prague in Danger*, 68.
6. Antonin and Mira Liehm, *The Most Important Art: Soviet and Eastern European Film After 1945*, 105.
7. Peter Hames, *The Czechoslovak New Wave* (Wallflower Press, 2005), 25.
8. Peter Hames, *The Czechoslovak New Wave*, 44.
9. Antonin and Mira Liehm, *The Most Important Art: Soviet and Eastern European Film After 1945*, 228.
10. Timothy Snyder, *Bloodlands: Europe Between Hitler and Stalin*, 262.
11. Peter Hames, *Czech & Slovak Cinema: Theme and Tradition* (Edinburgh University Press, 2010), 99.
12. Antonin and Mira Liehm, *The Most Important Art: Soviet and Eastern European Film After 1945*, 158.

13. Antonin and Mira Liehm, *The Important Art: Soviet and Eastern European Film After 1945*, 230.
14. Ewa Mazierka, *Masculinities in Polish, Czech and Slovak Cinema: Black Peters and Men of Marble* (Berghahn Books, 2010), 55.
15. Šárka Sladovníková, *The Holocaust in Czechoslovak and Czech Feature Films* (*ibid*.em-Verlag, 2018), 22–23.
16. Alice Němcová Tejkalová, "Ester Krumbachová," in Jill Nelmes and Jule (Eds.), *Women Screenwriters: An International Guide* (Palgrave Macmillan, 2015), 254.
17. Peter Hames, *Czech & Slovak Cinema: Theme and Tradition*, 102.
18. Antonin Liehm, *Closely Watched Films* (Routledge, 2018), 189.
19. Peter Hames, "*Enfant Terrible* of the Czech New Wave: Jan Němec's 1960s Films," *Kinoeye* (May 14, 2001), https://web.archive.org/web/20120609150809/http://www.ce-review.org/01/17/kinoeye17_hames.html.
20. Peter Hames, "*Enfant Terrible* of the Czech New Wave: Jan Němec's 1960s Films."
21. Antonin and Mira Liehm, *The Most Important Art: Soviet and Eastern European Film After 1945*, 284.
22. Known as *The Shop on the High Street* to British audiences.
23. Peter Hames, *Czech & Slovak Cinema: Theme and Tradition*, 49.
24. Ján Kadár, "*The Shop on Main Street*: Not the Six Million But the One," Criterion Collection (September 17, 2001), "https://www.criterion.com/current/posts/139-the-shop-on-main-street-not-the-six-million-but-the-one.
25. Ján Kadár, "*The Shop on Main Street*: Not the Six Million but the One."
26. Timothy Snyder, *Bloodlands: Europe Between Hitler and Stalin*, 274.
27. Martin Votruba, "Slovak Cinema," *KinoKultura* (special issue #3, December 2005), http://www.kinokultura.com/specials/3/votruba.pdf.
28. Antonin Liehm, *Closely Watched Films*, 175.
29. Peter Hames, *The Czechoslovak New Wave*, 2.
30. Jonathan Owen, *Avant-garde to New Wave: Czechoslovak Cinema, Surrealism and the Sixties* (Berghahn Books, 2013), 45.
31. Ivana Košuličová, "Drowning the Bad Times: Juraj Herz Interviewed, *Kinoeye* (January 7, 2002), " http://www.kinoeye.org/02/01/kosulicova01.php.
32. Herz argues that Steven Speilberg stole the same sequence a few years later for *Schindler's List*, a claim that is hard to deny.
33. Peter Hames, *The Czechoslovak New Wave*, 247.
34. Daniel Bird, "To Excess: The Grotesque in Juraj Herz's Czech Films," *Kinoeye* (January 7, 2002), http://www.kinoeye.org/02/01/bird01.php.

Chapter 11

1. Timothy Snyder, *Bloodlands: Europe Between Hitler and Stalin*, 160.
2. Antonin and Mira Liehm, *The Most Important Art: Soviet and East European Film After 1945*, 48.
3. Antonin and Mira Liehm, *The Most Important Art: Soviet and East European Film After 1945*, 48.
4. This does not solely refer to countries in Eastern and Central Europe, but also includes Asian territories and Cuba, which are obviously outside the scope of this chapter.
5. Antonin and Mira Liehm, *The Most Important Art: Soviet and East European Film After 1945*, 60.
6. Seán Allan and John Sandford (Eds.), *DEFA: East German Cinema, 1946–1992* (Berghahn Books, 1999), 62.
7. Antonin and Mira Liehm, *The Most Important Art: Soviet and East European Film After 1945*, 76–77.
8. Lida Oukaderova, *The Cinema of the Soviet Thaw: Space, Materiality, Movement* (Indiana University Press, 2017), 4.
9. Masha Shpolberg, "1957: *The Cranes Are Flying*," Senses of Cinema (December 2017), http://sensesofcinema.com/2017/soviet-cinema/the-cranes-are-flying-soviet-cinema/.
10. Masha Shpolberg, "1957: *The Cranes Are Flying*."
11. Anna Lawton, "Toward a New Openness in Soviet Cinema, 1976–1987," in Daniel Goulding (Ed.), *Post New Wave Cinema in the Soviet Union and Eastern Europe* (Indian University, 1989), 20.
12. Timothy Snyder, *Bloodlands: Europe Between Hitler and Stalin*, 379.
13. Julia Levin, "Ballad of a Soldier," *Senses of Cinema* (December 2002), http://sensesofcinema.com/2002/cteq/ballad_soldier/.
14. Julia Levin, "Ballad of a Soldier."
15. Dina Iordanova, "*Ivan's Childhood*: Dream Come True," Criterion Collection (January 22, 2013), https://www.criterion.com/current/posts/589-ivan-s-childhood-dream-come-true.
16. Timothy Snyder, *Bloodlands: Europe Between Hitler and Stalin*, 402.
17. Timothy Snyder, *Bloodlands: Europe Between Hitler and Stalin*, 342.
18. Antonin and Mira Liehm, *The Most Important Art: Soviet and East European Film After 1945*, 237.
19. Antonin and Mira Liehm, *The Most Important Art: Soviet and East European Film After 1945*, 241.
20. John Cunningham, *Hungarian Cinema: From Coffee House to Multiplex* (Wallflower Press, 2004), 110.
21. Antonin and Mira Liehm, *The Most Important Art: Soviet and East European Film After 1945*, 237.
22. Michael Koresky, "Eclipse Series 11: Larisa Shepitko," Criterion Collection (August

11, 2008), https://www.criterion.com/current/posts/507-eclipse-series-11-larisa-shepitko.

23. Antonin and Mira Liehm, *The Most Important Art: Soviet and East European Film After 1945*, 349.

24. David Paul, "Hungary," Daniel J. Goulding (ed.), *Post New Wave Cinema in Soviet Union and Eastern Europe* (Indiana University Press, 1989), 186.

25. Necati Sönmez, "Ordinary Compromises," *Kinoeye* (3.2, 3 Feb. 2003), http://www.kinoeye.org/03/02/sonmez02.php.

26. Timothy Snyder, *Bloodlands: Europe Between Hitler and Stalin*, 225.

27. Timothy Snyder, *Bloodlands: Europe Between Hitler and Stalin*, 242.

28. Timothy Snyder, *Bloodlands: Europe Between Hitler and Stalin*, 251.

29. Timothy Snyder, *Bloodlands: Europe Between Hitler and Stalin*, 182.

30. Mark Le Fanu, "*Come and See:* Orphans of the Storm," Criterion Collection (June 30, 2020), https://www.criterion.com/current/posts/7003-come-and-see-orphans-of-the-storm.

Bibliography

Allan, Seán, and John Sandford (eds.). *DEFA: East German Cinema, 1946–1992*. Berghahn Books, 1999.
Arendt, Hannah. *Eichmann in Jerusalem: A Report on the Banality of Evil*. Penguin Classics, 2006.
Arendt, Hannah. *The Jew as Pariah: Jewish Identity and Politics in the Modern Age*. Grove Press, 1978.
Atkinson, Michael. "Blunt Force Trauma: Andrzej Żuławski." In *Exile Cinema: Filmmakers at Work Beyond Hollywood*, edited by Michael Atkinson. State University of New York Press, 2008).
Bachmann, Ingeborg. *Wir müssen wahre Sätze finden: Gespräche und Interviews*. Piper, 1983.
Barker, Jennifer Lynde. *The Aesthetics of Antifascist Film: Radical Projection*. Routledge, 2012.
Bazin, André. "Le réalisme cinématographique et l'école italienne de la libération." In *Esprit*, January 1948, 61–62.
Benjamin, Walter. *The Correspondence of Walter Benjamin: 1910–1940*. University of Chicago Press, 1994.
Benjamin, Walter. "Theses on the Philosophy of History." In *Illuminations: Essays and Reflections*, Schocken Books, 2007.
Bertellini, Giorgio. *The Cinema of Italy*. Wallflower Press, 2005.
Bettelheim, Bruno. "Surviving." In *The New Yorker*, August 2, 1976.
Bird, Daniel. "Only the Images: A Profile of the Late Jan Lenica." In *Kinoeye*, November 12, 2001, https://www.kinoeye.org/01/06/bird06.php.
Bird, Daniel. "To Excess: The Grotesque in Juraj Herz's Czech Films." In *Kinoeye*, January 7, 2002, http://www.kinoeye.org/02/01/bird01.php.
Bohlen, Celestine. "Chabrol Offers a Cool-Eyed Look at a Stormy Issue." In *New York Times*, October 15, 1989, https://www.nytimes.com/1989/10/15/movies/film-chabrol-offers-a-cool-eyed-look-at-a-stormy-issue.html.
Bondanella, Peter. *The Films of Roberto Rossellini*, Cambridge University Press, 1993.
Bondanella, Peter. *Italian Cinema: From Neorealism to the Present*, Continuum, 2001.
Bondanella, Peter. *Rome, Open City* commentary track, Criterion Collection DVD, 2012.
Boston, William. "Burying the Past." In *Time*, October 1, 2003, http://content.time.com/time/magazine/article/0,9171,491731,00.html.
Bresson, Robert. *Bresson on Bresson: Interviews, 1943–1983*. New York Review Books, 2016.
Brody, Richard. "Hitchcock and the Holocaust." In *The New Yorker*, January 9, 2014, http://www.newyorker.com/online/blogs/movies/2014/01/hitchcock-and-the-holocaust.html.
Brunette, Peter. *Roberto Rossellini*. University of California Press, 1996.
Caldwell, Mark, and Dirk Bogarde. *Film Talk* (1975), https://www.youtube.com/watch?v=Kx6D5FjbpyU.
Camus, Albert. *Resistance, Rebellion, Death: Essays*. Vintage International, 1995.
Caute, David. *Joseph Losey: A Revenge on Life*. Oxford University Press, 1994.
Celli, Carlo, and Marga Cottino-Jones. *A New Guide to Italian Cinema*. Palgrave Macmillan, 2007.
Coates-Smith, Michael, and Garry McGee. *The Films of Jean Seberg*. McFarland, 2012.
Corrigan, Timothy. *"Young Törless."* In Criterion Collection, March 14, 2005, https://www.criterion.com/current/posts/669-young-torless.
Cowrie, Peter. *Hiroshima mon amour* commentary track, Criterion Collection DVD, 2010.
Cunningham, John. *Hungarian Cinema: From Coffee House to Multiplex*. Wallflower Press, 2004.
Danks, Adrian. "Border Crossings: Placing René Clément's *La Bataille du rail*." In *Senses of Cinema*, July 2003, http://sensesofcinema.com/2003/cteq/la_bataille_du_rail/.
Demetz, Peter. *Prague in Danger*. FSG Adult, 2009.
Dietz, George, and Nora Reinhardt. "Resurrecting Schlingensief at the Biennale." In *Der Spiegel*, June 3, 2011, http://www.spiegel.de/international/zeitgeist/death-in-venice-resurrecting-schlingensief-at-the-biennale-a-766151.html.

Dimbleby, Richard. "Audio Slideshow: Liberation of Belsen." In BBC News, April 15, 1945, http://news.bbc.co.uk/2/hi/in_depth/4445811.stm.
Dixon, Wheeler Winston. "The Power of Resistance: *Les Dames du Bois de Boulogne.*" In *Senses of Cinema*, March 2008, http://sensesofcinema.com/2008/feature-articles/dames-du-bois-de-boulogne/.
Dmytryk, Edward. *Odd Man Out: A Memoir of the Hollywood Ten*. Southern Illinois University Press, 1996.
Ebert, Roger. "The Trial." In RogerEbert.com, February 25, 2000, http://www.rogerebert.com/reviews/the-trial-1963.
Elaesser, Thomas. *Fassbinder's Germany: History, Identity, Subject*. Amsterdam University Press, 1996.
Elsaesser, Thomas. *New German Cinema: A History*. Rutgers University Press, 1989.
Erens, Patricia. *The Jew in American Cinema*. Indiana University Press, 1984.
Foster, Gwendolyn Audrey. *Women Film Directors: An International Bio-Critical Dictionary*. Greenwood, 1995.
Foucault, Michel. *The History of Human Sexuality, Vol. 1: An Introduction*. Vintage, 1990.
Freud, Sigmund. *On Metapsychology*. Gardners Books, 1991.
Friedländer, Saul. *Nazi Germany and the Jews, 1939–1945: The Years of Extermination*. Harper Perennial, 2008.
Friedländer, Saul. *Reflections on Nazism: An Essay on Kitsch and Death*. Indiana University Press, 2000.
Gaffney, Elizabeth. "Günter Grass, The Art of Fiction, No. 124." In *The Paris Review*, Issue 119, Summer 1991, https://www.theparisreview.org/interviews/2191/the-art-of-fiction-no-124-gunter-grass.
Gay, Peter. *Weimar Culture: The Insider as Outsider*. W.W. Norton & Company, 2001.
Goeschel, Christian. *Suicide in Nazi Germany*. Oxford University Press, 2009.
Gordon, Robert. *The Holocaust in Italian Culture, 1944–2010*. Stanford University Press, 2012.
Greene, Naomi. "Salò: Breaking the Rules." In Criterion Collection, October 4, 2011, https://www.criterion.com/current/posts/511-sal-breaking-the-rules.
Gumbel, Andrew. "Who Killed Pasolini?" In *The Independent*, September 23, 1995, http://www.independent.co.uk/arts-entertainment/who-killed-pasolini-1602381.html.
Guppy, Shusha. "Alain Robbe-Grillet, The Art of Fiction No. 91." In *The Paris Review*, Issue 99, Spring 1986, https://www.theparisreview.org/interviews/2819/the-art-of-fiction-no-91-alain-robbe-grillet.
Haggith, Toby, and Joanna Newman. *Holocaust and the Moving Image: Representations of Film and Television Since 1933*. Wallflower Press, 2005.
Halftof, Mirek. *Polish Film and the Holocaust: Politcs and Memory*. Berghahn Books, 2014.
Hames, Peter. *Czech & Slovak Cinema: Theme and Tradition*. Edinburgh University Press, 2010.
Hames, Peter. The Czechoslovak New Wave. Wallflower Press, 2005.
Hames, Peter. "Enfant Terrible of the Czech New Wave: Jan Němec's 1960s Films." In Kinoeye, May 14, 2001, https://web.archive.org/web/20120609150809/http://www.ce-review.org/01/17/kinoeye17_hames.html.
Hayward, Susan. Les Diaboliques. University of Illinois Press, 2005.
Hemingway, Bernard. "*The Devil Strikes at Night*." In *Senses of Cinema*, December 2003, http://sensesofcinema.com/2003/cteq/devil_strikes_at_night/.
Hewitt, Leah D. *Remembering the Occupation in French Film: National Identity in Postwar Europe*. Palgrave Macmillan, 2008.
Holm, Isak Winkel. "The Calamity of the Rightless: Hannah Arendt and Franz Kafka on Monsters and Members." In *Philosophy and Kafka*, edited by Brendan Moran and Carlo Salzi, Lexington Books, 2015.
Indiana, Gary. "*Léon Morin, Priest:* Life During Wartime." In Criterion Collection, July 26, 2011, https://www.criterion.com/current/posts/1935-l-on-morin-priest-life-during-wartime.
Insdorf, Annette. *Indelible Shadows: Film and the Holocaust*. Cambridge University Press, 2003.
Iordanova, Dina. "*Ivan's Childhood:* Dream Come True." In Criterion Collection, January 22, 2013, https://www.criterion.com/current/posts/589-ivan-s-childhood-dream-come-true.
Jackson, Julian. *France: The Dark Years, 1940–1944*. Oxford University Press, 2003.
Jewish Telegraphic Agency. "Hidden Jewish Children Being Reunited with Parents in France; Many Others Orphaned." October 5, 1944, https://www.jta.org/1944/10/05/archive/hidden-jewish-children-being-reunited-with-parents-in-france-many-others-orphaned.
Johnson, Ben, and Anna Maria de Dominicis. "Alberto Moravia, The Art of Fiction No. 6." In *The Paris Review*, Issue 6, Summer 1954, http://www.theparisreview.org/interviews/5093/the-art-of-fiction-no-6-alberto-moravia.
Jones, Kent. "*Hiroshima mon amour:* Time Indefinite." In Criterion Collection, July 13, 2013, https://www.criterion.com/current/posts/291-hiroshima-mon-amour-time-indefinite.
Kadár, Ján. "*The Shop on Main Street*: Not the Six Million But the One." In Criterion Collection, September 17, 2001, "https://www.criterion.com/current/posts/139-the-shop-on-main-street-not-the-six-million-but-the-one.
Kennelly, Kate. "Re-envisioning the Postwar Documentary, Alain Resnais's *Night and Fog* and *Hiroshima mon amour*." In *Bright Lights Film Journal*, March 6, 2015, https://brightlightsfilm.

com/re-envisioning-the-postwar-documentary-alain-resnaiss-night-and-fog-and-hiroshima-mon-amour/#.XyeFG_hKjVo.

Kern, Laura. "Eyeing Pornography That Uses the Holocaust as Titillation." In *New York Times*, April 9, 2008, https://www.nytimes.com/2008/04/09/movies/09stal.html.

Kirsch, Adam. "Primo Levy's Unlikely Suicide Haunts His Lasting Work." In *Tablet Magazine*, September 21, 2015, http://www.tabletmag.com/jewish-arts-and-culture/books/193650/primo-levis-complete-works.

Kirschner, Jonathan. "Dark Undercurrents: Claude Chabrol's Second Wave from *Les Biches* (1968) to *Innocents with Dirty Hands* (1975)." In *Bright Lights Film Journal*, March 25, 2018, https://brightlightsfilm.com/claude-chabrol-second-wave-les-biches-1968-innocents-dirty-hands-1975/#.XuKWM55KjVo.

Kline, T. Jefferson. "Double Projection." *Art Forum*, July 14, 2008, https://www.artforum.com/film/t-jefferson-kline-on-the-films-of-alain-robbe-grillet-20742.

Koresky, Michael. "Eclipse Series 11: Larisa Shepitko." In Criterion Collection, August 11, 2008, https://www.criterion.com/current/posts/507-eclipse-series-11-larisa-shepitko.

Košuličová, Ivana. "Drowning the Bad Times: Juraj Herz Interviewed." In *Kinoeye*, January 7, 2002, http://www.kinoeye.org/02/01/kosulicova01.php.

Lane, Anthony. "Jean-Pierre Melville's Cinema of Resistance." In *The New Yorker*, April 24, 2017, https://www.newyorker.com/magazine/2017/05/01/jean-pierre-melvilles-cinema-of-resistance.

Langford, Michelle. *Allegorical Images: Tableau, Time and Gesture in the Cinema of Werner Schroeter*. Intellect Ltd, 2006.

Lanzmann, Claude. *The Patagonian Hare: A Memoir*. Farrar, Straus and Giroux, 2013.

Lawton, Anna. "Toward a New Openness in Soviet Cinema, 1976–1987." In *Post New Wave Cinema in the Soviet Union and Eastern Europe*, edited by Daniel Goulding, Indian University, 1989.

Le Fanu, Mark. "*Come and See*: Orphans of the Storm." In Criterion Collection, June 30, 2020, https://www.criterion.com/current/posts/7003-come-and-see-orphans-of-the-storm.

Leibovitz, Liel. "Listless." In *Tablet Magazine*, December 13, 2011, https://www.tabletmag.com/sections/arts-letters/articles/listless.

Levi, Primo. "On Translating Kafka." In *La Stampa*, June 5, 1983.

Levin, Julia. "*Ballad of a Soldier*." In *Senses of Cinema*, December 2002, http://sensesofcinema.com/2002/cteq/ballad_soldier/.

Lezra, Jacques. *Wild Materialism: The Ethic of Terror and the Modern Republic*. Fordham University Press, 2010.

Liehm, Antonin. *Closely Watched Films*. Routledge, 2018.

Liehm, Antonin, and Mira Liehm. *The Most Important Art: Soviet and East European Film After 1945*. University of California Press, 1984.

Liehm, Mira. *Passion and Defiance: Italian Films from 1942 to the Present*. University of California Press, 1986.

Lim, Dennis. "Pasolini's Legacy: A Sprawl of Brutality." In *New York Times*, December 26, 2012, https://www.nytimes.com/2012/12/27/movies/pasolinis-legacy-a-sprawl-of-brutality.html.

Lloyd, Christopher. *Henri-Georges Clouzot: French Film Directors*. Manchester University Press, 2016.

Lopate, Phillip. "Night and Fog." In Criterion Collection, June 23, 2003, https://www.criterion.com/current/posts/288-night-and-fog.

Lord, James. *Six Exceptional Women: Further Memoirs*. Farrar, Straus and Giroux, 1994.

Marcus, Millicent. *Italian Film in the Light of Neorealism*. Princeton University Press, 1987.

Marrone, Gaetana. *The Gaze and the Labyrinth: The Cinema of Liliana Cavani*. Princeton University Press, 2000.

Marrone, Gaetana. "*The Night Porter*: Power, Spectacle, and Desire." In Criterion Collection, December 9, 2014, https://www.criterion.com/current/posts/3393-the-night-porter-power-spectacle-and-desire.

Mazierka, Ewa. *Masculinities in Polish, Czech and Slovak Cinema: Black Peters and Men of Marble*. Berghahn Books, 2010.

McCullers, Carson. *Reflections in a Golden Eye*. First Mariner Books, 2001.

McKibbin, Toby. "Alain Robbe-Grillet: Teasing the Real." In *Senses of Cinema*, October 2014, http://sensesofcinema.com/2014/feature-articles/alain-robbe-grilletteasing-the-real/.

Melville, David. "'The Fiery Beauty of the World': Wojciech Has and *The Hourglass Sanatorium*." In *Senses of Cinema*, August 2012, http://sensesofcinema.com/2012/cteq/the-fiery-beauty-of-the-world-wojciech-has-and-the-hourglass-sanatorium/.

Monaco, James. *The New Wave: Truffaut, Godard, Chabrol, Rohmer, Rivette*. Harbor Electronic Publishing, 2004.

Němcová Tejkalová, Alice. "Ester Krumbachová." In *Women Screenwriters: An International Guide*, edited by Jill Nelmes and Jule Selbo, Palgrave Macmillan, 2015.

O'Donoghue, Darragh. "Story of Women (Une affaire de femmes, 1988)." In *Senses of Cinema*, February 2017, http://sensesofcinema.com/2017/cteq/story-of-women/.

Oukaderova, Lida. *The Cinema of the Soviet Thaw: Space, Materiality, Movement*. Indiana University Press, 2017.
Owen, Jonathan. *Avant-garde to New Wave: Czechoslovak Cinema, Surrealism and the Sixties*. Berghahn Books, 2013.
Palmer, Tim. "An Amateur of Quality: Postwar French Cinema and Jean-Pierre Melville's Le Silence de la mer." In Journal of Film and Video, Vol. 59, No. 4, WINTER 2007, 3–19.
Pasolini, Pier Paolo. Heretical Empiricism. New Academia Publishing, 2005.
Paul, David. "Hungary." In *Post New Wave Cinema in Soviet Union and Eastern Europe*, edited by Daniel J. Goulding, Indiana University Press, 1989.
Paxton, Robert O. "Meville's French Resistance." In Criterion Collection, January 11, 2011, https://www.criterion.com/current/posts/1711-melville-s-french-resistance.
Pipolo, Tony. "*A Man Escaped*: Quintessential Bresson." In Criterion Collection, March 25, 2013, https://www.criterion.com/current/posts/2628-a-man-escaped-quintessential-bresson.
Pulver, Andrew. "The Brotherhood of Mann." In *The Guardian*, August 13, 2004, http://www.theguardian.com/books/2004/aug/14/featuresreviews.guardianreview7.
Rentschler, Eric. "The Place of Rubble in the Trümmerfilm." In *New German Critique*, No. 110, COLD WAR CULTURE, Summer 2020, 9–30.
Rentschler, Eric. "The Tin Drum: Schlöndorff's German Fresco." In Criterion Collection, May 9, 2004, https://www.criterion.com/current/posts/321-the-tin-drum-schl-ndorff-s-german-fresco.
Rossellini, Roberto. "Dix ans de cinema." In *Cahiers du cinéma* 50, August-September 1955.
Saryusz-Wolska, Magdalena. "New German Cinema's Forgotten Film: Hansjürgen Pohland's *Katz und Maus*." In *German Life and Letters*, 66:1 January 2013.
Schatz, Adam. "Who does that for anyone?" In *London Review of Books*, Vol. 41, No. 12, June 20, 2019, https://www.lrb.co.uk/the-paper/v41/n12/adam-shatz/who-does-that-for-anyone.
Scholz, Anne-Marie. "'Josef K von 1963…': Orson Welles' 'Americanized' Version of *The Trial* and the changing functions of the Kafkaesque in Postwar West Germany." In *European Journal of American Studies*, 4–1, 2009: Spring 2009, http://ejas.revues.org/7610.
Segel, Harold B. *The Columbia Guide to the Literatures of Eastern Europe Since 1945*. Columbia University Press, 2008.
Shandley, Robert. *Rubble Films: German Cinema in the Shadow of the Third Reich*. Temple University Press, 2001.
Sherr, Rebecca. "The Uses of Memory and the Abuses of Fiction: Sexuality in Holocaust Fiction and Memoir." In *Other Voices*, vol. 2, no. 1, February 2000, http://www.othervoices.org/2.1/scherr/sexuality.php.
Shirer, William. *The Rise and Fall of the Third Reich*. Simon & Schuster, 2011.
Shpolberg, Masha. "1957: *The Cranes Are Flying*." In *Senses of Cinema*, December 2017, http://sensesofcinema.com/2017/soviet-cinema/the-cranes-are-flying-soviet-cinema/.
Sladovníková, Šárka. *The Holocaust in Czechoslovak and Czech Feature Films*. ibid.em-Verlag, 2018.
Smith-Prei, Carrie. "'Their Adam's Apple Put Them on Screen': Hansjürgen Pohland's *Cat and Mouse* and the Narrative of the Male Body." In *Processes of Transposition: German Literature and Film*, edited by Christiane Schönfeld, Editions Rodopi, 2007.
Snyder, Timothy. *Bloodlands: Europe Between Hitler and Stalin*. Basic Books 2012.
Sönmez, Necati. "Ordinary Compromises." In *Kinoeye*, 3.2, 3 Feb. 2003, http://www.kinoeye.org/03/02/sonmez02.php.
Sontag, Susan. *Under the Sign of Saturn*. Farrar, Strauss, Giroux, 1980.
Sragow, Michael. "Deep Focus: *Leon Morin, Priest*." In *Film Comment*, May 11, 2017, https://www.filmcomment.com/blog/deep-focus-leon-morin-priest/.
Tippins, Sherill. *February House: The Story of W.H. Auden, Carson McCullers, Jane and Paul Bowles, Benjamin Britten, and Gypsy Rose Lee, Under One Roof in Brooklyn*. Mariner Books, 2006.
Topor, Roland. *The Tenant*. Centipede Press, 2006.
Truffaut, François. "André Bazin, the Occupation and I." In *French Cinema of the Occupation and Resistance: The Birth of a Critical Esthetic*, edited by André Bazin, Ungar, 1981.
Truffaut, François. *The Films in My Life*. De Capo Press, 1994.
Tsiolkas, Christos. "The Atheist's Shoah—Roman Polanski's *The Pianist*." In *Senses of Cinema*, May 2003, http://sensesofcinema.com/2003/feature-articles/pianist/.
Turk, Edward Baron. *Child of Paradise: Marcel Carne and the Golden Age of French Cinema*. Harvard Film Studies, 1989.
Tyler, Ralph. "The Savage World of Rainer Werner Fassbinder." In *New York Times*, March 27, 1977, https://www.nytimes.com/1977/03/27/archives/the-savage-world-of-rainer-werner-fassbinder-fassbinders-world.html.
United States Holocaust Museum. "The Biologcal State: Nazi Racial Hygeine, 1933–1939." In *Holocaust Encyclopedia*, http://www.ushmm.org/wlc/en/article.php?ModuleId=10007357.

United States Holocaust Museum. "France." In *Holocaust Encyclopedia*, https://encyclopedia.ushmm.org/content/en/article/france.

United States Holocaust Museum. "Nazi Medical Experiments." In *Holocaust Encyclopedia*, http://www.ushmm.org/wlc/en/article.php?ModuleId=10005168.

Vincendeau, Ginette. *Jean-Pierre Melville: An American in Paris*. British Film Institute, 2003.

Votruba, Martin. "Slovak Cinema." In *KinoKultura*, special issue #3, December 2005, http://www.kinokultura.com/specials/3/votruba.pdf.

Watson, Fiona. "Clouzot, Henri-Georges." In *Senses of Cinema*, July 2005, http://sensesofcinema.com/2005/great-directors/clouzot/.

Weedman, Christopher. "*Mr. Klein*." In *Senses of Cinema*, July 2010, http://sensesofcinema.com/2010/cteq/mr-klein/.

Welles, Orson, and Nicholas Fry. *The Trial: A Film By Orson Welles*. Lorrimer Publishing, 1970.

Wroe, David. "Son of 'Dr Death' Aribert Heim to escape charges for concealing Nazi father's existence." In *The Telegraph*, February 5, 2009, http://www.telegraph.co.uk/news/worldnews/europe/germany/4524580/Son-of-Dr-Death-Aribert-Heim-to-escape-charges-for-concealing-Nazi-fathers-existence.html.

Yakir, Dan. "An Interview: Andrzej Wajda." In *Film Comment*, November-December 1984, https://www.filmcomment.com/article/interview-andrzej-wajda/.

Zimmerman, Joshua D. *Jews in Italy Under Fascist and Nazi Rule, 1922–1945*. Cambridge University Press, 2009.

Ziv, Avner and Anat Zajdman. *Semites and Stereotypes: Characteristics of Jewish Humor*. Praeger, 1993.

Žižek, Slavoj. *Organs without Bodies: On Deleuze and Consequences*. Routledge, 2004.

Index

Ace of Aces (1982) 151
Akerman, Chantal 211–212
Ambulance (1961) 159–160
Angry Harvest (1985) 166–168
Arendt, Hannah 32, 96, 145–146, 178, 206
Army of Shadows (1969) 62–63, 71–75
The Ascent (1977) 203
Au revoir les enfants 151–152
Auden, Wystan 83–84
Autant-Lara, Claude 38–39

Ballad of a Soldier (1959) 195–198
La bataille du rail (1946) 26
Becker, Jurek 202
Bergman, Ingmar 102–103
The Berlin Affair (1985) 90
Berlin Alexanderplatz (1980) 98–99, 101, 103, 105–107, 109
Berri, Claude 136–138
Bertolucci, Bernardo 17, 79–83, 94
Birds and Greyhounds (1969) 200
The Blue Angel (1930) 77, 84–85, 88, 109
Der Bomberpilot (1970) 52–53
Bondarchuk, Sergei 196–197
Border Street (1948) 157–158
Borowczyk, Walerian 159, 162, 165
The Boxer and Death (1963) 176, 180
Brass, Tinto 115, 122
Brauner, Artur 44, 48
Brecht, Bertolt 21, 55, 59, 76, 96–97, 143, 191, 206
Bresson, Robert 26, 28, 37–38
Brynych, Zbyněk 177–180, 183
Brzozowski, Andrzej 160
By the Railway Track (1963) 160

Cabaret (1972) 7, 77, 83–86, 88, 102–103
Camus, Albert 46, 74–75, 81, 146

Carné, Marcel 25, 27–28
Cat and Mouse (1967) 51–52, 57
Cavani, Liliana 16, 77, 84, 86–90, 94
Chabrol, Claude 65–68
Chukhray, Grigory 195–196
Clément, René 26, 31, 68
Closely Watched Trains (1966) 183–184, 186
Clouzot, Henri-Georges 27–30
Coach to Vienna (1966) 184
Cocteau, Jean 25–27
Cold Days (1966) 201
Come and See (1985) 208–211
The Condemned of Altona (1962) 20–22
The Conformist (1970) 79–81, 83–84, 91, 93–94
Continental-Films 25, 27
Le corbeau (1943) 27–28
The Cranes Are Flying (1957) 193–198
The Cremator (1969) 178, 180, 185–186
Czech New Wave 170, 174, 176, 179–180, 185, 200, 204

Les Dames du Bois de Boulogne (1945) 26, 28
The Damned (1969) 20, 23, 76–79, 83–84, 90–91, 93–94, 103, 122, 128
Death Is Called Engelchen (1963) 176–177
The Death Mills (1945) 13, 133
DEFA 191–192, 202
De-Nur, Yehiel 114–115
De Sica, Vittorio 14–17, 19–22, 44, 79
Despair (1978) 90, 100–103, 109
The Devil Strikes at Night (1957) 47–48
Diamonds of the Night (1964) 177, 179–180
Dietrich, Marlene 59, 77, 84–85, 88, 100, 102–103, 109, 122
Distant Journey (1949) 171–174, 177, 180

Dmytryk, Edward 134–135
Duras, Marguerite 34–36

Eichmann, Adolf 32, 49, 61, 96, 114–115, 133, 136, 143, 178, 182
Einsatzgruppen 154, 208–210
Encounter at the Elbe (1949) 190
Europa Europa (1990) 167–168

Fassbinder, Rainer Werner 2, 21, 42, 53–54, 57–59, 89–90, 95–111, 165
Fate of a Man (1959) 196–197
The Fifth Horseman Is Fear (1964) 178–180, 183
Forbidden Games (1952) 31
Ford, Aleksander 157–158
Fosse, Bob 7, 31, 83–86

The Garbage, the City, and the Death (1976) 98–100, 109
The Garden of the Finzi-Continis (1970) 20, 23
General Della Rovere (1959) 14–17, 19–20, 23, 90
A Generation (1955) 157–158
German, Aleksey 202
Germany Pale Mother (1980) 58–59
Germany Year Zero (1948) 5, 10–12, 14, 16, 47, 212
Gestapo's Last Orgy (1977) 123–124
Goebbels, Joseph 6, 25, 59, 100, 110
Gombrowicz, Witold 155, 161, 162,
Grass, Günter 51, 56–58

Has, Wojciech 164
Hemmings, David 102–103
Herz, Juraj 185–186
Herzog, Werner 48, 52, 149
Heydrich, Reinhard 74, 111, 121, 154, 170–171, 173, 175, 188
Hiroshima mon amour (1959) 34–37

Index

The History of the Third Reich (1963) 16, 86–87
Hitler: A Film from Germany (1977) 54–55
Holland, Agnieszka 165–169, 205
Holocaust TV series 18, 55–56, 59, 99
The Honors of War (1960) 64
Hospital of the Transfiguration (1979) 164
Hourglass Sanatorium (1973) 164
How Far from Here, How Near (1972) 164

I, Justice (1968) 179
Ilsa: She Wolf of the SS (1975) 113, 117, 119–124, 127–128
In a Year with 13 Moons (1978) 103–104, 110–111
In Those Days (1947) 43
Isherwood, Christopher 83–86
Italian neorealism 6–24, 26, 40, 41, 56, 76, 78, 157, 192
Ivan's Childhood (1962) 197–199

Jakob the Liar (1974) 71, 202–203
Jakubowska, Wanda 156–157, 172, 181
Jancsó, Miklós 200–201, 205, 207
The Juggler (1953) 133–134
Just a Gigolo (1978) 102–103

Kadár, Ján 176–177, 180–183
Kafka, Franz 71, 145–148, 150, 155, 159, 161, 163, 164, 176, 178, 183, 186
Kalatozov, Mikhail 193–194
Kapo (1960) 16–20
Katzelmacher (1969) 96
Kawalerowicz, Jerzy 158, 166
Klimov, Elem 204, 208–211
Klos, Elmar 176–177, 180–183
Kluge, Alexander 48–49
Konwicki, Tadeusz 158, 161, 164
Kovács, András 201
Krejčík, Jiří 175
Krumbachová, Ester 179

Lacombe Lucien 66, 140–142, 152
Lang, Fritz 9, 27, 41, 44–45, 48, 55, 67, 74–75
Lanzmann, Claude 33, 54, 81, 108, 139, 161, 165–167
The Last Metro (1980) 151
The Last Stage (1948) 156–157, 172, 181
The Last Train (1973) 140
Lem, Stanisław 164

Lenica, Jan 159
Léon Morin, Priest (1961) 62–64
Levi, Primo 46, 108
Lili Marleen (1981) 102–103, 107–109
The Line of Demarcation (1966) 65–68
Lizzani, Carlo 14, 16, 19, 83
A Loaf of Bread (1960) 179–180
Lola (1981) 109
Long Is the Road (1949) 43–44, 191
Lorre, Peter 44–46, 48
Losey, Joseph 66, 71, 74, 143–146
The Lost One (1951) 44–46, 48
Love and Anarchy (1973) 91
Love Camp 7 (1969) 113, 116, 121
A Love in Germany (1983) 165–166
Lustig, Arnošt 177, 179–180

Maetzig, Kurt 191
Makaveyev, Dušan 205
Malle, Louis 66, 140–141, 144, 151–152
A Man Escaped (1956) 37–38
The Man Who Lies (1968) 68–71
Mann, Klaus 46–48, 206–207
Manon (1949) 27–30
Marriage in the Shadows (1947) 191–192
The Marriage of Maria Braun (1978) 58, 101, 103–105, 107–109
Melville, Jean-Pierre 2, 30–31, 50, 61–66, 71–75
Menzel, Jiří 183
Mephisto (1981) 205–208
The Merchant of the Four Seasons (1971) 97–98
Mr. Klein 66, 71, 74, 143–146, 150
Molotov-Ribbentrop line 154, 188, 198–199
Morgenstern, Janusz 159
Morituri (1948) 44
Munk, Andrzej 158–160, 166
Murderers Among Us (1946) 42–44, 191

Nazisploitation 88, 113–125, 128
Němec, Jan 177, 179–180
New German Cinema 2, 40–44, 48–59, 95–111
Night and Fog (1956) 3, 18, 31–34, 133
The Night Porter (1974) 18, 77, 86–94, 115, 123, 128

100 Years of Adolf Hitler: The Last Hours in the Bunker (1989) 59
Ophuls, Marcel 3, 69, 71, 73, 75, 138–141, 152, 165

Ordinary Fascism (1965) 201
The Organ (1965) 183

Paisan (1946) 5, 10–12, 26, 90
Pasolini, Pier Paolo 3, 17, 19, 59, 77–79, 88, 90–91, 112–114, 125–131
Passenger (1963) 159–160
The Pawnbroker (1964) 19, 69, 136
The Pianist (2000) 150, 168–169
Pioneers in Ingolstadt (1971) 96–97
Pohland, Hans Jürgen 51–52, 57
Polanski, Roman 149–150, 162, 164–165, 168, 211
Pontecorvo, Gillo 14, 16–19

Radok, Alfréd 171–174, 178
Resnais, Alain 2, 3, 31–37, 69
Riefenstahl, Leni 6, 172
Robbe-Grillet, Alain 68–71
Rome, Open City (1945) 5, 7–12, 26, 66, 167, 211
Romeo, Juliet and Darkness (1959) 174–175
Romm, Mikhail 201
Rossellini, Roberto 2, 5–17, 19, 26, 47, 66, 78, 90, 116, 167
rubble film 2, 11–13, 41–50, 191–192

Sade, Marquis de 112, 115, 129
Salò, or the 120 Days of Sodom (1975) 3, 77, 87, 112–115, 119, 121, 124–131, 212
Salon Kitty (1976) 115, 121–122, 124
Sanders-Brahms, Helma 58–59
Sandra (1965) 20, 22–23, 76, 81, 83
Sartre, Jean Paul 20–21, 27, 99
Schlingensief, Christoph 59
Schlöndorff, Volker 42, 48, 50–51, 56–58
Schroeter, Werner 52–53, 59
Schulz, Bruno 146, 155, 161, 164
Scola, Ettore 93–94
The Serpent's Egg (1977) 102–103
Seven Beauties (1975) 77, 91–94
Shadow of Angels (1976) 98–100
Shepitko, Larisa 203–204
Shoah (1985) 23, 33, 54, 108, 139, 161, 165–167
The Shop on Main Street (1965) 178, 180–183
Signs of Life (1968) 52
The Silence of the Sea (1949) 30–31, 61–62
Singing in the Dark (1956) 135–136
Siodmak, Robert 13, 44, 47–48
The Skin (1981) 90
Solan, Peter 176

Somewhere in Europe (1948) 192
The Sorrow and the Pity (1969) 3, 69, 73, 138–141, 143, 152, 212
A Special Day (1977) 93–94
The Spider's Stratagem (1970) 81–83
Stalag fiction 114–115
Stars (1959) 196
The Stationmaster's Wife (1977) 99–100
Stoyanov, Georgi 200
The Stranger (1946) 16, 133
Street Acquaintances (1948) 191–192
Stromboli (1950) 14
Syberberg, Hans-Jürgen 54–55, 58–59
Szabó, István 205–208

Tarkovsky, Andrei 197–198
The Tenant (1976) 149–150
The Third Part of the Night (1971) 58, 161–164

The Tin Drum (1979) 56–59, 102, 205
Topor, Roland 149–150
Transport from Paradise (1963) 177–179
The Trial (1962) 147–150
The Trip Across Paris (1956) 38–39
Truffaut, François 25, 29, 33, 151
The Two of Us (1967) 136–138, 152
Two Women (1960) 19–20

Uher, Štefan 183

Vadim, Roger 115–116
Vávra, Otakar 171
Vel d'hiv 24, 142–143
Veronika Voss (1982) 98–99, 101, 109–111
Vice and Virtue (1963) 115–116
Vichy government 24–31, 35, 67–68, 132–133, 137–139, 143

Visconti, Luchino 13–14, 22–23, 76–79, 81, 94

Wajda, Andrzej 44, 51, 157–158, 161, 164–167, 169
Weiss, Jiří 174–175
Welles, Orson 16, 133, 147–149
Wertmüller, Lina 77, 84, 90–94
Witkiewicz, Stanisław Ignacy 146, 155, 161–162
Women of the Resistance (1965) 86–87, 89

Young Törless (1966) 50–52
Yugoslav Black Wave 204

Żebrowski, Edward 164
Zhelyazkova, Binka 199, 201–202
Zinnemann, Fred 13
Żuławski, Andrzej 58, 161–165

www.ingramcontent.com/pod-product-compliance
Lightning Source LLC
Chambersburg PA
CBHW080803300426
44114CB00020B/2819